Violence in Popular Culture

Violence in Popular Culture

American and Global Perspectives

Laura L. Finley, Editor

 GREENWOOD™

An Imprint of ABC-CLIO, LLC
Santa Barbara, California • Denver, Colorado

Library of Congress Cataloging-in-Publication Data

Names: Finley, Laura L., editor.
Title: Violence in popular culture : American and global perspectives / Laura L. Finley, editor.
Description: Santa Barbara, California : Greenwood, [2019] | Includes bibliographical references and index.
Identifiers: LCCN 2018018612 (print) | LCCN 2018021242 (ebook) | ISBN 9781440854330 (ebook) | ISBN 9781440854323 (hard copy : alk. paper)
Subjects: LCSH: Violence in mass media. | Violence in popular culture.
Classification: LCC P96.V5 (ebook) | LCC P96.V5 V53 2019 (print) | DDC 363.3—dc23
LC record available at https://lccn.loc.gov/2018018612

ISBN: 978-1-4408-5432-3 (print)
       978-1-4408-5433-0 (ebook)

23 22 21 20 19   1 2 3 4 5

This book is also available as an eBook.

Greenwood
An Imprint of ABC-CLIO, LLC

ABC-CLIO, LLC
130 Cremona Drive, P.O. Box 1911
Santa Barbara, California 93116-1911
www.abc-clio.com

This book is printed on acid-free paper ∞

Manufactured in the United States of America

Contents

Preface

Violence is one of the most ubiquitous components of popular culture. Music, television, film, novels, video games, and other forms of popular culture often feature interpersonal and institutional violence. The frequent and increasingly gory nature of these depictions has been and continues to be the subject of great debate in the United States (Grossman & DeGaetano, 2014). In particular, there is great concern about the effects of violent popular culture on children and teens, given that kids age eight and under watch an average of 1 hour and 40 minutes of TV or DVDs a day and kids older than eight watch an average of 4 hours daily. Kids may begin playing video games as young as age four (Emmons, 2013).

Critics contend that violence in popular culture can result in copycats who seek to emulate characters with whom they identify. For instance, many school shooters, including Columbine killers Eric Harris and Dylan Klebold, were avid players of violent video games and consumers of violent films and television. Many have even stated that they were replicating the actions of their violent heroes. Other violent criminals have also been directly influenced by popular culture. James Holmes, the shooter who killed 12 and wounded 70 at a movie theater in Aurora, Colorado, on July 20, 2012, was obsessed with the Joker character played by Heath Ledger in *The Dark Knight* (Singular & Singular, 2015).

Most people do not directly copy what they see or hear in popular culture; however, it may still be harmful in that it might increase aggression. Several studies lend support to this notion but are far from conclusive. Additionally, critics maintain that violent popular culture increases fear of violence, or what psychologist George Gerbner has called "the mean world syndrome." For instance, studies have shown that viewing crime dramas actually increases fear of crime, especially among men (See Huesmann et al., 2003; Reith, 1999). This fear then shapes how we act in our daily lives.

Violent media and popular culture are also said to desensitize consumers, leaving us less empathetic to victims of violence and more prone to see it as a normal part of our lives. Again, many studies lend support to the desensitizing effect of violent popular culture. Some studies have even suggested that the effects of consuming violent popular culture persist past the short term.

Others contend that violent popular culture is not really harmful and can identify studies that support this conclusion. They point to limitations in studies finding negative effects, noting that samples are often small and that many studies fail to address whether more violent people are attracted to violent popular culture in the first place. It is possible, for example, that more aggressive individuals are attracted to playing the most violent video games (Emmons, 2013). Some forms of violent popular culture may even be helpful. For instance, depictions of various forms of violence can be a powerful tool for prompting public discussion of difficult topics, like domestic violence, sexual assault, and police brutality. Fantasy and dystopian stories and films, some assert, are important because they allow young people to grapple safely with challenging topics and to see themselves as having the power to make social change.

This edited volume is intended to further explore the debate about violence in American popular culture. It includes reviews of the scholarly literature on the topic as well as 110 entries that analyze specific films, television shows, novels, musical genres, and radio programs popular currently or historically in the United States and 30 sidebars on popular culture and violence outside the United States. Further, this volume provides readers with a chronology of important events and developments related to violence in American popular culture and an appendix with recommended resources for additional information.

FURTHER READING

Emmons, S. 2013. "Is Media Violence Damaging to Kids?" *CNN*, February 21, 2013. http://www.cnn.com/2013/02/21/living/parenting-kids-violence-media

Grossman, D., & DeGaetano, G. 2014. *Stop Teaching Our Kids to Kill*. New York: Harmony.

Huesmann, L., Moise-Titus, J., Podolski, C., & Eron, L. 2003. "Longitudinal Relations between Children's Exposure to TV Violence and Their Aggressive and Violent Behavior in Young Adulthood: 1997–1992." *Developmental Psychology, 39*(2), 201–21.

Reith, M. 1999. "Viewing of Crime Drama and Authoritarian Aggression: An Investigation of the Relationship between Crime Viewing, Fear, and Aggression." *Journal of Electronic and Broadcasting Media, 43*(2), 211–21.

Singular, S., & Singular, J. 2015. *The Spiral Notebook: The Aurora Theater Shooter and the Epidemic of Mass Violence Committed by American Youth*. Berkeley, CA: Counterpoint.

Acknowledgments and Dedication

I am so pleased to have been able to write this book, as I feel that the topic is both interesting and important. Popular culture influences us in ways that so many fail or refuse to acknowledge. As a criminologist, I believe this is an issue that deserves academic attention and that can and should inform what and how we teach.

Not only have I learned a lot, but I've been able to work with some truly wonderful people. Catherine Lafuente at ABC-CLIO was fabulous, offering timely feedback, suggestions to improve various entries, and flexibility with deadlines. I have very much enjoyed mentoring students through the writing process, and although some contributed actual entries (as attributed in the book), many others helped as research assistants. Thanks to the following Barry University students who offered their labor:

Wills Compere

Rinayah Davis

Gabby Desposito

Eddy Georges

Francesca Gerard

Tara Gleba

Shanquia Hilson

Alex Hunt

Aatiyah Malik

Jorge Martinez

Deanna Morency

Inelis Santana

Chante Teixeira

Randel Thompson

Theo Turner

Kyla Van Tull

Chelsea Wagner

This book is dedicated to all those educators, activists, students, and parents who are working to make the United States a less violent and more just nation. Royalties from sales will be devoted to four nonprofit organizations I work with that are helping to achieve that end.

Introduction: Violence in American Popular Culture

Since there have been published plays, short stories and novels, radio programming, television shows, films, and video games, there has been a concomitant concern that violence within these genres will negatively affect consumers. Decades of research has not entirely settled the debate. Another challenge is in determining what, if any, kinds of prohibitions or cautions should be placed on media that contains violent messages or imagery. In the United States, the First Amendment prohibits undue restrictions on freedom of speech, expression, and the press. Over time the Supreme Court has made decisions that provide some clarity on what may be deemed appropriate censorship of various types of media and popular culture, although some issues remain unaddressed.

This introduction begins by presenting data on consumption of popular culture in the United States. It then provides an overview of research about the effect of violent media, including television, film, music and music videos, and video games. Further, readers are introduced to some of the most controversial types of popular culture and some of the most sensational examples. Finally, the introduction addresses the challenges and controversies related to efforts to censor or prohibit violent popular culture and offers suggestions related to media literacy.

The U.S. Bureau of Labor Statistics found in 2015 that the average American spent 2 hours and 46 minutes watching television per day (Ingraham, 2016). Nielsen reported in 2015 that 95 percent of children and teens ages 2 to 17 watch TV approximately 20 hours per week, with many older viewers simultaneously using a "second screen," often a mobile phone. Nearly 90 percent of persons in that age group listen to the radio (Grow & Tell . . . , 2015). Although data suggest that people are going to the movies less often in 2018 than in previous eras, they are not necessarily watching fewer films. Rather, the availability of online film-viewing though services like Netflix or On Demand through cable television packages means consumers have more ways to view movies than ever before. Similarly, although many have argued that millennials don't like to read, in reality, people have more opportunities to read books, magazines, and news sources than in previous generations, with Kindles and other electronic readers, as well as the average iPhone, offering books and other literature for purchase, rent, or even free. Further, video games remain tremendously popular as a form of entertainment. In 2015, 50 percent of all adult males in the United States said they play video games, as did 48 percent of women. Of people ages 18 to 29, 77 percent of men and 57 percent of women said they played (Duggan, 2015). The Pew Research Center found in 2015 that 84 percent of teen boys and 59 percent of teen girls play video games (Lenhart, 2015). In sum, consumption of popular culture is a mainstay of daily life for most people in the United States.

Research has shown that, over time, many types of popular culture have become more violent. Some have proposed that television networks are in a competition to offer more violent content, as they believe it is what viewers want and that it will appeal to an increasingly global audience. Although it would seem logical that programming intended for adult consumers would contain more violence, a study by the Kaiser Foundation found more violence in children's television programming than in any other category. Before adulthood, the average child in the United States had observed at least 40,000 simulated murders and 200,000 acts of violence (Grossman & DeGaetano, 2014).

Although many still debate the effects of violent media, data seem clear that it does indeed have negative consequences of some sort. Three different scientific commissions since the 1970s have concluded that violent media increases violent behavior. The Surgeon General's Commission Report (1972), the National Institute of Mental Health Ten Year Follow-Up (1982), and the American Psychological Association's Commission on Violence and Youth (1994) all determined that viewing violence may not only increase violent behavior but may also desensitize consumers to real-life violent behavior (Media Violence, 2009).

In 2000, six professional organizations issued a joint statement about media violence. In that statement, the American Psychological Association, the American Academy of Pediatrics, the American Academy of Family Physicians, the American Psychiatric Association, the American Medical Association, and the American Academy of Child and Adolescent Psychiatry cited that more than 1,000 studies "point overwhelmingly to a causal connection between media violence and aggressive behavior in some children" (Grossman & DeGaetano, 2014, pp. 837–38).

How, precisely, violent media affects people is a complex issue, however. Colonel David Grossman and Gloria DeGaetano (2014) identified four main effects of media violence. First, they argue that media violence increases aggression, sometimes through directly copying what is depicted. Stephen and Joyce Singular (2015) note the case of James Holmes, who shot and killed 12 and wounded 70 at a movie theater in Aurora, Colorado, on July 20, 2012. Holmes was obsessed with the Joker character played by Heath Ledger in *The Dark Knight* (2008), and he was dressed in character when he perpetrated the massacre.

Violence media also increases fear of violence. This is true of both news media and popular culture. For example, a 2006 study found that youth ages 13 to 17 who watched more news coverage of the Iraq War were more fearful than were youth who watched less coverage. Media scholar George Gerbner has studied this for decades and found that both adults and young people who regularly watch violent media rate the world a more dangerous place, what he calls "the mean world syndrome." Empirical data show television crime dramas increase fear of criminal victimization, especially for men (Grossman & DeGaetano, 2014).

Additionally, heavy consumers of violent media often become desensitized to violence in the real world. For example, one study measured the skin conductance levels of 303 undergraduate students who either watched a sad film clip or a violent one. They found those who watched the violent clip showed evidence of desensitization, meaning it triggered less of a physiological response (Krahe et al., 2011). Other research has shown that people who consume violent media express less empathy for crime victims. Such studies often have viewers watch violent clips and then answer questions about stories or vignettes, and respondents who see the violence are less likely to assign blame to perpetrators and more likely to see victims as partially responsible.

It is clear as well that users of violent media seem to have an increased appetite for violence. A 2013 study analyzed PG-13 movies and found that they contain more violent scenes than did rated-R movies from the 1980s, which indicates that people are more accepting of violence, and of more of it, as time goes on.

Media critic Meenakshi Gigi Durham (2008) explains that although there may not be a causal relationship between media violence and violent behavior, media

> are culture mythmakers: they supply us, socially, with ideas and scripts into our consciousness over time, especially when the myths are constantly recirculated in various forms. They accentuate certain aspects of social life and underplay others. They are a part of a larger culture in which these myths are already at work, making it possible for the myths to find fertile ground in which to take root and flourish. They can reinforce certain social patterns and trends, and invalidate others. They can gradually and insidiously shape our ways of thinking, our notions of what is normal and what is deviant, and our acceptance of behaviors and ideas that we see normalized on television, in films, and in other forms of popular culture. (pp. 148–49)

An important part of the conversation is how the violence is depicted. Characters in popular culture use violence for a variety of purposes, and consumers are supposed to identify, or have allegiance with them, in large part due to the reasons for their violence. Yet critics maintain that this can be even more damaging, as violence is still violence, but might feel more acceptable if we identify with the characters' allegedly justifiable usage. Films like the *Star Wars* franchise tend to emphasize defeating dark, evil, and violent enemies through violent action. This is depicted as justified. "Evening up the score is a well-established justification for the use of violence, motivated, some would say, by an expressive or emotional urge to correct a deeply perceived wrong" (Neumann, 1998, p. 45). The *Harry Potter* books and film series show protagonist Harry and his supporters using similar forms of violence against those characters presented as "evil," yet it is supposed to be considered justified or acceptable because of its benevolent purpose. The 1999 Brad Pitt and Edward Norton film *Fight Club* has also influenced young men to see themselves as heroes for using violence, telling men that to be anything but average they must be hypermasculine. "Fight Club conveys the message that the way to have a real impact on society is to do something huge and bloody. And in some ways, it's a very difficult message to counter. The movie stars who embody this core message naturally become onscreen heroes and role models" (Singular & Singular, 2015, p. 103).

One widely used typology addresses instrumental and expressive violence as it is depicted in films. Instrumental violence is perpetrated for a particular purpose or goal. Instrumental violence is presented in the following 10 ways: 1) rebellion against injustice; 2) vengeance; 3) rebellion against bureaucracy; 4) problem solving; 5) extracting confessions; 6) demonstrate authority; 7) expose corruption; 8) establish order; 9) a higher morality; and 10) conflict resolution. Expressive violence is presented via 1) stereotyping of ethnic groups; 2) teenage rebellion; 3) nature; 4) the beast; 5) going it one better; 6) war; 7) fun; 8) mysticism; 9) the madman; 10) vengeance; and 11) sex (Neumann, 1998).

One of the problems with media violence is that it is typically presented as if there are no consequences. "It is 'clean.' There is a lack of blood, minimal suffering, and often, in the case of television and video games, the cartoon characters are invincible" (Groves, 2002, p. 26). Media scholar George Gerbner has referred to this as "happy violence" and notes that it is most common in children's programming. Cartoons often show characters getting beaten, falling off cliffs, blown up by dynamite, or facing other forms of violence then popping back up, same as always. Gerbner asserts that this is particularly problematic, as young people lack the ability to understand that, in real life, violence has very real consequences. Many studies have shown that the effects of media violence may vary but are true across many cultures (Tarabah et al., 2016).

TELEVISION

Some of the most popular television programming deals with crime and violence. Yet such programming has been found to overrepresent violent crimes like murder, as do reality-based television shows. As a result, viewers may overestimate how much violent crime occurs and misunderstand the nature of it. Not only does this make people more fearful of what they perceive to be a very dangerous world, but it changes our daily behaviors. People may avoid certain neighborhoods, purchase weapons or other devices for security, or even stay in more often out of fear that they will be victimized.

> If most of us get our knowledge of crime and criminal justice from the news media and TV programs, which tend to cover or portray only the most sensational kinds of crime and criminal justice activities, it's no surprise that many of us develop perceptions that may not reflect what is really happening in the world of crime and in the various stages of the criminal justice system. (Surette, 1992, p. 296)

Violence is often, although not exclusively, depicted in crime-related shows, which have constituted approximately one-third of all television programs since the 1980s. These shows provide important narratives about why crime happens, who is a perpetrator, and who is a victim. Studies have shown that victims are often presented in dramatic ways that result in viewers seeing them as dissimilar to themselves, which may result in increased victim blaming. Research suggests that most do not blame victims out of malice but instead out of a desire to believe that the world is just and thus people who are victimized are at fault, at least in part (Best, 1999). Research has also shown that crime-related television often emphasizes the victimization of white women by black offenders (Best, 1999). In reality, however, most crime is intraracial, or between people of the same race.

FILMS

Popular movies reinforce dangerous stereotypes about who commits crime and responses to it. Films are a significant source of people's ideas "about legality and illegality, the volume of various types of crime, and the motives of lawbreakers." Further, "[d]ue to the globalization of film markets, movies also play a major role internationally in the dispersion of images, myths, and values. For many of us, they are a significant source—perhaps the most significant source—of ideas about crime and criminals" (Rafter, 2000, p. vii). Yet "although film plays a central role in generating representations and understandings of crime, criminologists have traditionally ignored it, clinging to a narrow social science perspective that pays little attention to the interactions of crime and culture" (Rafter, 2000, p. 4). Additionally, the way police and social service agencies react or provide aid to such victims can certainly be shaped and altered by unfavorable depictions seen in media outlets. The "prescribed formula taken in primetime crime dramas, which includes an evil offender, a violent crime, at least one go-getter police officer who is willing to bend the rules to serve justice and a just resolution of the case at the end of the program can create powerful ideological images of crime, the efficiency of the criminal justice system, and characteristics of offenders and victims" (Britto, 2007, p. 40).

Studies have documented that violence in movies has increased. A 2013 study found that gun violence in 945 top-selling PG-13 films had increased and exceeded the violence in top-ranked R-rated movies. Both PG- and R-rated films featured violent encounters with guns at least twice per hour, the study found. The researchers critiqued the fact that the current rating system is harsher on the inclusion of sex acts than it is on violence. Further, critics express concern that much of the violence presented in films is gratuitous and senseless. A 2014 study found that 94 percent of movies released in that year featured gun fights (Bushman, Jamieson, Weitz, & Romer, 2013).

MUSIC AND MUSIC VIDEOS

Some studies have found that songs with violent lyrics increase aggression. In a series of five experiments involving over 500 college students, researchers from Iowa State University and the Texas Department of Human Services examined the effects of seven violent songs by seven artists, comparing them with eight nonviolent songs by seven artists. After listening to the songs the students were asked to perform a series of tasks to measure aggressive thoughts and feelings, including classifying words that can have both aggressive and nonaggressive meanings, such as rock and stick. The study also included songs with humorous lyrics to see how humor interacted with violent song lyrics and aggressive thoughts.

Results showed that violent songs led to more aggressive interpretations of ambiguously aggressive words, increased the relative speed with which people interpreted a word to be aggressive, and increased the proportion of word fragments (such as h_t) that were filled in to make aggressive words (such as hit, as opposed to hot). Even the humorous violent songs increased aggressive thoughts. Lead researcher Craig A. Anderson, PhD, of Iowa State University explained the importance of the study: "Aggressive thoughts can influence perceptions of ongoing social interactions, coloring them with an aggressive tint. Such aggression-biased interpretations can, in turn, instigate a more aggressive response—verbal or physical—than would have been emitted in a nonbiased state, thus provoking an aggressive escalatory spiral of antisocial exchanges." Anderson and colleagues recommended more research, however, to identify both short- and long-term effects of listening to violent lyrics. Anderson said, "One major conclusion from this and other research on violent entertainment media is that content matters. This message is important for all consumers, but especially for parents of children and adolescents" (Anderson & Carnagey, 2003).

Another study found different results. Thirty-nine music listeners aged 18 to 34 years were subjected to an anger induction, then were randomly assigned to listen to 10 minutes of extreme music from their own playlist or to 10 minutes of silence. Heart rate and their rating on the Positive and Negative Affect Scale (PANAS) were taken afterward. Results showed that ratings of PANAS hostility, irritability, and stress increased during the anger induction but decreased after the music or silence. Heart rate increased during the anger induction and held constant but did not increase for those who listened to extreme music and decreased in the silence condition. In sum, the findings indicated that listening to extreme music did not make angry participants angrier, although silence may still be more calming (Sharman & Dingle, 2015).

Music has also been used as a tool for torture. The Nazis used music both to torture and to cover up the screams of victims they were torturing. Jonathan Pieslak, in his 2009 book, *Sound Targets: American Soldiers and Music in the Iraq War*, documented how the U.S. military used music in their interrogations at Abu Ghraib prison and in other facilities. During the 2004 battle of Fallujah, speakers mounted on Humvees played Metallica and AC/DC. It was authorized by General Ricardo Sanchez in a 2003 memo. Soldiers used the theme song to the children's show *Barney and Friends*, Christina Aguilera songs, music in Arabic, and violent songs by Eminem and Drowning Pool, along with other tunes, played over and over. Influenced by the Nazis as well as by Cold War–era research into psychological methods of torture, music is a "no-touch" means to disintegrate someone's personality. In Israel, Palestinian detainees have been tied to kindergarten chairs, cuffed, hooded, and tortured with classic music. In Chile under the regime of dictator Augusto Pinochet, interrogators employed a variety of music, including the soundtrack to the violent film *A Clockwork Orange* (1971) (Ross, 2016).

VIDEO GAMES

Video games often feature violence, even those marketed to young children. One study found that 89 percent of games are violent, and even 98 percent of those rated appropriate for teens (Grossman & DeGaetano, 2014). One-third of all video games feature sexual themes, including sexual violence (Durham, 2008).

Studies generally seem to confirm that playing violent video games increases aggression, although new research has suggested that the effect may be more related to frustration than to the actual activity of the game. Playing violent video games is a common link among many school and mass shooters. Video games are particularly popular among young men, who are overwhelmingly responsible for violent crime in the United States. Eric Harris and Dylan Klebold, the Columbine shooters, were avid players, as was Adam Lanza, the shooter at Sandy Hook Elementary in Newtown, Connecticut.

A study conducted in 2010 which included 130,295 participants around the world found users of violent video games increased aggressive thoughts, physiological arousal, angry feelings, and aggressive behavior. Another study found that people who played violent video games were less inclined to help injured persons than were those who played nonviolent games (Anderson & Bushman, 2001). These and other studies have found that the earlier a youth is exposed to violent media and the more frequent involvement increase the effects.

As Grossman and DeGaetano (2014) explain, "There is a generation out there that has been fed violence from its youngest days, and has been systematically taught to associate pleasure and reward with vivid depictions of inflicting human death and suffering" (p. 5). Many times video game violence is also gendered, and women in the games are demeaned and degraded. For instance, a description of *Grand Theft Auto* states, "You can pick up a hooker, take her out in the woods, have sex with her, pull over, beat her with a bat, then you can get into the car and run her over" (Durham, 2008, p. 141).

CENSORSHIP ISSUES

Some argue that the United States should do more to censor or prohibit violent media, in particular when it comes to children. Yet First Amendment advocates, along with those in the television, film, radio, and other industries, resist such limitations, arguing they are unconstitutional and unfairly restrict businesses from producing products the public has a right to consume. The Federal Communications Commission (FCC) restricts certain media, but it is mostly concerned with obscenity, profanity, and indecency, rather than violence specifically. The Motion Picture Production Code, often referred to as the Hays Code, set standards for film, but also focuses more on sex than on violence particularly. Similarly, efforts to censor television via designating hours for "family" time and the introduction of the V-chip have been only mildly successful, at best. The FCC established "Family Viewing Hour" in 1975, designating 8:00 to 9:00 p.m. as being devoted to family-friendly programming. Yet given the lack of emphasis on violence in any of these policies, as well as the popularity of cable television and alternative sources to watch TV, such as Hulu, it remains easy for young people to see violent programming.

Attempts to prohibit certain video games have been deemed unconstitutional, and efforts to hold filmmakers, video game producers, and others in the industry legally accountable for violence perpetrated by consumers have never been successful. In *Brown v. Entertainment Merchants Association* (2011), the court struck down a 2005 California law that banned the sale of certain violent video games to children without parental supervision, deeming it a violation of the First Amendment. Occasionally, however, scandals have resulted in companies refusing to carry games or pulling them from the shelves. In 1976, an advanced version of *Pong*, called *Death Race*, was taken off the market after outcry about the killing of gremlins. Video game historian Steve L. Kent said, "What got everyone upset about Death Race was that you heard this little 'ahhhk' when the person got hit, and a little gravestone came up." In 1993, *Mortal Kombat* was released as the first video game to feature realistic, life-like violence, but the industry's creation of the Entertainment Software Ratings Board (ESRB) quelled some of the concerns, and it remained on the shelves amidst protests. In 1995, some retail stores banned the game *Phantasmagoria* due to the rape scene in the game that involves a helpless female protagonist. In 1997, attorney Jack Thompson filed the first lawsuit against the video game industry on behalf of three children who were killed by a school shooter at Heath High West, Paducah, Kentucky. The shooter, Michael Carneal, was an avid player of violent games, including *Doom*, *Quake*, and *Redneck Rampage*. The suit was dismissed in July 2008. The Columbine massacre of 1999 reinvigorated charges that video games were in part responsible for violent attacks, and another lawsuit was filed but also dismissed (A Timeline . . . , 2018).

Bans on controversial books have occurred throughout U.S. history, but critics contend that these are not only in contrast to First Amendment rights but ineffective if the goal is to keep young people from learning about controversial topics. Many books that are considered "classics" have faced bans or calls for censorship. Mark Twain's *The Adventures of Huckleberry Finn*, Alex Haley's *The Autobiography of Malcolm X*, Toni Morrison's *Beloved*, Dee Brown's *Bury My Heart at Wounded Knee*, Joseph Heller's *Catch-22*, Jack London's *The Call of the Wild*, J. D. Salinger's *The Catcher in the Rye*, and Ray Bradbury's *Fahrenheit 451* are among the most banned books in U.S. history.

Controversies over violent lyrics have resulted in congressional hearings and parental advisories, which critics contend merely make these albums more popular. In 1985, amidst concerns about sex and violence in popular music, Tipper Gore, wife of Senator Al Gore, and three other powerful women formed the Parents Music Resource Council (PRMC), which famously listed the "filthy 15." In November 1985, the Recording Industry Association of America (RIAA) agreed to put warning stickers on inappropriate albums. They initially wanted a "V" to mark violent records, an "O" for satanic or music that was anti-Christian, and "D/A" for music about drugs and alcohol. In addition to the fact that the label served as the proverbial "forbidden fruit," critics contended that the white artists were given more leeway than were black artists. Pop critic Chris Molanphy said, "If you were a white rock act, you could get away with a couple of F-bombs or a couple of curses on your album and not get stickered. But if you were a rapper or even a hard R&B singer and you said something as daring as 'pee,' you could get labeled." Given how easy it is to download music, most contend that the labels are worthless today (Schonfeld, 2015).

MEDIA LITERACY AND OTHER ALTERNATIVES

Because censorship is not terrifically effective and generates concerns about constitutionality, many have proposed that instead, we should teach people to be more informed media consumers. Media literacy helps identify controversial issues and informs consumers how to understand the social, political, and economic factors that underlie why or how a piece is being debated. Some media literacy programs are general, focusing on critical thinking and analysis, and others are tied to specific pieces of media, such as a young adult novel.

Ultimately, it is consumers who have the biggest voice in terms of the amount and type of violence presented in popular culture. If people stopped going to violent movies; refused to buy violent video games, books, or music; and tuned in to only nonviolent television programming, the industry would surely respond. Media critics like Jean Kilbourne and Jackson Katz have long maintained that it says a lot about American culture that we continue to be so fascinated by violence.

FURTHER READING

Anderson, C., & Bushman, B. 2001. "Effects of Violent Video Games on Aggressive Behavior, Aggressive Cognition, Aggressive Affect, Physiological Arousal, and Prosocial Behavior: A Meta-Analytic Review of the Scientific Literature." *Physiological Science, 12*(5), 353–59.

Anderson, C., & Carnagey, N. 2003. "Exposure to Violent Media: The Effects of Songs with Violent Lyrics on Aggressive Thoughts and Feelings." *Journal of Personality and Social Psychology, 84*(5): 960–71.

"Banned Books That Shaped America." n.d. http://www.bannedbooksweek.org/censorship/bannedbooksthatshapedamerica

Best, J. 1999. *Random Violence: How We Talk about New Crimes and New Victims.* Berkeley, CA: University of California Press.

Britto, S. 2007. "Does "Special" Mean Young, White and Female? Deconstructing the Meaning of "Special" in Law & Order: Special Victims Unit." *Journal of Criminal Justice and Popular Culture, 14*(1), 39–57.

Bushman, B., Jamieson, P., Weitz, I., & Romer, D. 2013. "Gun Violence Trends in Movies." *Pediatrics,* 1014–1018.

Duggan, M. 2015. "Who Plays Video Games and Identifies as a 'Gamer.'" Pew Research Center, December 15. http://www.pewinternet.org/2015/12/15/who-plays-video-games-and-identifies-as-a-gamer

Durham, M. 2008. *The Lolita Effect: The Media Sexualization of Young Girls and What We Can Do about It.* New York: The Overlook Press.

Grossman, D., & DeGaetano, G. 2014. *Stop Teaching Our Kids to Kill.* New York: Penguin.

Groves, B. 2002. *Children Who See Too Much: Lessons from the Child Witness to Violence Project*. Boston, MA: Beacon.

"Grow and Tell: As Children Age from Toddlers to Teens, Their Media Palate Changes." *Nielsen*, March 3. http://www.nielsen.com/us/en/insights/news/2015/grow-and-tell -as-children-age-from-toddlers-to-teens-their-media-palate-changes.html

Huesmann, L. R., Moise-Titus, J., Podolski, C., & Eron, L. D. 2003. "Longitudinal Relations Between Children's Exposure to TV Violence and Their Aggressive and Violent Behavior in Young Adulthood: 1977–1992." *Developmental Psychology, 39*: 201–21.

Ingraham, C. 2016. "Americans Are Watching More TV and Working Less, Federal Data Show." *The Washington Post*, June 28. https://www.washingtonpost.com/news /wonk/wp/2016/06/28/americans-are-watching-more-tv-and-working-less-new -federal-data-show

Krahe, B., Moller, I., Huesmann, L., Kirwil, L., Felber, J., & Berger, A. 2011. "Desensitization to Media Violence: Links with Habitual Media Violence Exposure, Aggressive Cognition, and Aggressive Behavior." *Journal of Personal and Social Psychology, 100*(4), 630–46.

Lenhart, A. 2015. "Chapter Three: Video Games Are Key Elements in Friendships for Many Boys." *Pew Research* Center, August 6. http://www.pewinternet.org/2015/08 /06/chapter-3-video-games-are-key-elements-in-friendships-for-many-boys

Media Violence. 2009. American Academy of Pediatrics. Retrieved August 29, 2018 from http://pediatrics.aappublications.org/content/pediatrics/124/5/1495.full.pdf

Neumann, I. 1998. "Pop Goes Religion: Harry Potter Meets Clifford Geertz." *European Journal of Cultural Studies, 9*, 81–100.

Rafter, N. 2000. *Shots in the Mirror: Crime Films and Society*. New York: Oxford University Press.

Ross, A. 2016. "When Music Is Violence." *The New Yorker*, July 4. https://www.newyorker .com/magazine/2016/07/04/when-music-is-violence

Schonfeld, Z. 2015. "Does the Parental Advisory Label Still Matter?" *Newsweek*, November 10. http://www.newsweek.com/does-parental-advisory-label-still-matter-tipper -gore-375607

Sharman, L., & Dingle, G. 2015. "Extreme Metal Music and Anger Processing." *Frontiers in Human Neuroscience, 9.* https://www.ncbi.nlm.nih.gov/pmc/articles/PMC4439552

Singular, S., & Singular, J. 2015. *The Spiral Notebook: The Aurora Shooter and the Epidemic of Mass Violence Committed by American Youth*. New York: Counterpoint.

Surette, R. 1992. *Media, Crime, and Criminal Justice: Images and Realities*. Pacific Grove, CA: Brooks/Cole Publishing.

Tarabah, A., Badr, L., Usta, J., & Doyle, J. 2016. "Exposure to Violence and Children's Desensitization Attitudes in Lebanon." *Journal of Interpersonal Violence, 31*(18), 3017–3038.

"A Timeline of Video Game Controversies." 2018. *National Coalition Against Censorship.* http://ncac.org/resource/a-timeline-of-video-game-controversies

Chronology: Violence in American Popular Culture

1897

The state of Maine enacts legislation prohibiting the showing of films depicting prizefighting.

1915

The U.S. Supreme Court determines in *Mutual Film Corporation v. Industrial Commission of Ohio* that films are commerce, not art, and therefore are not protected by the First Amendment. The decision was overturned in 1952 in *Joseph Burstyn, Inc. v. Wilson*.

1915

D. W. Griffith's racist *The Birth of a Nation* features violent men in blackface and heroic KKK members.

1927

William A. Wellman's *Wings* about WWI is the only silent film to win a Best Picture Oscar.

1930, March 31

The Motion Picture Producers and Distributors Association adopts the Production Code, or what is often called the Hays Code, to outline moral guidelines for film production.

1938, October 30

Radio airing of Orson Welles's "War of the Worlds," warning of an alleged alien attack, results in panic and calls for action by the Federal Communications Commission.

1939, April 20

Billie Holiday records "Strange Fruit," a powerful critique of lynching in the South.

1958

Concertgoers in Berlin and London trash facilities and fight with authorities during concerts by Bill Haley and the Comets.

1958
The city of Boston bans rock concerts after an altercation at a daylong festival led by DJ Alan Freed.

1960, September 8
Alfred Hitchcock's *Psycho* is released. The film is considered by many to be the origin of the horror/slasher genre.

1962
The Chrystal's "He Hit Me and It Felt Like a Kiss," written by Gerry Goffin and Carole King about the abuse endured by their babysitter, singer Little Eva, features lyrics that seem to condone abuse.

1964
Nina Simone's "Mississippi Goddamn" offers an emotional response to the 1963 bombing at Sixteenth Street Church in Birmingham, Alabama, which killed four black girls.

1966
The Kinks video for "Dead End Street" is the first pop music video to be banned by the BBC because it featured pallbearers and a corpse that jumped out of a coffin.

1967
Release of *Bonnie and Clyde*, which depicts the murder spree of Bonnie Parker and Clyde Barrow, who were killed in a shootout with police in 1934.

1968
Release of Roman Polanski's *Rosemary's Baby*, which depicts a woman having the devil's baby. The film was nominated for Best Screenplay and Best Supporting Actress, and Ruth Gordon won the latter.

1969
Sam Peckinpah's *The Wild Bunch* is considered one of the most violent Westerns.

1969, March
John Lennon and Yoko Ono stay in bed for a week to protest violence and suffering in the world in their famous "bed-in."

1969, December 6
Hell's Angels, hired to conduct security, turn violent during a Rolling Stones performance at Altamont Music Festival, resulting in four deaths.

1971
Release of John Lennon's most famous song, "Imagine," which critiques capitalism and greed.

1971
Stanley Kubrick's *A Clockwork Orange* shocks and disturbs. Graphic rape scenes were banned in the United States, and in the UK the film was said to have inspired a British teenager to copycat it.

1971, December 4
A Swiss casino is burned to the ground during a Frank Zappa concert after a fan fired a flare gun and the crowd went wild.

1972
U.S. Surgeon General issues a statement documenting the public health effects of media violence.

1973
Release of *The Exorcist*, about a possessed child. It was nominated for nine Oscars and won two, for Best Sound and Best Screenplay. It was the first horror film to be nominated for the Best Picture award.

1975, June 20
Release of *Jaws* to one of the widest audiences at the time and the highest-grossing movie until *Star Wars* in 1977. It is considered by many to be the start of the summer Hollywood blockbuster model.

1976, November
Writers Guild of America W., Inc. v. FCC determines that networks cannot be forced to host "family hours" in which only certain types of programming are available.

1977, May 25
Star Wars, later renamed *Star Wars Episode IV: A New Hope*, featuring the epic battle against the Empire and its various evil characters like Darth Vader, sets new opening records it held until the 1982 release of *E.T. the Extra-Terrestrial*.

1977
The Sex Pistol's "God Save the Queen" refers to British royalty as a fascist regime. Despite being banned by the BBC, it reached number two on the charts.

1978
I Spit on Your Grave is considered by some to be a feminist critique of male sexual violence and by others a worthless glorification of violence.

1978
The Deer Hunter wins five Academy Awards for its depiction of soldiers from small-town America who are captured by the Vietcong.

1979, November 19
Ronny Zamora, 15, with his father and mother, sued the National Broadcasting Company, Columbia Broadcasting System, and American Broadcasting Company claiming that since he was 5, Ronny had been addicted to and "completely subliminally intoxicated" by televised violence on these three networks. On June 4, 1977, Zamora shot and killed his 83-year-old neighbor in Miami, Florida. The claim was dismissed.

1980
Bassist Geezer Butler of Black Sabbath is hit by a bottle during a concert in Milwaukee, resulting in a prompt end to the show.

1980
Italian director Ruggero Deodato's *Cannibal Holocaust* is so violent it is banned in many nations. Deodato is arrested because Italian authorities believe the on-screen violence was so extensive that he must have murdered one or more of his actors.

1980, December 8
Mark David Chapman murders musician John Lennon outside of his home in New York City.

1982, April 23
The Clash release "Know Your Rights" on their album *Combat Rock*. It is a cautionary song about police abuse of authority.

1984, September 16
First episode of *Miami Vice* airs on NBC. The hugely popular show featured two Miami police officers, Sonny Crockett (Don Johnson) and Ricardo Tubbs (Phillip Michael Thomas). The show, filmed largely in Miami, ran for five seasons.

1986
Oliver Stone's *Platoon* wins five Oscars and 18 awards.

1987
Robocop becomes the first film to receive an X-rating for violence alone.

1988
A high school student in California holds his humanities class hostage, claiming he was influenced by Stephen King's story *Rage*. One year later, a Kentucky student holds his class hostage, emulating the book.

1988
Motorhead's video for "Killed by Death" is banned from MTV due to its excessive and senseless violence, including a scene where the lead singer is electrocuted.

1988, August 9
Release of NWA's "F**k tha Police," heralded as one of the most influential protest songs about police corruption and brutality. Critics contended it incited violence, whereas proponents emphasized that the song discussed real problems in urban communities.

1989, April 19
The vicious beating and rape of Trisha Meili, who came to be called the Central Park Jogger, leads to the arrest of five juvenile males. Media describes their actions as "wilding," and all were given lengthy prison sentences. The convictions were later overturned when DNA identified another perpetrator, and the boys were all released in 2002. Coverage of the incident and the boys' arrest helped usher in an era of harsh laws for juvenile offenders.

1990, September 13
Original airing of *Law & Order*, which ran for 20 seasons. The police procedural and legal drama set in New York City is the longest-running crime drama, and plots

were often based at least loosely on real cases. It won many Emmy awards, and its success spawned several spinoffs.

1991

Garth Brooks's video for "The Thunder Rolls," in which he depicted a violent, cheating husband, was banned by The Nashville Network and Country Music Television. Brooks won a Country Music Award for video of the year.

1991

After Axl Rose of Guns & Roses dives into the crowd to stop a photographer during their St. Louis concert, the crowd goes berserk, resulting in dozens of injuries.

1991, May 6

In *Waller v. Osbourne* (1991), Thomas and Myra Waller alleged that heavy metal artist Ozzy Osbourne was partly responsible for their son, Michael Jeffrey Waller's, suicide through his song "Suicide Solution." The court ruled that the plaintiffs failed to show that Osbourne's music incites imminent lawless activity.

1991, September 25

Rapper Tupac Shakur released the song "Trapped" on his album *2pacalypse Now*. The song describes police harassment and brutality of black men.

1992

Violence ensues after Axl Rose takes more than two hours to take the stage during a Montreal concert. Dozens were injured, the facility and surrounding area were trashed, and police eventually used tear gas to dispel the mob.

1992

John Woo's cop flick *Hard Boiled* features 307 on-screen deaths. It is ranked by MTV as the fourth most violent film of all time.

1992

Body Count releases "Cop Killer" just after the LA riots after the LAPD's assault on Rodney King and makes reference to Police Chief Daryl Gates and to King. Police accused the band of igniting tensions that erupted after the four white officers were acquitted of assaulting King. Front man Ice-T defended the song and denounced police brutality.

1993, December 10

The first-person-shooter video game *Doom* is released to tremendous popularity, with an estimated 15 to 20 million players in its first two years. It is considered a pioneer in 3D graphics as well as in multiplayer gaming, and has been widely criticized for its graphic violence. Many school shooters, including Columbine killers Eric Harris and Dylan Klebold, were frequent players.

1992, November 2

Rage Against the Machine releases "Killing in the Name" on their album *Rage Against the Machine*. The song discusses institutionalized racism and police brutality.

1993, September 10
First airing of *The X-Files*, a science fiction horror series that ran for nine seasons and resulted in two films. It focuses on two FBI agents Fox Mulder (David Duchovny) and Dana Scully (Gillian Anderson) as they solve cases involving the paranormal.

1994
The video for Nirvana's "Heart-shaped Box," which features a little girl, dressed in KKK robes, picking fetuses from a tree and an old man wearing a Santa hat climbing a crucifix, generates huge controversy yet wins the 1994 MTV Music Video Award.

1994, August 26
Oliver Stone's *Natural Born Killers* is released to acclaim and criticism for his excessive violence. Fans appreciated its satirical look at how media glorifies violence, whereas critics noted that it reinforced the same glorification. Several lawsuits were filed by persons and family members harmed in alleged copycat assaults, although none were successful.

1995, October 2
The televised trial of O. J. Simpson for the murder of his former wife, Nicole, and her friend, Ronald Goldman, is referred to as the "trial of the century." Simpson's acquittal generated great controversy and resulted in an increase in television shows focusing on crime and courtroom dramas.

1996
Passage of the Telecommunications Act of 1996 required installation of V-chips, which block certain types of programming, in television sets in subsequent years.

1996, February 2
Barry Loukaitis kills his algebra teacher and two students at his Moses Lake, Washington high school. Loukaitis was a fan of the Stephen King story *Rage* and the films *Natural Born Killers* and *Basketball Diaries*.

1996, October 25
Ozzy Osbourne's first Ozzfest, a heavy metal festival, helps elevate that musical genre.

1996
Tupac Shakur's "Hit 'Em Up" inflamed the tensions between East Coast and West Coast rappers, with lyrics that have been called the "biggest diss of all time."

1996, September 7
Tupac Shakur is murdered in a drive-by shooting in Las Vegas.

1997
The Prodigy's video for "Smack My B**** Up" is banned by the BBC.

1997, March 9
Rapper Christopher Wallace, known as Notorious B.I.G. or Biggie Smalls, is shot four times in a Los Angeles drive-by. He dies an hour later.

1997, December 1
Michael Carneal kills three and injures five at his Paducah, Kentucky high school. Carneal was an avid consumer of violent films, pornography, and video games.

1998
Saving Private Ryan depicts soldiers enduring the violence of war to rescue others. It was nominated for 11 Academy Awards and won for Best Director, Best Cinematography, Best Film Editing, Best Sound Editing, and Best Sound Mixing.

1999
Parents of three victims of Michael Carneal's 1997 shooting spree at Heath High School in Paducah, Kentucky, file a lawsuit against two Internet pornography websites, several video game manufacturers, and distributors of the 1995 film *The Basketball Diaries*, asserting that they were significant factors in Carneal's rampage. The suit was dismissed in 2001.

1999, January 10
First airing of *The Sopranos* on HBO. A crime drama, the show focused on fictional Italian mobster Tony Soprano (James Gandolfini), showing both his criminal and family life, much of which was described via his sessions with his therapist Jennifer Melfi (Lorraine Bracco). It won several Peabody, Emmy, and Golden Globe awards and is considered by some to be the best television show ever. It is applauded for altering the stereotypes of organized crime.

1999
Release of *Fight Club*, a film based on the 1996 Chuck Palahniuk novel that critiques capitalism while depicting brutal fighting as a form of psychotherapy.

2000
The crowd rushes the stage as Pearl Jam begins to play at Danish open-air Roskilde festival. Nine were killed and 23 suffered serious injuries.

2000
The Federal Bureau of Investigation (FBI) releases a report documenting media violence as a factor in school shootings.

2000
Japanese director Kinji Fukasaku's *Battle Royale* is a more violent version of *Lord of the Flies*. Many have compared it to *The Hunger Games* series, although the former is much more gory.

2001
Madonna's "What It Feels Like for a Girl," produced by her then-husband Guy Ritchie, is banned by MTV and VH1 because it depicts the artist on a crime spree that ends in suicide.

2001, April 24
Bruce Springsteen releases "American Skin (41 Shots)," about the police shooting of Guinean immigrant Amadou Diallo. Police mistook Diallo's reach for his wallet to show identification as an attempt to reach for a weapon. The

Patrolmen's Benevolent Association in New York City called for a boycott of Springsteen's show. Eventually, the city paid $3 million to Diallo's family in a wrongful death suit.

2002, October 11
Michael Moore's film *Bowling for Columbine* is released. The film problematizes U.S. gun culture and examines media and violence in an attempt to explain the April 20, 1999, massacre at Columbine High School in Littleton, Colorado.

2003, February 20
One hundred fans are killed and 230 suffer injuries when a fire breaks out at the Great White Concert in West Warwick, Rhode Island.

2003
Author Joyce Carol Oates's novel *Rape: A Love Story* shows the dangers of rape myths.

2003
Metallica releases "St. Anger," with the video filmed at San Quentin prison.

2004
Mel Gibson's *The Passion of the Christ* spends nearly 100 minutes graphically depicting the torture and death of Jesus.

2005
Release of *The Devil's Rejects* by Rob Zombie, which MTV ranked as the ninth most violent film of all time.

2005
Hostel ushers in an era of "torture pornography" that is particularly popular among adolescents.

2007
Federal Communications Commission releases report noting the "strong evidence" that media violence increases aggressive behavior among children.

2007
Zack Snyder's *300* graphically retells the Battle of Thermopylae. It is ranked by *Time* as one of the most ridiculously violent films of all time.

2008
Actor Christina Hendricks's character in *Mad Men* is raped in what she calls one of the most disturbing scenes she has ever filmed.

2008
Jamie Foxx and T Pain's song "Blame It" features lyrics that seem to suggest drunkenness is an excuse for rape.

2008
Release of *Rambo*, ranked by MTV as the eighth most violent film of all time due to the high body count. Two hundred and thirty-six people die in the film, more than the three previous Rambo films combined.

2009, May 8
Brawls during an Iron Maiden concert in Colombia are so bad military troops are called in and 111 people are arrested.

2009, August 26
Musician Chris Brown is sentenced to five years of probation and 1,400 hours of community service for violently attacking his girlfriend, musician Rihanna.

2010
Frustrated fans who couldn't get tickets for Metallica's show in Santiago, Chile, start a riot. Chile's paramilitary is called in and 160 people are arrested.

2010
Quentin Tarantino releases his two-volume epic, *Kill Bill*. It is considered by many to be a campy, bloodthirsty rampage.

2010
M.I.A.'s "Born Free" video is banned by YouTube. The video depicted the genocide of redheaded individuals, showing one young man getting blown up and another shot in the head.

2010, October 31
First airing of *The Walking Dead*, a horror series based on a comic book series of the same name and depicting a world that has been taken over by zombies. A group of survivors unite and engage in constant fights with the zombies, called walkers, and rival survivors. It is very popular and has received several awards as well as resulted in a spinoff, *Fear the Walking Dead*.

2010
Eminem and Rihanna team up for "Love the Way You Lie," which domestic violence advocates say repeats dangerous misconceptions about abuse.

2011, April 17
First airing of *Game of Thrones*, the award-winning, violent HBO series adaptation of the novels by George R. R. Martin.

2011, June 27
Supreme Court rules in *Brown v. Entertainment Merchant's Association* (2011), striking down a 2005 California law prohibiting the sale of certain violent video games to children without parental supervision.

2013
American Psychological Association (APA) report notes a link between playing violent video games and aggression.

2013
Release of *12 Years a Slave*, which receives both accolades and criticism for its depiction of violence against slaves.

2013
Syfy airs *Sharknado*, a violent but comical cult classic that has spawned three sequels.

2013
Robin Thicke's song and video "Blurred Lines" generates huge controversy, as it is seen by many to glorify sexual exploitation.

2014
Musician Cee Lo Green pleads no contest to charges of giving Ecstasy to a woman who then accused him of sexual assault.

2015
Straight Outta Compton chronicles the career of gangsta rap group N.W.A.

2016
Mel Gibson's *Hacksaw Ridge* uses tremendous violence to tell the story of a conscientious objector during WWII.

2016
Nate Parker releases a remake of *The Birth of a Nation*, refashioned as a slave rebellion film. It won the Jury Prize and Audience Award at the 2016 Sundance Festival but generated controversy as it was revealed that Parker was accused of rape 17 years prior.

2018, February 14
Nikolas Cruz shoots 17 and injures 15 more at Marjorie Stoneman Douglas High School in Parkland, Florida. President Donald Trump issues statement blaming violent video games.

1

Violence in Radio

Introduction

From controversial stories, to comments by hosts, to questionable lyrics in the songs selected, violence in radio broadcasts has long been a source of debate. When broadcast radio was introduced in the 1920s, proponents maintained that it was an important new vehicle to give people of all ages information about the world. Critics contended that it would corrupt young people and discourage them from their studies, their faith, and otherwise interfere with healthy pursuits. Indeed, newspapers reported of children having nightmares after listening to "lurid" radio programs, although in reality radio has always been more controlled by the federal government than have other mediums. In the 1930s and 1940s radio was criticized for broadcasting shows about crime and violence. Some of the radio programs in this era were horror themed, although they were definitely not marketed to children. Shows like *Inner Sanctum* and *Lights Out* were known for their particularly gruesome stories, while the premier show of the era, *Suspense*, was more of a scary thriller without as much gore. *Escape* was narrated by Vincent Price, launching his career. Stephen King, the master of horror novels, has said that radio is the perfect medium for these creepy and violent tales.

Radio has always been censored by the Federal Communications Commission (FCC). Federal law prohibits the airing of obscene, indecent, or profane information. It will fine commentators, hosts, and stations for violating these laws. Comedian George Carlin made fun of this censorship in his classic skit, "Seven Dirty Words."

One of the earliest controversies about radio violence occurred after the broadcast of "War of the Worlds" on October 30, 1938. An adaptation of H. G. Wells's novel by the same name, it was directed and narrated by director and future filmmaker Orson Welles and told the story of an alien invasion. Welles told the story in a way that made it sound as though an actual invasion was happening at that moment. There were reports that so many people believed an attack was occurring that a panic ensued, whereby thousands of New Yorkers and even people in other cities fled their homes. People allegedly jumped to their deaths rather than face the purported alien invasion. This crazed response has been a part of American folklore ever since, although there is no evidence such a widespread panic occurred. Rather, a few people fired guns in the air. Although records show some people called the hospital to inquire about donating blood, there is no evidence that anyone committed suicide because of the broadcast.

Sports radio has also endured controversies, as commentators sometimes say things that are racist, sexist, or condone violence. Alternatively, sport commentators have also called for an end to gun violence and used their platform to advocate nonviolence. For instance, ESPN host Max Kellerman was suspended in 2014 for a conversation he had on ESPN-LA Radio. The conversation on the *Mason & Ireland* show occurred just three days after another ESPN commentator, Stephen A. Smith, was suspended for comments he made about NFL player Ray Rice and the release of videotape that Rice had knocked out his girlfriend in an elevator. Kellerman admitted to hitting his girlfriend several years prior. ESPN had cautioned their hosts not to discuss the issue in light of the controversy around Smith's suspension (Raissman, 2014). San Francisco 49ers team radio broadcaster Ted Robinson was suspended for two games for making comments about the Rice domestic violence situation as well. He criticized Janay Palmer, who married Rice after the incident.

The 1980s saw the rise of "shock jocks" in the United States. These are controversial radio hosts who say intentionally provocative things and who discuss topics that are often taboo. Many have asserted that in their heyday, these shock jocks incited violence, although such allegations are difficult to prove. Some shock jocks like Howard Stern are known for sexually provocative content and guests, while others like Rush Limbaugh are known for their conservative political commentary. Stern has come under fire for making fun of tragedies, for instance, in 1982 when he joked about a plane crash that killed 74 people. He was fired from radio station DC101 in Washington, D.C., six months later. He was fired from another station in 1985 for hosting a stunt he called "Bestiality Dial-A-Date." After the Columbine massacre in April 1999, Stern again drew heat for making sexual comments about the girls fleeing the shooters. The Colorado state legislature issued an official censure against Stern.

Limbaugh has referred to the NFL as the "thug league" and likened players to violent gang members. He attacked Sandra Fluke, who testified before Congress about the need for insurance coverage to include birth control, calling her a "slut." He also mocked actor Michael J. Fox, who suffers from Parkinson's disease.

Another controversial shock jock is Bubba the Love Sponge (born Todd Clem) Clem. In 2001, Clem aired a segment called "Bubba's Road Kill Barbecue." It involved the killing of a feral hog, "Andy," that had been captured by a hunter. The realistic sound effects of hogs feeding led many listeners to believe the hog was actually being tortured. The animal was indeed killed. Clem and Executive Producer Brent Lee Hatley, as well as two loyal listeners, were arrested and charged with felony animal cruelty. Clem and the others argued that the hog was slaughtered in keeping with all required law. All four were acquitted. Clem was fined multiple times by the FCC for other stunts. He was removed from his show in

Tampa, Florida, in August 2014. For several years after and as of May 2017, he has been embroiled in a lawsuit against *Nielsen Audio* and Cox Media Group that alleges he manipulated ratings. Clem has countersued, claiming that Nielsen and Cox conspired with his competition to remove him from the air.

Shock jock Don Imus was eventually fired for referring to the members of the NCAA championship-winning female basketball team as "nappy-headed hoes" in 2004. Two shock jocks known as Marconi and Tiny Imus signed a multiyear contract with Citadel Broadcasting in 2007. On June 17, 2013, the three hosts of the show—Steak Shapiro, Chris Dimino, and Nick Cellini—were trying to taunt their division rivals, the New Orleans Saints when they mocked former Saints player Steve Gleason, who speaks using a voice box that he controls with his eyes because he has amyotrophic lateral sclerosis (ALS). Despite issuing apologies, all three were fired.

Marconi and Tiny were a pair of shock jocks who did the morning show on KNRK-FM in Portland, Oregon. They got into some trouble on May 12, 2004, when they played an audiotape of American Nick Berg, who'd been murdered in Iraq. They were both fired because they made jokes about Berg's grizzly beheading.

The influence of shock jocks has waned in recent years, especially among younger people, many argue, because radio is not the preferred medium. One-third of people ages 18 to 34 do not have an AM/FM radio in their homes (Jackson, 2016). Many shock jocks have gravitated to satellite radio, which has more limited listenership but is not governed by the FCC regulations. During the presidential campaign of 2016, tapes of then-nominee Donald Trump making misogynistic comments on *The Howard Stern Show* some years prior generated great debate and, among many, disgust. Conservative talk show hosts have fared better, as their listeners skew older.

Perhaps the biggest scandal in radio history involved the murder of Denver liberal radio host Alan Berg. On June 18, 1984, the 50-year-old radio host was shot 13 times in his driveway while returning home after dinner with his ex-wife. The murder happened just days after Berg had called out the Order, a white supremacist group. Four members of the Order, an Aryan Nation splinter group, were arrested. Prosecutors alleged that these men targeted Berg because he was Jewish and that he had repeatedly ridiculed their group and other white supremacist organizations on his show. Two were convicted. David Lane was sentenced to 150 years in prison for driving the getaway car (he died in 2007), and Bruce Pierce was sentenced to 252 years. Reports are that he remained involved with the Order from behind bars.

White supremacist groups have long used radio as a tool to spread their doctrine of hate. Today, however, more are using the Web and social media. In March 2016, Huffington Post reported that white supremacists were broadcasting from Donald Trump rallies.

One radio program that has been applauded in the United States is *This American Life.* It is a weekly public radio show that airs on more than 500 stations, reaching some 2.2 million listeners. It is also one of the most popular podcasts, which are downloaded weekly by another 2.5 million people. Each episode focuses on a specific theme, some of which are related to crime and violence. For instance, Episode 164, which aired on July 7, 2000, focused on crime scenes and crime scene analysis. Episode 604, which aired on December 9, 2016, focuses on Samantha

Broun's interviews with inmates, politicians, police officers, and family members who were involved or affected by the murder of Broun's mother 20 years prior. A television version of *This American Life* aired from 2006 to 2008, and in 2014 the spinoff podcast series *Serial* was launched.

Serial is both popular and lauded by critics. It is a podcast series hosted by investigative journalist Sarah Koenig. It won a Peabody Award in April 2015 for the telling of a long-form fiction story. Episodes, which initially aired weekly then every other week, focus on issues of crime and justice. Season One, for instance, took on the case of 18-year-old Hae Minn Lee, who was murdered in 1999 in Baltimore, Maryland. Her ex-boyfriend, Adnan Masud Syed, was convicted and sentenced to life in prison despite declaring his innocence. Three weeks after the end of Season One, the Maryland Court of Special Appeals allowed Syed to appeal his conviction. In June 2016, the conviction was set aside, and Judge Martin P. Welch called for a new trial. Season Two focuses on the case of Army Soldier Beau Bergdahl, who was held for five years by the Taliban then released, only to face charges of desertion in the United States.

Outside the United States, radio has definitely been used to incite violence. Although various media outlets were used to promote dangerous stereotypes about the Tutsis in the 1990s, the private radio station, Radio Television Libre des Mille Collines, was at the forefront of the problem. At one point the station called for a "final war" to "exterminate the cockroaches," which led to the genocide that killed some 800,000 Tutsis and moderate Hutus (Smith, 2003). Alternatively, radio campaigns have been used in many countries as part of awareness campaigns about various forms of violence.

Laura L. Finley

Further Reading

Breech, J. 2014. "49ers Suspend Radio Announcer Ted Robinson for Ray Rice Comments." *CBS Sports,* September 10. http://www.cbssports.com/nfl/eye-on-football/24704860/ers-suspend-radio-announcer-ted-robinson-for-ray-rice-comments

Brite, J. 2002. "Florida Shock Jock Faces Animal Cruelty Charges." *CNN*, February 25. http://edition.cnn.com/2002/LAW/02/25/ctv.florida.bubba.suit/index.html

Chilton, M. 2016. "The War of the Worlds Panic Was a Myth." *The Telegraph*, May 6. http://www.telegraph.co.uk/radio/what-to-listen-to/the-war-of-the-worlds-panic-was-a-myth

Dukakis, A. 2014. "Murder of Colorado Radio Man Still Resonates 30 Years Later." *Colorado Public Radio*, June 18. http://www.cpr.org/news/story/murder-colorado-radio-man-alan-berg-still-resonates-30-years-later

Jackson, D. 2016. "The Last Days of Shock Jocks." *Thrillist*, October 18. https://www.thrillist.com/entertainment/nation/radio-shock-jocks-howard-stern

Malloy, S. n.d. "The 20 Most Racist Things Rush Limbaugh Has Ever Said." *Alternet*. http://www.alternet.org/20-most-racist-things-rush-limbaugh-has-ever-said

Raissman, B. 2014. "ESPN Suspends Max Kellerman for Inappropriate Conversation on Domestic Violence." *New York Daily News*, August 8. http://www.nydailynews.com/sports/more-sports/espn-suspends-max-kellerman-inappropriate-conversation-domestic-violence-article-1.1897365

Serial: https://serialpodcast.org

Smith, R. 2003. "The Impact of Hate Media in Rwanda." *BBC*, December 3. http://news
.bbc.co.uk/2/hi/africa/3257748.stm

Sullivan, D. 2017. "In Countersuit, Bubba the Love Sponge Accuses Nielsen, Cox Media
of Conspiracy to Boot Him from Radio." *Tampa Bay Times*, January 17. http://www
.tampabay.com/news/courts/civil/in-countersuit-bubba-the-love-sponge-accuses
-nielsen-cox-media-of/2309894

This American Life: https://www.thisamericanlife.org/about

Wilkie, C. 2016. "White Supremacists Are Broadcasting from Inside Trump Rallies." *Huffington Post*, March 2. http://www.huffingtonpost.com/entry/white-supremacists
-donald-trump-rallies_us_56d663cfe4b03260bf789a09

Bubba the Love Sponge

Born Todd Alan Clem, Bubba the Love Sponge is a controversial radio host most
known for his *Bubba the Love Sponge Show*. He legally changed his name to
Bubba the Love Sponge in 1999.

Bubba the Love Sponge began his radio career at Indiana State University, then
moved on to WGRD in Grand Rapids, Michigan. He has long been criticized for
making sexist comments and for graphic discussions of sex and drugs, although
this was in part what attracted his fan base. He has been fired from many positions, first in 1988 after he made sexual remarks about another radio host in town.

In 2001, Bubba and colleagues engaged in a controversial skit on WXTB in
Tampa. They used sound effects to make it seem as though they were slaughtering
a wild boar on air. Bubba, along with his Executive Producer Brent Hatley and two
others were charged with animal cruelty but all were acquitted.

In 2004, Bubba was fined by the Federal Communications Commission (FCC),
along with four stations owned by Clear Channel Communications, for material
that was offensive. One of the controversial pieces involved a skit in which the cartoon characters George Jetson, Scooby Doo, and Alvin and the Chipmunks were
discussing various sex activities. Clear Channel fired Clem shortly after the fine
was announced.

Bubba faced another lawsuit in 2006, when a porn film actress known as Hope
Miler, claimed that during a segment with another porn actress, Melissa Harrington,
Bubba had commanded Harrington to penetrate her with a large sex toy. The case
was eventually dismissed.

One year later, Bubba was sued by a competing DJ, Todd Schnitt, who alleged
that he made disparaging remarks about his family on air. The two reached a settlement in 2013.

In 2010, Bubba announced via Twitter that he had been hired to be a backstage
interviewer with Total Nonstop Action Wrestling. He participated in several backstage interviews on Monday night's *TNA Impact!* but was fired after he made disparaging remarks about Haitian people. Just days after the January 12, 2010, magnitude
7.0 earthquake that left as many as 316,000 people dead and millions devastated,
Bubba wrote on Twitter: "F**k Haiti" and referred to the earthquake as a "cleanse."
On January 19, 2010, Bubba claimed to have been assaulted by wrestler Awesome
Kong while working backstage; then a little over a month later Kong filed a lawsuit

alleging that Bubba had threatened him during a phone call. The two argued on Tampa Bay radio host Mike "Cowhead" Calta's show, and Bubba is said to have used racial slurs against Kong. His time with TNA was not entirely over, however. He rejoined as a personal interviewer for the Band, a group of professional wrestlers, only to again be fired on April 30 when the Cowhead show issue came to light.

A 2012 sex scandal gained Bubba much attention. Gawker released a video in which his then-wife, Heather Clem, was having sex with former professional wrestling star Hulk Hogan, born Terry Bollea, a friend of Clem's. Heather admits to the act, but denies that they intended to film the incident. Hogan filed the suit due to being illegally videotaped. Hogan sued Bubba, Heather, and Gawker for invasion of privacy, eventually reaching a settlement of just $5,000 (Griffin, 2016). Hogan also sued Gawker Media and was initially awarded $140 million, but eventually a settlement of $31 million was reached.

In 2013 Bubba allegedly made racist remarks during the filming of a commercial for Vermont Teddy Bear Company. He claims that the audio was doctored; the video was removed from YouTube but is still available on TMZ.

Bubba faced another lawsuit in 2015 when Nielsen alleged that he had tampered with the radio ratings. The organization claimed that he lied about how many listeners he had, and Bubba admitted to paying one of the Nielsen panelists to say they listened to his show but denied that he bribed anyone else.

In 2017, Bubba signed on to host his show on WWBA 820 AM, which many saw as a huge step down from his heyday. The network does include many conservative talk show hosts, including Laura Ingraham and Dennis Miller (Kludt, 2016).

Outside of his show, Bubba has faced trouble with the law. On February 23, 2017, his former girlfriend, Nicole "Nikki" L'Ange, filed for a restraining order against Bubba in Pinellas County, Florida, alleging that for the four years they lived together he had been violent toward her. The incident that prompted her application for the restraining order allegedly involved him strangling her, hitting her in the back of the head, throwing her to the ground, and threatening her if she left or called the police. L'Ange claims that Bubba harassed her, her father, and her friends after she left him, and she also says that he cancelled her health insurance and prevented her from obtaining unemployment benefits. She also says that Bubba is "unstable," has a "horrible temper," and made disparaging remarks about her on his show (Staff Reports, 2017).

Laura L. Finley

See also: Cumia, Anthony; *Opie & Anthony Show, The*; Stern, Howard

Further Reading

Bubba the Love Sponge Show: http://www.btls.com/

Griffin, J. 2016. "Bubba the Love Sponge Clem Is Off the Air at Tampa Bay's WBRN-FM 98.7." *Tampa Bay Times*, December 12. http://www.tampabay.com/news/business /bubba-the-love-sponge-clem-is-off-the-air-at-tampa-bays-wbrn-fm-987/2305988

Inside Radio Staff. 2017. "Bubba Takes New Gig in Home Market—on AM." *Inside Radio,* February 9. http://www.insideradio.com/free/bubba-takes-new-gig-in-home-market -on-am/article_ffd415ac-eef6-11e6-986c-43226507cd58.html

Kludt, T. 2016. "Why Hulk Hogan Settled for $5,000 with the Man Who Made His Sex Tape." *CNN*, March 12. http://money.cnn.com/2016/03/12/media/hulk-hogan-gawker-settlement/index.html

Staff Reports. 2017. "Bubba the Love Sponge Hit with Restraining Order for Domestic Violence." *Saint Petersburg Blog,* http://saintpetersblog.com/bubba-love-sponge-hit-restraining-order-domestic-violence/

Coast to Coast AM

Coast to Coast AM focuses on the paranormal and other odd experiences, airing on more than 600 stations in the United States and in Mexico and Guam. It is heard by nearly 4.5 million listeners each night and features two main hosts, George Noory and George Knapp, whose programs air overnight (About Coast to Coast AM, 2018).

Noory was recruited by Premier Radio Network to guest host on *Coast to Coast with Art Bell*. After Bell retired in 2003, Noory took over as the permanent host and has grown the listening audience. His show covers topics such as alien abductions, ghosts, time travel, and conspiracies. Noory, who became interested in these issues when he read Walter Sullivan's book *We Are Not Alone* at age 13, says, "I've wanted to cover stories that the mainstream media never touch—the unusual, the paranormal and things like that. I learned that broadcast was the best business for exploring these issues, and I've been doing it for 33 years." Noory started his radio career on Detroit's WCAR-AM, and his first interview was with UFO expert and physicist Stanton Friedman. He moved on to serve as news producer and executive news producer at WJBK-TV from 1974 to 1978, then at age 28 was the youngest news director of a major news market when he worked at KMSP-TV in Minneapolis. Noory also served as director of news planning and development at KSTP-TV in that city, then director of news at KSDK-TV in St. Louis. He received three Emmy Awards for his work as a news executive.

Noory is the co-author of four books. In 2006, Noory released a book he co-wrote with William J. Birnes, called *Worker in the Light: Unlock Your Five Senses and Liberate Your Limitless Potential*, which emphasizes personal empowerment and happiness. The two co-authored a second book in 2009, *Journey to the Light*, which presents the firsthand accounts of ordinary people who made major spiritual growth and changed their lives. Noory's third book, co-authored by Rosemary Ellen Guiley, was released in 2011. *Talking to the Dead* focuses more on the topics of his show. His latest book, released in 2015 and co-authored with Richard Belzer and David Wayne, called *Someone Is Hiding Something: What Happened to Malaysia Airlines Flight 370?* argues that something paranormal or a conspiracy is likely responsible for that tragedy.

GAIAM TV launched a new series in 2012 that is hosted by Noory. *Beyond Belief with George Noory* is a one-hour, weekly show that features some of his favorite radio guests and topics. Noory has also appeared on SYFY, the History Channel's *Ancient Aliens*, the Larry King show, and many other radio and television programs.

George Knapp started his career in journalism. He served for many years as a news anchor on KLAS TV Las Vegas. Knapp has twice received the prestigious

Peabody Award. He also won the Dupont Award from Columbia University, the Edward R. Murrow Award, and 25 regional Emmy Awards for his news writing, investigative reporting, and environmental reporting. Knapp's reports about Nevada's Area 51 military base and aliens won him the UPI's Best Individual Achievement by a Reporter Award in 1989. Since 2007, he has been a weekend host of *Coast to Coast*. On *Coast to Coast*, Noory is known for his lengthy discussions with both callers and experts. Noory is proud of his work, saying, "I've brought in new topics, seeking more answers and the truth" (Noory, 2018). Not only does he focus on aliens and paranormal topics, but he has broadened the show's content to cover computer security, bird flu, and other important scientific and political topics. Still, tales of visits by ghosts remain the most common, especially from callers. Noory is a believer, who claims he had an out-of-body experience as a child. He says, "If they [callers] think their dead grandmother is visiting them at night, more power to them. They don't need me telling them (it's) true or not true. There are those few people who may challenge the facts and say some of the stuff may not be true. I say to them, 'Chill out, relax and have an open mind'" (Wired Staff, 2006).

Scientists do not shy away from the show, even if they disagree with its hosts. Frequent guest Michael Shermer, publisher of *Skeptic* magazine, explains that he and other scientists go on the show because, "We want to chase out bad ideas with good ideas, and just explain what science is. Why don't most scientists accept psychic powers as real or UFOs are real? Why do we have high standards of evidence before you accept something?" Others are more prone to scoff at the show openly, as Peter Ward, an author and paleontologist at the University of Washington, does, saying the stories told on it are "so outrageous that you have to really be a nincompoop to take the far-out stuff seriously" and referring to it as "entertainment with some good science in it" (Wired Staff, 2016).

Laura L. Finley

See also: "War of the Worlds"

Further Reading
About Coast to Coast AM. 2018. https://www.coasttocoastam.com/pages/about
Knapp, G. 2018. Coast to Coast AM. https://www.coasttocoastam.com/pages/george-knapp
Noory, G. 2018. Coast to Coast AM. https://www.coasttocoastam.com/pages/george-noory
Wired Staff. 2016. "Coast to Coast AM Is No Wack Job." *Wired*, February 15. https://www.wired.com/2006/02/coast-to-coast-am-is-no-wack-job/

Cumia, Anthony

Anthony Cumia is a radio "shock jock" whose program has long been accused of being racist and promoting violence. For almost 20 years, he hosted a show with Greg "Opie" Hughes. The show was known for crazy skits, its support of upcoming comedians, and the hosts' outlandish comments. They grew a large following on FM radio before moving to Sirius XM in 2007.

Cumia once expressed on his show, *The Opie & Anthony Show*, that he always seeks a dentist of his own race because he trusts them more. He has repeatedly argued that people are too kind to black Americans and that he believes they are mostly criminals. He has made the argument that black people have more power than white people because they can cry that any problem is due to racism. Cumia also claimed most blacks in the United States aren't descendants of slaves and that blacks use slavery as an excuse to sell drugs and commit crimes. He often yelled at black fans on his show, typically using curse words.

Cumia was fired from his show in 2014 after he called a black woman disparaging and racist names. He claims she punched him while he was taking photos in Times Square because she objected to being in the frame. Cumia referred to black people as "savages" and "animals" and claimed that she was lucky he didn't shoot her. SiriusXM called his rant "abhorrent" and "wholly inconsistent with what SiriusXM represents." Cumia responded by ranting further on Twitter, at one point saying that black Americans "are not people" (Warren, 2014). In a July 2, 2014, tweet, he wrote, "It's a jungle out in our cities after midnight. Violent savages own the streets. They all came 2 defend this pig. I had to yell like at dogs" and then wrote, in response to a fan who asked why he was fired, "I was white" (Morrisey, 2014). His partner Opie and a third co-host, comedian Jim Norton, expressed outrage that Cumia was fired, but SiriusXM refused to allow him to continue with the show.

Cumia had been fired twice before, but always with Opie. The duo were let go from WAAF in Boston after a skit in which they claimed, for April Fool's Day, that the mayor of Boston had died. In 2002 they were fired after hosting a contest on their show in which fans were dared to have sex in St. Patrick's Cathedral (Collins, 2002). Immediately after Cumia was fired, things seemed OK with Opie, but then some time later he spoke to several outlets expressing dismay that his partner hadn't fought harder for him. Opie responded that he indeed did all he could and was upset that Cumia was disparaging him on social media. "Since he got fired nine months ago, he's been passive-aggressively taking shots at me on podcasts, allowing people on his show to trash me," Opie said (Mosendz, 2015). Opie also explained that when the two started hosting together they were best friends, but a fallout in 1999 made the subsequent years less collegial. Cumia had gotten an ugly divorce, and Opie's girlfriend was good friends with his ex-wife. Cumia did not appreciate that Opie regularly invited his girlfriend to show events. Contract negotiations with SiriusXM also stressed the relationship (Mosendz, 2015). Cumia said after the firing that he no longer considered Opie a friend, while Opie referred to Cumia as a former friend. Opie said he would consider another show together should the right situation arise, but Cumia has said absolutely not (Mosendz, 2015).

In real life Cumia is no stranger to controversy, either. In 2016, he pleaded guilty to third-degree assault against his girlfriend, Dani Golightly, as well as to criminal obstruction of breathing. She broadcast on the social media site Periscope after the incident. Although the video shows him searching the home for a handgun, he did not face firearms charges. Cumia was ordered to complete six months of rehabilitation for alcoholism and a batterer's intervention program (Merlan, 2016).

Laura L. Finley

See also: Bubba the Love Sponge; Edwards, James; *Opie & Anthony Show, The*; Stern, Howard

Further Reading

Collins, D. 2002. "DJs Dumped over Church Sex Stunt." *CBS News,* August 21. https://www.cbsnews.com/news/djs-dumped-over-church-sex-stunt

Merlan, A. 2016. "Anthony Cumia Pleads Guilty in Domestic Abuse Strangulation Case, Gets a Very Nice Deal." *Jezebel,* June 27. http://jezebel.com/anthony-cumia-pleads-guilty-in-domestic-abuse-strangula-1782662811

Morrisey, T. 2014. "Opie & Anthony Host Has a Long History of Racism." *Jezebel,* July 3. https://jezebel.com/opie-anthony-host-has-a-long-history-of-racism-1599685595

Mosendz, P. 2015. "Opie and Anthony No More: Inside the Nasty Breakup of Radio's Most Notorious Shock Jocks." *Newsweek,* April 9. http://www.newsweek.com/opie-and-anthony-no-more-inside-nasty-break-radios-most-notorious-shock-jocks-321186

Warren, L. 2014. "New York Radio Host Fired after Racist Twitter Tirade Against Black Woman 'Who Punched Him in the Face in Times Square.'" *Daily Mail,* July 4. http://www.dailymail.co.uk/news/article-2679686/Radio-host-unleashes-racist-Twitter-tirade-punched-face-black-woman-Times-Square.html

Edwards, James

James Edwards, whose show is called *The Political Cesspool*, is a conservative talk show host. The show is syndicated by Liberty News Radio Network and Accent Radio Network and has aired since 2004. It is also simulcast on Stormfront Radio, which is run by the white nationalist group Stormfront. Starting in 2011 it is also featured on WLRM in Millington, Tennessee, which is a Christian station. Not only is the show controversial because of the perspectives espoused by the host and guests, but also for its sponsors, which include the white separatist group Council of Conservative Citizens and a Holocaust denial group, Institute for Historical Review. It, and Edwards, have long attracted the attention of the Southern Poverty Law Center, which monitors hate groups, and the Anti-Defamation League, which addresses anti-Semitism. Edwards himself has said he is a white nationalist and disavows homosexuality (About James Edwards, n.d.). The mission statement for *The Political Cesspool* says it "stands for the Dispossessed Majority" and is "pro-white." It says the show rejects "homosexuality, vulgarity, loveless sex, and masochism" and believes "secession is a right of all people and individuals." It also states, "We wish to revive the White birthrate above replacement level fertility and beyond to grow the percentage of Whites in the world relative to other races" (About James Edwards, n.d.).

Guests on Edwards's show include leaders of white nationalist and white supremacist groups as well as conservative political, religious, and community leaders. Long-time Ku Klux Klan leader David Duke, conservative religious pundit Pat Buchanan, and Holocaust denier Willis Carto are among the guests who frequent the show. Outside of the show, Edwards has espoused what many believe to be racist views. On a panel on CNN's *Paula Zahn Now* show in 2007, Edwards denounced what he called "forced integration" and claimed that African Americans are violent and commit too much crime. Two years later on the same show he made similar comments and has referred to slavery as "the greatest thing that ever happened to African-Americans" (Wilkie, 2016). In a February 2007 show, Edwards said,

"A lot of their motivation is that they hate Christianity. They hate what we call the WASP establishment . . . and they're using pornography as a subversive tool against us. Jews are by and large dominant in the porn industry" (About James Edwards, n.d.). In March 2015, Edwards claimed, "I am firmly of the belief that race relations were better during Jim Crow, and even better in the antebellum south, than they are now" (About James Edwards, n.d.).

Edwards is also a member of the American Freedom Party, which advocates white nationalism. In 2010 Edwards published a book, *Racism, Schmacism: How Liberals Use the "R" Word to Push the Obama Agenda*, in which he denounced racism as politically correct. To celebrate the 10th anniversary of the show in October 2014, Edwards hosted an event with some of the most well-known white nationalists and ended it with a salute to Nathan Bedford Forrest, the Civil War general and first grand dragon of the Ku Klux Klan, whom Edwards idolizes (About James Edwards, n.d.).

Edwards interviewed Donald Trump Jr., President Donald Trump's oldest son, in March 2016. That the Republican frontrunner and later winner of the election's son would agree to be on a show that has, among its objectives, "to grow the percentage of Whites in the world relative to other races," generated a great deal of controversy. Edwards was also issued press credentials and a VIP parking pass at a Trump campaign event, although a spokesperson said at the time that the Trump campaign did not know about Edwards's personal views and also strongly condemns them. Edwards made several comments on his show in support of Trump, praising his "masculine attitude" as a "prototypical alpha male" and the candidate's approach to immigration (Pilkington, 2016). Edwards has expressed pride that he may have helped Trump win the 2016 election.

Laura L. Finley

See also: Cumia, Anthony; Limbaugh, Rush; *Opie & Anthony Show, The*

Further Reading

About James Edwards. n.d. *Southern Poverty Law Center.* https://www.splcenter.org/fighting-hate/extremist-files/individual/james-edwards

Pilkington, E. 2016. "Donald Trump Jr. Grants Interview to Prominent White Supremacist." *The Guardian,* March 2. https://www.theguardian.com/us-news/2016/mar/02/donald-trump-jr-james-edwards-radio-interview-white-supremacist

Wilkie, C. 2016. "Here's What Happened during Donald Trump Jr.'s Interview with a White Nationalist." *Huffington Post,* March 3. https://www.huffingtonpost.com/entry/donald-trump-jr-james-edwards-interview_us_56d8854ae4b0000de403a77f

Limbaugh, Rush

Talk-radio host Rush Limbaugh has made a long career out of being controversial. He has repeatedly been accused of making racist and sexist comments and of advocating violence in various situations. Without a doubt Limbaugh has a great deal of influence, as his three-hour radio show is aired five days a week on more than 600 radio stations.

Rather than directly advocate violence, Limbaugh's broadcasts generally focus on creating the conditions for violence, or as he typically describes it, "chaos." He also uses a variety of rhetoric tactics to frame those he sees as opponents, in particular, the political left, as the enemy. He frequently tells listeners that the left is a violent threat to them and their lifestyle. Limbaugh blames the left for the so-called breakdown of morality in society, describing them as ignorant. He has even alleged at times that the left burns their cars and houses and kills their children more than the right does.

Limbaugh has, according to John K. Wilson (author of *The Most Dangerous Man in America: Rush Limbaugh's Assault on Reason*), repeatedly used his website to call for violence. For instance, he commented about the 2009 military coup in Honduras that overthrew the democratically elected president as "what many of you wish would happen here," then just days later issued a similar call for a coup against President Obama. He asked, "Do you realize, ladies and gentlemen, what we are living through right now is exactly why the Revolutionary War was fought," implying that the Obama administration was cause for revolution (Wilson, 2011). He supported these calls with regular accusations and insinuations that President Obama and others in his administration were engaged in some type of conspiracy to harm the American people. Further, Limbaugh penned a song, to the tune of "Puff the Magic Dragon" that used age-old stereotypes to make fun of Obama. His "Barack the Magic Negro" was a hit with his listeners.

One topic that Limbaugh took up frequently was the falsehood that the Affordable Care Act Obama helped enact would result in "death panels" that essentially authorized murder of the elderly. "This is what dictators do . . . there's a reason, if you go back to world history, you go back to Cambodia, you go back to Mao Tse-tung in China, you go to Cuba, you go to old Soviet Union, one of the things they did was target—Hitler, health care—target the elderly. Target them. Why? Because they vote, they are more likely it [sic] vote, and they're more educated, they have more experience, they know more, they have been alive longer. You get rid of the people who know the past. You get rid of people who know how great the eighties were with a conservative economic policy, get rid of those people" (Malloy, 2013).

Before the November 2016 election, Limbaugh called on listeners to vote in the Democratic primaries as a way to divide the party and, he asserted, result in street riots at the Denver Democratic convention. He predicted that Donald Trump would win (which he did) and maintained that the political left would turn to "levels of violence that we have not seen." He, like Mr. Trump, criticized the mainstream media, arguing that they would fail to condemn violent protestors. Although many did indeed protest the results, very little violence ensued.

Limbaugh responds defensively to concerns about his show and website. For instance, he equated the criticism of himself and others for their violent rhetoric to the poor treatment of rape victims: "Yeah, that's what they used to tell women who were raped, isn't it? 'Just sit back and enjoy it'" (Malloy, 2016).

Limbaugh has equated conservatives with rape victims numerous other times. In discussing a man who made death threats to Speaker of the House Nancy Pelosi, Limbaugh asked, "Do you people in the White House, do you people in the media, do you ever stop to consider that you have an intelligent, informed electorate who simply doesn't like being raped, and being raped is what is happening to people in this country by their government. No other way to put this" (Myers, 2012).

Limbaugh minimizes sexual assault and jokes about the need for consent. In February 2012, Limbaugh ignited controversy when he referred to college student Sandra Fluke, who was testifying before Congress about the need for the inclusion of birth control in health insurance coverage, as a "slut" and a "prostitute" (Wemple, 2013). When allegations of sexual assault were levied against then-Republican presidential candidate Donald Trump, Limbaugh denounced liberals as the "rape police" (Chumley, 2016).

Many of his comments involve dangerous racial stereotypes. Days after the 2009 inauguration of President Obama, Limbaugh warned his viewers that "angry minorities" who now felt empowered would seek revenge against whites. He has denounced the NBA, referring to it as the Thug Basketball Association, and poked tasteless fun at the victims who suffered from Hurricane Katrina in New Orleans. He refers to the NAACP as a racist organization. Limbaugh also denounced the Black Lives Matter movement as a terrorist group and repeatedly cites statistics that reinforce the image that violent crime in America is out of control and is largely perpetrated by blacks. Similarly, he has laughed at the argument that Native Americans experienced a genocide in the United States and calls Spanish the "language of the ghetto" (Malloy, 2016).

Limbaugh's fans argue that he is not responsible for any act of violence and that he is merely giving voice to the conservative viewpoint in the United States.

Laura L. Finley

See also: Cumia, Anthony; Edwards, James; *Opie & Anthony Show, The*

Further Reading

Chumley, C. 2016. "Rush Limbaugh Warns of Massive Leftist Violence If Trump Elected." *World News Daily,* July 1. http://www.wnd.com/2016/07/rush-limbaugh-warns-of -massive-leftist-violence-if-trump-elected/#gwmsCUEbp4m4Gaql.99

Feldman, J. 2008. "Did Limbaugh Try to Incite Violence? *Huffington Post,* May 7. http:// www.huffingtonpost.com/jeffrey-feldman/did-limbaugh-incite-viole_b_100586 .html

Malloy, S. 2013. "The 20 Most Racist Things Rush Limbaugh Has Ever Said." *Alternet,* January 21. http://www.alternet.org/20-most-racist-things-rush-limbaugh-has-ever -said

Myers, R. 2012. "How Rush Limbaugh Gets Away with Fomenting Violence and Hate Against Liberals; the Poor; Minorities." *Daily Kos,* October 7. http://www.dailykos .com/story/2012/10/7/1141320/-How-Rush-Limbaugh-gets-away-with-fomenting -violence-and-hate-against-liberals-the-poor-minorities

Wemple, E. 2013. "Rush Limbaugh's Legacy on Sandra Fluke." *The Washington Post,* October 11. https://www.washingtonpost.com/blogs/erik-wemple/wp/2013/10/11/rush -limbaughs-legacy-on-sandra-fluke/?utm_term=.bdba33ca9138

Wilson, J. 2011. "Limbaugh and Violent Rhetoric." *Daily Kos,* January 12. http://www .dailykos.com/story/2011/1/12/935692/-

Wilson, J. 2011. *The Most Dangerous Man in America: Rush Limbaugh's Assault on Reason.* New York: Thomas Dunne Books.

Opie & Anthony Show, The

Gregg "Opie" Hughes and Anthony Cumia were co-hosts of the *Opie & Anthony* radio show, which started in 1995 and ended in 2014. Jim Norton joined as co-host in 2001. They are known for the controversial gags and jokes they made on the show. More than violence, their skits often featured sexist jokes and sexual content.

The *Opie & Anthony Show* first ran on WAAF in Boston. It became nationally syndicated by Infinity Broadcasting in 2001. Opie and Anthony were twice fired for their antics. First, in 1998, WAAF fired the duo for an April Fool's Day prank in which they told their listeners that the mayor of Boston had died. They were fired again in 2002 after the skit "Sex for Sam," in which they incited listeners to have sex in St. Patrick's Cathedral, including a live account of one couple doing it (Collins, 2002). Opie said about the incident, "I wish [the company] had hung in there and rode out the controversy. I mean, [the church stunt] was in bad taste and all that. We get that. But the attention we received would have translated into huge, huge ratings if they had stuck with us." He went on, "I know we did an FCC-friendly show. Nothing graphic was ever described. It was very tame on the air. But it was a different time. We put the FCC in a bad position" (Farhi, 2006).

After the second firing, Opie and Anthony returned in October 2004 on XM Satellite Radio, which became SiriusXM Satellite in a 2007 merger with Sirius. The show ended when Cumia was fired in July 2014. They have said that they are simply comedians, not shock jocks (Farhi, 2006).

Cumia issued a series of racist tweets about a black woman who he claims punched him in the face when he was taking photos in Times Square. He referred to her as an "animal pig face worthless meat sack," among other epithets (Leopold, 2015). Spokespeople for SiriusXM denounced Cumia's tweets as inconsistent with their brand. Hughes and Norton defended Cumia, although Cumia has said he does not think they did enough to help him keep his job. Fans reacted by starting a Change.org petition and alleging they would boycott Sirius until Cumia was reinstated. Cumia has never apologized, instead defending himself by saying, "Sirius decided to cave and fire me," he wrote in a Twitter post on Friday morning that now appears to have been deleted. "Welcome to bizarro world. Fired for s*** that wasn't even on the air & wasn't illegal. So, who's next?" (Coleman, 2014). Opie and Anthony had been having troubles with the network before the firing, as Cumia and Norton wanted longer contracts than Opie had asked for. The two co-hosts bickered frequently about it. Opie has said he might consider doing another show with Anthony, but Cumia says absolutely not.

Not long after his firing, Cumia was arrested when his girlfriend, Danielle Brand, said he pushed her against a wall, tried to strangle her, and stomped on her hand in their New York home (Coleman, 2014). A video of the incident was uploaded to the streaming site Periscope (Mosendz, 2015).

Laura L. Finley

See also: Bubba the Love Sponge; Cumia, Anthony; Edwards, James; Stern, Howard

Further Reading

Coleman, M. 2014. "Opie and Anthony Host Anthony Cumia Fired after Racist Twitter Tirade." *Rolling Stone*, July 6. https://www.rollingstone.com/culture/news/opie -anthony-host-anthony-cumia-fired-after-racist-twitter-tirade-20140706

Collins, D. 2002. "DJs Dumped over Church Sex Stunt." *CBS News,* August 21. https:// www.cbsnews.com/news/djs-dumped-over-church-sex-stunt

Farhi, P. 2006. "Opie & Anthony Get the Last Laugh." *The Washington Post,* June 26. http:// www.washingtonpost.com/wpdyn/content/article/2006/06/25/AR2006062500957 .html

Leopold, T. 2015. "Anthony Cumia of 'Opie and Anthony' Arrested." *CNN,* December 21. http://edition.cnn.com/2015/12/21/entertainment/anthony-cumia-arrested-feat /index.html

Mosendz, P. 2015. "Opie and Anthony No More: Inside the Nasty Breakup of Radio's Most Notorious Shock Jocks." *Newsweek*, April 9. http://www.newsweek.com/opie-and -anthony-no-more-inside-nasty-break-radios-most-notorious-shock-jocks-321186

Serial

Serial is a radio podcast that is hosted by Sarah Koenig. It is a spin-off from the popular *This American Life* radio series, and over an entire season told a real-life murder mystery. Some asserted that the telling of the murder is a mix of *The Sopranos* and Sherlock Holmes. The story is that of 32-year-old Adnan Syed, who is serving life in prison for the murder of 18-year-old Hae Min Lee, but who may have been wrongly convicted. The podcast provides listeners with various perspectives on the case in an attempt to solve the mystery of what happened on January 13, 1999.

Koenig was contacted by a woman named Rabia Chaudry, a friend of Syed's, and who was a friend of a defense attorney whom Koenig had written about in the past. After investigating for a year she chose to focus on the case for the first season, even though they were still gathering information when the show opened. Ira Glass introduced the show on *This American Life*, saying that the intent was to hunt down what really happened, learning as Sarah revealed the details never heard by the jury. He told listeners that Sarah and the other producers, Dana Chivvis, and Julie Snyder, changed their mind about Syed's guilt as they investigated the case.

Hae was murdered on January 13, 1999, during her senior year in high school. She was found strangled and buried in a park in Baltimore. Syed was her exboyfriend and immediately a person of interest. Some of the material that Koenig and her colleagues acquired proved inconclusive, and each episode featured material that showed how flawed people are, in their memory and in their actions. Witnesses who were interviewed were likeable but imperfect. For instance, Jay, the chief witness for the prosecution, had testified that he had helped Adnan bury Hae's body. He led the police to her car. But he was also known to be a drug dealer, liked punk rock, and worked at a porn video store. Several times he provided conflicting stories about the details of the murder He seemed genuinely traumatized by his involvement, however. Similarly, even Hae's boyfriend Don admitted that he found it hard to believe that Syed, whom he liked, killed her.

In the final episode, Koenig interviews Don, whose alibi seems less airtight than it had to the jury, given that his boss testified he was at work was his mother. Further, he had not tried to contact Hae after she disappeared, which could imply guilt when exhibited by Syed. Koenig also interviews Josh, Jay's co-worker at the porn video store, who tells her about his anxious behavior the week of the murder. Another exciting turn is when Koenig takes a call from Deirdre Enright, of the Innocence Project, who tells her that a serial killer who had been in prison in Baltimore may have been in the area where the murder occurred in January 1999. Koenig concludes that Jay leading the police to Hae's car is really the only credible piece of evidence against Syed and that it shouldn't be nearly enough to sentence a 17-year-old to life in prison. She said, "As a juror, I vote to acquit Adnan Syed," she said. As a person, she has doubts. That's an essential distinction. "I feel like shaking everyone by the shoulders like an aggravated cop" (Leszkiewicz, 2016). Critics applauded the show, calling it more than a murder mystery and really an exposé of the flaws in the justice system. The show was also acclaimed for drawing attention to the issues of wrongful incarceration and police profiling, especially at a time when the United States was reeling from many police shootings of young black men, including that of Michael Brown in Ferguson, Missouri, which generated widespread protest and condemnation of the excessive police response by the U.S. justice system.

Critics contend, however, that Koenig's focus on Syed's possible innocence means Hae Min Lee is virtually lost in the story. Rather than bringing justice for Hae and her family, the emphasis is on justice for Syed. Koenig did reach out to Hae's family and they were not responsive. Hae's part of the story, then, is told only from letters or extracts from her diary. The comments about her ex-boyfriend Syed do imply that he was at times controlling, showing up at places when she was to be with her friends, and critics note that despite these obvious signs of dating violence, and the fact that prosecutors alleged it was their recent breakup that prompted Syed to kill Hae, Koenig fails to interview or otherwise obtain the perspective of a domestic violence expert. She spends a lot of time addressing possible racism or prejudice but not this important angle. Critics also asserted that the general premise—a young women's death—should not be the focus of an entertaining podcast heard by millions. Someone claiming to be Hae's brother wrote on Reddit:

> To you listeners, it's another murder mystery, crime drama, another episode of CSI. You weren't there to see your mom crying every night, having a heart attack when she got the news that the body was found, and going to court almost every day for a year seeing your mom weeping, crying and fainting. You don't know what we went through. Especially to those who are demanding our family response [sic] and having a meet up . . . you guys are disgusting. Shame on you. I pray that you don't have to go through what we went through and have your story blasted to [five million] listeners. (Leszkiewicz, 2016)

Additionally, some critics took issue with the lack of objectivity in the podcast. While Koenig and crew claimed to have been uncovering facts and sharing them, regardless of perspective, some believe the show was always swayed toward a presumption of Syed's innocence. Koenig even said, "I don't think the state's story is the correct story" (Leszkiewicz, 2016) Further, critics contend that in real-life murder stories like *Serial*, the investigative team tends to get far too close to their subjects. Koenig admitted that her relationship with Syed was "Definitely [. . .] weird and hard to define. It's a personal relationship. It's not truly professional" (Leszkiewicz, 2016). As well, critics assert that the show prompted listeners to take matters into their own hands, encouraging them to sleuth for their own information, as many did on the Internet after each episode aired.

Laura L. Finley

See also: Murder, She Wrote; Scandinavian Crime Novels; *This American Life*

Further Reading

Larson, S. 2014. "What "Serial" Really Taught Us." *The New Yorker*, December 8. http://www.newyorker.com/culture/sarah-larson/serial-really-taught-us

Leszkiewicz, A. 2016. "From Serial to Making a Murderer: Can True Crime as Entertainment Ever Be Ethical?" *The New Statesman,* January 15. http://www.newstatesman.com/culture/tv-radio/2016/01/serial-making-murderer-can-true-crime-entertainment-ever-be-ethical

Sanghani, R. 2014. "Serial: How a Schoolgirl's Brutal Murder Became Casual Entertainment." *The Telegraph,* December 21. http://www.telegraph.co.uk/women/womens-life/11304281/Serial-podcast-How-a-schoolgirls-murder-became-entertainment.html

Serial: https://serialpodcast.org/

Stern, Howard

Howard Allan Stern is most known as a radio shock jock and host of *The Howard Stern Show*. He is also a television personality, producer, author, actor, and photographer. He is a controversial and outspoken figure who has been fined and fired numerous times for his sexual gags.

Stern was born in 1954 and knew at age five he wanted a career in radio. His first radio job was at Boston University, and then from 1976 to 1982 he hosted on WRNW in Briarcliff Manor, New York; WCCC in Hartford, Connecticut; WWWW in Detroit, Michigan; and WWDC in Washington, D.C., where he built up a following for his bawdy antics. He began working for WNBC in New York City in 1982 and was fired in 1985. He then began a 20-year run on WXRK in New York City, with his morning show entering syndication in 1986. In 1992, Stern and Infinity Broadcasting were fined $600,000 by the Federal Communications Commission (FCC) for his on-air comment, "The closest I came to making love to a black woman was [when] I masturbated to a picture of Aunt Jemima on a pancake box" (Mariker, 2012).

Although he was not fired or fined, Stern generated controversy in March 1995, when he made fun of the fans of Latin musician Selena, who had been shot and killed. Just one day before her funeral he played gunshots over her music and mocked her fans using a thick Spanish accent. He said, "Spanish people have the worst taste in music. . . . This music does absolutely nothing for me. Alvin and the Chipmunks have more soul." A week later Stern apologized, but many were not mollified. Then, just one day after the Columbine High School shooting, Stern talked about the girls who had fled the school while Dylan Klebold and Eric

Harris shot and killed 13 people, then themselves, saying, "There were some really good-looking girls running with their hands over their heads," and asking, "Did those kids try to have sex with any of those good-looking girls? They didn't even do that? At least if you're going to kill yourself and kill the kids, why wouldn't you have some sex? If I was going to kill some people, I'd take them out with sex" (Mariker, 2012).

Another controversy was in an interview with The Who's Pete Townshend when Stern's co-host brought up the child pornography charges the guitarist faced in 2003. Townshend walked out, Stern apologized, and the two seemed to patch it over. Other controversies are related to the guests he has had on his show, from President Donald Trump to white supremacist Jewish Center shooter Frazier Glenn Miller, and Ku Klux Klan members (Lowry, 2014).

At its peak, *The Howard Stern Show* attracted 20 million listeners. Stern has won numerous awards, including Billboard's Nationally Syndicated Air Personality of the Year eight times. Not only is Stern the first host to have the number-one morning show in Los Angeles and New York at the same time, but he is also the most fined radio host. His show has cost Stern and station owners $2.5 million in indecency fines from the FCC. In 2004, Stern was dropped by Clear Channel Radio, the company that carried his show in six major markets, after they were fined $495,000 by the FCC. The fine was for a conversation with Rick Salomon, who was the co-star of the scandalous sex tape of actor Paris Hilton, in which the two talked frankly about anal sex and a caller used a racial epithet. That same year, Stern signed a five-year deal with Sirius worth $500 million, making him the best-paid radio host of all time. That medium is free from FCC regulations. In 2012, Stern was inducted into the National Radio Hall of Fame.

Stern's photography has appeared in several magazines, and his two books, *Private Parts* (1993) and *Miss America* (1995), sold over 1 million copies. *Private Parts* was made into a feature film in which Stern himself starred. It topped the U.S. box office in 1997 and grossed well (Staff Reporter, 2015).

In addition to the controversial topics he addresses on his show, Stern himself is not shy to engage in odd behavior. He appeared at the 1992 MTV Music Video Awards wearing a gold Spandex superhero costume that exposed his butt cheeks. Calling himself Fartman, Stern descended from the ceiling and simulated a large gas attack that resulted in an explosion on the stage. Stern did not apologize and even thought of turning Fartman into a movie but never did. MTV never invited him back to the awards show.

Stern's long-time co-host Robin Quivers brought up during the 2016 presidential campaign Donald Trump's comment, from his show some years prior, that if you are a celebrity "You can grab 'em by the p****." Quivers asked Stern whether he liked Trump and thought such comments were "locker room talk." Stern responded, "A lot of the show that I've been doing for my entire life, radio show publicly, is an effort to sort of do 'locker room talk,' to express all kinds of s*** and just not even care what anyone thinks. But this idea of 'locker room talk' . . . all the times I've been around guys—and believe me when I'm around guys 85 percent of the times you're talking about p****—but I have never been in the room when someone has said, 'Grab them by the p****'" (Chen, 2016).

Laura L. Finley

See also: Bubba the Love Sponge; Cumia, Anthony; *Opie & Anthony Show, The*

Further Reading

Chen, J. 2016. "Howard Stern on Donald Trump Locker Room Talk: 'I've Never Heard a Guy Say "Grab Them by the P****."'" *US Magazine,* October 17. http://www.usmagazine.com/celebrity-news/news/howard-stern-donald-trumps-grab-them-by-the-p—sy-isnt-locker-talk-w445315

Lowry, B. 2014. "Howard Stern's White Supremacist Interview Suddenly Doesn't Look So Funny." *Variety,* April 14. http://variety.com/2014/voices/columns/howard-sterns-white-supremacist-interview-suddenly-doesnt-look-so-funny-1201157977

Marikar, S. 2012. "Howard Stern's Five Most Outrageous Offenses." *ABC News*, May 14. http://abcnews.go.com/Entertainment/howard-sterns-outrageous-offenses/story?id=16327309

Staff Reporter. 2015. "Howard Stern: Most Controversial Moments after Shock-Jock Signs New Contract." *IB Times*, December 15. http://www.ibtimes.co.uk/howard-stern-most-controversial-moments-after-shock-jock-signs-new-contract-1533519

This American Life

Produced by Chicago Public Media and hosted by Ira Glass, *This American Life* is a weekly public radio show that is broadcast on more than 500 stations to some 2.2 million listeners. It is also available in podcast, with each episode downloaded by more than 2.5 million people. It started in 1995 in Chicago and has won all of the major broadcasting awards, including the Peabody, the DuPont-Columbia, the Murrow, and the Overseas Press Club. For two years, between 2006 and 2008, Showtime produced a television version of *This American Life*, which won three Emmy Awards. The creators are also responsible for the blog and podcast, *Planet Money*, and in 2014, they launched another podcast, *Serial*, which is hosted by Sarah Koenig and unravels the story of the murder of a teenage girl and the incarceration, some believe wrongly, of her ex-boyfriend for the crime. Another podcast, *S-Town*, was launched in 2017.

Each episode of *This American Life* focuses on a particular theme and features a variety of stories, mostly journalistic but sometimes comedy or essays. Many famous writers have had their work featured on the show, including David Sedaris, Dave Eggers, Nick Hornby, Alex Kotlowitz, Lindy West, and Dan Savage. Host Ira Glass was named the best radio host in the country by *Time* magazine and has received the Edward R. Murrow Award.

A search for "violence" in the show archives reveals that many episodes were devoted to that topic. Episode 81, called "Guns," which aired on October 24, 1997, featured an interview with Geoffrey Canada, author of the book *Fist Stick Knife Gun: A Personal History of Violence in America*, who discussed what it's like to carry a gun. Canada described how, growing up in the South Bronx area of New York, kids settled their arguments with fistfights that occurred under formal rules they created. Today, he critiqued, violent conflicts are settled with firearms in a far more deadly fashion. The episode also includes conversations with people who have survived gun violence as well as gun enthusiasts, who describe why they enjoy shooting. Further, the episodes addresses how illegal guns end up in the hands of youth in Chicago.

Episode 487, called "Harper High School, Part One," aired on February 15, 2013. The show's team spent five months in Chicago's Harper High School, which in the previous year saw 29 current and former students shot. Reporter Alex Kotlowitz interviewed kids, staff members, and community residents to better understand the violence. Although many see it as gang related, the episode makes clear it is about much more than that. Part Two, which aired a week later, includes an interview with a young man who accidentally shot and killed his brother, as well as interviews with youth to find out how they acquire guns and the impact gun violence has on their physical and mental well-being.

Several episodes focus on U.S. involvement in the war in Iraq, both during and after the war was over. On November 3, 2006, Episode 320 "What's in a Number" addressed the estimates of Iraqis who died during the U.S. invasion. Interviewers spoke with Iraqis, all of whom knew someone who had been killed during the war. It also explores why the British Journal *The Lancet* came up with a much higher number of civilian casualties—650,000—than the U.S. government had stated. Episode 416, "Iraq After Us," aired on October 15, 2010. Interviewers not only spoke to soldiers who had returned from Iraq, but also went there to interview local politicians and residents about the after-effects of the war and the country's stability.

Episode 451, titled "Back to Penn State," aired on November 18, 2011. The episode's team went to Penn State University, where they had been two years prior when it was named the number-one party school in the United States, this time to see how the school and its students were handling the fallout of the child sex abuse scandal involving one of the football team's coaching staff members, Jerry Sandusky. In 2009, many students said that the best thing about the beloved football team and its long-time coach, Joe Paterno, were the moral standards it set. Yet Paterno, as well as the university's president, resigned in wake of the Sandusky scandal.

Episode 210, titled "Perfect Evidence," aired on April 19, 2002. It addressed the issue of wrongful convictions and how DNA had, at the time, freed more than 100 incarcerated individuals. Glass spoke with Huy Dao of the Innocence Project, which has been a national leader in using DNA and other evidence to draw attention to wrongful convictions. Other interviews in the episode address additional cold cases that have been reopened and their impact on the justice system. The episode also critiques police and prosecutors for the actions that result in wrongful convictions.

In Episode 127, "Pimp Anthology," which aired on April 16, 1999, the focus is on the story of how one man and his three friends became pimps in the 1970s in Oakland, California. He explains how he failed as a pimp because he could not handle the violence that inevitably comes with that industry.

Although these and other episodes focus on crime and violence, they do not glorify it, nor depict gory details. Rather, the intent of *This American Life* is to educate and inform listeners about the most pressing topics in the United States today.

Laura L. Finley

See also: Serial

Further Reading

Silman, A. 2014. "From 'the Greatest Podcast Ever Made' to 'Shamelessly Exploitative': A Guide to the Serial Backlash." *Salon,* November 17. http://www.salon.com/2014 /11/17/from_the_greatest_podcast_ever_made_to_shamelessly_exploitative_an _introduction_to_the_serial_backlash

This American Life: https://www.thisamericanlife.org/

"War of the Worlds"

The "War of the Worlds" is a radio broadcast that was adapted from H. G. Wells's novel *The War of the Worlds* (1898). It was part of the Mercury Theater on the Air program for Halloween. It aired on October 30, 1938, on the Columbia Broadcasting System radio network and was narrated by actor Orson Welles. It was recorded as a series of news bulletins that announced a series of odd explosions on Mars, followed by an unusual object falling from the sky and landing on a farm in New Jersey. The bulletins then announced an alien invasion of the United States and the world that was said to have caused mass hysteria. That panic has been proven to be more fiction than reality, however, given that there were really not that many listeners. The show aired at 8 p.m., which was primetime for radio, but most listeners were tuned into Edgar Bergen, the ventriloquist, and his dummy "Charlie McCarthy," at least until the "War of the Worlds" episode was well under way. A survey conducted by C. E. Hooper rating service of listenership found that 98 percent of persons surveyed were listening to something else that night. Regardless, the legend of the panic lives on and even grew over time, allegedly involving some 1 million crazed listeners (Pooley & Socolow, 2013).

Many complained in the days following the broadcast, arguing that the news bulletin style was deceptive. Some even called for some type of action by the Federal Communications Commission (FCC). Welles, who was just 23 at the time, admits that he selected that format specifically so it could appear that a crisis was actually happening. The FCC did investigate but found that neither Welles nor the network had broken any laws. Welles was worried that the scandal would hurt his career, but it actually helped. Shortly after he secured a contract with a Hollywood studio, and in 1941 he directed, wrote, produced, and starred in *Citizen Kane*. In later interviews Welles indicated that they had intended to scare listeners to remind them not to believe everything they heard (Schwartz, 2015).

Some have argued that the panic was really created by the news media. Radio had taken over much of the newspaper industry's advertising revenue, so newspapers were looking for something to gain attention and to convince readers that radio was not to be trusted. The myth of the panic has lived on in scholarly publications as well as in popular culture, in large part due to the distrust people have of media and the concern that it remains too influential.

The language used in the broadcast was indeed scary. After the crash on the farmer's land, an announcer described a Martian emerging from a metal cylinder.

"Good heavens, something's wriggling out of the shadow like a gray snake. Now here's another and another one and another one. They look like tentacles to me . . . I can see the thing's body now. It's large, large as a bear. It glistens like wet leather. But that face, it . . . it . . . ladies and gentlemen, it's indescribable. I can hardly force myself to keep looking at it, it's so awful. The eyes are black and gleam like a serpent. The mouth is kind of V-shaped with saliva dripping from its rimless lips that seem to quiver and pulsate" (1938: Welles scares nation, n.d.). The Martians went on to fire heat-rays at the humans, decimating a force of 7,000 National Guardsman, then releasing poisonous gas into the air. When he received word that some people were panicking, Welles reminded listeners that the show was fiction.

Laura L. Finley

See also: Alien Franchise; *Coast to Coast AM*; *Star Trek*; *Star Wars* Franchise; *X-Files, The*

Further Reading

n.d. "1938: Welles Scares Nation." *History.com*. http://www.history.com/this-day-in-history/welles-scares-nation

Pooley, J., & Socolow, M. 2013. "The Myth of the War of the Worlds Panic." *Salon,* October 28, 2013. http://www.slate.com/articles/arts/history/2013/10/orson_welles_war_of_the_worlds_panic_myth_the_infamous_radio_broadcast_did.html

Schwartz, T. 2015. "The Infamous "War of the Worlds" Broadcast Was a Magnificent Fluke." *Smithsonian,* May 6. https://www.smithsonianmag.com/history/infamous-war-worlds-radio-broadcast-was-magnificent-fluke-180955180

2

Violence in Film

Introduction

As long as there have been films, there has been concern about violence depicted in them. "When the cinema was introduced, in 1895, it laid claim to a more extensive and intimate view of death. One of Edison's kinetoscopes, those brief films viewed individually through an eyepiece, presented the viewer with the execution of Mary, Queen of Scots. . . . The first true narrative movie in history, *The Great Train Robbery* (1903), had several murders" (Goldberg, 1998, p. 49).

Violence was especially common in the gangster films of the 1930s. These stories were often based on reality, as were the popular detective stories. Western films and films about the two World Wars also featured a great deal of violence, and the depictions grew increasingly realistic with new technologies and filming techniques.

World War II remains one of the most frequent topics of films. The War Department actually commissioned more than 200 propaganda films before and after the war. Most of the World War II films attempted to accurately depict the dangers of war while also showing the United States and its allies as needing to engage the Nazis in order, ironically, to keep the peace.

> In the years after the war, when the audience had become acquainted with the real thing, violent death on-screen began to change. In the 1950s, some of the exaggerated violence and death that had been the domain of adolescent boys and lower-class types edged into mainstream movie houses. Late in the decade, partially in response to the threat of the atom bomb, the science-fiction film was crossbred with the horror film, and new ways to die were invented—in the jaws of monsters, in the embrace of a protoplasmic blob of vegetable matter. The industry has become ever more inventive about means of death as film technology and special effects advance, so that now men may die from alien creatures bursting out of their breasts or from powerful rays that make them simply disappear. (Goldberg, 1998, pp. 49–50)

Westerns were the most popular genre immediately after World War II. Most Westerns featured some type of struggle between good and evil, with good prevailing.

Although the good characters often used violence to defeat their enemies, it was depicted as both necessary and good and made heroes out of popular Western actors like John Wayne.

Domestic violence and sexual assault are common topics for films. Some focus the plot on these incidents, whereas it may be just a small part of other films. Hollywood does not always do a good job of depicting rape or abusive relationships, however. Many films use what is called rape myths (Burt, 1980), or myths and misconceptions, in the way that they represent the victims, the offenders, and the context of the situation. Rape victims are often shown as either "virgins or vamps"; that is, they are innocent and likeable and in no way responsible, or they are flirty, provocative, and unlikeable and therefore brought on their victimization. Likewise, offenders are often presented as mentally ill or pure evil. Black rapists appear far more often, and film historian Donald Bogle (2004) referred to these characters as "brutal black bucks," describing them as "big, baaaaad n******, oversexed and savage, violent and frenzied as they lust for white flesh" (Bogle, 2004, p. 14). The film reified the myth of the black rapist, which was often presumed true even if no rape actually happened. One early example of this was D. W. Griffith's *The Birth of a Nation* (1915), which made it appear that "the idealized white woman under assault by a sexually lusting black man was the biggest threat to the nation" (Haggard, 2014, p. 83).

Another related category of films is what scholars call "rape-revenge films." These feature a person seeking revenge against a rapist. Sometimes that person is the victim, whereas in other cases it is someone else, like a parent, police officer, or friend. Portrayals of rape victims' revenge can be found as early as the 1930s. In *Shanghai Express* (1932), the main character, Hue Fei, kills her perpetrator, Cheng. Rape-revenge films became very popular in the 1970s. *I Spit on Your Grave* is perhaps the goriest. It shows professional writer Jennifer being gang-raped by four men near a country house she rented for the summer. Instead of going to the police, Jennifer decides to seek vengeance against the men by viciously murdering them. Critics denounced the level of violence, with Gene Siskel and Roger Ebert "warn[ing] that the film inspired violence against women" (Schubart, 2007). Ebert (1980) said in his article in the *Chicago Sun-Times* that the film was "sick, reprehensible and contemptible" (para. 1) and said that anyone who enjoyed the film "suffered a fundamental loss of decent human feelings" (para. 8).

The 1960s saw violent death in films become even more commonplace and more explicit and gory. Alfred Hitchcock's 1960 film *Psycho* used a camera close-up to show the stabbing of the primary female character in the shower. It also used rapidly changing film angles such that the audience felt off-balance and scared, even though the knife never actually entered her skin on film. In 1967, the film *Bonnie and Clyde*, starring Warren Beatty as Clyde Barrow and Faye Dunaway as Bonnie Parker, detailed with great violence the crime spree of the two protagonists and their demise "with so many bullets at the end that they performed a virtual dance of death" (Goldberg, 1998, p. 50). Two years later, Sam Peckinpah's *The Wild Bunch* (1969), a new kind of Western, featured "a veritable deluge of death, with bodies flying through the air and blood in quantities unseen before" (Goldberg, 1998, p. 50).

The final scene reportedly used some 90,000 rounds of blank ammunition, which was more than was used in the Mexican revolution of 1913. Film historian Laurent Bouzereau wrote about *The Wild Bunch*, "When the smoke clears, it seems we can almost smell the blood" (Bouzereau, 2000, p. 20).

Films continued to get more violent through the 1970s and into the 1980s, epically with the rise of what is known as the slasher-horror genre. These films generally featured crazed serial killers who preyed on young women and committed gory murders at high rates. The *Halloween* series, the *Nightmare on Elm Street* series, the *Friday the 13th* series, the *Child's Play* series, and many others were very popular with teen and early adult audiences. Critics expressed concern not only at the ubiquitous violence but also at the misogynistic perspectives that were often part of this genre. Female characters are often stalked throughout these films, and although there may be fewer incidents of violence against the females than the males, studies have shown that the violence against female characters has a decidedly sexual nature and takes up more screen time (Welsh, 2009). Teens are the biggest consumers of what has been called "torture porn" films like the *Saw* and *Hostel* series. These films are notorious for their depictions of graphic sexual violence.

Serial killers are a frequent topic of films, with more than 1,000 made since 1990. Although most of these are horror films, crime dramas, or documentaries, some depictions of serial killers are comedies, for instance, *So I Married an Axe Murderer* (1993) and *Scary Movie* (2000). The popularity of films of this nature reflects a broader infatuation with serial killers, as is evidenced by the many collector's items available. This "murderabilia" includes art, body parts (hair, fingernail clippings, and more), t-shirts, calendars, trading cards, and more (Jarvis, 2007).

Even films marketed to children often feature a great deal of violence. Disney films often show various forms of violence, including murders and violence within families. The popular film *The Lion King* shows many battles over who will lead the pride of lions. *Beauty and the Beast* shows crazed villagers assaulting an old man and the beast. The *Harry Potter* films show violence by the evil characters, including Lord Voldemort, but also by the good characters who must defeat them, including protagonist Harry Potter and his closest friends, Hermione Granger and Ron Weasley. "In fact, the hero almost invariably confronts the villain with the same sorts of deception and violence that the villain wields" (Forbes, 2011, pp. 16–17).

The 1980s also saw significant focus on violent movies due to the arrival of the VCR. Many states added violence to their statutes related to obscenity. For instance, Missouri banned the sale or rental to minors of videos that the average adult would find "cater or appeal to a morbid interest in violence for persons under the age of seventeen; depict violence in a 'patently offensive' way, according to contemporary adult community standards with respect to what is suitable for persons under the age of seventeen; and, taken as a whole, lack serious literary, artistic, political or scientific value for persons under the age of seventeen" (Heins, 2001, p. 134). The law was invalidated in a challenge by the Video Software Dealers Association. Movies and TV were the primary targets, but attention was also focused on trading cards, as some companies had produced such cards depicting serial killers.

As a result, the mid-1980s saw a dramatic increase in official support for censorship of film and other media genres. The conservative Reagan administration took on pornography with a commission headed by Attorney General Edwin Meese. Antipornography activists Andrea Dworkin and Catharine MacKinnon brought a new wave of attention to sexual entertainment, asserting that it contributes to violence against women. Vice President Al Gore's wife Tipper Gore made it her mission to denounce sexually explicit music that she and her fellow members of Parents' Music Resource Center found inappropriate. The Meese Commission's final report in 1986 found a connection between violent pornography and aggressive behavior, and prompted great outcry by antipornography activists as well as criticism from social scientists, who claimed their work had been misinterpreted in the report and by the entertainment industry (Heins, 2001).

Yet violence in film did not decrease as a result of these efforts. A 2013 study found that gun violence in 945 top-selling PG-13 films had increased and exceeded the violence in top-ranked R-rated movies. Both PG- and R-rated films featured violent encounters with guns at least twice per hour, the study found. The researchers critiqued the fact that the current rating system is harsher on the inclusion of sex acts than it is on violence. Further, critics express concern that much of the violence presented in films is gratuitous and senseless (Wilson & Hudson, 2013).

Compared to other countries, the U.S. system of rating for films is somewhat simple. Films that are rated "G" are appropriate for a general audience, including children. "PG" films may contain some material unsuitable for children so parental guidance is recommended, and those rated "PG-13" may be inappropriate for viewers under the age of 13. "R"-rated films are restricted to those over 17 or minors accompanied by an adult guardian.

Further Reading

Bogle, D. 2001. *Toms, Coons, Mulattoes, Mammies and Bucks: An Interpretive History of Blacks in American Films.* New York: Continuum International.

Bouzereau, L. 2000. *Ultra Violent Movies.* New York: Kensington Publishing.

Burt, M. 1980. "Cultural Myths and Support for Rape." *Journal of Personality and Social Psychology, 38*(2), 217–230.

Ebert. R. 1980. *I Spit On Your Grave.* https://www.rogerebert.com/reviews/i-spit-on-your -grave-1980

Finley, L., & Mannise, K. 2014. "Potter Versus Voldemort: Examining Evil, Power and Affective Responses in the *Harry Potter* Film Series." In *Evil and Popular Culture,* edited by S. Packer & J. Pennington, 59–72. Santa Barbara, CA: ABC-CLIO.

Forbes, D. 2011. "The Aesthetic of Evil." In *Vader, Voldemort, and Other Villains,* edited by J. Heit, 13–27. Jefferson, NC: McFarland & Company.

Goldberg, V. 1998. "Death Takes a Holiday, Sort Of." In *Why We Watch: The Attractions of Violent Entertainment*, edited by J. Goldstein, 27–52. New York: Oxford University Press.

Haggard, N. 2014. "The Birth of the Black Rapist: The 'Brutal Black Buck' in American Culture." In *A History of Evil in Popular Culture,* edited by S. Packer & J. Pennington, Vol. 1, 83–94. Santa Barbara, CA: ABC-CLIO.

Heins, M. 2001. *Not in Front of the Children: "Indecency," Censorship, and the Innocence of Youth.* New York: Hill & Wang.

Heller-Nicholas, A. 2011. *Rape-Revenge Films.* Jefferson, NC: McFarland & Company.

Jarvis, B. 2007. "Monsters, Inc.: Serial Killers and Consumer Culture." *Crime, Media, Culture, 3*(3), 326–44.

Olson, S. 2014. "Children's Cartoons Contain 2.5 Times More Death Than Adult Horror Movies: Violence from 'Snow White' to 'Frozen.'" *Medical Daily,* December 16. http://www.medicaldaily.com/childrens-cartoons-contain-25-times-more-death -adult-horror-movies-violence-snow-314600

Schubart, R. 2007. *Super Bitches and Action Babes.* Jefferson, NCL McFarland.

Welsh, A. 2009. "Sex and Violence in the Slasher Horror Film: A Content Analysis of Gender Differences in the Depiction of Violence." *Journal of Criminal Justice and Popular Culture, 16*(1), 1–25.

Wilson, J., and Hudson, W. 2013, November 11. "Gun Violence in PG-13 Movies Has Tripled." *CNN.* https://www.cnn.com/2013/11/11/health/gun-violence-movies/index .html

Alien Franchise

The *Alien* Franchise is a collective of movies that date from 1979 to the latest *Alien* movie, which was released in 2017 and directed by Ridley Scott. The story was written by Dan O'Bannon and Ronald Shusett. James Cameron, David Fincher, and Jean-Pierre Jeunet have directed previous films in the franchise. The films are typically categorized as a blend of science fiction and horror, all with their fair share of goriness. According to special effects supervisor for the movie, Neil Corbould, the latest *Alien* movie was the goriest of the franchise to date, with a classic mixture of sci-fi and horror being displayed throughout the film (Schaefer, 2017).

In the first movie of the franchise, *Alien,* which was released in 1979 and directed by Ridley Scott, the crew of a commercial spaceship are travelling back home when on the way they pick up distress signals from a distant moon. As the crew is obligated to answer the call, they land on the moon. The crew members soon realize that they have stumbled across the colony of an unknown life form. Later, they realize they are in trouble as they are not alone on the spaceship and must deal with the soon-to-be-life-threatening consequences. The main characters are Ellen Ripley (Sigourney Weaver), her fellow officers on the ship, and the aliens they battle. People loved this movie, and it was a box office success, grossing more than $78,900,000, according to IMDb. One of the scenes from this movie got voted the second scariest movie moment of all time on Bravo's "The 100 Scariest Movie Moments." This was the scene where the crew members were gathered around the dining table eating dinner, when out of nowhere, one of the members started to have a seizure of some sort. Then, within minutes, an unidentified creature came bursting through his chest.

Seven years after the first *Alien* movie was released, the sequel *Aliens* debuted in 1986. In this movie, the lone survivor from the first film, Ellen Ripley (Sigourney Weaver), is called back to help a group of Marines who are stranded on a moon trying to fight off extraterrestrials. While she is at the space colony trying to help defend both herself and the Marines, she stumbles across the sole survivor of the colony, a young girl, who she must then protect. Like the first movie, this film did very well in the box office, generating a gross of $85,160,248. Some critics said that the movie was a roller-coaster ride of violence. Others contend, however, that the violence shown in the *Alien* movies is very much different from the violence that occurs in real life; in these movies, unidentified life forms burst out of people's chests, and alien-like creatures kill with supernatural ease.

The third film in the *Alien* franchise was *Alien 3* (1992). This movie was directed by David Fincher and written by David Giler, Walter Hill, and Larry Ferguson, which was created from the story by Vincent Ward. The film also stars Sigourney Weaver as Ellen Ripley. The plot begins when Ripley crash-lands at a maximum-security prison, with a wave of weird and deadly events shortly following her arrival. Ripley then starts to realize that she wasn't alone and that she had brought along an extra passenger who causes nothing but problems for her. This movie didn't do as well as the other two at the box office, with a gross income of $55,475,600.

The next movie in the franchise is *Alien: Resurrection* (1997), which was directed by Jean-Pierre Jeunet and written by Dan O'Bannon and Ronald Shusett. Like the previous movies in this collection, the main character is still Ellen Ripley, and she's still played by Sigourney Weaver. Ellen is resurrected as a human/alien hybrid clone after being dead for centuries. She has been brought back to life so that she can continue the fight in her deadly, ongoing war against the aliens. Of all the *Alien* movies released to date, this contribution to the franchise had the lowest gross income, with box office sales coming in at $47,748,610. Many critics said that if it were not for Weaver's presence and performance in the film, it was a unwatchable film—it was that much of a letdown to critics and fans alike. The violence portrayed in this movie was typical for the franchise and included humans shooting at the aliens and aliens attacking the humans, ripping their bodies to bits like pieces of meat.

Prometheus (2012) is the next installment in the franchise, once again directed by Ridley Scott and written by Jon Spaihts and Damon Lindelof. The main character, David (Michael Fassbender), plays an android in the film. Unlike the previous *Alien* movies, *Prometheus* is set in 2093, where a team finds a colony on a distant moon, but after a short time they realize that they are not alone. Things quickly change to survival mode when the team discovers what is actually there: aliens. This movie excelled in box office sales, reaching a staggering $126,477,084, which exceeded previous box office sales for the other movies in this franchise.

The most recent addition to the roster of films is *Alien: Covenant* (2017). Directed once again by Scott and written by Dan O'Bannon, the film in the eyes of many critics was one of the more gruesome movies from the collection, with acts of violence occurring throughout the movie. It starts onboard a colony ship wherein thousands of humans on board are in a state of hibernation. They will remain so until they reach their destination, where they will start a new world. Along the way, the ship's crew stumbles across an uncharted planet, which at first seems promising. However, they realize that once again, they are not alone and must do their best to survive and escape before it's too late. Michael Fassbender once again plays the main role in this movie as David. This movie did well at the box office (though not as profitable as the previous movie in this collection), with sales coming in at $74,243,930.

Alien: Covenant was extremely violent. Even Katherine Waterston, who played Daniels, admits that the film is horrifically violent (Den of Geek, 2009). She does admit, though, that although the violence shown in this movie is intense, fans will still likely enjoy it. The violence in this movie is very unrealistic; at the end of the day, it's a science fiction/horror movie, which attracts viewers who expect some degree of violence to occur.

Several of the films in the *Alien* franchise have received several accolades. The first two won Academy Awards, including an Oscar for visual effects.

Laura L. Finley

See also: Jaws; *Star Trek*; *Star Wars* Franchise; "War of the Worlds"; *X-Files, The*

Further Reading

Anderson, J. M. 2017. "Alien: Covenant—Movie Review." *Common Sense Media*, May 14. https://www.commonsensemedia.org/movie-reviews/alien-covenant

Anonymous. n.d. "Alien Franchise." IMDb. http://www.imdb.com/title/tt0078748/

Anonymous. 2009. "The Plot-Obstacles to an Alien Prequel." *Den of Geek*, May 31. http://www.denofgeek.com/us/movies/alien/14431/the-plot-obstacles-to-an-alien-prequel

Schaefer, S. 2017. "Alien: Covenant Will Be the Goriest Alien Movie Yet." *Screenrant*, February 28. https://screenrant.com/alien-covenant-rating-blood-violence/

Arab Media

Historically, the Arab media has been one of the most closed media systems in the world, and by extension, has suffered from a lack of research by media scholars. As such, little is known about how media operates in Arabic-speaking countries. There are many stereotypes of the Arab world that influence media consumers in the United States, who often see little to counter these depictions. Yet many living in Arab countries are accustomed to and believe in censorship, such that some 70 percent of adults in Arab countries believe that governments should do more to censor sexual and violent content in film and TV, and a similar amount believes they should be banned if the local culture finds them offensive. Yet many of the most popular films in Arab countries like the United Arab Emirates (UAE) include violent action flicks like *Fast and Furious* (2001), *Iron Man* (2008), *Skyfall* (2012), and *GI Joe* (2009).

Some films distributed in Arab countries are heavily censored. For instance, nearly one quarter of the film *The Wolf of Wall Street* (2013) was removed due to depictions of sexual activity or illegal drug use (McGinley, 2014). A study of 6,000 people, including both nationals and expatriates, in Qatar, Saudi Arabia, Lebanon, Egypt, Tunisia, and the United Arab Emirates found that 45 percent of respondents say they watch Hollywood movies, but 34 percent say American films have content that is "harmful to morality." Only 15 percent say U.S.-made films are good for morality, according to the survey, whereas 71 percent feel that Arab movies are. Two-thirds of respondents said that people benefit from watching movies from different parts of the world, but 65 percent say they prefer films that portray their own culture. More than half (54 percent) said films are an important source of information about their own culture. Respondents favored censorship of both romantic content and violent films, with more than two-thirds favoring bans on films deemed to be offensive. There were significant differences by country. Saudi Arabian and Egyptian respondents supported censorship at the highest rates, over 75 percent, whereas Tunisians were least supportive. Still, over 50 percent of Tunisians supported film censorship. The dean and CEO of Northwestern University in Qatar explained, "These apparently contradictory findings really are not, but reflect how the Arab world is coping with globalization and still grappling to preserve local culture" (Kwok, 2014).

Qatar, the UAE, and Bahrain censored the film *Noah* (2014), as it is taboo in Islam to depict prophets. UAE censored *Sex and the City 2* (2010), as it showed a scene with Carrie Bradshaw and her friends wearing Arabian clothing riding camels through a Middle Eastern desert. It was deemed not to fit the country's cultural values, according to its National Media Council. Iran banned the film as well. Yet despite these efforts, uncensored films tend to be easily available as bootleg DVDs for a few dollars, as there is no copyright law protecting against such pirating. The state-controlled television station in Iran also allows certain films, generally censoring those with romantic or sexual scenes but allowing those depicting violence. On the other hand, Turkey, which is more secular, is far less restrictive than many of the other Arab countries. Lebanon is also more open.

A different controversy that emerged in Arab media in 2015 was a television show in which Moroccan actress Maisa Maghrabi was shown wearing dark glasses, then removing them to reveal a dark-purple black eye on the left side of her face. Maghrabi is leading an educational campaign about domestic violence called "Don't hide the violence towards you." Whereas some believe this can be a significant component of raising awareness about abuse, others criticized it for being too gory for television. It is not the first time that Arab media was criticized for covering domestic violence. In 2004, a Moroccan Dutchman, Mohammad Bouveri, murdered a filmmaker, Theo van Goghon, on a street in Amsterdam because Goghon had made a short film raising awareness about domestic violence in Islamic culture. Stereotypical or offensive depictions of Islam or Islamic leaders have long created problems, and in some cases have been the genesis for serious acts of violence.

Laura L. Finley

See also: Blues Music; Global Censorship; Islam, Depictions of

Further Reading

Ajami, F. 2012. "Why Is the Arab World So Easily Offended?" *The Washington Post*, September 14. https://www.washingtonpost.com/opinions/in-the-arab-world-why-a-movie-trailer-can-lead-to-violencewhy-cant-the-arab-world-accept-offenses-without-violence/2012/09/14/d2b65d2e-fdc8-11e1-8adc-499661afe377_story.html

Bruce, M. D. 2016. "Sensational Pictures: An Analysis of Visual Structure on Five Transnational Arab News Channels." In *Digital Technology and the Future of Broadcasting: A Global Perspective*, edited by J. V. Pavlik, 1-26. London: Routledge.

Bruce, M., & Conlin, L. 2016. "Images of Conflict and Explicit Violence on Arab TV: A Visual Content Analysis of Five Pan-Arab News Networks." *Athens Journal of Mass Media and Communications, 2*(3):151–67.

Fahmy, S. 2010. "Contrasting Visual Frames of Our Times: A Framing Analysis of English- and Arabic-Language Press Coverage of War and Terrorism." *The International Communication Gazette, 72*: 695–717.

Jasperson, A. E., & El-Kikhia, M. O. 2003. "CNN and Al Jazeera's Media Coverage of America's War in Afghanistan." In *Framing Terrorism*, edited by K. Hafez, 133–32. New York: Routledge

Kwok, Y. 2014. "Hollywood Movies in Arab Countries: A Love and Hate Relationship." *CNN*, April 23. http://www.cnn.com/2014/04/23/world/meast/middle-east-hollywood-films-censorship-survey/index.html

McGinley, S. 2014. "70% of Arabs Call for More Film and TV Censorship." *Arabian Business*, April 17. http://www.arabianbusiness.com/70-of-arabs-call-for-more-film-tv-censorship-546868.html

Murphy, M. 2010. "Muslim Countries Vary Greatly on Censorship of Hollywood Films." *Fox News*, October 21. http://www.foxnews.com/entertainment/2010/10/19/muslim-countries-vary-greatly-censorship-hollywood-films.html

Blaxploitation Films

Blaxploitation is a genre of films that largely featured Black characters. It gained popularity in the 1970s and remains controversial, in that many of the films rely on dangerous stereotypes but at the same time allow Black actors to move out of the roles as sidekicks. These films also featured funk and soul music, introducing that genre to new viewers. Produced initially for an urban, Black audience, the genre quickly gained popularity with others. The term blaxploitation is said to have been coined by former film publicist and head of the Los Angeles chapter of the National Association for the Advancement of Colored People (NAACP), Junius Griffin. The first true blaxploitation film is said to have been *Sweet Sweetback's Baadasssss Song* in 1971. Other widely known blaxploitation films include *Shaft* (1971), *The Mack* (1973), *Superfly* (1972), *Blacula* (1972), and *Coffy* (1973).

The films of the 1970s did well at the box office. *Shaft,* which was made on a budget of somewhere between $500,000 and $1.5 million, grossed $12 million. *Superfly* did well, too.

Blaxploitation films often use shock value to provoke thought. This includes outlandish clothing, dialogue, and frequent sex; violence; pimps; prostitutes; and drug dealing. The protagonists typically overcame racism in some way, and they were, as many note "badasses." Mostly males, they were hypersexual and macho. Many addressed important issues like discrimination and police brutality. Some are action films, whereas others are comedies, dramas, Westerns, and even horror films. Most critics and scholars believe the genre was influenced by the black power movement of the 1960s and 1970s. Later blaxploitation films were less intense in this regard than those produced in the 1970s. The later films often featured popular hip-hop artists, including Ice-T, Too Short, Slick Rick, and Snoop Dogg. These artists have also frequently paid tribute to the genre in their lyrics.

Whereas *Shaft* was a standard detective story, albeit with a black detective, *Sweet Sweetback's Baadasssss Song*, directed by Melvin Van Peebles, received an X rating for its profanity and sex, yet it sat at the top of the box office for two weeks after it opened. Reportedly the Black Panthers required members to watch it. Audiences were stunned to see a Black protagonist, and one that actually lived until the end of the film, as usually Black characters were killed off much earlier.

Whereas many saw, and still see, the genre as empowering, others feel it furthers stereotypes. In the 1970s, the NAACP, the National Urban League, and the Southern Christian Leadership Conference created the Coalition Against Blaxploitation, and their efforts helped to decrease the influence of the genre in the later 1970s. Critics contend that the genre did little to address problems in urban areas that are faced by people of color, instead reinforcing an individualistic philosophy that one "badass" man can change things instead of a whole community. Further, they argue that blaxploitation paints urban, Black life one-dimensionally, implying that crime, drugs, and violence are endemic in these communities. Women are generally depicted as sex objects. Although as Foxy Brown in *Coffy*, Pam Grier was a tough and capable woman, she was also sexualized.

The genre largely faded by 1976, due to the efforts by the Coalition Against Blaxploitation, as well as the rise of summer studio blockbusters like *Jaws* and *The Exorcist*. Many modern directors have been influenced by the genre. Notable among them is Quentin Tarantino, whose *Jackie Brown* (1997) featured blaxploitation star Pam Grier and was in the spirit of the genre. *Undercover Brother* (2002) is a comedic parody of blaxploitation. In *Austin Powers: Goldmember* (2002), the main character goes back in time and works with, and has a relationship with, a blaxploitation character, Foxy Cleopatra, obviously a sendup to Foxy Brown.

Although the genre is applauded for opening doors for black actors, most blaxploitation films were produced by White people, and many assert that the actors were mistreated or taken advantage of. A 2003 documentary, *BaadAsssss Cinema*, examined the genre. In it, actor Samuel L. Jackson says, "The black heroes were antiheroes . . . they were pimps, drug dealers, gangsters. But they were all fighting against The Man." Filmmaker Isaac Julien commented, "On the surface, a film like *Blacula* is hysterical. But if you deconstruct the film, it reveals, in a cinematic sense, the anxiety about race relations in the United States"; yet Elvis Mitchell, an African American film reviewer for the *New York Times* who consulted on the documentary, said, the films were made "purely from a commercial impulse to get as many Afros in the theater as humanly possible" (Lambert, 2003). The years 2017 and 2018 saw talks of reboots of blaxploitation films. Remakes of *Shaft, Superfly, Cleopatra Jones*, and *Foxy Brown* are all in the works. Dr. Todd Boyd, the Katherine and Frank Price Endowed Chair for the Study of Race and Popular Culture in the USC School of Cinematic Arts, argues that the state of race relations in 2018 is not that different from the blaxploitation era and that Hollywood is seeking to better connect to disenfranchised viewers (Boyd, 2018).

Laura L. Finley

See also: Lee, Spike; Silent Films; Superhero Films; Tarantino, Quentin

Further Reading

Bausch, K. 2013. "Superflies into Superkillers: Black Masculinity in Film from Blaxploitation to New Black Realism." *Journal of Popular Culture, 46*(2), 257–76.

Boyd, T. 2018. "The Return of Blaxploitation: Why the Time Is Right to Bring Back Shaft and Foxy Brown." *The Guardian,* January 11. https://www.theguardian.com/film/2018/jan/11/blaxploitation-shaft-foxy-brown-film

Dunn, S. 2008. *Baad Bitches and Sassy Supermamas: Black Power Action Films.* Champaign: University of Illinois Press.

Guerrero, E. 1993. *Framing Blackness: The African American Image in Film.* Philadelphia: Temple University Press.

Lambert, C. 2003. "The Blaxploitation Era." *Harvard Magazine.* https://harvardmagazine.com/2003/01/the-blaxploitation-era

Sims, Y. 2006. *Women of Blaxploitation.* Jefferson, NC: McFarland and Company.

Whitty, S. 2012. "Looking Back at 'Blaxploitation' Films." NJ.com, January 16. http://www.nj.com/entertainment/tv/index.ssf/2009/07/looking_back_at_blaxploitation.html

Bollywood

Bollywood is the name given to India's film industry. Most films are recorded in Hindi, although many are released with dubbing for English-speaking audiences. Its revenue in 2016 was $1.78 billion, with experts predicting 11 percent annual growth (Frater, 2016). Although it is mostly known for its vibrant costumes and propensity for breaking into song, many have criticized Bollywood for brutal depictions of police violence, its stereotypical portrayals of women, and its insensitive depiction of sexual assault and domestic violence. A woman is raped every 22 minutes in India, and some have said that Bollywood depictions do little to help reduce the rate of sexual assault (Brook, 2014).

Gangaajal (2003) tells the story of a town full of violent crime and the police officers who are as brutal and corrupt as the criminals. One scene, based on real incidents, shows a police officer pouring acid on the eyes of an accused. The main character, Amit Kumar, realizes that a local politician, Sadhu Yadav, is the primary beneficiary of the corruption. The incidents that influenced the film occurred in the early 1980s and involved 30 or more prisoners being blinded by acid by guards and police.

Ugly (2014) is a crime thriller that generated much controversy for its lack of gory violence, which were hallmarks of the films of director Anurag Kashyap. It tells the story of a 10-year-old girl who is kidnapped and focuses on its impact of those around her. Rather than blood and guts, *Ugly* focuses on the inner turmoil of the characters. Reviewers say it leaves them feeling guilty and with a sense of loss, but admire it for its cinematography.

Lakshmi (2014), directed by Nagesh Kukunoor, features intense verbal abuse and brutal depictions of rape and torture in the industry of child trafficking. A 14-year-old girl is kidnapped from her village, raped, and then sold to a brothel. She is eventually rescued by an undercover agent and then courageously testifies in court against her assailants, which lands them in prison. It is allegedly based on a true story and rings true in the fact that India has a serious problem with the trafficking of children into brothels. Kukunoor had visited with several nongovernmental organizations (NGOs) that assist victims before making the film.

Hazaaron Khwaishein Aisi (2005) is a love story that also features some brutal scenes. It focuses on three students. Geeta is in love with the revolutionary, Siddharth, who seeks to end caste-based discrimination. He breaks her heart when he chooses his ideology over her. Vikram is questioning his father's Gandhian pacifism. He loves Geeta. Years later, Vikram is a powerful man, Geeta is unhappily married to someone else, and Siddharth is still waiting for his revolution. Geeta has an affair with Siddharth, and she sends their child to live with her parents in London. The police capture her and Siddharth for his revolutionary activities, and while Geeta is bailed out of prison by her husband, she believes Siddharth was killed by the police. Vikram tries to help but ends up being brutally beaten and almost killed by police. Director Sudhir Mishra says the film is about his struggle to understand the end of the Nehru era in India, which was a time of great change and upheaval (Hazaaron Khwaishein Diary, 2017).

Jag Mundhra's *Provoked* (2006) is based on the real-life story of Kiranjit Ahluwalia, who killed her abusive husband after a decade of physical, psychological, and sexual abuse. The marriage was arranged, and almost immediately after the wedding her husband, Deepak, began to abuse her. Together they had two sons, who often witnessed the abuse of their mother. Unable to take the repeated abuse, Kiranjit Ahluwalia, sets fire to her husband's feet while he sleeps, accidentally killing him. She is charged with murder and gets assistance from an NGO, Southall Black Sisters. Initially, Ahluwalia was convicted of murder and sentenced to life in prison. The prosecution suggested that, rather than self-defense, she was jealous because Deepak had numerous affairs. The conviction was overturned in 1992, and her case is said to have made a tremendous difference in how India sees domestic violence.

Mehndi (1998) is the story of a woman who is abused by her husband and his family after they do not receive the promised dowry. She refuses to be intimidated; thus the film draws attention to the abuse women receive under the dowry system, but also to their resilience.

Raja Ki Ayegi Baraat (1997) is the story of a man who rapes a girl because she slaps him, then in a court hearing it is determined that justice will be served if he marries her.

Laura L. Finley

See also: Blues Music; *Law & Order*; *Mad Max* Films; Nollywood; Rape Films

Further Reading

Bindel, J. 2007. "I Wanted Him to Stop Hurting Me." *The Guardian,* April 4. https://www.theguardian.com/world/2007/apr/04/gender.ukcrime

Brook, T. 2014. "Does Bollywood Incite Sexual Violence in India?" *BBC*, October 21. http://www.bbc.com/culture/story/20140205-does-bollywood-incite-sex-crimes

Frater, P. 2016. "Bollywood Forecast to Grow 11% Annually, Report." *Variety*, January 6. http://variety.com/2016/biz/asia/bollywood-forecast-to-grow-11-annually-report-1201673182/

"Gangajaal Plot." n.d. *IMDb.* http://www.imdb.com/title/tt0373856/plotsummary

"Hazaaron Khwaishein Diary." 2017. *Outlook India*, April 24. https://www.outlookindia .com/magazine/story/hazaaron-khwaishein-diary/298742

Kamath, S. 2016. "A Fictional Account of a True Story." *The Hindu*, October 18. http:// www.thehindu.com/features/cinema/A-fictional-account-of-a-true-story/article 11641545.ece

Kaushal, S. 2014. "Ugly Review: A Dark, Gripping Movie That Is a Must Watch." *Hindustan Times*, December 28. https://www.hindustantimes.com/movie-reviews/ugly -review-a-dark-gripping-movie-that-is-a-must-watch/story-GscpDadkQJZ9g8 YcRCgegL.html

Bonnie and Clyde

Bonnie and Clyde (1967) tells the story of the real couple and features Warren Beatty as Clyde Barrow and Faye Dunaway as Bonnie Parker. The film begins in 1931, when Barrow is about to steal Bonnie's mother's car. Bonnie decides that Clyde is more interesting than her life and follows him into a life of crime, where the two rob stores, gas stations, and banks. The pair later connect with C.W. (Michael J. Pollard) who adds car heisting to their list of offenses. Then, they are joined by Clyde's brother Buck (Gene Hackman), who was recently released from prison, and Buck's wife, Blanche (Estelle Parsons). The gang continues their crime spree across the country, from Texas to Missouri, Kansas to Nebraska, and as they do so, the violence escalates. They capture one of their pursuers, Sheriff Hamer (Denver Pyle) and while they humiliate him they do not kill him. He becomes their arch-nemesis. When they are captured and try to escape, Buck is killed and Blanche is recaptured. Bonnie, Clyde, and C. W. seek refuge with C. W.'s father, Malcolm (Dub Taylor), in Louisiana, and Malcolm tries to negotiate with Sheriff Hamer. Blanche had told Hamer the gang's location, however, and Bonnie and Clyde ride into an ambush. As in real life, when the two were killed with thousands of police bullets in 1934, the film shows an equally bloody end. The only difference is that in the film they are shot after they surrendered, whereas in reality they had attempted to fight, which resulted in the barrage of bullets.

There are some distinct differences between real life and the cinematic portrayal. "In real life, Bonnie and Clyde were not as glamorous as their on-screen portrayal. Clyde was sadistic. Even as a child he liked to torture animals, and by the time he and Bonnie hooked up with their young recruit, Clyde had already murdered at least two men" (Bouzereau, 2000, p. 4). The 1967 film depicts Bonnie and Clyde as victims of their time, but the two were, in reality, not very likeable. Yet

> the film's power arises from the fact that we, the audience, follow the story from the antiheroes' point of view. At first, even their acts of violence are bumbling, which enhances the sympathy we feel for them. But as the violence becomes increasingly graphic, we tend to distance ourselves from the couple. But the film's piece de resistance was the last scene, the bloody shoot-out and ultraviolent killing of Bonnie and Clyde. The death of Bonnie and Clyde was perfectly choreographed by Arthur Penn. The carnage is haunting; this brief moment of ultra-gore got mixed reactions from the critics and public alike. Penn wanted to get the spasm of death on film, and he used four cameras, each one set at a different speed (24, 48, 72 and 96 frames per

second). Different lenses were also used to get the shock value of a "ballet of death," in Penn's words. Penn wanted two kinds of death: Clyde's had to be rather like a ballet, and Bonnie's had to have a physical shock about it. There is a sense of realism about that scene that is both captivating and repulsive, especially when a piece of Beatty's head comes off. (Bouzereau, 2000, pp. 6–7)

The film's violence was definitely remarkable for its time. Charles Champlin wrote in the *Los Angeles Times*, "Under the old [Production] Code, you would see somebody be shot but you never saw the body torn apart. You didn't make the link. Bonnie and Clyde, as [reviewer] Joe Morgenstern said, suggested that killing kills, that it's violent and painful. Violence is not an everyday thing without effect" (Bouzereau, 2000, p. 3). Film critic Pauline Kael was upset with those who attacked the film. She wrote in her *The New Yorker* review "But the whole point of Bonnie and Clyde is to rub our noses in it [violence], to make us pay our dues for laughing. The dirty reality of death—not suggestions but blood and holes—is necessary" (Bouzereau, 2000, p. 9). Yet other critics found it deeply disturbing. Henry Miller, the famous author, wrote, "I had intended to sit down and let loose a stream of vitriol the morning after I saw Bonnie and Clyde, which is now three weeks ago, alas, and in the meantime I have cooled off somewhat. Nevertheless, I am still furious, more toward the public which acclaims the film and enjoys it than toward the produce and director, though I hold them fully responsible for this monstrous piece of entertainment" (Bouzereau, 2000, p. 9). Other words used to describe the film included "tasteless," "grisly," "stomach-turning," "reprehensible," and "gross and demeaning" (Hoberman, 1998, p. 116). *Time* magazine issued mixed reviews. It first critiqued the film for its excessive violence, then weeks later referred to it as the "sleeper of the decade." It was the first film to be featured on the cover of *Time*. When asked about the film's bloody end, Penn says he was influenced by media reports and images of the Vietnam War. These were broadcast daily during the filming of the movie. He said, "It was a time where, it seemed to me that if we were going to depict violence, then we would be obliged to really depict it accurately; the kind of terrible, frightening volume that one sees when one genuinely is confronted by violence" (Gross, 2008). Warren Beatty also co-produced the film and defended its violence as being necessary to the emotional response they were intending. In defending the film, Penn expressed that violence is part of the American character.

Bonnie and Clyde immediately inspired a new style of filming violence, and according to many, was supplanted within two years by Sam Peckinpah's *The Wild Bunch*, which had more slow motion and more graphic violence. Yet more than 25 years after its release, political pundit David R. Boldt attacked the film in an August 1, 1993, editorial in the *Philadelphia Inquirer*, referring to it as "pornoviolence," and asserting that "I think we went wrong with the release of Bonnie and Clyde . . . the first in a wave of movies that came to the screen immediately after Hollywood's self-policing apparatus was dismantled in 1966" (Hoberman, 1998, p. 117). In 1995, Senator Bob Dole denounced *Natural Born Killers*, a modern *Bonnie and Clyde*, as "a nightmare of depravity" (Hoberman, 1998, p. 118).

Bonnie and Clyde grossed $22.7 million, which was 10 times its budget and the 13th highest-grossing American film to that date. It received 10 Academy Award nominations in 1968 and won 6: Best Actress in a supporting role for Estelle Parsons; Best Cinematography for Burnett Guffy; Best Picture for Warren Beatty; Best Actor in a Leading Role for Beatty; Best Actress in a Leading Role for Faye Dunaway; and Best Actor in a Supporting Role for Gene Hackman. The National Catholic Office for Motion Pictures named it the Best Film of the Year for Mature Audiences.

The film was said to also influence fashion, and several companies created *Bonnie and Clyde*–themed advertisements. Groups recorded songs about the film and the story, and "The Ballad of Bonnie and Clyde" became a top-40 hit.

Laura L. Finley

See also: Cop Films; *Dukes of Hazzard*; Gang Films; *Natural Born Killers*

Further Reading

Bouzereau, L. 2000. *Ultra Violent Movies* (2nd ed.). New York: Kensington Publishing.

Gross, T. 2008. "Arthur Penn, Realistic Violence in Bonnie and Clyde." *NPR*, March 28. http://www.npr.org/templates/story/story.php?storyId=89164831

Hoberman, J. 1998. "A Test for the Individual Viewer: Bonnie and Clyde's Violent Reception." In *Why We Watch: The Attractions of Violent Entertainment*, edited by J. Goldstein, 116–43. New York: Oxford University Press.

Coen Brothers Films

Joel and Ethan Coen, often referred to as the Coen brothers, are writers, directors, and film producers. Their work is often darkly comedic, but they have also produced violent dramas. Highly acclaimed, the Coen brothers have received 13 Academy Award nominations for their work as well as numerous other awards.

Blood Simple (1984) was the Coen brothers' first film. It tells the story of Abby (Frances McDormand), who is cheating on her husband, Julian Marty (Dan Hedaya), with Ray (John Getz). The husband hired a private detective, Lorren Visser (M. Emmet Walsh), who photographs her in a hotel tryst. He authorizes the detective to kill her and Ray after his attempt to kidnap her is a failure. As Marty opens his safe to pay the detective, Visser shoots him, making it look like Abby did it. Ray finds Marty's body and tries to hide it, assuming Abby murdered him, only to find as he drives that Marty is alive. He buries Marty alive. Ray and Abby distrust one another, presuming the other is at fault, while Visser continues to follow them. In the end, Abby brutally stabs Visser to death. The film was praised by critics and established the Coen brothers' reputation for dark humor.

Miller's Crossing (1990) is a gangster film that has been widely praised for its beautiful cinematography while depicting a classic story of Irish mobster violence. Gabriel Byrne as the protagonist, Tom Reagan, and John Turturro as grifter Bernie Bernbaum also received applause for their performances. The scene that many cite as among the most violent in a Coen brothers film involves a shooting set to the tune of the Irish ballad "Danny Boy."

Fargo was praised for its comedy, satire, and suspense. Violence is central to the plot but integrated humorously. Based on a true story from Minnesota in 1987 and filmed there and in North Dakota, it tells the story of Jerry Lundegaard (William H. Macy), who, desperate for money, hires two lowlifes, Showalter (Steve Buscemi) and Grimsrud (Peter Stormare), to kidnap his wife (Kristin Rudrud) with a promise to split the ransom. Their plan goes awry. They unexpectedly kill some people during the kidnapping, and the bodies are found, frozen by the highway, the next day. The police chief, pregnant Marge Gunderson (Frances McDormand), leads the investigation. She quickly traces the kidnapping to Lundegaard, and ask that he call off the kidnappers, but because he does not know their phone numbers, he cannot do so. One of the most violent scenes is not actually shown on film. Rather, in the tradition of Alfred Hitchcock, viewers know but do not see bodies being fed into a woodchipper. Film credit heaped praise on *Fargo*, claiming it was "why he loves the movies" (Ebert, 1996). *New York Times* critic Janet Maslin wrote, "'Fargo' is a crime tale in which somebody's foot is seen sticking out of a wood chipper. And the Coens can present that image so that its salient feature is the victim's white sock," and "As 'Fargo' plays out the kidnapping and its aftermath, it sometimes turns grisly with the sharp ferocity that is another staple of the Coens' noir style. The violence is so quick it appears cartoonish, but there's no mistaking the fact that this tale is fundamentally grim. Yet the film makers' absurdist humor and beautifully honed storytelling give it a winning acerbity, a quirky appreciation of the sheer futility captured on screen" (Maslin, 1996).

No Country for Old Men is considered by many to be the Coens' most violent film. Critics praised the film, which is set on the U.S.-Mexico border in 1980. Two of the main characters are an aging sheriff played by Tommy Lee Jones, and a mysterious killer—and Jones's nemesis—played by Javier Bardem. Bardem's character is searching for $2 million that went missing when a drug deal went bad, resulting in a shootout. His primary target is a former hunter, played by Josh Brolin. It is based on a novel by Cormac McCarthy. Although some saw the film as a commentary on modern violence, the Coens disavowed that connection. Instead, they believe it offers a greater commentary on aging, as Jones's character struggles with the aging process and his abilities throughout the film.

The Coen brothers have collaborated several times with actor and director George Clooney. These credits include *O Brother, Where Art Thou?*, *Intolerable Cruelty*, *Burn After Reading*, *Hail, Caesar*, and *Suburbicon*. The latter stars Matt Damon as Gardner Lodge, a suburban father in the 1950s who decides to take the law into his own hands after his home is violently invaded. Like much of the Coens' work, it features a significant amount of deadpan, dark humor.

Laura L. Finley

See also: Tarantino, Quentin

Further Reading

Collette-White, M., & Davidson, M. 2007. "Coen Brothers Show Violent and Humorous Film in Cannes." *Reuters,* May 20. https://uk.reuters.com/article/uk-cannes-coens/coen-brothers-show-violent-and-humorous-film-in-cannes-idUKL20297771 20070520

Ebert, R. 1996. "Fargo." *Rogerebert.com*, March 8. https://www.rogerebert.com/reviews/fargo-1996

Guardian Film. 2017. "Suburbicon Trailer: Matt Damon Gets Bloody in George Clooney's Latest Comedy." *The Guardian,* June 27. https://www.theguardian.com/film/2017 /jul/27/suburbicon-trailer-matt-damon-george-clooney-coen-brothers

Hoad, P. 2017. "How We Made Blood Simple." *The Guardian,* November 6. https://www .theguardian.com/film/2017/nov/06/how-we-made-blood-simple-coen-brothers -barry-sonnenfeld

Maslin, J. 1996. "Film Review: Deadly Plot by a Milquetoast Villain." *The New York Times,* March 8. http://www.nytimes.com/movie/review?res=9803e1da1f39f93ba35750c0 a960958260

Orr, C. 2014. "30 Years of Coens: Miller's Crossing." *The Atlantic,* September 10. https:// www.theatlantic.com/entertainment/archive/2014/09/30-years-of-coens-millers -crossing/379895/

Turan, K. 2007. "Violence Overwhelms 'No Country.'" *NPR*, November 9. https://www .npr.org/templates/story/story.php?storyId=16143451

Cop Films

Crime films have long been among the most popular with viewers and most frequently feature a dedicated officer or officers who pursue the offenders. In some cases, however, the officers themselves are vigilantes, sometimes likeable, and other times the antiheroes of the story.

Perhaps the most famous of all cinematic police officers is Clint Eastwood's Dirty Harry. Harry Callahan is a San Francisco cop who plays by his own rules, yet no one doubts his integrity. The original *Dirty Harry* film, released in 1971, begins with a sniper shooting an innocent woman in a swimming pool. The killer calls himself Scorpio and threatens to kill others if the police don't give him $100,000. Callahan learns that his boss, Lt. Bressler (Harry Guardino), and the mayor (John Vernon) intend to pay the killer. Scorpio shoots another innocent victim, and Harry and his partner Chico (Reni Santoni) see him, but he escapes, then demands even more money under threat of more killing. Harry delivers it but is attacked by the sniper, and from there goes on a personal quest to catch him, torturing him in the end. Although it seems dated now, the entire plot, along with Harry's famous line, "Do you feel lucky, punk," was innovative at the time. In subsequent Dirty Harry films the main character takes on more of a superhero status, but in this one he is more ruthless.

Critics denounced the film for its violence. Garrett Epps in the *New York Times* wrote that it was "a film without mercy. . . . We do not need any more laws governing what can be shown and what cannot; but we can all place some pressure on producers and distributors to stop offering us Fascist propaganda and sadomasochistic wet dreams. If we do not, we may soon find our screens completely filled with screaming faces, broken teeth, and rivers of red, red blood" (in Bouzereau, 2000, p. 166). It was accused of encouraging vigilante behavior. Eastwood responded that the film was a reaction to the many previous that had been, in his assessment, overly concerned with the rights of the accused. Dirty Harry, Eastwood argued, was most worried about the rights of victims. Director Don Siegel responded to the critics, "I dimly remember that at the end of Hamlet there are five bodies lying around, so that's balderdash. This constantly plainted ditty against violence—if people don't want it, they wouldn't go to the movies. I loathe the gratuitous violence. I fight very hard against it. My violence is very sharp and abrupt" (Bouzereau, 2000, p. 167).

The film made Eastwood a star, and he reprised his role in *Magnum Force* (1973). In *Magnum Force*, Harry tracks down a spree of killings committed by police officers who were showing their resentment of judges who free criminals. They want Harry to join them but he refuses, and finally Harry kills all of them. This film also features some well-known lines, including "There's nothing wrong with shooting as long as the right people get shot" (Bouzereau, 2000, p. 170). It is considered by fans to be the best of the sequels, but critics were still harsh in their assessment. There were three other sequels: *The Enforcer* (1976), *Sudden Impact* (1983), and *The Dead Pool* (1988).

The 1980s saw a variety of other cop films to compete with Dirty Harry, many featuring male "buddy" officers who added some comedic elements. The *Die Hard* series starring Bruce Willis and the *Lethal Weapon* series starring Mel Gibson and Danny Glover were commercially popular, and the hard-core vigilantes played by Steven Seagal, Sylvester Stallone, and Jean-Claude Van Damme were more graphically violent than Harry. The 1980s also saw rogue cop movies in *Renegades* (1989), *Robocop* (1987), and *Dead Bang* (1989), among others.

A critically acclaimed cop film about officers gone bad is *Training Day* (2001). Scriptwriter David Ayer grew up in the area of Los Angeles that was policed by the Los Angeles Police Department's Rampart Unit, and was inevitably influenced by the corruption of its Community Resources Against Street Hoodlums (CRASH) team in the late 1990s involving at least 70 officers. A veteran LAPD officer in an elite narcotics unit, Alonzo Harris (Denzel Washington) mentors rookie Jake Hoyt (Ethan Hawke) as they police a gang-infested community during a 24-hour period. Harris teaches Hoyt that justice looks different in this community and routinely pockets drugs and money. Hoyt refuses to take part, and later Harris abandons him, leaving him to be beaten by the Russian mafia. He tries to arrest Harris but a gunfight ensues, and Harris is killed by the Russian mafia as he tries to flee to the airport, with broadcasts referring to him as a hero officer. Washington won an Academy Award for Best Actor, and Hawke was nominated for Best Supporting Actor. Critics raved about Washington's performance as the tough guy, a sizeable departure from most of his previous roles. The film was also praised because most of the earlier films about corrupt cops (*Serpico* [1973], *Prince of the City* [1981], and *Q & A* [1980], for instance) featured white officers. Critics were bothered by the last 15 minutes, however, asserting that director Antoine Fuqua tried to do too much and left it feeling implausible. A 2012 film titled *Rampart*, starring Woody Harrelson, also depicted the corruption in the LAPD. The popular TV series *The Shield* is said to also have been loosely based on the Rampart scandal.

That violent and vigilante cop movies are so popular reflects on the powerlessness and hopelessness many feel in trying times, according to Jeanine Basinger, who was a professor of film studies at Wesleyan University.

Laura L. Finley

See also: Bonnie and Clyde; British Television; *Charlie's Angels*; Gang Films; *Hill Street Blues*; Italian Films; *Law & Order*; Mafia Films; *Miami Vice*; Rambo Films

Further Reading

Basinger, J. 1989. "Why Do We Cheer Vigilante Cops?" *New York Times,* July 3. http://www.nytimes.com/1989/07/03/opinion/why-do-we-cheer-vigilante-cops.html

Bouzereau, L. 2000. *Ultra Violent Movies.* New York: Kensington Publishing.

Mitchell, E. 2001. "Training Day: This Is Not a Mentoring Program to Emulate." *New York Times,* October 5. http://www.nytimes.com/movie/review?res=9C00E7DE163CF936A35753C1A9679C8B63

Patterson, J. 2012. "Rampart, the LAPD and Hollywood." *The Guardian,* February 17. https://www.theguardian.com/film/2012/feb/18/rampart-woody-harrelson-lapd-hollywood

Rafter, N. 2000. *Shots in the Mirror: Crime Films and Society.* New York: Oxford University Press.

Disney Films

Walt Disney Studios was established on October 16, 1923. Its divisions, including Pixar Animation Studios, Walt Disney Pictures, Marvel Studios, and Walt Disney Animation Studios, are responsible for the production of Disney films. Although they are intended to appeal largely to children, Disney films often contain a great deal of violence. Dr. Ian Colman and Dr. James Kirkbride found that children's cartoons contain 2.5 times more violence than do adult horror films (Olson, 2014). They analyzed 45 of the top-grossing children's cartoon films released between 1937 and 2013, which included many Disney films. Many Disney films also portray rather harsh realities that lead one to question whether they are even appropriate for children. It turns out that violent themes such as miscarriages, the death of loved ones, and even deadly family rivalries are more common in Disney films than is often thought.

The Lion King, released June 15, 1994, produced by Walt Disney Feature Animation, and directed by Roger Allers and Rob Minkoff, may be one of Disney's most famous films, grossing $967 million, but it is also one of the most violent. *The Lion King* tells the tale of a pride of lions set in the grasslands of Africa. The head of the pride, or king, is Mufasa (James Earl Jones), who is resented by his brother Scar (Jeremy Irons). Scar then plans to kill both his brother the king and his nephew (Simba) the heir, which he makes clear in a musical number called "Be Prepared," sung against a backdrop very similar to the fiery pits of hell, describing the impending doom he plans to bring to his family members. With the help of malicious hyenas, Scar succeeds in starting a wildebeest stampede that literally tramples Mufasa to death, while his son Simba watches. Scar then convinces Simba that he was responsible for his father's death. In shame, Simba runs away from his pride and spends the next few years living with Timon the meerkat (Nathan Lane) and Pumbaa the warthog (Ernie Sabella), who teach him how to live with the motto "Hakuna Matata" (no worries). Eventually, Simba runs into a member of his old pride, Nala (Moira Kelly), with whom he falls in love. She then informs Simba of Scar's reign of terror and persuades him to return home and fight for his rightful place on the throne. A fight ensues between Scar (backed up by the hyenas) and Simba (with the lionesses). The fight scene includes slow motion hits and bursting through flames, concluding with the hyenas physically tearing apart Scar.

The Lion King displays examples of both domestic violence and military violence. Even though society often sees domestic violence as spouse against spouse, domestic violence is defined as violent or aggressive behavior within the home. Therefore, other forms of family relationships such as brother against brother fall under the category of domestic violence. In *The Lion King,* the pride is the home and the relationship between scar and Mufasa is domestic. In the stampede scene, Mufasa attempts to save himself by leaping to a nearby cliff, but finds himself in need of his brother's assistance to help him up onto the cliff. He cries out to his brother Scar but receives no aid. Instead, Scar digs his claws into Mufasa's and whispers "long live the king," as he watches Mufasa plummet back into the stampeding wildebeest. The death of Mufasa, directly influenced by his brother's hands, solidifies the notion of domestic violence in this movie. It is also important to call attention to the fact that Scar then proceeds to make Simba think the death of his father was his own fault. Oftentimes in domestic violence cases the victim views themselves as the problem, rather than the one who is being victimized.

Military violence is also prevalent in *The Lion King.* The "good" lionesses fight against the "bad" hyenas in order to secure Simba's reign. The image of Scar turning the foolish hyenas into a structured militarized order is also featured in the film.

A more recent Disney film that utilizes violence while bringing to light a number of political and social issues is *Zootopia.* Released March 4, 2016, and directed by Byron Howard, Rich Moore, and Jared Bush, *Zootopia* is the story of how Judi Hopps (Ginnifer Goodwin), the first rabbit police officer from a rural farming town, finds her footing in the big city of Zootopia. She uncovers a major conspiracy that has been coursing through the city of Zootopia. Assistant Mayor Bellwether (Jenny Slate) plots to take over Zootopia by systematically spreading propaganda through the media, which convinces the public that predators (the minority of this population) were genetically predisposed to aggressive or violent behavior. This makes the population become fearful of predators and breeds hatred toward them. Judi, however, stumbles onto the truth by accident when she is given an "impossible" case to solve by her overbearing boss Chief Bogo (Idris Elba).

Zootopia points out many social issues, including police brutality, racism, and the distribution of drugs into minority neighborhoods. It also highlights the violence in the criminal justice system toward minorities and violence in the media. For example, after Judi confirms the assistant mayor was behind drugging the predators in order to make them appear as though they are violent by nature, she goes to great lengths in order to keep her involvement in the conspiracy a secret. Bellweather corners Judi and her accomplice Nick Wilde (Jason Bateman) in an attempt to kill them and keep her secret. In fact, she planned to drug Nick, a fox, with the same substance she was using on the other predators, which would make him go feral and kill Judi.

Violence against minorities is also a prevalent theme in *Zootopia.* From childhood, Nick is treated as though he is inferior because he is a predator. He was kicked out of "normal" social groups and was forced to make a living in an unconventional way because of the discrimination he faced.

Lastly, *Zootopia* also exhibits a great amount of violence in the media. This can be seen when the mayor and Judi give the official report on the news that the predators have been going "savage" because they are genetically predisposed to do so. Not only were they indirectly sending the message to the public that it was okay to fear these animals; they were showing images and videos of these animals going "savage." In addition, the news was flooded with these images, which made the public assume that the only problems in society are those brought on by predators.

Megan-Marie Pennant

See also: Family Guy; *Harry Potter* Books and Film Series; *South Park*; War Films

Further Reading

Acuna, K. 2012. "Disney's Darkest Hours: The 10 Most Horrific Movies the Mouse House Ever Made." *Business Insider,* March 17. http://www.businessinsider.com/disneys -dark-side-the-10-most-horrific-movies-the-mouse-house-ever-made-2012-3

Bahar, C. 2016. "30 Facts about The Lion King." *Mental Floss,* January 4. http://mentalfloss .com/article/57386/30-facts-about-lion-king

Gellar, J. 2016. "10 Shocking Controversial Messages in Disney Films." *Screenrant,* April 18. https://screenrant.com/most-controversial-disney-movies-video-list/

Olson, S. 2014. "Children's Cartoons Contain 2.5 Times More Death Than Adult Horror Movies: Violence from 'Snow White' to 'Frozen.'" *Medical Daily,* December 16. http://www.medicaldaily.com/childrens-cartoons-contain-25-times-more-death -adult-horror-movies-violence-snow-314600

Dystopian Young Adult Literature and Film

Critics have expressed concern that young adult dystopian literature, some of which is later made into feature films, is too violent and dark. Dystopian novels and films typically depict a world that is governed by fear and surveillance, with protagonists that generally struggle against this oppression. Proponents maintain that these novels and their film adaptations merely depict issues of importance to youth. Further, they note that many popular children's books, including the Grimm's fairy tales, Roald Dahl's stories, and the Beatrix Potter books, also depicted violence. Stories like *Alice in Wonderland* feature calls for executions. Later, violence was routine in the widely popular *Harry Potter* fantasy series by J. K. Rowling and was used by both good and evil characters to achieve their goals. Although the violence is frequent, it is rarely of a graphic or gory nature, although it is certainly intended to be scary. In addition, given the themes of most dystopias, institutional violence is frequently depicted. Some of the most popular dystopian series that have been made into films are Veronica Roth's *Divergent* series, Suzanne Collins's *Hunger Games* trilogy, and James Dashner's *Maze Runner* series.

Roth's *Divergent* series is set in a highly structured society consisting of five groups or factions: Abnegation, Amity, Erudite, Candor, and Dauntless. These factions allegedly consist of people with similar traits and beliefs, and therefore they perform specific jobs in the society. The factions were started after a terrible war that leaders believe was due to selfishness, aggression, ignorance, cowardice, and duplicity; hence they tried to create an alternative society. At age 12, young people take a test that places them in a specific faction. If they choose to join it, they must leave behind their family and friends. Beatrice/Tris is one of the few whose test results are unclear, so she is known as a divergent. She joins the Dauntless, known for their bravery, and meets Four, formerly known as Tobias. He, too, is divergent. The Dauntless also train to be fighters and exert brutal defeats on weaker members. Although at first it sounds like a utopia, it clearly is not. Those who fail the initiation into their faction, called the factionless, are left to perform the jobs no one else in the society wants and suffer extreme poverty and discrimination. Government leaders, desperate for control, utilize serums, tests, and simulations to control the minds of the citizenry. They are particularly concerned about the divergent and force them to undergo a series of emotionally and physically painful tests and simulations in order to assess why they are resistant to the mind control. At the end of the first novel, Tris and others are beginning to realize that they have been lied to and challenge the control executed by their leadership.

Suzanne Collins was motivated to write *The Hunger Games* while watching television coverage of the war in Iraq. The *Hunger Games* is set in Panem, a country that rose from the ashes of what was once North America and that is divided into districts and a Capitol. The book opens on the day of the Reaping, a ceremony in which a boy and a girl from each of the districts are chosen in a brutal lottery to fight to death in the Hunger Games. The Games are a televised spectacle of brutality that are to be watched by all as a warning and a way to quiet dissent. The protagonist, Katniss Everdeen, volunteers as tribute to replace her young sister (who was chosen in the lottery) in the Games. After preparing to fight in the Games, Katniss and her District 12 partner, Peeta Mellark, enter the horrifying arena, where Capitol controllers send terrifying weather, horrific animal hybrids, and the other tributes to kill them in what seems like a gladiator arena. One scholar wrote, "Today, our 'games' are less gladiatorial, yet they harbor the same voyeuristic gains for those who choose to watch them," explaining that "[l]ike Capitol fans who watch the Hunger Games, insulated by their own apathy and far from any 'real' danger or consequences, our audiences relish in the ruin and humiliation, the unpredictability, and the spectacle that unfold in the lives of their beloved reality television stars" (Mortimore-Smith, 2012, p. 159).

Katniss and Peeta win the Games—the first time there were two winners—because they refuse to kill one another. This represents a major threat to the power of President Snow, and Katniss becomes an idol and leader, resulting an uprising that spreads across the districts in the second two books and three films.

The Capitol is far from benevolent, as it keeps the districts in control through surveillance, control, militarism, and deprivation while its own residents live in opulence. President Snow resorts to increasing levels of violence to stave off the growing rebellion. Katniss at first works with the leader of District 13, but she soon realizes that President Coin is as power-hungry and violent as is President Snow.

Throughout the series, Katniss also uses violence, although it is seemingly justified to fight oppression and for self-defense. Unlike the "bad" characters, she grapples with it, even struggling with the deaths she is responsible for as an adult, when she and Peeta are married with children.

Dashner's *Maze Runner* trilogy focuses on a group of boys who wake up in a cement maze with no memories of how they got there. In "the Glade," as they call it, the boys form a society, with each taking on particular functions. Although they want to escape, they realize the area is guarded by horrifying creatures they call Grievers that will maim and kill without hesitation. They receive a box of supplies each week, so they know someone is orchestrating the situation. After the arrival of a girl, Teresa, they learn that they have been part of an elaborate experiment by a governing agency called "WICKED"—World in Catastrophe Killzone Experiment Department. WICKED has been instrumental in the segregation of a postapocalyptic society in an attempt to cure the human race from a plague, "The Flare," that killed much of the population. In the second book, *The Scorch Trials,* the boys have escaped the Glade so WICKED has adjusted the situations they must face. In the finale, *The Death Cure,* the boys must use the memories they have finally pieced together to challenge WICKED once and for all.

In addition to concerns that the books and films are too violent for the age group to which they were marketed, critics note that the violence depicted is nowhere near realistic in that there is no racial or gender violence, both of which are exceedingly common in real life. Although they may make readers and viewers uncomfortable—at least the parents of those readers and viewers—critics contend that they are not nearly radical enough in their critique of hyperviolent, mass-mediated culture. Instead, critics contend that these books, and even more, the films, play into it, with their huge marketing budgets and consumer products.

Laura L. Finley

See also: Brave New World; *Fahrenheit 451*; *Fight Club*; *Harry Potter* Books and Film Series; Japanese Films; *Lord of the Flies*; *Mad Max* Films; *1984*; South Korean K-Pop; *Twilight* Saga, The; Zombie Films

Further Reading

Bruton, C. 2014. "Violence in Teen Fiction Goes on The Dock." *The Guardian*, November 13. https://www.theguardian.com/books/2014/nov/13/violence-teen-fiction-ya-novels-glamorise-crime-catherine-bruton

Craig, A. 2012. "The Hunger Games and The Teenage Craze for Dystopian Fiction." *The Telegraph*, March 14. http://www.telegraph.co.uk/culture/books/9143409/The-Hunger-Games-and-the-teenage-craze-for-dystopian-fiction.html

Finley, L. 2014. "Teaching Peace with Young Adult Fantasies and Dystopias: Nine Themes for Educators." *Peace Studies Journal*, 7(2), 77–95.

Finley, L., & Bellian, D. 2015. "Challenging Militarism through Young Adult Dystopian Literature: Using *The Hunger Games* Trilogy to Teach Peace and Justice." In *Teaching Peace through Popular Culture*, edited by L. Finley, J. Connors, & B. Wien. Charlotte, NC: Information Age.

McCarry, S. 2014. "May the Box Office Be Ever in Your Favor: How Divergent and The Hunger Games Avoid Race and Gender Violence." *Bitch Media*, March 10. https://bitchmedia.org/post/may-the-box-office-be-ever-in-your-favor-how-divergent-and-thehunger-games-and-divergent-avoid-pp.

Mortimore-Smith, S. 2012. "Fueling the Spectacle: Audience as 'Gamemaker'." In *Of Bread, Blood and the Hunger Games*, edited by M. Pharr & L. Clark, 158–66. Jefferson, NC: McFarland & Co.

Regan, L. 2014. "Violent, Dystopian Fiction Is Nothing New." *The Conversation*, May 22. http://theconversation.com/violent-dystopian-childrens-fiction-is-nothing-new -27007

Fight Club

In the film *Fight Club* (1999), director David Fincher tells the story of an insomniac known as the Narrator (Edward Norton), who meets soap salesman Tyler Durden (Brad Pitt). The Narrator moves in with Durden, and the two have a complicated relationship where they routinely physically fight one another for therapeutic reasons. They begin to hold these fights in front of audiences full of men who also participate in what comes to be known as the "fight club." Durden subsequently establishes the following rules for their gatherings:

> You don't talk about fight club.
> You don't talk about fight club.
> When someone says stop, or goes limp, the fight is over.
> Only two guys to a fight.
> One fight at a time.
> They fight without shirts or shoes.
> The fights go on as long as they have to.
> If this is your first night at fight club, you have to fight. (Palahniuk, 1999)

Unbeknownst to the Narrator, Durden begins establishing other fight clubs with other men in a variety of locations. When he finds out that Durden has excluded him, he becomes upset, and even more so when Durden gets romantically involved with Marla (Helena Bonham Carter). The film, which is based on the book by Chuck Palahniuk, is a criticism of hypermasculinity, consumerism, narcissism, and capitalism as a whole.

Tyler Durden is narcissistic and hypermasculine; the Narrator is simply average, and he idolizes Durden. He is unfulfilled at his job, and he just wants to be recognized and find meaning in his life. The way to do so, according to the film, is to be extreme and violent, as the world has essentially "feminized" men (Morgan, 2017).

The movie is full of white males showing off their bodies and fighting, often incurring bloody injuries that make them feel more alive. Critics note that these displays are similar to the historical displays of white power exemplified by the Nazis. In one scene, you see the characters dragging a Korean clerk out onto the street and threating to kill him. They are using their privileges as white males and using force to achieve their desired goal.

Consumerism and the way the characters spend money on goods and services is a major theme of the movie. From the beginning, the Narrator is tied to consumerist things. One particular quote from the movie explains this. Durden asks the Narrator what a duvet is. The Narrator responds, "It's a comforter." Durden then says, "It's a blanket. Just a blanket. Now why do guys like you and me know what a duvet is? Is this essential to our survival, in the hunter-gatherer sense of the word? No. What are we then? We are consumers. We're the by-products of a lifestyle of obsession." He then goes on explaining how his furniture describes him. "The things you own end up owning you" (Fincher, 1999). In sum, you toil away at your job to get the possessions you think you want, only to have to spend your whole life paying them off. The film criticizes the dehumanization that is common in the corporate world, where employees are seen as just another commodity.

Capitalism revolves around the idea of power and the exchange of currency and commodities. Durden tells his fight club members they are victims of their commodity-obsessed society wherein fathers are absent and men in general have been emasculated. Whether a man works in the restaurant business washing dishes or holds a high-level executive position, Durden preaches that they are all slaves to the system. With that said, they form a sort of anticapitalistic army known as Project Mayhem in order to rid the world of the big corporations. The plan is to target the big credit buildings and destroy them so that all the debt will be erased and everyone will be financially equal.

Just like in the military, there are strict rules in place, and the weak-willed will not survive. Durden tries to train the men to be more masculine. He makes them wait outside the house like they are animals to see how fit and determined they are and turns them away if they are weak. In one scene, Durden goes outside to tell two people standing on the porch that they are either too fat or too old and to get away from him. He demands a prohibition on speaking and total compliance to their cause. They also have no names, so they're all uniform and equal, rather than individuals.

The Narrator also uses violence and fear to gain power at his workplace. During a discussion with his boss, he is told that his performance, his appearance, and more are unacceptable. Rather than acquiesce or apologize, the Narrator instead demands 52 weeks of paid leave and several other conditions. When his boss responds that he is out of his mind, the Narrator proceeds to intentionally beat himself up, making it seem that his boss did it to him when his security arrives. From that depraved action, his demands are met, and he walks out the office with his head high. He has successfully used violence to get exactly what he wants, without consideration of who he might hurt to get it.

In another critique of capitalism, Durden steals liposuction byproducts from plastic surgery offices and uses it to make soap. His philosophy is that he steals the literal fat from rich women, then makes soap out of it to sell right back to them. He sells the soap at a high cost to department stores, who gush about the quality of the product. Although not overt, this is a form of violence against women, who obviously don't know that they are bathing with soap made from human flesh.

At the end of the film, the Narrator realizes that he and Durden aren't two people. Rather, they're the same person, as his insomnia drove him into a fugue state. It dawns on him that it was he who has been romantically involved with Marla, and he who has always been in charge of Project Mayhem. The film ends with the Narrator and Marla holding hands as they watch skyscrapers collapse in front of them, the work of Project Mayhem coming to fruition.

Laura L. Finley

See also: Dystopian Young Adult Literature and Film; *Natural Born Killers*; Tarantino, Quentin; *Walking Dead, The*

Further Reading

Fincher, David, dir. *Fight Club.* 1999; Chatsworth, CA: 20th Century Fox, 2002. DVD.

Henderson, G. 2011. "What Was Fight Club? Theses On the Value Worlds of Trash Capitalism." *Cultural Geographies, 18*(2), 143–70.

Locke, B. 2014. "'The White Man's Bruce Lee': Race and the Construction of White Masculinity in David Fincher's Fight Club (1999)." *Journal of Asian American Studies, 17*(1):61–89.

Morgan, K. 2010. "Fight Club Ten Years Later." *Huffington Post,* March 18. https://www.huffingtonpost.com/kim-morgan/fight-club-ten-years-late_b_364581.html

Palahniuk, Chuck. 1996. *Fight Club.* New York: Norton.

Gang Films

Although there were earlier gang films, *The Warriors* (1979) is said to have given rise to the modern gang film. The genre was especially popular in the 1990s, with many of the gang films controversial yet successful at the box office. "More than any other ultraviolent movies, gang movies are a mirror of our society. The violence depicted in these films can be viewed every night on the six o'clock news. Some of these movies have even been accused of generating and inspiring gang violence on our street. . . . And *The Warriors* (1979), in a sense, started it all" (Bouzereau, 2000, p. 113). The promotion for Walter Miller's film claimed "These are the armies of the night. They are 10,000 strong. They outnumber the cops five to one. They could run New York City. Tonight they're out to get The Warriors" (Bouzereau, 2000, p. 113). The film is credited with spawning more actual violence than any other, and even more than what was depicted on the screen. It opened on February 9, 1979, in 670 theaters, and by the middle of March three people had been killed in Warriors-inspired fights and several other brawls had broken out at screenings. The first killing occurred just three days after the opening, at a Palm Springs drive-in theater. A citizens group in South Central Los Angeles demanded that the film be recalled, claiming it was prompting racial violence in the city. After these incidents, Paramount Pictures offered to pay the security tabs for any theater that wanted it. And within two weeks of its release, Paramount cancelled its $100,000 ad campaign, which featured all the gangs depicted in the film posing together, and launched a new campaign that showed only the title of the film written in spray paint, graffiti-style. It generated broader conversations about the effect of violent movies, and A. Alan Friedberg, president of the National Association of Theatre Owners (NATO), stipulated, "There is no causal relationship between movies and real life. Motion pictures are a mirror, a reflection of the real world in which we live" (Bouzereau, 2000, p. 117). Yet it did well at the box office, grossing $4.7 million in just six days.

In the opening, viewers are introduced to the nine members of the Coney Island gang called the Warriors. They are clad in leather vests and headed to a gang convention in the Bronx, where a gang leader named Cyrus has declared a truce so that all the gangs can march as one against city officials. Most seem to agree, until Luther, the psycho leader of a gang called the Rogues, shoots Cyrus, inciting a melee. Everyone blames the Warriors for Luther's murder, and they must then fight off various gang attacks as they try to get back to Coney Island. They even fight a gang of girls, called the Lizzies. The Warriors are depicted as the heroes in the film, and the truth finally prevails when they have a confrontation with the Rogues and it is revealed that Luther murdered Cyrus.

The film was shot on location in Manhattan, Brooklyn, Queens, and Coney Island. Hill, producer Larry Gordon, and executive producer Frank Marshall decided not to cast actual gang members as extras, which upset gangs in the area. Much of it was shot in slow motion, following the style popularized by *Bonnie and Clyde* and the Sam Peckinpah films like *The Wild Bunch*.

Variety magazine praised the film's "bonecracking violence, dialogue consisting mostly of expletives, and an emphasis on the more degrading aspects of human nature. Under Walter Hill's forceful direction, the Paramount release should do well with the bare-knuckle crowd, along with those anxious about this subculture" (Bouzereau, 2000, p. 115). Whereas some asserted that it glorified violence, other critics responded like Stephen Farber in the *New West*, "at least it doesn't try to deny this, as the sanctimonious gang movies of the fifties often did" (Bouzereau, 2000, p. 115). Paramount was later sued by the family of one of the boys who was killed. The court rejected the argument that *The Warriors* was responsible, noting that although it did contain violent scenes, it was not advocating or encouraging violence.

Dennis Hopper's *Colors* (1988) stars Sean Penn and Robert Duvall as police officers in the Los Angeles Police Department's special Community Resources Against Street Hoodlums Unit, known as CRASH. They are working in an environment full of drugs, gangs, and violence. Producer Robert Solo intended for "social realism" in the tradition of *Blackboard Jungle* (1955). The LAPD hated the film, fearing that it depicted the police as inept in curtailing the gang warfare between the Crips and Bloods in Los Angeles, which had taken some 387 lives in the year prior to the film's release. They feared that gangs would show up at the film screenings and additional violence would ensue. The LAPD asked Hopper not to use the real names of the gangs, although the gangs were happy for the attention. He did, however, include some actual gang members as extras. Several groups protested the film, including the National Association for the Advancement of Colored People (NAACP) and the Los Angeles County Sheriff's Department. One theater even put up a sign reading "If you are wearing gang-related clothing, you will not be admitted" (Bouzereau, 2000, p. 120). Yet opening weekend was packed, and despite one fistfight in Culver City, California, there was no reported violence. Weeks later, however, a 19-year-old gang member was killed outside a theater showing the film in Stockton, California. Hopper responded, saying, "The best I can do [. . .] is point my finger at the problem and say, 'Look!'" (Brower, 1988). It was considered by many to be the second most controversial film of 1988, behind Mel Gibson's *The Last Temptation of Christ*.

There were mixed reactions to *Colors*. Some asserted that it glorified violence, whereas others said it showed the stupidity of gang violence, which is so often related to turf and gang symbols like colors, hence the name of the film. Robert

Solo responded to the criticism, noting "The film is not a film that is going to stir someone to violence. More violence, perhaps, over the years has been stirred by horror movies and chop-shockery movies and ax-murder movies than anything like this" (Bouzereau, 2000, p. 119). Film critic Roger Ebert wrote in his April 15, 1988, review, "There are many good moments in 'Colors,' but the one I will remember the longest is in the scene where a group of Los Angeles gang members are trying to explain why the gang is so important to them. Talking to a couple of cops, they describe the feeling of belonging—of feeling for the first time in their lives that they were part of a 'family' that cared for them and was ready to die for them. The product of their family is, of course, tragic. Their gang deals in drugs, defends its turf and murders to enforce its authority" (Ebert, 1988). He noted that the film accurately addressed the hopelessness in these communities, and in particular, the challenges for police in solving gang-related crimes. He also noted that movies about gangs tend to romanticize them or demonize them, but Colors avoided both. Instead, it addressed the circumstances that create gang involvement, although its depiction of police, Ebert argued, was pretty routine. Despite the expected duo of street-smart veteran (Duvall) and hot-headed rookie (Penn), Ebert argued that the quality of acting made for a better depiction than most of cops.

The year 1991 saw the release of *New Jack City*, which chronicles the rise and fall of American mobster and drug lord Nino Brown, played by Wesley Snipes. It focuses on how the drug trade in disadvantaged communities helps create and sustain gang activity. Director Mario Peebles was influenced by real stories of black gangsters. It was well received, with critics noting its antidrug message. Yet it, too, triggered a series of violent incidents and riots, including a two-hour rampage in Los Angeles and the fatal shooting of a 19-year-old in Brooklyn. The producers responded that the violence was not the result of the film but rather due to ongoing disputes. They noted, "The real cause of violence at the theaters is not cinematic images of drug culture but decades of poverty in our communities. Chronic unemployment, inadequate education, dilapidated housing, poor health care, a lack of public services, and an apathetic bureaucracy do not breed civility" (Bouzereau, 2000, p. 121).

That same year, John Singleton's *Boyz N the Hood* also focused on gang life, drugs, and violence in inner cities. Like *New Jack City*, *Boyz* also had an antiviolence message, and the main character, Tre Styles (Cuba Gooding Jr.), rejects the gang life in South Central Los Angeles, watching in dismay as his friend falls prey to it. Yet it, too, triggered violent sprees, with at least one person dead after a midnight showing at a drive-in and more than thirty wounded. Other incidents occurred in different parts of the country. Columbia Pictures agreed to pay for security at theaters wishing to add it. Singleton was upset about the violent reaction but denounced any responsibility, saying," I didn't create the conditions in which people just shoot each other" (Bouzereau, 2000, p. 123).

Juice is a movie based on a group of best friends, who called themselves the "Wrecking Crew." They live in Harlem, and the film documents the way they survive the streets. Bishop (Tupac Shakur), Quincy "Q" (Omar Epps), Raheem (Khalil Kain), and Steel (Jermaine Hopkins) have been best friends since the second grade. Their lives were not easy, as school was a joke and they were constantly harassed by police. A rival Puerto Rican gang harasses them daily. The boys were simply fed up and wanted respect.

The boys decide to rob a local corner store. Bishop, the mastermind, brings a gun, which the others believe is just for show. Instead, he shoots the store owner and they all flee. Raheem confronts Bishop about the gun, and Bishop shoots Raheem. He threatens to kill Q and Steel if they tell anyone. They try to stay away from Bishop, but he keeps trying to pull them in and is increasingly violent. Steel confronts Bishop, who is trying to frame him for the murders and is shot but survives, and he then tells Q's girlfriend what has happened. Q decides to confront Bishop, unarmed, and the two scuffle. After a chase and more scuffling, Bishop falls to his death. Again, violence ensued after film screenings, with at least one 14-year-old girl killed during an outbreak in Chicago. Paramount again offered to pay for additional security. *Juice* was a box office success, grossing more than $2 million in its opening, and showings have been held in communities with significant gang presence as a way to teach youth about the dangers of gang involvement.

One year later, a gang film by twin brothers Allen and Albert Hughes called *Menace II Society* was released. The brothers had grown up in a gang-infested portion of Detroit, and their mother had tried to keep them from joining gangs by giving them a video camera. Their intent was to shock audiences into understanding the realities of inner-city life and the daily violence. Film critic David Smith wrote in the *Hollywood Reporter*, that *Menace II Society* is "the most brutal and affecting film yet to deal with the dead-end existence in the ghetto" (Bouzereau, 2000, p. 124). The violence even had to be cut back so that the film could avoid an NC-17 rating. It tells the story of Caine (Tyrin Turner) who is being raised by his grandparents in a housing project in Watts, Los Angeles. He is implicated in the murder of a local grocer, which starts his descent into a life of gang violence.

Other popular gang films of the 1980s and 1990s include *The Outsiders* (1983), *American Me* (1992), *Blood In, Blood Out* (1993), *A Bronx Tale* (1993), *Friday* (1995), *Clockers* (1995), and *American History X* (1998).

Laura L. Finley

See also: Bonnie and Clyde; Broadway Musicals; Cop Films; Latin American MCs; Lee, Spike; *Lonesome Dove*; Mafia Films

Further Reading

Anonymous. 1992. "Prosecutor Says Film Juice Partly to Blame for Girl's Death." *UPI*, January 19. http://www.upi.com/Archives/1992/01/19/Prosecutor-says-film-Juice -partly-to-blame-for-girls-death/1216695797200/

Bouzereau, L. 2000. *Ultra Violent Movies*. New York: Kensington Publishing.

Ebert, R. 1988. "Colors." April 15. http://www.rogerebert.com/reviews/colors-1988

Global Censorship

Laws on media censorship vary tremendously around the globe. Precisely what is banned, what is subject to censorship or restrictions, and who gets to decide differ from country to country.

In the United Kingdom, local councils may show any films they choose, but generally elect to follow the classifications set by the British Board of Film Classification (BBFC). Established in 1912, the BBFC was created as an autonomous body for classifying films. In 1984, parliament made it responsible for classifying videos as well. Flexible to public opinion, the BBFC's standards for film and video are routinely updated as a result of public consultations. It rarely cuts films, and usually at the request of a film distributor that wants to lower the age classification assigned to its film. The only real law related to what films are prohibited in the UK is the Obscene Publications Act, which bans material that "tends to deprave or corrupt persons who are likely to read, see or hear it" (Clarke, 2002).

Arabic-speaking countries in the Middle East and North Africa generally block content that is "harmful to morality." A study of 6,000 people in Qatar, Saudi Arabia, Egypt, Lebanon, Tunisia, and the United Arab Emirates (UAE) found that the majority of respondents support some degree of censorship. More than two-thirds of the respondents agreed that films and other entertainment should be banned for offensive content, with more than three-quarters of respondents from Saudi Arabia and Egypt supporting such censorship. Whereas a majority enjoy Hollywood films, 34 percent of the respondents said they were harmful to morality. Arab movies are considered more appropriate, with 71 percent of the respondents indicating they were good for morality. Eighty percent of the respondents favored films made in Arabic-speaking countries. Many films in Arabic-speaking countries are cut dramatically, like *The Wolf of Wall Street*, which lost nearly 40 minutes (Kwok, 2014).

For more than three decades, Saudi Arabia completely banned cinemas. That ban was lifted in 2014, paving the way for theater chains to open in the country with a large population of people under the age of 25. Content is still censored, although experts predict a gradual lifting of restrictions. Like neighboring Kuwait, which censors movies containing sex, homosexuality, and religious issues, films shown in Saudi Arabian theaters are often shorter due to segments that were cut (Vivarelli, 2017).

Lebanon, considered one of the most liberal countries in the Middle East, banned the film *Wonder Woman* in 2017 after displaying posters, showing trailers, and even hosting advance screenings of it. Although the country may ban films due to sexual or other content, the most frequent cause, as in this case, was that the film originated in Israel. The star of the film, Gal Gadot, is Israeli, although other films she was in were not banned. Critics contend that this sets a dangerous precedent and that it is confusing, as in addition to earlier Gadot films being released, films starring Israeli Natalie Portman were allowed. Defenders claim that the ban is appropriate because Gadot is the star of the film and she served time in the Israeli army and is an outspoken supporter of it.

In 2002, Chile lifted its restrictions on films. Prior to the new law, nearly 1,100 films had been banned, largely for being pornographic in a country that is heavily influenced by the Catholic Church. During the leadership of dictator General Augusto Pinochet, between 1973 and 1990, military leaders often issued bans on films or ordered cuts to them at their whim. *Fiddler on the Roof* (1971) was banned because too many characters were Russian, as were films like *Missing* (1982) about the disappearance of an American citizen in Chile during the coup that brought Pinochet to power. Other films were banned because they were allegedly blasphemous, including Monty Python's *The Life of Brian* (1979) and Oliver Stone's *Salvador* (1986). The new law created a board to assign films to one of four classifications. Rather than simply political or military leaders, the new board of 21 includes film directors, critics, and even psychologists.

Laura L. Finley

See also: Arab Media; Global Video Games; Islam, Depictions of; Italian Films; Japanese Films; *Natural Born Killers*

Further Reading

Biltereyst, D., & Vande Winkel, R., eds. 2013. *Silencing Cinema: Film Censorship around the World.* New York: Palgrave Macmillan.

Clarke, S. 2002. "Explained: Film Censorship in the UK." *The Guardian*, March 13. https://www.theguardian.com/film/2002/mar/13/filmcensorship.seanclarke

Kwok, Y. 2014. "Hollywood Movies in Arab Countries: A Love and Hate Relationship." *CNN*, April 23. http://edition.cnn.com/2014/04/23/world/meast/middle-east-hollywood-films-censorship-survey/index.html

McKernan, B. 2017. "Wonder Woman and a Dangerous Precedent for Censorship in Lebanon." *The Independent*, June 2. http://www.independent.co.uk/news/world/middle-east/wonder-woman-banned-israel-lebanon-beirut-censorship-accusations-a7770146.html

Rohter, L. 2002. "After Banning 1,092 Movies, Chile Relaxes Its Censorship." *The New York Times*, December 13. http://www.nytimes.com/2002/12/13/world/after-banning-1092-movies-chile-relaxes-its-censorship.html

Vivarelli, N. 2017. "Five Key Questions about Saudi Arabia's Decision to Reintroduce Movie Theaters." *Variety*, December 12. http://variety.com/2017/film/global/five-key-questions-about-saudi-lifting-its-ban-on-movie-theatres-after-35-years-1202637894/

Harry Potter Books and Film Series

J. K. Rowling's seven *Harry Potter* fantasy books have been among the most widely read books of all time. The series saw success previously unheard of for children's books, so large that the *New York Times* had to change the way they list bestsellers, as otherwise the books would have dominated the list. The series was popular not only in the United States and in Rowling's home country of England but internationally as well, such that "Ms. Rowling, a single mother when she started writing the series, is now one of the richest women in Britain" (Harry Potter, 2011). Equally popular was the film series (2001–2011) based on the books, which has been called the "cultural mass phenomenon of the age." The books are full of action, excitement, humor, and horror.

It is not just readers and viewers who have taken an interest in the *Harry Potter* series. Scholars have examined myriad facets of the books, including psychological themes; religion and spirituality; and even radical analyses of gender, race, class, and social issues.

Like most works of fantasy, it is relatively easy to spot the "good" and "bad" characters. They look and dress differently, and music in films often introduces the bad characters with scary tropes. However, there are relatively few differences in the behavior exhibited by the bad and good characters. "Sometimes we characterize acts of force, violence, and deception as evil, but frequently both good and evil characters will resort to these methods. Indeed, the use of force often seems necessary in order to defeat the forces of evil, and characters who attempt to negotiate peacefully with villains are frequently depicted as woefully naïve. And we find the hero almost invariably confronts the villain with the same sorts of deception and violence that the villain wields" (Forbes, 2011, pp. 16–17).

The books and films tell the story of how Tom Riddle becomes Voldemort, an evil and violent character destined to take all the power. Voldemort is so evil he is referred to as "he who shall not be named," as even saying his name conjures desperate fear. He is countered throughout with young sorcerer Harry Potter, who survived Voldemort's attack that killed his parents and who is therefore the only one who can truly counter him.

Voldemort is hideous, looking and acting like a snake, and he surrounds himself with an army of creepy characters who do his bidding. None are hesitant to use magical spells, to assault Harry and anyone else who gets in their way, or even to kill. In fact, Voldemort is the only character who doesn't hesitate to use the most twisted, violent, and prohibited spells. Voldemort tells Harry, there "is no good or evil, only power and those too weak to seek it." It is clear that he will use anyone and anything to get what he wants.

One of Voldemort's primary subordinates is Bellatrix Lestrange. She seems to enjoy inflicting violence, as does Dolores Umbridge, who ends up leading Harry's school (Hogwarts) in *The Order of Phoenix.* She is small in stature and dresses in all pink, but is as power-hungry as Voldemort. She enjoys punishing the students, and in particular, Harry.

Another one of Voldemort's followers is Lucius Malfoy, who is in his army he calls "Death Eaters." Malfoy's son, Draco, is Harry's primary nemesis at Hogwarts School of Witchcraft and Wizardry, and it becomes clear early on that Draco will likely turn out bad. One of the first things that happens when young people who supposedly have wizarding powers arrive at the school is that they are sorted into houses, somewhat like teams. Harry ends up in Gryffindor, with his soon-to-be lifelong friends, Ron Weasley and Hermione Granger. Draco is sorted to Slytherin, a house full of bullies and brutes.

Professor Severus Snape is a complex character, although in the first books and films it is suspected that he is a follower of Voldemort or is otherwise evil. He wears all-black clothing and never smiles. Snape seems to have a particular problem with Harry, and he also has disdain for the smart and hard-working Hermione. It is only as the series develops that it is revealed that he loved Harry's mother Lily and had actually been helping to protect Harry.

As the primary protagonist, Harry is likeable: he is brave, loyal, and kind. Although Harry struggles with internal battles due to the little bit of Voldemort that is inside him from when his mother sacrificed her life to save him, he constantly chooses to do the right thing. He does, however, build and train an army to fight Voldemort, so it is clear that Harry does not disavow violence. Like guns, wands may make kids feel powerful. Jones explained: "Her [Rowling's] characters use magic wands to defeat their foes and defend themselves (making them much more acceptable to gun-sensitive parents), but most of the time those wands function exactly like guns in children's fantasies; Harry and his friends whip them out, aim, fire, blow things up, knock down monsters, sometimes miss or have their shots blocked, or comically mis-fire and accidentally shoot themselves" (Jones, 2002, p. 49).

Albus Dumbledore, the head of Hogwarts, is also depicted as a wise, kind, and caring soul who mentors Harry. Yet as the series develops, it becomes clear that things are not always as they seem and that Dumbledore is not purely good. It is clear at the end that he manipulated both Snape and Harry, resulting in Snape's death.

In addition to the interpersonal violence depicted throughout the series, *Harry Potter* features a great deal of institutional violence. It is clear that the Ministry of Magic becomes little but a stooge for Voldemort, and that even the precious Hogwarts is about controlling and disciplining students. Hideous Dementors, which fly in swarms and look like gray ghosts, possess souls and they cart people off to the terrifying prison, Azkaban. The books and films make it seem as though only those with special, magical powers are capable of ending crime and obtaining justice for victims. The series ultimately leaves readers and viewers with the idea that justice can only be achieved by killing the worst offenders.

Laura L. Finley

See also: Crucible, The; Disney Films; Dystopian Young Adult Literature and Film; Nollywood; *Twilight* Saga, The

Further Reading

Finley, L., & Mannise, K. 2014. "Potter versus Voldemort: Examining Evil, Power and Affective Responses in the *Harry Potter* Film Series." In *Evil and Popular Culture*, edited by S. Packer & J. Pennington, 59–72. Santa Barbara, CA: ABC-CLIO.

Forbes, D. 2011. "The Aesthetic of Evil." In *Vader, Voldemort, and Other Villains*, edited by J. Heit, 13–27. Jefferson, NC: McFarland & Company.

Harry Potter. 2011. *The New York Times,* January 21. http://topics.nytimes.com/top/reference /timestopics/complete_coverage/harry_potter/index.html?scp=1-spot&sq=harry %20potter&st=cse

Heit, J. 2011. "Introduction." In Vader, Voldemort, and Other Villains, edited by J. Heit, 3–13. Jefferson, NC: McFarland & Company.

Jones, G. 2002. *Killing Monsters: Why Children Need Fantasy, Super Heroes, and Make-Believe Violence.* New York: Basic.

Hitchcock, Alfred

"There is no terror in the bang, only in the anticipation of it."

—Alfred Hitchcock

Alfred Hitchcock (1899–1980) is known for being the "master of suspense." Born in Leytonstone, England, Hitchcock was one of three children. It is said that he had a lonely childhood due to obesity, which left him isolated and sheltered away from others. His parents had unusual methods of discipline and often sent him to the local jail for the police to lock him up for misbehaving. Afterward, they would force him to stand for hours and to explain his lack of good judgement. Many believe that his strange upbringing had a big impact on the way in which he constructed his films.

In 1925, he directed his first feature film, *The Pleasure Garden* (1925), a tale of adultery and murder, which displayed his future brilliance as a director. He then produced *Blackmail* in 1929, which tells the story of a woman who stabs an artist to death when he tries to seduce her. Hitchcock further expounded on the themes of sex and violence in 1930 with the film *Murder*, which introduced the technique of recording a character's thoughts onto the soundtrack. *Alfred Hitchcock Presents* was a TV show he hosted that aired from 1955 to 1965. It featured dramas, thrillers, and suspense. By the time it premiered on October 2, 1955, Hitchcock had been directing films for over three decades. *Time* magazine named the show one of "The 100 Best TV Shows of All Time."

Hitchcock's filmmaking typically includes themes like desperation, fear, suspicion, and paranoia. He invented camera tricks and film editing techniques that are still being used in movies. One thing to take into consideration about Hitchcock's films is the big influence that he had on other directors, including Brian De Palma and the Wachowski sisters. His films definitely elevated the medium of film as a form of art more than any other director.

One of Hitchcock's greatest artistic achievements was the commercially successful movie *Psycho* (1960), a groundbreaking popular-culture sensation that caused a great deal of controversy. Made for just $800,000, *Psycho* grossed more than $32 million. *Psycho* was directed and produced by Alfred Hitchcock and is based on the novel by Robert Bloch. The film is about a beautiful blonde secretary, Marion Crane (Janet Leigh), who ends up at an isolated motel after stealing money from her employer. She comes into contact with the motel's disturbed owner, Norman Bates (Anthony Perkins). The film *Psycho* forever changed the scope of the silver screen. With its shocking bursts of violence and unreserved sexual undertones, the film tested the strict censorship boundaries of the day and introduced a new wave of violence in films. The film announced that it was taking the audience to places it had never been before. David Thomson, author of *The Moment of Psycho*, said that "Alfred Hitchcock taught America to love murder."

The movie was filmed in black and white in order to manage the graphicness of the murder scenes. Hitchcock was very aware that the movie would not have gotten shown if it was in color, showing bright red blood splattering the walls and floors. Even though it was in black and white, however, the film seemed more graphically violent than it actually was. It is said that it was not the graphic violence in film that created the horror, but that it was something subconscious within the minds of the audiences who identified with the characters in the film. It is the hidden levels of violence in *Psycho* that places it among the most reputable and profound horror films ever made. The most iconic scene from the film was controversial, in that it showed Bates stabbing Crane while she was showering. The music by

Bernard Herrmann is one of the most recognizable scores in film history. That Janet Leigh was filmed in her underwear was unusual for the time, as was the fact that she was killed only 30 minutes into the film. Many consider *Psycho* to be the precursor to the subgenre of slasher horror movies. These types of films involved violent psychopaths murdering people, typically using large-bladed knives, and similar to Hitchcock's film *Psycho*, they also seek to ignite an emotional reaction from the audience by playing on their fears. In 2012, Anthony Hopkins played Hitchcock in a film with that title. It depicts the making of *Psycho* and shows insights into the director's life.

In *The Birds* (1963), a flock of crazed birds terrorize a small town. It was the film debut for Tippi Hedren, who plays young socialite Melanie Daniels. Hedren later accused Hitchcock of sexually assaulting her. *The Birds* featured several grisly scenes of corpses, which was unusual at the time. Hitchcock worked with Hermann again, only in this film they did not create a score but rather disturbing caws, screeches, and rustling wings. Fans applauded Hitchcock's depiction of the mental unease experienced by the characters in the film.

Hitchcock's *Frenzy* (1972) is considered by many to be his last great film. It is the story of a serial killer in London who is raping and killing women. Although the audience knows early on that the perpetrator is Robert Rusk (Barry Foster), his friend Richard Blaney (Jon Finch) is arrested and jailed.

Gina Thompson

See also: Kubrick, Stanley; Lee, Spike; Poe, Edgar Allan; Silent Films; Tarantino, Quentin

Further Reading

Allen, J. 1985. "The Representation of Violence to Women: Hitchcock's *Frenzy.*" *Film Quarterly, 38*(30), 30–38.

Coyle, J. 2012. "After 'Psycho,' a Shower of Violence in Movies." *CNSNews,* November 2. https://www.cnsnews.com/news/article/after-psycho-shower-violence-movies

Sooke, A. 2015. "The Birds, Review: 'Disturbing.'" *The Telegraph,* January 9. http://www.telegraph.co.uk/culture/film/filmreviews/11334674/The-Birds-review-disturbing.html

Strauss, M. 2007. "The Painted Jester: Notes on the Visual Arts in Hitchcock's Films." *Journal of Popular Film & Television, 35*(2), 52–56.

Thompson, K., & Bordwell, D. 2010. *Film History: An Introduction* (3rd ed.). New York: McGraw-Hill.

Holocaust Films

The first films depicting issues relevant to the Holocaust emerged in 1940s Germany and generally presented the discrimination and violence against Jewish people and others targeted by the Nazis as warranted and appropriate. *Jud Süss* (1940) depicted a Jewish man attempting to take over the duchy of Württemberg in the 18th century. It was shown to Nazi officials at concentration camps as a tool for inciting their hatred. That same year, *The Eternal Jew* compared Jews to rats and depicted them as responsible for violence, class warfare, fraud, and corruption. *Terezin: A Documentary Film from the Jewish Settlement Area* (1944) was shown to

Red Cross officials to fool them into believing that the Jews in concentration camps and ghettos were being treated well.

The mid-to-late 1940s saw a series of films made by the Allies to depict the horrors of the war, and the concentration camps specifically. Prisoners of war and German civilians watched these films as a tool for re-education and reconciliation. These films were made in both Germany and other countries.

During the Cold War era, additional films were made about World War II, including George Stevens's three-time Academy Award winner *The Diary of Anne Frank*. These films tended not to depict the horrors of the war or of the concentration camps, however, instead focusing on more emotional stories. *The Pawnbroker* (1965) told the tale of Sol Nazerman and showed the parallels between the discrimination of the Third Reich and that in the United States during the civil rights movement. *Judgment at Nuremberg* (1961) presented a fictionalized version of the trials of Nazi officials for war crimes and crimes against humanity.

Films in the 1970s and 1980s grappled more directly with the Holocaust. In 1978, Marvin Chomsky's four-part miniseries *Holocaust*, broadcast on NBC, followed two fictional families. One perpetrated atrocities and the others were victims. The series chronicled the development of the ghettos and the use of gas chambers. Meryl Streep starred as Inga Helms-Weiss of the victimized family. The series was not universally applauded, however, as Holocaust survivor Elie Weisel criticized it for turning the atrocities into a soap opera. Another lengthy examination of the Holocaust can be found in the French-British nine-hour documentary *Shoah* (1985). *Sophie's Choice* (1982) also featured Meryl Streep as a Holocaust survivor who reveals her survival story to her new lover, Nathan (Kevin Kline).

Perhaps the most impactful of all the Holocaust films is *Schindler's List* (1993). It chronicles the story of Oskar Schindler, a German industrialist who saved more than 1,000 Polish Jews. The black and white filming gave *Schindler's List* a feeling of both reality and brutality. One of the most controversial scenes in the film takes place in a shower, where people at concentration camps expecting to be gassed are showered with water.

Life Is Beautiful (1997) also generated controversy, as it told the story of a father who protected his son from the horrors of the concentration camps by turning the experience into a game. *The Pianist* (2002) is historical fiction that won three Oscars (Best Director, Roman Polanski; Best Adapted Screenplay, Ronald Harwood; and Best Actor, Adrien Brody). It tells the story of a pianist who was sent to a concentration camp and who helped lead a resistance movement.

The period 2008–2009 saw several Holocaust films released, including *Valkyrie*, which starred Tom Cruise as the German officer who attempted to kill Adolf Hitler in 1944; *The Reader*, a fictional tale starring Kate Winslet as a woman on trial for war crimes; *Good*, in which Viggo Mortenson plays a professor caught up in the zeal of Nazism; *The Boy in the Striped Pajamas*, about a German boy who befriends a Jew and learns the horrid truth about what was happening; and *Defiance*, which tells the story of three brothers who escape the Nazis to lead a Jewish uprising in Belarus. Quentin Tarantino, no stranger to hyperviolent film, took on a Holocaust story in his 2009 *Inglorious Basterds*. It is a revenge fantasy in which a Jewish cinema owner and a group of Jewish soldiers craft a plan to execute Nazi leaders. Critics claim that the film demonstrates everything that Tarantino tried to critique in earlier films, and offers nothing new as a Holocaust film. It was definitely popular, though, grossing $37 million in its opening weekend (Siegel, 2009). *The Book Thief,* based on Markus Zusack's 2005 novel, was a popular film from 2013. It is one of only a few Holocaust films to feature a female character and does not graphically depict violence in the way that other films in this genre do.

German filmmaker Uwe Boll, who has been described as a "schlockmeister" and "the world's worst film director," ignited controversy with his 2010 film *Auschwitz*, which graphically depicted prisoners suffocating in gas chambers and being loaded into ovens as their teeth are pulled. Critics vowed to boycott the film, but Boll maintained that the more graphic depiction was necessary so that desensitized audiences would never forget the Holocaust.

Laura L. Finley

See also: German Punk Music; Tarantino, Quentin; War Films

Further Reading

Baron, L. 2005. *Projecting the Holocaust into the Present: The Changing Focus of Contemporary Holocaust Cinema.* Lanham, MD: Rowman & Littlefield.

Connolly, K. 2010. "German Director's Holocaust Film Causes Outrage." *The Guardian,* November 12. https://www.theguardian.com/world/2010/nov/12/uwe-boll-auschwitz-film-causes-outrage

Eaglestone, R., & Langford, B. 2008. *Teaching Holocaust Literature and Film.* Basingstoke, UK: Palgrave Macmillan.

"Film and the Holocaust." (n.d.). *The National Holocaust Centre and Museum.* https://www.nationalholocaustcentre.net/film-and-the-holocaust

Insdorf, A. 2008. "The Holocaust and Hollywood." *Newsweek,* November 27. http://www.newsweek.com/holocaust-and-hollywood-84803

Kerner, A. 2011. *Film and the Holocaust: New Perspectives on Dramas, Documentaries, and Experimental Films.* New York: Continuum.

Loshitzky, Y. 1997. *Spielberg's Holocaust: Critical Perspectives on Schindler's List.* Bloomington: Indiana University Press.

Siegel, L. 2009. "Tarantino's Hollow Violence." *The Daily Beast,* August 23. http://www.thedailybeast.com/articles/2009/08/24/tarantinos-hollow-violence.html

Islam, Depictions of

Despite the fact that Islam was a significant part of the foundation of the modern West, its cultural influence is often minimized or overlooked. Depictions of Muslims or the Islamic religion in U.S. popular culture run the gamut from exoticizing to demonizing, with a smaller percentage offering realistic and detailed portrayals. Since the September 11, 2001, terrorist attacks, the most frequent depiction is that of terrorist, although that type of portrayal predated the incident. If not terrorists, Muslims are depicted as duplicitous spies. Former president Barack Obama once said, "[O]ur TV shows should have Muslim characters that are unrelated to national security" (Schilling, 2016).

Before the emphasis on Islamic terrorists, the most common popular-culture depiction of Muslims was that of the exotic, such as in films like *The Arabian Nights*

(1942). Characters were mystical and magical, albeit often brutal and hypersexual. *The Sheik* (1921) starred Rudolph Valentino as Ahmed Ben Hassan, who meets and falls in love with a white woman. In *The Son of the Sheik* (1926) he reprises his role, this time raping a white woman and killing most of her town. Even Disney's *Aladdin* (1992) draws on this emphasis of seduction and violence.

The second half of the 20th century saw Muslims depicted as backwards and uncouth, in particular compared to the "civilized" Westerners. For instance, in *Lawrence of Arabia* (1962), considered one of the greatest films of all time, the Arabs are ignorant tribesmen, and the Western-educated main character must educate and refine them. Likewise, Steven Spielberg's *Raiders of the Lost Ark* (1981) shows that even the Nazis are more civilized than the Arabs. Films based on real situations also fueled these stereotypes, as *Not Without My Daughter* (1991), the story of a woman who must escape her abusive Iranian husband, shows him as a monster.

In the 1960s and 1970s, the rise of Black Muslims and the increased political volatility in the Middle East furthered the stereotype of militant Islam. *Back to the Future* (1985) featured aggressive Libyans trying to steal plutonium, for instance. Other depictions show the Muslim population occupying a postapocalyptic wasteland, including films based on reality, such as *Argo* (2012), *Lone Survivor* (2013), and *American Sniper* (2014).

Equally problematic is the depiction of the pious Muslim. Such portrayals may be intended to help counter negative ones but still often serve to trivialize the religion. For example, many films suggest that the biggest oppression in Arab countries is the prohibition on alcohol.

Still another issue is that depictions of Muslims often have them uttering guttural sounds or gibberish, suggesting ignorance. Nor are all their exchanges with other individuals violent or contentious. Likewise, although there are indeed some issues related to the oppression of women in Arab society, Islam itself is quite progressive in terms of gender equality. Cinematic portrayals tend to present it as though women are always subjugated.

Occasionally, Muslims are depicted as noble warriors, as in *The 13th Warrior* (1999), *Three Kings* (1999), and *Kingdom of Heaven* (2005). *Syriana* (2005) and *Babel* (2006) are praised for showing a more complex world and contextualized Muslim violence.

Because depictions of the prophets are prohibited, there have been many controversies related to television, film, novels, comic books, and other forms of popular culture. Although the Qur'an does not forbid such portrayals explicitly, it does forbid graven images. Portraying Muhammad in a vulgar or disrespectful manner is considered blasphemy. For example, a Dutch newspaper, *Jyllands-Posten*, published a series of editorial cartoons depicting the Prophet Muhammed. Four Muslim men were convicted of attacking the newspaper's Copenhagen office in late 2010. When the French magazine *Charlie Hebdo* displayed the Prophet Muhammad on its cover, its office was burned to the ground with Molotov cocktails. In 2001 and again in 2010, the cartoon *South Park* aired episodes featuring the Prophet Muhammad, generating a series of threats.

Laura L. Finley

See also: Arab Media; Global Censorship, Soccer/Football Hooligans; *South Park*; War Films

Further Reading
Burke, D. 2015. "Why Images of Muhammed Offend Muslims." *CNN*, May 4. https://www .cnn.com/2015/05/04/living/islam-prophet-images/index.html

Jhally, S. 2006. *Reel Bad Arabs: How Hollywood Vilifies a People.* Documentary film. Media Education Foundation.

Mozaffer, O. 2016. "Islam in Western Cinema, Part 1: The Exotic Muslim, From the Exotic Land." *RogerEbert.com*, August 8. https://www.rogerebert.com/far-flung-corres pondents/islam-in-western-cinema-part-1

Mozaffer, O. 2016. "Islam in Western Cinema, Part 2: The Violent, Militant Muslim." *RogerEbert.com,* August 15. https://www.rogerebert.com/far-flung-correspondents /islam-in-western-cinema-part-2—the-violent-militant-muslim

Mozaffer, O. 2016. "Islam in Western Cinema, Part 3: The Pious Muslim." *RogerEbert.com*, August 22. https://www.rogerebert.com/far-flung-correspondents/islam-in-western -cinema-part-3—the-pious-muslim

Mozaffer, O. 2016. "Islam in Western Cinema, Part 4: The Journey Through American Islam." *RogerEbert.com*, August 29. https://www.rogerebert.com/far-flung-corres pondents/islam-in-western-cinema-part-4—the-journey-through-american-islam

Our Foreign Staff. 2015. "Prophet Mohammed Cartoons Controversy: Timeline." *The Telegraph,* May 4. http://www.telegraph.co.uk/news/worldnews/europe/france/11341599 /Prophet-Muhammad-cartoons-controversy-timeline.html

Schilling, D. 2016. "Bloodthirsty Terrorists and Duplicitous Spies: Does TV Have a Muslim Problem?" *The Guardian,* May 4. https://www.theguardian.com/tv-and-radio /tvandradioblog/2016/feb/04/muslim-television-characters-us-tv-shows-terrorist -spy-24-homeland-obama

Trifunov, D. 2012. "Prophet Muhammad in Pop Culture Can Lead to Violent Consequences." *PRI,* May 4. https://www.pri.org/stories/2012-09-12/prophet-muhammad -pop-culture-can-lead-violent-consequences

Italian Films

Crime films have long been popular in Italy, as in the United States. In general, Italian crime films feature dark themes, bad cops, and tense showdowns. American directors like Quentin Tarantino say they were widely influenced by Italian crime films, with Tarantino calling Fernando Di Leo's *Milan Caliber 9* (1971) "the greatest Italian noir of all times" (Celluloid Liberation Front, 2014).

The late 1960s saw many Italian heist films, and poliziotteschi, action films influenced by American police and vigilante works, became very popular in the 1970s and remain so today. These films tend to depict brutal and graphic violence and usually feature working-class protagonists who help address the crime and violence that corrupt and bureaucratic systems cannot. These films reflect the time period, as Italy was suffering from political unrest, political terrorism, kidnappings, bombings, and violent crime by organized groups such as the Sicilian mafia. The films reflected the anger the public felt at the violence in the major cities of Italy. Critics have expressed concern that such films negatively depict political activists and endorse "tough on crime" perspectives as well as glorify vigilantism. Others maintain that poliziotteschi generally feature protagonists from both the right and left wings, and that they offer differing views on the causes of, and solutions to, violent crime. Another subgenre of crime film in Italy, giallo, generally focuses on murder mysteries (Celluloid Liberation Front, 2014). Dario Argento's *Deep Red* (1975) tells the story of a music teacher who, after witnessing the death of a psychic woman, teams up with a reporter to investigate. Argento's *Suspiria* (1977) focuses on a ballet student who attends a school full of witches who unleash all manner of terror.

One of the most controversial films ever made is the Italian horror film *Cannibal Holocaust* (1980). It is said to have been one of the first to use "found footage" and graphically depicts violence against people and animals. The movie focuses on a team of American filmmakers who travel into the Amazon basin in search of a previous expedition, who disappeared while investigating cannibal tribes and features a "degrading onslaught of rapes, murders, torture, salacious sex, genocide, castration and even news footage of real-life executions" (Rose, 2011). The director, Ruggero Deodato, was actually arrested on obscenity charges, although he was later cleared. *Cannibal Holocaust* was banned in Italy, Australia, and other countries. Deodato said, "My producer in Italy was showing dailies in the film markets and getting an amazing response, so he was ringing me every day in the jungle telling me: 'Do more! Do more! Keep filming! Kill more people! Don't worry, your message will come though" (Rose, 2011).

Another renowned Italian film is the horror show *Black Sunday* (1960). It focuses on a witch who returns from her gruesome death to seek revenge on the descendants of her killers. A bronze mask with stakes was nailed to her face, and then she was burned at the stake. Mario Bava's film is also said to have influenced directors in the United States. Director Tim Burton once said, "Mario Bava's *Black Sunday* is one of the first films that made me understand the power of cinema in the sense of images as part of the story" (Thompson, n.d.). In another Bava film, *Castle of Blood* (1964), a writer accepts a bet to spend the night in a haunted house, where the ghosts of his past lovers pursue him. Bava's *Twitch of the Death Nerve* (1971) is said to have helped give rise to the modern horror-slasher film. Thirteen people are brutally slashed to death as they fight over a piece of real estate that is to be inherited.

Quentin Tarantino was a huge fan of director Lucio Fulci's film *The Beyond* (1981). Tarantino helped re-release the film, which is about a New Orleans hotel that is really a gateway to hell replete with revolting and brutal zombies.

One of the most widely known Italian directors is Pier Paolo Pasolini. His films often featured pimps and controversial characters and were said to have influenced American filmmaker Martin Scorsese. His life was full of drama as well. In 1949, Pasolini was charged with corruption of minors and engaging in obscene acts in public. He received a suspended prison sentence for blasphemy for his film *La Ricotta* (1963). He was murdered in November 1975. His body was found in a Rome shanty town where he had been beaten and run over by his own Alfa Romeo. Pasolini's last film, *Salò, or the 120 Days of Sodom* (1975), was released after his death. It focuses on Italy's Nazi-Fascist past and, although it is not considered his best, it is among the most violent.

Laura L. Finley

See also: Cop Films; Global Censorship; Japanese Films; Tarantino, Quentin; Zombie Films

Further Reading

Casalena, E. 2017. "15 Controversial Movies That Have Been Banned or Delayed." *Business Insider*, August 4. http://www.businessinsider.com/movies-unreleased-due-to-controversy-2017-7

Celluloid Liberation Front. 2014. "The Best Cop Movies You've Never Heard Of: 'Polizioteschi' Films Get Their Due." *Indiewire*, June 19. http://www.indiewire.com/2014/06/the-best-cop-movies-youve-never-heard-of-poliziotteschi-films-get-their-due-25140/

Rose, S. 2011. "Cannibal Holocaust: 'Keep Filming! Kill More People!'" *The Guardian*, September 15. https://www.theguardian.com/film/2011/sep/15/cannibal-holocaust

Shipka, D. 2011. *Perverse Titillation: The Exploitation Cinema of Italy, Spain and France, 1960–1980.* Jefferson, NC: McFarland & Co.

Thomson, I. 2013. "Pier Paulo Pasolini: No Saint." *The Guardian*, February 22. https://www.theguardian.com/film/2013/feb/22/pier-paolo-pasolini

Thompson, L. n.d. "TCM Imports—The Films of Mario Bava." *TCM.* http://www.tcm.com/this-month/article/430%7C0/Black-Sunday.html

Timpone, T. 2016. "13 Italian Horror Films You Must See." *Syfy*, October 19. http://www.syfy.com/syfywire/13-italian-horror-films-you-must-see

Japanese Films

Japan has produced some of the most controversial movies in film history. Starting in the 1970s, Japanese films were often brutally violent, with some featuring samurai, the organized crime group the Yakuza, and others straight horror. Among the most provocative are the following films.

Kotoko (2011) tells the story of a pregnant woman's rapidly declining mental health. As her condition worsens, she risks losing her baby. She meets a novelist, and their relationship seems as though it will help her, but she stabs him with a fork and beats him while screaming and slashing her own wrists. Like many Japanese films, it juxtaposes moments of intense terror and bloodshed with serenity and beauty. Director Shinya Tsukamoto was already famous for his 1989 film *Tetsuo*, which has been described as "the cinematic equivalent of a jackhammer to the brain: harsh, loud, violent and unrelenting" (Schilling, 2012).

Sion Sono's *Suicide Club* (2001) opens with a tremendous act of violence: 54 high school girls, all in uniform, join hands and hurl themselves into an oncoming train. Their blood splashes everywhere, including on the camera. Police try to figure out why these girls committed suicide and find disturbing evidence that even more are planned.

In the Realm of the Senses (1976) is based on a real story. Prostitute Abe Sada was arrested and her lover's severed penis was found in her mouth. Sada begins working for an innkeeper, Kichi, and the two begin an affair. Sada seems to be in control, and the two engage in increasingly violent sex.

Director Kinji Fukasaku's *Battle Royale* (2000) was banned in several countries, in part due to the timing of its release, which was shortly after the massacre at

Columbine High School in Littleton, Colorado. It is a satire about teens. The plot pits two groups of high school students against one another in a fight to the death. Critics were concerned that actual teens were used in the violent, bloody film. It was not released in the United States or Canada for 11 years, and Japanese authorities attributed an increase in youth crime to the film. Many have noted similarities between *Battle Royale* and *The Hunger Games*. In both, the kids are chosen by a lottery system and then sent to secret locations where they are provided with weapons and other equipment making it easier to kill. After *The Hunger Games* was released, *Battle Royale* saw a boost in sales. *Hunger Games* author Suzanne Collins claims she had never heard of *Battle Royale*. In contrast, in *Battle Royale* all the children are the same age and no one is betting on a winner, as in *Hunger Games*. Although *Hunger Games* was definitely violent, *Battle Royale* featured much more gory and bloody scenes with the youth who perpetrate them seemingly finding great joy in killing.

Emily Casalena of ScreenRant rates the film *Premonition* (2004) as the scariest Japanese horror film. A teacher and his wife stop to use a phone and see a newspaper that shows a headline about their daughter's death moments in the future. She is subsequently killed in a car accident, just as the headline said. The couple end up divorced due to the trauma of coping with their daughter's death, and the wife, Ayaka, finds a series of headlines with premonitions about violent deaths (Casalena, 2016).

Japanese director Akira Kurosawa is considered one of the country's best in history. He was known for adapting European literary classics to contemporary Japan, as he did with *The Idiot* (1951), as well as for his violent masterpieces, including *Rashomon* (1950), *Seven Samurai* (1954), *Throne of Blood* (1957), *Yojimbo* (1961), and *Sanjuro* (1962). *Time* magazine film critic Richard Corliss said Kurosawa "was one of the first to aestheticize violence, to make it sexy, make it hurt" (Corliss, 1998).

Laura L. Finley

See also: Dystopian Young Adult Literature and Film; Global Censorship; Italian Films

Further Reading

Acuna, K. 2012. "Here's Why 'The Hunger Games' Is Not 'Battle Royale.'" *Business Insider*, April 3. http://www.businessinsider.com/the-hunger-games-is-not-battle-royale-despite-many-similarities-2012-4?r=US&IR=T&IR=T

Casalena, E. 2016. "The Sixteen Best Japanese Horror Movies of All Time." *Screen Rant*, September 8. https://screenrant.com/best-japanese-horror-movies/

Corliss, R. 1998. "Long Live the Emperor." *Time*, September 21. http://content.time.com/time/world/article/0,8599,2054200,00.html

Lee, M. 2015. "10 Provocative Japanese Films That Are Worth Your Time." *Taste of Cinema,* June 10. http://www.tasteofcinema.com/2015/10-provocative-japanese-films-that-are-worth-your-time/

Murguia, S., ed. 2016. *The Encyclopedia of Japanese Horror Films.* Lanham, MD: Rowman & Littlefield.

Schilling, M. 2012. "Kotoko." *Japan Times*, April 6. https://www.japantimes.co.jp/culture/2012/04/06/films/film-reviews/kotoko/#.WqfvyudG02w

Walters, B. 2010. "Akira Kurosawa: 10 Essential Films for the Director's Centenary." *The Guardian*, March 23. https://www.theguardian.com/film/filmblog/2010/mar/23/akira-kurosawa-100-google-doodle-anniversary

Jaws

Critics said that the film *Jaws* is not actually about a shark. Despite having a shark in it, in all its marketing, and even though the film scared generations of watchers that they might be bitten in half while swimming, the underlying story is one of morality. It is not hyperviolent, but the type of violence depicted had a dramatic impact on viewers. The technology that made *Jaws* seems antiquated and rudimentary, and the idea that a monster shark could be in anything but a B-movie was unheard of, yet when it was released in 1975 it was a genre-defining blockbuster that changed the face of modern cinema. It redefined the summer film as one that could be a marketable cultural phenomenon at a time when most of the big hits were released over the Christmas holidays.

Jaws began as a 1974 book with the same title. Author Peter Benchley's story is about a seaside resort named Amity that is terrorized by a great white shark. Police chief Martin Brody (Roy Scheider) orders the beaches to be closed, but the mayor and local businessmen insist they stay open. Of course, the result is tragic. Eventually, Brody joins professional shark hunter Quint (Robert Shaw) and ichthyologist Matt Hooper (Richard Dreyfuss) to hunt down the shark and save the town. After potential director Dick Richards reportedly blew his chances by repeatedly referring to the shark as "a whale," the producers turned to Steven Spielberg to direct the film.

One of the most violent scenes is when Hooper dives underwater to dig a tooth out of a sunken boat and Ben Gardner's mutilated head floats up. This and other intense, gory sequences earned *Jaws* the reputation of being the most shocking movie ever to be awarded a family-friendly PG rating in the United States. Some disagreed. In his *Los Angeles Times* review, critic Charles Champlin wrote that "the PG rating is grievously wrong and misleading . . . *Jaws* is too gruesome for children and likely to turn the stomach of the impressionable at any age" (Rosen, 2015). Film critic Roger Ebert gave it four stars. He wrote "*Jaws* is a sensationally effective action picture, a scary thriller that works all the better because it's populated with characters that have been developed into human beings we get to know and care about. It's a film that's as frightening as 'The Exorcist' and yet it's a nicer kind of fright, somehow more fun because we're being scared by an outdoor-adventure saga instead of by a brimstone-and-vomit devil" (Rosen, 2015). Vincent Canby of the *New York Times* wrote, "If you think about *Jaws* for more than 45 seconds you will recognize it as nonsense, but it's the sort of nonsense that can be a good deal of fun, if you like to have the wits scared out of you at irregular intervals" (Rosen, 2015).

According to David Brown, one of the film's producers: "Almost everyone remembers when they first saw *Jaws*. They say, I remember the theatre I was in, I remember what I did when I went home—I wouldn't even draw the bathwater"

(Kermode, 2015). Brown said they deliberately released the film when people would be heading off to the beach, and one of the film's most memorable tag lines was "See it before you go swimming!" In fact, Steven Spielberg has said that he always had a fear of water, not being a great swimmer, and that his fear likely influenced him. Further, the release of *Jaws* took advantage of the rapid growth of mall movie theaters, where young people would often see their favorite films multiple times. They also spent an unprecedented amount on advertising and promotions. Some $2.5 million was devoted to promotion, with a lot of it on television advertisements, which were not previously used much. They also used promotional items, like *Jaws*-themed ice creams, t-shirts, pendants, and the like. It opened in more than 400 theaters, which was a lot at the time. In its first 38 days, *Jaws* sold 25 million tickets, and rentals in 1975 set a new record at $102.5 million. It was also a new type of family film, the first to be scary. Although it had a tremendous influence on the box office, reports were that the film had a negative effect on beach attendance and served to demonize sharks for decades to come.

The production did not go off without a hitch, however. When they began in May 1974, there was still no script, the cast had not been fully selected, and the actual shark was yet to be constructed. Filming began in Martha's Vineyard, and many of the upper-class residents were not happy to have a film crew invading their space. Today, however, the film has helped popularize the area. Once the mechanical shark was constructed, there were additional problems, as every time it was in the saltwater it malfunctioned. One time the shark sank to the bottom of the ocean; in total the crew used three sharks. Storms and crew seasickness also set back the production. By the time the filmmakers had enough usable footage, the production was more than 100 days over schedule and they had spent closer to $9 million, with $3 million on special effects alone. Some say, however, that the limited shots of the shark, due to its repeated malfunctioning, forced Spielberg to use different techniques. In fact, it isn't until 81 minutes into the film that the shark emerges. The limitations with the mechanical shark also inspired a *Psycho*-like score that actually made it much more scary. Composer John Williams used just two notes to create the shark theme music, and reportedly Spielberg inquired as to when he'd hear the actual score after he first heard the now-quintessential riff.

Jaws was nominated for four and won three Academy Awards. It grossed $7 million in its opening weekend and more than $470 million worldwide since its release. That translates to more than 1 billion if adjusted for inflation. It spent 14 weeks as the number-one film in America.

The success of the summer blockbuster *Jaws* was followed two years later with the opening of George Lucas's *Star Wars*, then again years later with his sequels *The Empire Strikes Back* and *Return of the Jedi*. Lucas and Spielberg became some of the most influential people in Hollywood. *Jaws* has lived on in popular culture and even in academics. De Montfort University in Leicester held a *Jaws* 40th Anniversary Symposium, where academics debated issues of masculinity, villainy, environmentalism, and more.

Jaws continues to serve as a significant influence for filmmakers of a variety of genres. Kevin Smith, the filmmaker best known for *Clerks* (1994) and *Chasing Amy*

(1997), saw it as a child and said rather than the shark, which did indeed scare him, it was the "bromance" between Brody, Matt Hooper, and Captain Quinn that really influenced how he crafts relationships in his films. Further, *Jaws* inspired a number of copycat films, including *Piranha, Orca, The Deep*, and *Tentacles. Jaws II* and *Jaws 3-D* were lesser hits.

Laura L. Finley

See also: Alien Franchise; Slasher Films

Further Reading

Ebert, R. 1975. "Jaws." January 1. http://www.rogerebert.com/reviews/jaws-1975

Kermode, M. 2015. "Jaws, 40 Years On: 'One of the Truly Great and Lasting Classics of American Cinema." *The Guardian,* May 31. https://www.theguardian.com/film/2015/may/31/jaws-40-years-on-truly-great-lasting-classics-of-america-cinema

Labrecque, J. 2014. "Jaws: The Best Summer Blockbuster of All Time." *Entertainment Weekly,* April 29. http://ew.com/article/2014/04/29/jaws-best-summer-blockbuster/

Rosen, C. 2015. "Jaws 40th Anniversary: What Critics Thought in 1975." *Entertainment Weekly,* June 20. http://ew.com/article/2015/06/20/jaws-40th-anniversary/

Kubrick, Stanley

Stanley Kubrick (1928–1999) was an American film director, producer, screenwriter, cinematographer, photographer, and editor. He is considered to be among the most influential directors in film history. Known for their unique cinematography, creative use of sound, realism, and dark humor, some of Kubrick's most widely known films include *Lolita* (1962), *Dr. Strangelove* (1964), *2001: A Space Odyssey* (1968), *A Clockwork Orange* (1971), *The Shining* (1980), and *Full Metal Jacket* (1987). Kubrick's first major film was *The Killing* (1956), which follows a band of thieves who end up betraying one another, followed by the World War I antiwar film *Paths of Glory* (1957) and *Spartacus* (1960). *Spartacus* received six Academy Award nominations and won in four categories. Kubrick never won an Academy Award for best director, however.

Lolita is Kubrick's interpretation of Vladimir Nabokov's book by the same name. Kubrick, at the time a little-known director, and producing partner James Harris, bought the film rights for $150,000 in 1958, before the book had even found an American publisher. As had most publishers, studios turned down the film due to the controversial nature of the story, which is focused on a middle-aged college professor who is infatuated with a 12-year-old girl. In order to get the film produced, Kubrick had to edit some of the more controversial components of the story, which to many depicted sexual assault.

Dr. Strangelove or How I Learned to Stop Worrying and Love the Bomb is a satire of the Cold War fears of nuclear conflict between the United States and the USSR. Kubrick himself even considered moving to Australia out of fear of nuclear attack, and it is said that he studied more than 40 military and political books before writing the script, which is loosely based on Peter George's novel *Red Alert*. The story follows a bizarre U.S. Air Force general who orders a nuclear strike on Russia, and the efforts of the president of the United States and his advisors as they try to recall the bombers. As such, it addresses violence perpetrated by the state. Kubrick's *Full Metal Jacket* also focused on the violence of war, in this case, the conflict in Vietnam. It focused on the costs of war by detailing the torturous basic training endured by recruits and the impact service has on those who engage in violent conflict. His 1957 film *Paths of Glory* was a critique of war as well, as it showcased a group of French soldiers who refuse to continue on a suicidal attack and their commanding officer, played by Kirk Douglas, who defends them.

2001: A Space Odyssey is a futuristic tale. The movie was the third-highest grossing of 1968, after *The Graduate* and *Funny Girl,* and is often featured on lists of the best films ever. Kubrick won the Best Visual Effects Oscar for the film in 1969.

A Clockwork Orange is one of Kubrick's most controversial films. Kubrick wanted it to address why people are attracted to brutal violence. The film features Alex (Malcolm McDowell), a sadistic delinquent who leads a group of teens on nightly acts of ultraviolence. Kubrick repeatedly said that Alex represented the Freudian concept of the id, or unchecked and often dangerous impulses. He is eventually arrested, and an equally violent form of aversion therapy is used to treat him. In 1973, amidst protests about the film and death threats to himself and his family, Kubrick asked Warner Brothers to withdraw distribution in the UK. In 2000, it was finally released for British audiences. The film has been linked to several copycat incidents in London, where assailants wearing similar costumes and makeup have raped and tortured their victims. It is one of only two X-rated films to be nominated for the Best Picture Academy Award. Kubrick ended up trimming 30 seconds from the film so that it could receive an R-rating. In all, *A Clockwork Orange* received four nominations.

The Shining is known as Kubrick's horror film. It is based on the novel by Stephen King, who has said he did not like Kubrick's adaptation featuring Jack Nicholson as Jack Torrance, a writer who takes the job as a caretaker at a hotel. He learns that the previous caretaker had lost his mind, and Jack himself slowly becomes possessed by the evil that remains at the hotel. King took issue with the coldness of Kubrick's film and the depiction of Wendy Torrance (Shelley Duvall) as a stupid prop who screams frequently. Further, King critiqued Nicholson's depiction of Jack as too crazy early in the film, as his goal with the character was to get readers to relate to the character, to see that it could be them. King also saw the book as a statement about domestic violence, but Kubrick's film merely depicts it occurring.

Kubrick died in 1999, just days after finishing his film *Eyes Wide Shut.*

Laura L. Finley

See also: Hitchcock, Alfred; Lee, Spike; *Natural Born Killers*; Russian Popular Culture; Tarantino, Quentin

Further Reading

Bradshaw, P. 2000. "The Old Ultra-Violence." *The Guardian,* March 3. https://www .theguardian.com/film/2000/mar/03/fiction

Libby, B. 2002. "Masterpiece: '2001: A Space Odyssey.'" *Salon,* March 5. http://www.salon.com/2002/03/05/2001_3/

Miller, L. 2013. "What Stanley Kubrick Got Wrong about 'The Shining.'" *Salon,* October 1. http://www.salon.com/2013/10/01/what_stanley_kubrick_got_wrong_about_the_shining/

Moviefone Staff. 2012. "'Lolita': How Stanley Kubrick Turned Vladimir Nabokov's Novel into a Mainstream Hit." *Moviefone,* June 11. https://www.moviefone.com/2012/06/11/lolita-stanley-kubrick-vladimir-nabokov/

Robey, T. 2016. "A Clockwork Orange: The Look That Shook the Nation." *The Telegraph,* February 3. http://www.telegraph.co.uk/film/what-to-watch/a-clockwork-orange-stanley-kubrick-controversy/

Lee, Spike

Spike Lee is a Black American actor, writer, director, and producer. He has made 35 films since 1983. Lee is credited with helping to redefine what a "race movie" could be and expanding the types of stories and roles for Black people.

In *She's Gotta Have It* (1983), Tracy Camilla Johns plays a promiscuous young commercial artist juggling three boyfriends: a professional, a model, and a bike messenger. It is a comedy-drama in which the main character, Nola, concludes that monogamy is a form of slavery. The film was Lee's first and was both applauded and critiqued for its frank examination of female sexuality and its reversing of traditional gender stereotypes.

In *School Daze* (1988), Lee addressed racial discrimination, although its focus is on bias within Black culture. It is considered a musical-comedy-drama and focuses on fraternity and sorority members at a historically Black college during homecoming weekend. Characters who are lighter skinned clash with those who are darker skinned or who keep their hair more natural. The women taunt each other with racial epithets, including "pickaninny," "Barbie doll," "tar baby" and "high-yellow heifer" (Freedman, 1991).

In 1989, Lee made *Do the Right Thing,* which he considers his masterpiece. He also stars in the comedy-drama, which is set in a Brooklyn neighborhood amidst rising racial tensions. Things come to a head on a hot summer day, when a fight results in police presence and an officer ends up killing one of the Black men who had been fighting and a riot ensues. Lee was nominated for an Academy Award for Best Original Screenplay, and Danny Aiello was nominated for Best Supporting Actor. Before *Do the Right Thing,* Lee was often considered a "Black Woody Allen," but through this film "Lee positioned himself as one of Hollywood's most outspoken and polarizing opinionators on the issue of race relations, with subsequent interviews and public feuds (with Clint Eastwood, Tyler Perry, Charlton Heston, and others) cultivating a popular image of him having no love lost for white folks. It's an image that persists today" (Bailey, 2012).

In another film to take on race relations, *Jungle Fever* (1991), Lee took up the issue of interracial relationships. It opens with a photograph of Yusuf K. Hawkins, the black teenager killed by a white mob in the Bensonhurst section of Brooklyn in 1989. Hawkins was shot because he was thought to be the companion of a local girl who the community disavowed because she dated blacks and Hispanics. Wesley Snipes plays Flipper Purify, who begins a relationship with a white woman, Angie Tucci (Annabella Sciorra). Neither Flipper's Harlem nor Angie's Bensonhurst appreciate the interracial relationship—and neither do their families. The film also addresses drug abuse, as Gator Purify, played by Samuel L. Jackson, is a crack addict who steals to finance his habit.

In 1992, Lee made *Malcolm X*, based on the book *The Autobiography of Malcolm X*. Denzel Washington played the role of Malcolm X, the controversial and influential Black Nationalist leader. It was released just a few months after the trial of the four white officers who beat Rodney King in Los Angeles but were acquitted on all charges. Roger Ebert called it "one of the great biographies" (Ebert, 1992). It showcases the early life of Malcolm Little, whose father was murdered, likely by the KKK; his mistreatment by white educators as a bright student; and his conviction for burglary and time in prison, which is when he adopted the Nation of Islam and changed his name to Malcolm X. It ends with the tragic assassination of Malcolm X in 1965. Ebert applauded the film, saying, "Walking into 'Malcolm X,' I expected an angrier film than Spike Lee has made. This film is not an assault but an explanation, and it is not exclusionary; it deliberately addresses all races in its audience. White people, going into the film, may expect to meet a Malcolm X who will attack them, but they will find a Malcolm X whose experiences and motives make him understandable and finally heroic" (Ebert, 1992).

Clockers (1995) focuses on crime among Black Americans. White cops show up to hassle the Black drug dealers, called "clockers." One character, Strike (Mekhi Phifer), is asked by his "boss," Rodney (Delroy Lindo), to commit murder, and feeling as though he has no other option, Strike tries to persuade his brother Victor (Isiah Washington) to do the killing. Victor confesses to the crime, which isn't actually depicted, and the white cop Rocco Klein (Harvey Keitel) doesn't believe he did it. Similarly, *Chi-Raq* (2015) examines crime in the inner city, this time in Chicago, which is so overrun with drugs and violence that the women, taking a hint from the Greek tragedy *Lysistrata*, begin a sex strike. Critics had mixed reviews, and Lee became engaged in a verbal war with Chance the Rapper, who criticized him for negatively depicting Chicago.

Lee has made some films that do not specifically address race. For instance, *Summer of Sam* (1999) is about the serial killer who called himself the Son of Sam, David Berkowitz, and focuses on a group of Italian Americans who are panicked about the killings.

Laura L. Finley

See also: Ancient Greek Literature and Culture; Blaxploitation Films; Gang Films; Hitchcock, Alfred; Kubrick, Stanley; Tarantino, Quentin

Further Reading
Bailey, J. 2012. "When Spike Lee Became Scary." *The Atlantic*, August 22. https://www.theatlantic.com/entertainment/archive/2012/08/when-spike-lee-became-scary/261434/

Child, B. 2015. "Spike Lee Rebuffs Chicago-Based Rapper's Criticism of Chi-Raq." *The Guardian*, December 11. https://www.theguardian.com/film/2015/dec/11/spike-lee -chi-raq-chance-rapper-chicago

Ebert, R. 1992. "Malcolm X." *RogerEbert*, November 18. https://www.rogerebert.com /reviews/malcolm-x-1992

Freedman, S. 1991. "Film; Love and Hate in Black and White." *The New York Times*, June 2. https://www.nytimes.com/1991/06/02/movies/film-love-and-hate-in-black-and -white.html

Mad Max Films

The original *Mad Max* film (1979) was made in Australia and was directed by George Miller. It is a futuristic tale featuring Mel Gibson as Max Rockatansky in what some say is an Australian version of *Dirty Harry*. The films show a decayed society in which police battle with nomad bikers. Max is a dedicated officer, but after a road chase ends in the death of a crazed biker known as the Knightrider (Vince Gill) Max becomes the target of his friends' wrath. Led by psychotic Toecutter (Hugh Keays-Byrne) they seek revenge. Max and his partner Jim Goose (Steve Broley) arrest one of the gang, Johnny the Boy, who raped a young couple. Johnny is released on a technicality, and he and the guys hunt down Goose and burn him alive in his car. In horror, Max quits the police and takes his wife Jessie (Joanne Samuel) and child on vacation. The gang catches up to them and kills Max's son. Jessie is tortured and left essentially brain dead. Max goes mad and vows to hunt down and kill each of the bikers. What follows has been considered "an orgy of nonstop violence" (Bouzereau, 2000, p. 176).

The film was initially banned in New Zealand due to its violence and the fear that people might emulate the antisocial behavior. France gave it an X-rating, which meant it had a 33 percent surtax. The distributor delayed its release for two years. Critics contend, however, that the actual violence isn't depicted; rather, it is only the beginning and the aftermath of it that is shown. Even when the baby is killed, the film only shows his shoes flying and falling to the ground.

The sequel, released as *Mad Max Two: The Road Warrior* in the United States in 1981, shows a further decayed society. Gangs fight for control of fuel, the most precious commodity. Max has joined a commune which is under constant threat by marauding gangs, in particular, one led by a man name Humungus. Max ends up destroying the enemy in a hyperviolent clash. It is more graphic than the first film, with scenes including a boomerang cutting through a biker's skull and then slicing the fingers of a man who tried to catch it. There are numerous scenes involving rape, torture, and killing. *Mad Max: Beyond Thunderdome* (1985) was co-directed by Miller and George Ogilvie. The story was a bit lighter, as the directors were seeking a broader audience. Gibson's Max partners with Auntie Entity (Tina Turner). Max comes across the city of Bartertown and is forced to endure a battle to death in the thunderdome. He survives but is exiled to the desert, then saved by a group of wild children who help him seek revenge on Auntie Entity.

When asked about the violence in his films, director George Miller once said, "People say 'You must be very interested in violence.' And in a way I am, but in relationship to death, in confronting death. I worked as a doctor for two years; six months were in big-city emergency wards, where you see people die in a fairly extreme state. People die; babies are born. I know this is reflected in the two Mad Max films, which are fairly preoccupied with extreme situations. In that sense I see them as a lot of elements of horror films" (Bouzereau, 2000, p. 178).

In *Mad Max: Fury Road* (2015), Max (Tom Hardy) joins Imperator Furiosa (Charlize Theron) in a revolt of female concubines to wage high-speed war. Death and disfigurement are the result. It has been called one of the most grotesque and, at the same time, most perfect dystopias ever presented on screen. There were many calls for the film to be banned, which has been applauded and critiqued for its heavy female cast and its beautiful cinematography coupled with its brutal violence. It shows young boys willing to kill themselves to get to paradise, shootings and dismemberings, and alludes to rapes. Mark Olsen wrote in the *Los Angeles Times*, "*Fury Road* is both a caricatured screed and nuanced depiction of chaos, camaraderie, violence, hatred, resolve and an ability to overcome fear through resilience and understanding" (Olsen, 2015). It was nominated for 10 Academy Awards and won 6, the most of any film nominated in 2016.

Laura L. Finley

See also: Bollywood; *Brave New World*; Dystopian Young Adult Literature and Film; *Fahrenheit 451*; *1984*; *Rambo* Films; Superhero Films; Vonnegut, Kurt; Zombie Films

Further Reading

Bevis, K. 2016. "The Presence of the Womb in Mad Max: Fury Road." *Huffington Post*, November 24. http://www.huffingtonpost.co.za/kerri-ann-bevis/the-presence-of-the -womb-in-mad-max-fury-road/

Bouzereau, L. 2000. *Ultra Violent Movies* (2nd ed.). New York: Kensington.

Mason, P. 2015. "The Ultra-Violent World of Mad Max No Longer Shocks Us—It's Too Close to Reality." *The Guardian,* May 17. https://www.theguardian.com /commentisfree/2015/may/17/the-ultra-violent-world-of-mad-max-no-longer -shocks-us-its-too-close-to-reality

Olsen, M. 2015. "Why" 'Mad Max: Fury Road' is the Film of the Year. *Los Angeles Times*, December 11. http://www.latimes.com/entertainment/movies/la-ca-mn-1213-year -end-mark-olsen-20151213-story.html

Mafia Films

The 1930s saw a rise in films depicting the mafia and gangsters, which is not surprising given the mob activity during the Prohibition era. The increase in mafia films prompted calls on the Hays Office (the organization that maintained a moral code for films) to more strictly censor film violence, as many asserted that such films gave ideas to would-be criminals and glorified the mobster lifestyle. It was amidst this outcry that producer Howard Hughes and director Howard Hawks made *Scarface* (1932), their gangster epic based loosely on the life of famous

Mafioso Al Capone. Hughes was asked to remove many scenes and to ensure that an antigun message appeared in the film. The Hays Office even asked for a different ending, focusing on the main character, Tony Camante, played by Paul Muni, facing trial. The film even ran with a disclaimer at the end, "This picture is an indictment of gang rule in America and of the callous indifference of the government to this constantly increasing menace to our safety and our liberty. Every incident in this picture is the reproduction of an actual occurrence, and the purpose of this picture is to demand of the government: 'What are you going to do about it?' The government is your government. What are *you* going to do about it?" (Bouzereau, 2000, p. 100). Despite the controversies, *Scarface* was considered the best film portrayal of the mob to that date, perhaps due to its realistic depiction of crime and violence and high body count.

Brian De Palma re-created *Scarface* in 1983, albeit with a somewhat different storyline, and the new product, written by Oliver Stone, also faced much controversy. Al Pacino plays Tony Montana, who is a Cuban refugee released by Fidel Castro in May 1980, along with 125,000 other prisoners. Montana learns that drug dealing would likely be the easiest way for him to make it, and he and his best friend Manny (Steven Bauer) become allies with Frank Lopez (Robert Loggia). Lopez is a cocaine kingpin. The troubles begin when Lopez learns that Montana wants to take over not only his cocaine empire but also his girlfriend Elvira (Michelle Pfeiffer). Lopez tries to kill him, but Montana shoots Lopez. Montana is asked by another drug dealer, Alejandro Sosa (Paul Shenar), to kill a delegate at the United Nations who is attempting to expose his drug trade. Montana refuses when he realizes he would also need to kill the man's wife and children, and things spiral downhill. Montana is eventually killed by Sosa's guards. Miami's Cuban community protested the film, asserting it depicted them in an unflattering light. The crew ended up shooting the film in Los Angeles so as to avoid disturbances. De Palma reportedly received death threats from real-life mobsters when the film was released. De Palma and producer Martin Bregman were also frustrated that the Motion Picture Association of America (MPAA) gave the film an R-rating due to violence and profanity, although it almost received an X-rating. They had to endure many challenges before it was determined that the R-rating was appropriate. Bregman was particularly frustrated with the concerns about profanity, saying, "You go to any playground in New York City and listen to the nine-year-olds. You'll hear some words. A kid going to this movie isn't going to go out and contact his local cocaine dealer. We painted the world as bad as it is" (Bouzereau, 2000, p. 103). Critics noted that, although the film was violent, "De Palma doesn't linger on gore. Any recent horror movie is more graphically grisly" (Bouzereau, 2000, 105).

The popular *Godfather* series features the story of the mafia family the Corleones. The first film, *The Godfather*, was released in 1972. Don Vito Corleone (Marlon Brando) is head of the family. He is shot when he refuses to join a rival family, the Tattaglias, in the narcotics trade. Although he survives, his son Michael (Al Pacino) vows to avenge his father's shooting and kills the two men responsible for it. He is sent to Italy and gets married but is betrayed, and his wife is killed by a car bomb that was intended for him. After a rival family kills his brother Sonny

(James Caan) a peace agreement is negotiated between the five mafia families. But when Vito dies, Michael attacks the heads of the others and uses the violence to consolidate his empire. Film writer Laurent Bouzereau (2000) argues that "the most violent moment in *The Godfather* is, without a doubt, Sonny's assassination. He dies a la Bonnie and Clyde when he is ambushed at a highway tollbooth and is riddled with machine-gun bullets. The scene was shot in one take. About 110 brass casings containing gunpowder squibs, and packets of blood were rigged on actor James Caan's body, face, and hair. His car had about two hundred predrilled holes filled with squibs that detonated during the attack" (107–08). Other scenes show a character's eyes popping out after he is garroted and Michael Corleone shooting a police officer between the eyes, through his glasses. Another shocking scene shows Hollywood producer Woltz (John Marley) waking up to discover the head of his beloved horse beside him. They had originally intended to use a fake head, but instead obtained a real head from a slaughterhouse in New Jersey because they thought the fake looked way too fake. It was this scene that outraged people more than any other, despite the fact that 23 characters died, almost all violently, in the film.

Critics loved *The Godfather*. Vincent Canby of *The New York Times* wrote that *The Godfather* was "one of the most brutal and moving chronicles of American life ever designed within the limits of popular entertainment" (Bouzereau, 2000, p. 109). It received 10 Oscar nominations and won 3: Best Picture, Best Actor for Marlon Brando, and Best Screenplay for the adaptation by Mario Puzo and Francis Ford Coppola. Despite its box office success and acclaim, Coppola initially had no intention of directing a sequel. He suggested to Paramount Pictures that Martin Scorsese replace him. But when the studio offered him $1 million, big money at the time, Coppola agreed to make *The Godfather II* (1974).

The Godfather II carried on the story of Michael Corleone while it also reflected back on the life of Don Vito Corleone, played as a younger man by Robert De Niro. This film won six Oscars: Best Picture; Best Director; Best Supporting Actor for Robert De Niro; Best Screenplay for Puzo and Coppola; Best Score for Nino Rota and Carmine Coppola; and Best Art and Set Decoration for Dean Tavoularis, Angelo Graham, and George R. Nelson. *The Godfather II* included 16 violent deaths. Sixteen years later, *The Godfather III* (1990) focused on an aging Michael Corleone who is trying to leave the mafia life but keeps getting sucked back in. Twenty-one people died violently in *The Godfather III*, which did not receive as much critical acclaim but was still a box office success.

Martin Scorsese's *Goodfellas* (1990), adapted from the book *Wiseguy*, is another acclaimed mafia film. It tells the true story of Henry Hill, who narrated it to Nicholas Pileggi for the book while he was in the federal Witness Protection Program. Henry (Ray Liotta) is taken under the wings of mobster Cicero (Paul Sorvino) when he is just a young man in mid-1950s Brooklyn. He meets other mafia heroes, including James Conway (Robert De Niro) and the psychopath Tommy DeVito (Joe Pesci). It follows the crew for 30 years, showing how Hill was first enamored with his involvement and then the romance ended. In 1980, Hill agreed to testify against the mob and entered the Witness Protection Program. It is more brutally violent than the *Godfather* trilogy, starting with De Niro and Pesci "whacking," or murdering, someone in the trunk of a car. Pesci stabs him with a kitchen knife and De Niro shoots him. The scene is shown twice in the film, the second time in slow motion. In another scene Pesci shoots a kid in cold blood, and there are many beatings and deaths. The film greatly upset many in the Italian American community, who felt it was ruthless and depicted them inaccurately. It was nominated for six Academy Awards, and Pesci won the Oscar for Best Supporting Actor. Roger Ebert gave it five stars, and *Rolling Stone* critic Peter Travers called it "a prodigious achievement" (Travers, 1990).

Casino (1995) was another collaboration between Martin Scorsese and Nicholas Pileggi. It is based loosely on the life of Frank "Lefty" Rosenthal, a casino manager, and the rise of gambler Sam "Ace" Rothstein (Robert De Niro) in glitzy 1970s Las Vegas. De Niro is romantically involved with Ginger McKenna (Sharon Stone) and friends and partners with Nicky Santoro (Joe Pesci). It is basically considered to be *Goodfellas* in Vegas. The violence includes a man's head being crushed in a vice, Joe Pesci stabbing someone with a pen, a man's hand being smashed with a hammer, and another when Pesci is beat up and left half-dead in a grave. Stone was nominated for the Best Actress Academy Award in 1996.

Other popular mafia films include *On the Waterfront* (1954), *Mean Streets* (1973), *Once Upon a Time in America* (1984), *The Untouchables* (1987), *A Bronx Tale* (1993), *Pulp Fiction* (1994), *Donnie Brasco* (1997), *Gangs of New York* (2002), *The Departed* (2006), and *American Gangster* (2007).

Laura L. Finley

See also: Cop Films; Gang Films; *Sopranos, The*

Further Reading

Bouzereau, L. 2000. *Ultra Violent Movies.* New York: Kensington Publishing.

Renga, D. 2011. *Mafia Movies: A Reader.* Toronto: University of Toronto Press.

Travers, P. 1990. "Goodfellas." *Rolling Stone*, September 19. http://www.rollingstone.com /movies/reviews/goodfellas-19900919

Natural Born Killers

Natural Born Killers is a 1994 film directed by Oliver Stone and produced by Jane Hansher, Don Murphy, and Clayton Townsend. The story was written by filmmaker Quentin Tarantino. Its release generated a great deal of controversy due to the film's graphic and excessive violence. In 2006, *Entertainment Weekly* declared it the eighth most controversial film of all time. It was banned upon release in Ireland, and its release was delayed in Britain due to the controversial depictions.

The film stars Woody Harrelson as Mickey Knox and Juliette Lewis as Mallory Wilson Knox. The two, both from traumatized and abusive backgrounds, become lovers who go on a killing spree not dissimilar to that of Bonnie and Clyde. Their violence is glorified by media, making them stars. Robert Downey Jr. plays Wayne Gale, the sleazy host of a reality show called *American Maniacs* who will do anything to get the next juicy interview. Tom Sizemore is sex-obsessed detective

Jack Scagnetti, who attempts to arrest Mickey and Mallory. Tommy Lee Jones is warden Dwight McClusky. It was received well in the box office, grossing more than $50 million.

Whereas some applauded *Natural Born Killers* for examining the role of sensationalistic news journalism and 24/7 news coverage in normalizing violence, others critiqued it for becoming that which it was attempting to problematize. Additionally, critics expressed concern about the excessive uses of product placement. Further, critics have noted that the film was implicated in more than 30 real murders. Even Quentin Tarantino, whose films often feature various forms of violence, distanced himself from *Natural Born Killers*. Tarantino had hoped to make *NBK*, as it was generally known, himself, but funding was scarce so he sold the script to Hamsher and Murphy. Tarantino reportedly even tried to buy back the screenplay and block the film from production.

Director Oliver Stone was influenced by the media coverage of the Menendez brothers murder case in 1989, the 1991 Rodney King incident, and other high-profile acts of violence and trials that received excessive media coverage. He believed that the media had become too pervasive and that it marketed violence and suffering in order to increase ratings. Stone therefore undertook a reworking of the film's focus, which further angered Tarantino.

Stone wanted another actor, Michael Madsen, to play the role of Mickey Knox, but Warner Brothers insisted on someone less intimidating. Oddly it was revealed that the amiable Woody Harrelson's father had been a professional hitman and was serving two life sentences for the murder of a federal judge. He died in prison in 2007. Singer Tori Amos, known for her music as well as for sharing her background of sexual abuse and violence, initially agreed to play the role of Mallory but declined once Stone shared his idea that every time Mallory killed someone it would be set to Amos's song "Me and a Gun," an account of her real-life rape. She reportedly slapped Stone in public and then wrote about it in another song. Other high-profile actors who Stone had in mind were turned off by the script. Tim Roth and Steve Buscemi both declined roles after Tarantino threatened to never cast them again. Other actors who agreed to be in the film stipulated certain conditions, including Rodney Dangerfield, who played Mallory's sexually abusive father, only on the condition that he could rewrite all of his lines.

In the first five weeks of filming, the filmmakers used actual prisoners from the Stateville Correctional Center outside of Chicago as extras in the prison scenes. Raymond Sojak, convicted of beating his wife and children to death with a lead pipe, was one of the men cast in the film. Critics noted that director Stone lost control, with many of the inmates carrying on their simulated violence after the filming. Riot officers in full body armor were called in to quell what appeared to be a potential uprising during filming in 1993, and the entire prison was placed on lockdown. Two guards and several prisoners ended up hospitalized, and at least one member of the film crew was injured. Some 200 paid extras were bussed in to finish the filming.

It wasn't just the prisoners who got out of control. During the prison escape scene Juliette Lewis broke Tom Sizemore's nose after slamming him into a wall. In another scene Mickey and Mallory were tromping through a field full of rattlesnakes, all of which were real. Producer Jane Hamsher referred to Stone as a "maniac" and noted that on a location scouting trip prior to shooting the entire crew took psychedelic mushrooms and were nearly arrested. Harrelson and Lewis fought off screen, and he once threw her onto the hood of a car while twisting her arm into a half-nelson. Sizemore got into a verbal disagreement that ended in a fistfight with the captain of the plane transporting the cast and crew and was at one point charged with air piracy, although the charges were later dropped.

Natural Born Killers relies heavily on symbols to share its message that violence is pervasive and exacerbated by media. In one scene, Mickey and Mallory end up on a Native American reservation after their car runs out of gas. They stand in the glow of the fire, unable to communicate with the chief who does not speak English, when words, supposedly translations, flash on their chests, "Demon" and "watched too much TV" among them. Stone has commented that not only did he want the film to be a critique of media violence but also of the criminal justice system and the propensity to label people as criminals via a system that is violent itself. Yet some say his approach is overly moralistic and, because it offers no feasible solutions to the violence, it therefore reinforces the same authoritarian power structures. For instance, Stone's depiction of the abusive behavior against Mallory by her father echoes that of many conservative groups that blamed the dissolution of the family for crime and violence. In order to get its R-rating, some 150 scenes reportedly had to be cut.

Perhaps most importantly, critics point to a host of murders they believe were copycats of the film. On the morning of March 6, 1995, teen lovers Ben Darras and Sarah Edmondson left Oklahoma and headed east to Mississippi, where they shot and killed a local businessman, Bill Savage. Moving on to Louisiana, they shot convenience-store cashier Patsy Byers, paralyzing her from the neck down. Darras and Edmondson said that they had prepared for the trip by dropping acid and screening *Natural Born Killers* on a continuous loop throughout the night. A teen in Texas decapitated a classmate, claiming he wanted to be famous like "the natural born killers." Two youth from Paris who were big fans of *NBK* killed three police officers and then a taxi driver. Byers filed a lawsuit in July 1995 against Stone and Time Warner, alleging that, as in other product liability cases, they had distributed a film that they knew or should have known would cause and inspire violence. Author John Grisham supported the suit, noting a direct and causal link between the movie and the attack on Byers and others. A judge dismissed the suit in March 2001, a decision that was upheld by the Louisiana Court of Appeal some years later. Stone denounced the suit, claiming it was unfair to scapegoat a film or filmmaker for violence. A similar controversy surrounded Stanley Kubrick's *A Clockwork Orange* in the early 1970s, although Kubrick responded very differently; he had the film taken out of circulation. Later, there were allegations that several school shooters, including Michael Carneal's killing of three students at his West Paducah, Kentucky school on December 1, 1997, and the Columbine massacre of April 20, 1999, in which Eric Harris and Dylan Klebold, huge fans of *NBK*, killed 12 students and one teacher before committing suicide. Kimveer Gill, who killed 1 and injured 19 at the entrance to Dawson College in Montreal, also listed the film as a favorite. In 2006, 23-year-old Jeremy Allan Steinke and his 12-year-old girlfriend murdered her parents and 8-year-old brother. Steinke had allegedly watched the film the night before the incident and had bragged to friends that he planned to go "Natural Born Killer" on his girlfriend's family, since they did not approve of the relationship. Steinke was found guilty on three charges of first-degree murder and sentenced to life in prison without parole. Richardson was also found guilty on three counts of first-degree murder and was sentenced to 10 years in prison.

Even those who were critical of the film did admire its technical aspects. The special effects, colors, angles, filters, and music were carefully selected to evoke a particular tone.

Laura L. Finley

See also: *Bonnie and Clyde*; *Fight Club*; Global Censorship; Kubrick, Stanley; Rape Films; Western Films

Further Reading

Bell, C. 2015. "Mayhem, Murder and Movies: The Saga of Natural Born Killers." *The Telegraph*, September 8. http://www.telegraph.co.uk/film/natural-born-killers/making-of-murders-controversy/

Brooks, X. 2002. "Natural Born Copycats." *The Guardian,* December 20. https://www.theguardian.com/culture/2002/dec/20/artsfeatures1

Jenkins, P. 1994. *Using Murder: The Social Construction of Serial Homicide.* New York: Aldine de Gruyter.

Niessel, J. 1994. "Natural Born Killers: A Review." *Journal of Criminal Justice and Popular Culture,* 2(5), 113–17.

Parker, S. 2014. "In Praise of . . . Natural Born Killers." *Esquire,* October 15. http://www.esquire.co.uk/culture/film/news/a7192/natural-born-killers/

Travers, P. 1994. "Natural Born Killers." *Rolling Stone,* August 26. http://www.rollingstone.com/movies/reviews/natural-born-killers-19940826

Nollywood

Nollywood is Nigeria's Hollywood. Although lesser known in the United States, it is comparable to India's Bollywood in terms of volume and financial success, a remarkable feat given that it is a relatively new industry in that country. In 2009, Nigeria's film productivity surpassed that of the United States, and is second to India. More than 1,000 films are produced in Nigeria annually, although many are shot cheaply and then burned onto DVDs. Nigerian filmmakers have been influenced by American artists but also reflect their own culture. Many feature bawdy humor, which appeals to a public seeking escape from the depressing poverty that is their daily life. Moviemaking is now one of Nigeria's largest industries, and Nollywood stars are revered in the country and beyond. This is despite the fact that Nigeria often lacks even a reliable supply of electricity, so the barriers to filming are many.

Plots in Nollywood films tend to be similar, and storylines structured in relatively the same way. Movies tell the stories of moral dilemmas, like jealousy and betrayal, often with odd and unrealistic plot twists. "Black magic" is a common theme. In *Leyin Igbeyawo* (2014), a woman's new boyfriend becomes ill and it is revealed that she was responsible, as she had used black magic on him. She did so because she pined for her previous love and felt he should suffer since he pursued her when she was still with the other man. In *Iwa* (2014), a man uses black magic on a pastor, killing him, because he was jealous of the pastor's relationship with a woman. Women are generally portrayed as caretakers, as weak and submissive, and as using their femininity and black magic to manipulate men. Although verbal violence is the most common type found in Nollywood films, other forms of violence occur frequently as well.

Domestic violence is a common theme in Nollywood films. *A Private Storm* (2010) tells the story of a seemingly happy couple, Alex and Gina. In reality, Alex is verbally and physically abusive, and ultimately Gina leaves him. *Sinking Sands* (2010) shows a man who becomes abusive after he is left scarred due to an accident. *Damage* (2011) shows the effect of domestic violence on children, as the married couple's son begins acting violently as well.

Critics contend that the films are bad, with silly plots and poor acting and filming. Further, they contend that Nollywood movies reinforce dangerous stereotypes about African beliefs and spells. Mr. Kayode Aiyegbusi, head of the Performing Arts Department of Cyprian Ekwensi Centre for Arts and Culture, said, "The impression is that all our movies are targeted at witches, nudity, bad mothers-in-law, 419, rituals, money rituals and all sorts of negative things" and urged Nollywood filmmakers to make movies that showcase the country in a positive light (Giwa, 2010). One of the concerns about the quality of Nollywood productions is that they are made on low budgets and produced very quickly. On average, it costs $15,000 to make a film in Nollywood and takes only 20 days (Giwa, 2010). A group called the Witchcraft and Human Rights Information Network (WHRIN), which lobbies for human rights of persons who believe in witchcraft and spirit possession, sent a report to the United Nations High Commission for Human Rights in 2013, arguing that Nollywood films promote stereotypes of people with albinism and are partly responsible for the murders of many albinos, who are often killed for their body parts in Tanzania, Burundi, the Democratic Republic of the Congo, and Kenya. People mistakenly believe that those with albinism have special powers but that they also bring bad luck to the community. Given that witchcraft and black magic are common themes in Nollywood films, the WHRIN believes these films promote stereotypes that encourage discrimination and even killing of albinos.

Proponents note that Nollywood films offer an important perspective, given that so many films set in Africa depict a European worldview. They tell Nigerian stories, by Nigerians, and thus can give voice to persons who are misunderstood.

Laura L. Finley

See also: American Horror Story; Bollywood; *Buffy the Vampire Slayer*; *Harry Potter* Books and Film Series; *Twilight* Saga, The

Further Reading
Foxcroft, G. 2013. "Exploring the Role of Nollywood in the Muti Murders of Persons With Albinism." *WHRIN*. http://www.whrin.org/wp-content/uploads/2013/08/Exploring

-the-Role-of-Nollywood-in-the-Muti-Murders-of-PWA-Report-for-the-UNOHCHR -FINAL.pdf

Giwa, T. 2010. "Nollywood: A Case Study of the Rising Nigerian Film Industry—Content & Production." *Southern Illinois University Carbondale Research Papers.* http:// opensiuc.lib.siu.edu/cgi/viewcontent.cgi?article=1667&context=gs_rp

Izuzu, C. 2014. "Top Five Nollywood Films on Domestic Violence." *Pulse*, May 11. http:// www.pulse.ng/entertainment/movies/pulse-countdown-top-5-nollywood-movies -on-domestic-violence-id2986947.html

Rice, A. 2012. "A Scorsese in Lagos." *The New York Times*, February 23. http://www .nytimes.com/2012/02/26/magazine/nollywood-movies.html

Vanguard. 2014. "Nollywood Films Sending Positive, Negative Messages to Viewers. *Vanguard*, May 28. http://www.vanguardngr.com/2014/05/nollywood-films-sending -positive-negative-messages-viewers/

North Korean Films

North Korea is a dictatorship, and like others, censorship is a way of life, as is state-run propaganda. Yet North Korea is complex in the sense that its former leader, Kim Jong-il, loved film. Films about North Korea made in the United States have drawn heavy criticism from that country's leaders.

Reports are that current leader Kim Jong-un's family created a series of propaganda films, called "Nation and Destiny," designed to scare citizens from defecting to South Korea. One, produced by the leader's father, the late Kim Jong-il, shows South Korea full of poverty and violent thugs. The leaders ordered that these films be shown twice a day for nine years in 200 cinemas. More than 50 films were produced (Burke, 2017).

Kim Jong-il so loved film that he spent a great deal of time developing that industry in North Korea. One of the best-known North Korean films is *The Flower Girl* (1972), supposedly based on the writings of Kim Il-sung and his son, Kim Jong-il. The film is set during the time of Japanese rule in the 1920s and 1930s, and followed a woman and her family who are mistreated by their landlord. Kim Il-sung and his communist army save the day in yet another example of the glorification of the state. Another famous North Korean film is *Pulgasari* (1985), which is set in medieval times and features a group of feudal villagers who are oppressed by the governor who owns their land. They fight back when a townsman makes an effigy of a monster that comes to life and eats anything and everything. The governor tries but fails to control the beast.

North Korea began investing in films after World War II, as part of its competition with the South. South Korea produced its first feature film in 1964, but North Korea was hot on its tail. Yet too many restrictions made it hard for the industry to thrive, until Kim Jong-il came along and invested heavily in it.

In yet another example of how involved the state is with film production in North Korea, Kim Jong-il forced director Shin Sang-ok to make seven films before he and his wife escaped to South Korea. One of his films, *Hong Kil Dong* (1986), focuses on a Robin Hood–type character who defends villagers from oppression with his kung-fu skills.

Hollywood films have, especially in recent years, depicted North Korea as the antagonist. *Olympus Has Fallen* (2013) and the remake of *Red Dawn* (2012), for instance, paint North Korea as violent and brutally oppressive. One of the most controversial U.S. films was *The Interview* (2014), which is about a pair of journalists, played by James Franco and Seth Rogen, who are able to score an interview with Kim Jong-un (Randall Park). The CIA asks the pair to murder the dictator. Things go horribly awry, Kim is killed but not by them, and the journalists end up being rescued by three Navy SEALs. It was fairly well received in the United States, but not surprisingly, ignited fury in North Korea. The United States even claims that North Korea hacked Sony Pictures in response, which at first pulled the film amidst threats but then released it on Christmas Day. The country's National Defense Commission lashed out against President Barack Obama for allowing its release, calling him "reckless" and "a monkey," and called the film a "dishonest and reactionary movie hurting the dignity of the supreme leadership of the DPRK [North Korea] and agitating terrorism" (BBC, 2014).

Laura L. Finley

See also: China Beach; *M*A*S*H*; *Rambo* Films; South Korean K-Pop; War Films

Further Reading

BBC. 2014. "North Korea Berates Obama Over the Interview Release." *BBC News*, December 27. http://www.bbc.com/news/world-asia-30608179

Burke, D. 2017. "Bizarre North Korean Propaganda Films Show How Kim Jong-un's Family Tried to Terrify Citizens to Prevent Them from Defecting." *The Mirror*, December 8. https://www.mirror.co.uk/news/world-news/bizarre-north-korean-propaganda-films-11660014

Fowler, S. 2014. "The Five Best North Korean Films." *The Guardian*, August 15. https://www.theguardian.com/world/2014/aug/15/five-best-north-korean-films

Rosenberg, A. 2015. "How Hollywood Blundered into the Korean Culture Wars." *The Washington Post*, January 28. https://www.washingtonpost.com/news/act-four/wp/2015/01/28/how-hollywood-blundered-into-the-korean-culture-wars/

Rambo Films

David Morrell was a 26-year-old graduate student at Penn State University when he wrote the novel *First Blood* that became the Rambo film series. He had been watching television coverage of the Vietnam War and thought it would be interesting to write a story in which the war came home to the United States. The central character, he decided, would be a former Green Beret Medal of Honor winner who suffers from post-traumatic stress disorder. He is wrongfully arrested and escapes, to be tracked by a police chief who is a Korean War veteran. Both men are trained in guerilla warfare, but Rambo's skills are far better. Morrell finished the novel in 1970, and it was sold to a publisher within three weeks. A review in *Time* called it "carnography, violence's answer to pornography" (Bouzereau, 2000, p. 156). It was sold shortly after that to be made into a film, but it took 10 years before it reached the screen under Canadian director Ted Kotcheff, with Sylvester Stallone selected to play the leading role.

In the film version, the directors and Stallone chose to portray his character as reluctant to use violence. Stallone "wanted Rambo to be portrayed as a sympathetic victim, not a killing machine" (Bouzereau, 2000, p. 157). In fact, on the screen Rambo kills one man by accident, and there's another incident with a car crash, a far lower body count than in the novel. Unlike in the novel, Rambo lives at the end of the film, a choice made by test audiences.

Yet despite there being little real violence, criticism exploded. Film critic Jane Maslin wrote in the *New York Times*, "Vietnam is to *First Blood* as rape was to *Death Wish*. It's the excuse for a rampage of destruction," while Peter Rainier of the *Los Angeles Times* called it "a sado-masochistic revenge fantasy that might have been cooked up by the *Soldier of Fortune* crowd" (Bouzereau, 2000, p. 157). It was a box office success when it was released in 1982, however. Rambo became a cult hero, and two sequels, *Rambo: First Blood Part II* (1985) and *Rambo III* (1988), followed, then in 2008 *Rambo IV* was released to much criticism.

In the second film, Rambo is in a penitentiary and is offered a mission: return to Vietnam to find soldiers who are missing in action and presumed to be held as prisoners. He is captured and tortured, dunked into leach-infested water, and almost has his eyes carved out with a red-hot knife. He is saved by Co, played by Julia Nickson, and seeks revenge against those who tortured him and those who betrayed him. *Rambo: First Blood Part II* is much more violent than the first film, and the success and cult status of Rambo made it more controversial, as the toys, animated TV series, and other consumer products were appealing to children. Vietnam War veterans were also angered by the film, which they said was inaccurate and unrealistic. Copycat incidents followed. In England, a 27-year-old dressed in Rambo garb went on a killing spree before killing himself. *Daily Telegraph* columnist Leslie Garner wrote that the Rambo character "is the current icon of human destructiveness. . . . In the aftermath of Hungerford, it is sheer intellectual cowardice to pretend that these images . . . have no effect on behavior" (Associated Press, 1987). Charles Champlin wrote in the *Los Angeles Times*: "I tried a body count the other afternoon, but gave up after two dozen because there was no reliable way even to estimate how many fell to the bombs, rockets, and perpetual load automatic weapons. The deaths by knife and steel were easier to assess. I can't believe the full toll is less than 100" (Bouzereau, 2000, p. 158).

Rambo III tells the story of the kidnapping of the wife and daughter of Colonel Trautman, Rambo's former superior, played by Richard Crenna. Rambo has been living a solitary life with Buddhist priests but is compelled to help his old friend and goes on a one-man rescue mission. It was even more violent than the second film, prompting British officials to require 24 cuts. In America it was considered one of the most violent films to date, with an estimated double the amount of violence from *Rambo II*. Rambo uses knives, guns, and explosives routinely. Antiwar activists protested the film, and critics noted that the hypermacho Rambo was a reflection of the U.S. approach to foreign relations under the Reagan administration when it was released. Morrell and Stallone continued to defend the film as being no more violent than real life.

In the fourth installment, an aging Rambo comes out of retirement to save some Christian aid workers who have been trapped in Burma. The *Philadelphia Inquirer* called it a "slab of action porn" (Staff and Agencies, 2008). Stallone and other members of the cast spoke to the press about the atrocities they saw while filming in Burma. They saw survivors with injuries from landmines and wounds infested with maggots. The cast and crew even had shots fired over their heads and were threatened if they continued to film there.

Laura L. Finley

See also: China Beach; Cop Films; *Mad Max* Films; *M*A*S*H*; North Korean Films; Russian Popular Culture; Superhero Films; War Films

Further Reading

Associated Press. 1987. "TV Violence, Rambo Films Assailed as British Killings Toll Rises to 17." *Los Angeles Times*, August 22. http://articles.latimes.com/1987-08-22/news/mn-1039_1_john-rambo

Bouzereau, L. 2000. *Ultra Violent Movies*. New York: Kensington Publishing.

Donovan, B. 2009. *Blood, Guns, and Testosterone: Action Films, Audiences, and a Thirst for Violence*. Lanham, MD: Scarecrow Press.

Staff and Agencies. 2008. "Critics Draw First Blood as New Rambo Hits U.S." *The Guardian*, January 25. https://www.theguardian.com/film/2008/jan/25/news

Rape Films

One of the biggest concerns about films that depict rape is the widespread use of rape myths. Martha Burt (1980) first defined rape myths as "prejudicial, stereotyped, or false beliefs about rape, rape victims, and rapists" that create an environment hostile to rape survivors (p. 217), and others define them as "attitudes and beliefs that are generally false but are widely and persistently held, and that serve to deny and justify male aggression against women" (Lonsway & Fitzgerald, 1994, p. 134). These myths focus on victims' behaviors, assumptions about offenders, and the context of rape. For instance, rape myths suggest that the way victims dress or act can precipitate rape, or that offenders are most often strangers, or that victims must physically resist for it to be "real" rape.

Historically, female film characters who challenged traditional gender role stereotypes were most likely to be sexually assaulted. Rape was a punishment, essentially, for acting out of place. For instance, the iconic scene from *Gone with the Wind* shows Rhett carrying Scarlett up the stairs to her bedroom and, despite her obvious protestations, the sexual activity is presented as normal.

Films also make it seem as though consent is difficult for men to identify. In the 2006 action movie *Crank*, Jason Statham's character grabs for his girlfriend, played by Amy Smart, in the middle of Los Angeles's Chinatown. He demands that she have sex with him right then, and when she says no, he rapes her. Despite showing her verbal and physical resistance, she eventually begins moaning with pleasure, suggesting that she really did want to have sex and therefore he didn't rape her. Similarly, the 2009 comedy *Observe and Report* starring Seth Rogen depicts rape as something the character desires, even though the victim is a vomit-covered, passed-out character played by Anna Faris.

Even highly regarded films like the Academy Award–nominated *The Accused*, which is based on a true story, use rape myths. The message is that women who dress scantily or who flirt with men are inviting rape. Viewers only learn what really happened at Big Dan's bar the night Sarah (played by Jodie Foster) was gang-raped through a series of flashbacks.

One of the oldest rape myths is that rape is perpetrated predominately by Black males. The 1915 landmark film *The Birth of a Nation* helped reinforce the notion that white women were under attack by hypersexualized black men. Although there is no actual sexual assault depicted in the film, viewers know that the black character Gus pursued and assaulted the white woman, Flora Cameron. She commits suicide, and he is tried and then lynched. The film secured the image of the "brutal black buck" in the minds of many viewers for decades to come.

Films rarely show males as victims of rape, and when they do it is often the butt of a joke. The film *Get Hard*, directed by Ethan Cohen and starring Will Ferrell and Kevin Hart, features a variety of rape jokes. Hart, who is a decent man, is employed by the white-collar criminal Ferrell to teach him how to endure the prison sentence he has just been assigned. It is clear that he is chosen only because he is black. In one scene, Ferrell's character is in a gay restaurant and attempts to perform oral sex on a man to "ready himself" for prison rape. This is supposed to be amusing. Cinematic storylines often imply or sometimes even state that a man is lucky if he is raped by an attractive woman.

One exception is John Boorman's (1972) *Deliverance*. Lewis, played by Burt Reynolds, and his friends Ed, played by Jon Voight; Bobby, played by Ned Beatty; and Drew, played by Ronny Cox, are on a canoeing trip when on the second day, Ed and Bobby are held at gunpoint by two rednecks and one sodomizes Bobby, telling him to "squeal like a pig." The other is about to rape Ed when Lewis rescues his friends, shooting one of the rapists. They bury the body, and the four men head down the rapids before their canoes capsize. Things go haywire when Drew disappears overboard and they believe he was shot by the rapists. They find the man who was intending to rape Ed and kill him, before finally making their way to land. Despite a suspicious sheriff, they are not held, but the men have nightmares about the experience. John Boorman explained, "What I wanted was not to show violence in itself—you don't see too much blood in the film—but to confront both characters and spectators with the reality of violence. It's very important for me, for example, that the victim takes a long time to die: it was intended as an antidote to the kind of death one normally sees on the screen, happening so quickly, so banal as to be hypocritical" (Bouzereau, 2000, p. 149).

Popular culture often depicts victims seeking revenge against their rapists, or other people seeking revenge on their behalf. *I Spit on Your Grave* is one of the goriest rape-revenge films. After Jennifer is repeatedly gang-raped by four men near a country house she rented for the summer, which is graphically depicted in three scenes, she decides to seek revenge against the men by finding and murdering each of them in terrifying fashion. She castrates one in the bathtub then leaves him to bleed to death.

Thelma and Louise (1991) is one of the most famous films that depicts rape-revenge. On June 24, 1991, *Time* magazine featured it on its cover, and it received both criticism and praise. The rape scene takes place in a parking lot, and it is what drives the plot. When the man, Harlan, gets aggressive Thelma resists, and he slaps her and tries to rape her. Louise shoots Harlan and the two women flee. They go on to exact various forms of revenge on other males who harass women.

Death Wish shows a man seeking revenge against the men who murdered his wife and raped his daughter. It was widely popular, especially among white men, who enjoyed the main character's vigilantism. Critics condemned it for that exact reason. Vincent Canby wrote in *The New York Times*, "Its message, simply put, is: KILL. TRY IT. YOU'LL LIKE IT," while *Variety* called it a "poisonous incitement to do-it-yourself law enforcement" (Bouzereau, 2000, p. 140). The 2000s saw a resurgence of the rape-revenge film, and many were big hits. These include *Law-Abiding Citizen* (2009) and *The Girl with the Dragon Tattoo* (2009). *The Girl with the Dragon Tattoo*, based on a popular Swedish book in a series, reveals that the main character, Lisbeth Salander, is seeking revenge for the rape committed by her guardian, corrupt and sadistic Nils Bjurman. She invades his home, rapes him with a dildo, and makes him watch the DVD he made when he was raping her. She then tattoos, "I am a rapist and a sadistic pig" on his stomach.

Laura L. Finley

See also: *American Horror Story*; Blues Music; Bollywood; *Game of Thrones*; *Natural Born Killers*; Scandinavian Crime Novels; Silent Films; Slasher Films; *X-Files, The*

Further Reading
Bouzereau, L. 2000. *Ultra Violent Movies.* New York: Kensington Publishing.

Burt, M. 1980. "Cultural Myths and Support for Rape." *Journal of Personality and Social Psychology, 38*(2), 217–30.

Haggard, N. 2014. "The Birth of the Black Rapist: The 'Brutal Black Buck' in American Culture." In *A History of Evil in Popular Culture,* edited by S. Packer & J. Pennington, Vol. 1, 83–94. Santa Barbara, CA: ABC-CLIO.

Haskell, M. 1987. *From Reverence to Rape: The Treatment of Women in the Movies.* Chicago: The University of Chicago Press.

Heller-Nicholas, A. 2011. *Rape-Revenge Films.* Jefferson, NC: McFarland & Company.

Lonsway, K., & Fitzgerald, L. 1994. "Rape Myths: In Review." *Psychology of Women Quarterly, 18*(2), 133–64.

Russian Popular Culture

When the Soviet Union was a dictatorship, popular culture largely amounted to state-run propaganda. After the fall of the Soviet Union, censorship declined, and film, television, and other outlets became somewhat more progressive, including works that featured sex and violence.

Novels like *You're Just a Slut, My Dear!* (*Ty prosto shliukha, dorogaia!*), which focuses on sexual slavery and the harvesting of organs for sale; a trilogy of books called *Nympho* that feature a sex-addicted soldier; and books and films like the *MadDog* and *Antikiller* series, which showcase a Russian "Rambo," all became popular. Not only were such works a relief from every-day woes, but they built hope and nationalism, in that they emphasized heroics in the most challenging of situations. Further, they helped citizens make sense of the overwhelming collapse of Russia. One commentator wrote, "The full sense of collapse required a panoptic view that only the media and culture industry were eager to provide, amalgamating national collapse into one master narrative that would then be readily available to most individuals as a framework for understanding their own suffering and their own fears" (Borenstein, 2007).

One of the most controversial stories of all time is the novel by Russian author Vladimir Nabokov, *Lolita*. Lolita, the main character, is a woman who is the target of an older man's obsession. Humbert Humbert, her stepfather, rapes her and essentially comes to own her. Many have considered Humbert Humbert to be one of the greatest fictional characters of all time, due to his charisma. Yet it is clear that he knows what he is doing and is aware of the vulnerability of the young Lolita, whose mother was killed. The book barely got published in the United States due to the scandalous topic, and once it was, it was subjected to many attempts at censorship. In 1962, Stanley Kubrick made a film version of the story, starring Sue Lyon as Lolita, and adding to the controversy by depicting her as a "sex kitten," despite the character being just 12 years old. Modern readers tend to see Humbert as a pedophile rather than in a romantic sense.

In fall 2017, Hollywood erupted with accusations that directors and actors had long sexually harassed and assaulted women. These accusations spawned movements like #MeToo and #TimesUp. But in Russia, they were not received in quite the same fashion. Media moguls criticized the women as overplaying their hand, and even blamed the victims because, as Russian actress Agniya Kuznetsova said, "[T]hey shouldn't be acting like prostitutes. I feel sorry for this poor man (Harvey Weinstein). Women were created for schemes like this. Give them the chance, and they'll weave some plot or turn on you" (The World Staff, 2017).

Like other communist countries, Russia remains deeply concerned about depictions that might undermine authority or negatively portray the country. The film *Matilda*, directed by Russian Alexei Uchitel, is about the actual romance between the future Nicholas II and Mathilde Kschessinska, a teen ballerina, in the early 1900s. Nicholas II was executed, along with his family, by communist rebels in 1918 and was posthumously canonized by the Russian Orthodox Church in 2000. Some claim that the film is blasphemous, in that it portrays love scenes involving the holy tsar, and Christian State-Holy Rus, a radical Russian Orthodox movement, warned that "cinemas will burn" if *Matilda* were screened. The premier of the film was delayed due to a bomb threat, and a second screening in Moscow was cancelled when two cars outside of the law firm that represented the film studio were set afire, with a note reading "Burn for Matilda" left at the scene. A cinema in Yekaterinburg was burned, and a man who had protested the film was arrested for the attack. Natalia Poklonskaya, a prominent MP with Vladimir Putin's ruling United Russia party, has said the film "insults the feelings of religious believers," which is a criminal offense. She has called for it to be banned (Bennetts, 2017).

Another controversy ensued in 2016, when it was announced that a new Russian reality TV show was planning on allowing rapes and murders. *Game 2: Winter*, which sends 30 male and female contestants to the Russian wilderness to survive the frigid cold, bears, and wolves for nine months in order to hopefully win a $1.6

million prize, has boasted that anything will be allowed and said that contestants must sign a waiver acknowledging that fact. An advertisement for the show reads: "Each contestant gives consent that they could be maimed, even killed. 2,000 cameras, 900 hectares and 30 lives. Everything is allowed. Fighting, alcohol, murder, rape, smoking, anything" (Bulman, 2016). Contestants are warned, however, that police are free to arrest anyone who commits a crime during the show. Contestants are given survival training from a former special operative elite and are allowed to have knives but not guns.

Laura L. Finley

See also: Kubrick, Stanley; *Rambo* Films

Further Reading

Bennetts, M. 2017. "Heavy Security for Love Story of Russia's 'Holy Tsar' and Teenage Ballerina." *The Guardian*, September 11. http://www.theguardian.com/world/2017/sep/11/alexei-uchitel-matilda-film-about-russia-holy-tsar-premieres-after-threats#img-1

Borenstein, E. 2007. *Overkill: Sex and Violence in Contemporary Russian Popular Culture.* Ithaca, NY: Cornell University Press.

Bulman, M. 2016. "Russian Reality Show to 'Allow' Rape and Murder as Contestants Compete for Cash Prize." *The Independent*, December 15. http://www.independent.co.uk/arts-entertainment/tv/news/russian-reality-tv-show-allows-rape-murder-a7478346.html

Levitt, M., & Novokov, T., eds. 2007. *Times in Trouble: Violence in Russian Literature and Culture.* Madison, WI: University of Wisconsin Press.

Martin, R. 2016. "Depicting Sexual Predators as Villains in Fiction Is Tricky." *NPR*, September 25. https://www.npr.org/2016/09/25/495358007/depicting-sexual-predators-as-villains-in-fiction-is-tricky

The World Staff. 2017. "Russians Look at the Harvey Weinstein Scandal and Say 'What's the Big Deal?'" *USA Today*, October 24. https://www.usatoday.com/story/news/world/2017/10/24/russians-look-harvey-weinstein-scandal-and-say-whats-big-deal/793425001/

Silent Films

Silent films were popular from the 1890s until the early 1930s. The release of the first "talkie" in 1927 led to the demise of the silent film. Many were comedies that made the careers of stars like Charlie Chaplin and Buster Keaton. Some featured slapstick, comedic violence, but most did not depict brutal or gory violence. The term slapstick was coined in 1902, when silent film actor Hilary Platt actually slapped someone with a stick. Silent films featured ever bigger and more spectacular stunts or gags, and performers had to be physically skilled to pull them off. Many of the stunts were quite dangerous, and the actors lacked the protections of those in film today. In addition to slapstick violence, silent films often used racist stereotypes, including featuring actors in blackface.

Many actors were lucky to emerge from silent film sets without significant injuries. For instance, Buster Keaton survived a two-story house crashing on him in

Steamboat Bill, Jr. (1928) only because a window perfectly framed his body. Keaton said the shoot was exciting, even though he saw a cameraman praying beforehand. In *Wings* (1927), Dick Grace hung from a rope ladder out of a cockpit. He broke his neck shooting the film, which one the first Oscar for Best Picture. Yakima Canutt, a former rodeo star, was violently thrown from a horse during the filming of *Devil Horse* (1926). The horse tried to trample him in one scene. Stuntman Harvey Parry, standing in for Harold Lloyd, hung from an enormous, 12-story clock, flipping and twisting perilously in one of silent films' most iconic images in *Safety Last* (1923). Two stuntmen appearing in *The Trail of '98* (1928) died in the filming about gold rush prospectors in Canada. They were thrown from their canoes and swallowed by the rapids, and two others are presumed dead, as their bodies were never found.

People of color were typically depicted as black-faced savages with primitive features. For instance, *Ham the Explorer* (1916) depicted an African tribe that used stereotypical grunts like "oogabooga." Asians were shown as the "yellow threat," such as in *Do Your Stuff* (1923), which featured a yellow-faced Chinatown. *Rough Sailing* (1924) depicted violent turbaned Turks. Whereas many critics have condemned silent films for their racism, others see it somewhat differently. Jake Romm, a culture writer, explained, "The racism is so over the top, so outrageous, that it lacks the sort of invasive power of more subtle forms of racism. . . . One of the values of viewing this kind of exaggerated racism, despite the nasty taste it leaves, is that we can see in these films the roots of many of our current racist film tropes" (Romm, 2017).

The Great Train Robbery (1903) is a silent Western film that features a band of outlaws who board a train and kidnap, rob, and kill before a final shootout. It is just 12 minutes long but was considered a milestone in filmmaking in that it used a number of innovative filming tactics, including on-location shooting, frequent camera movement, and composite editing. In the final shot, the outlaw played by George Barnes looks directly into the camera and audiences felt as though he was firing his gun at them. Although it may be no more than legend, audiences reportedly fired back at the screen in showings in the West. Women were said to have covered their ears because the shooting seemed so realistic, even though the film was silent. The level of violence was clearly shocking to audiences at the time, and it was taboo to show anyone actually dying on screen.

Famous director Alfred Hitchcock, known for his creepy murder mysteries, also directed 10 silent films. Hitchcock once said, "The silent pictures were the purest form of cinema" (Jones, 2013). His *Blackmail* (1929), which was later retrofitted with sound, told the story of a woman who was blackmailed after she killed the man who raped her.

Laura L. Finley

See also: Blaxploitation Films; Hitchcock, Alfred; Rape Films

Further Reading

Demain, B. 2011. "6 Dangerous Stunts of the Silent Movie Era." *Mental Floss,* August 4. http://mentalfloss.com/article/28422/6-dangerous-stunts-silent-movie-era

Jones, K. 2013. "Silent Hitchcock." *The Wall Street Journal.* June 26. https://www.wsj.com
/articles/SB10001424127887323683504578565833917463370

LaSalle, M. 2004. "Early Film Violence Startled Even Though It Was Silent." *San Francisco Gate,* January 2. http://www.sfgate.com/entertainment/article/Early-film
-violence-startled-even-though-it-was-2818319.php

Lumenick, L. 2013. "Silent But Violent." *New York Post,* June 23. http://nypost.com/2013
/06/23/silent-but-violent/

Romm, J. 2017. "Vintage Slapstick Movies Show Just How Much, and How Little, Racism
Has Changed." *Forward,* January 25. fromhttp://forward.com/culture/361155
/vintage-slapstick-movies-show-just-how-much-and-how-little-racism-has-chang/

"Top Ten Silent Films." 2013. *The Guardian,* November 22. https://www.theguardian.com
/film/filmblog/2013/nov/22/top-10-silent-movies-films

Slasher Films

The popularity of the slasher genre of horror films peaked in the mid-1980s. Some
of the top-grossing 1980s slasher films include the *A Nightmare on Elm Street* series,
the *Friday the 13th* series', *Child's Play,* the *Halloween* series, and *Psycho II* and
III. These movies contain significant amounts of violence, with much of it eroticized violence against female characters. These films generally feature an antagonist who kills multiple characters. Studies show that although there are fewer acts
of violence against the female characters, the scenes of violence are much longer
than those involving male characters. That is because they are usually stalked or
followed throughout the movie, whereas the male characters are often victimized
right away and usually die. Another common characteristic is that the female characters are most likely to be partially nude or fully nude when the acts of violence
occur.

Many have asked why people watch slasher horror films. One study suggests
that viewers do not watch them because they are attracted to the aggression in the
film, but rather because they are inspired by the idea of confronting these situations in their real life. According to researchers from the University of Ausberg in
Germany, "[F]ilms with scenes of extreme violence appeal more to people who
believe there is value in facing violent aspects of life head-on" (Collins, 2013, p. 1).
Viewers realize that a lot worse could happen to them—for instance, they could be
killed by a serial killer, which makes their real problems seem like they are not
so bad.

One of the most successful horror films of the 1980s was *Halloween II.* This
movie is about an unlikeable psychopath, Michael Myers, who has been released
from the mental institution where he had been held for 15 years. He is released on
the anniversary of the date that he killed his older sister. Myers goes back to where
he grew up and goes on a killing spree. Later in the movie it becomes clear that
Michael Myers has a fixation on his younger sister. As investigators try to solve
the crime spree, they are able to unseal a file about Myers and find out this crucial
information. Unlike the previously cited research about the length of screen violence against female characters, Michael Myers makes his killings very quick and

does not stay with one victim very long. However, he does fixate on the main character because she is indeed his younger sister. Michael Myers is a very violent character, yet he can also be viewed as comical because it is so unrealistic that such an insane person would ever be allowed to leave the mental institution.

A Nightmare on Elm Street played a big role in popularizing horror films. The director, writer, producer, and actor of *A Nightmare on Elm Street*, Wes Craven, is known for his pioneering work in the genre of horror films, particularly slasher films. The main character in this movie is Freddy Krueger. He is a disfigured midnight mangler who preys on teenagers in their dreams. He is supposed to be dead because he was a child molester when he was alive, but he got out of jail on a technicality. The neighborhood parents of the kids who Freddy Krueger molested and murdered hunted him down and burned him alive in a boiler room. The boiler room is where the teenagers go when Freddy first makes his appearance in their dreams. A lot of time in *A Nightmare on Elm Street* is spent on torturing the two main female characters; there is not as much violence toward the male characters as there is toward the two women. Right after she had sexual relations with her boyfriend, one of the female characters was murdered, which is consistent with the previously cited studies.

According to Andrew Welsh, the sample size of many of the studies about horror films is very small, limiting the ability to generalize the conclusions. Also, some of the samples may have been biased. For instance, one study only picked the most commercially successful films from that time period, rather than reviewing lesser-known films. Some of the experiments did not have a clear selection of their unit analyses. For example, some of their units of analyses were not even on the violent acts that occurred in the film. The most serious limitation is the lack of clear operationalization of the variables in each of the experiments. Andrew Welsh's research was an attempt to fill in the gaps in research on this topic. The purpose of his study was to examine the frequency of violence in slasher films, the seriousness of that violence and the degree of harm from it, how graphically it was depicted, the duration of the violent incidents, and the degree to which the violence is coupled with sex or sexually provocative imagery. Fifty movies were analyzed in the study. The results of the violent interactions were measured using PAT (Perpetrator-Act-Target)–level measures. PAT-level measures is when each violent interaction that occurs within the movie is measured by seven variables in the coding protocol and then classified as either a antagonistic or defensive act of violence. The results of the study were that 1,363 violent PAT-level measures were identified across the 50 films. This indicates that there is a lot of violence depicted in horror films.

Laura L. Finley

See also: Jaws; Rape Films

Further Reading

Collins, N. 2013. "'Slasher' Films Encourage Empathy with Victims." *The Telegraph*, March 28. http://www.telegraph.co.uk/news/science/science-news/9959629/Slasher-films-encourage-empathy-with-victims.html

Dirks, T. 2016. Halloween II (1981). *Filmsite*. http://www.filmsite.org/series-halloween2.html

Dirks, T. 2016. A Nightmare on Elm Street (1984). *Filmsite.* http://www.filmsite.org/series
-nightmare.html

Welsh, A. 2009. "Sex and Violence in the Slasher Horror Film: A Content Analysis of Gender Differences in the Depiction of Violence." *Journal of Criminal Justice and Popular Culture, 16*(1), 1–25.

Star Wars **Franchise**

Star Wars is an American space opera media franchise, centered on a film series created by George Lucas. This franchise began in 1977 with the release of its first film, *A New Hope*. Forty years later this media franchise is still a worldwide phenomenon. In December 2015 it was reported that the series has taken in $7.3 billion at the box office, and that was before another film was released in December 2017, *The Last Jedi* (Chew, 2015). The series describes an epic fight for control of the empire and pits good against evil via a series of characters.

This science fiction franchise has fans of all ages. It has also generated controversy over the depiction of characters and the violence they use, in particular since the films are marketed to families. Both the good and bad characters use violence to achieve their goals. The following showcases just some of the violence featured in the films.

Episode IV: A New Hope

- The main character, Luke Skywalker (Mark Hamill), trains to be a Jedi to defeat the Empire, led by Darth Vader (David Prowse/James Earl Jones). Luke discovers his Uncle Owen and Aunt Beru were burned by Stormtroopers and takes their skeletal remains from the front door of his house across the plains of Tatooine.

- In a scene at a cantina, a character called Ponda Baba engages in a physical altercation with Luke. Because Luke used Obi-Wan's (Alec Guinness) lightsaber as a weapon, Ponda Baba's arm was slashed off and a pool of blood gathered.

- Another main character on the good side, bounty hunter Han Solo (Harrison Ford), has a conversation with Greedo, another bounty hunter. Han shoots Greedo before Greedo could shoot him to collect the bounty on him.

- Obi-Wan, the wise older Jedi, engages in a fight with Darth Vader to settle the score between them. Darth Vader wins the fight and Obi-Wan dies.

Episode V: The Empire Strikes Back

- Darth Vader (David Prowse/James Earl Jones) and the Empire torture Han Solo (Harrison Ford) mercilessly to show the people of Cloud City that consequences will be levied against those acting against the Empire's interest.

- During a duel between Darth Vader and Luke Skywalker (Mark Hamill), Darth Vader cuts off Luke's hand.

Episode VI: Return of the Jedi

- Luke Skywalker (Mark Hamill) is confronted by Jabba the Hutt's pet, the rancor, and is forced to kill it out of self-defense because the pet tries to eat him.

This occurs shortly after Luke and his friends were sent to be executed at the Sarlacc Pit.

- At one point, Luke rejects the evil Emperor Palpatine's (Ian McDiarmid) invitation to join the dark side. Since Luke denies the temptation of the dark side, Palpatine attempts to kill him slowly and painfully.

Episode I: The Phantom Menace

- Obi-Wan (Ewan McGregor) and Master Qui Gon (Liam Neeson) attempt to create a peaceful negotiation with the Trade Federation. The Federation responds by gassing the chamber Obi-Wan and Master Qui Gon are standing in.
- Obi-Wan engages the brutal Darth Maul (Ray Park) in a dual after Master Qui Go is killed.
- The Trade Federation attempts to forcibly make the Queen of Naboo (Natalie Portman) sign a treaty legalizing their vision of Planet Naboo.

Episode II: Attack of the Clones

- After Anakin Skywalker (Hayden Christensen) rescues his mother from the Tuskin Raiders, she dies in his arms. Eager for revenge, Anakin slaughters an entire tribe, including children and women. Word of his deeds spreads to others as he progresses on his journey toward the dark side.
- In the beginning of the episode, the threat of Queen Padme (Natalie Portman) being assassinated looms over the atmosphere, as assassins make two attempts on her life, both nearly successful.

Episode III: Revenge of the Sith

- Emperor Palpatine (Ian McDiarmid) orders his army to execute "Order-66" to kill all the Jedi. Anakin Skywalker (Hayden Christensen) is sent on a private mission to the Jedi temple to kill all the Jedi children in training. A young Jedi boy asks Anakin for help and was killed for doing so.
- Anakin and Obi-Wan (Ewan McGregor) challenge Count Dooku (Christopher Lee), and Obi-Wan is incapacitated. Anakin severs Dooku's head from his body after being defeated.
- After Anakin is irreversibly burned and scarred during his battle against Obi-Wan, Anakin must undergo painful surgery without anesthetics to replace his missing limbs and heavily scared tissue. Throughout the episode, you can hear his screams of agonizing pain.

Star Wars: The Force Awakens

- Finn (John Boyega) defects from the Stormtroopers because he does not want to inflict violence upon others.
- Kylo Ren (Adam Driver) tortures Rey (Daisy Ridley) with the Force to get information from her.
- Kylo Ren murders his father, Han Solo (Harrison Ford) by stabbing him with a light saber, then lets him fall off of a bridge.

- Kylo Ren severely beats Finn, leaving him incapacitated at the end of the film.

Rogue One: A Star Wars Story

- Jyn Erso's (Felicity Jones) mother attempts to kill an Empirical officer for trying to take the Erso family into custody because of her knowledge of the Death Star plan. Jyn's mother (Valene Kane) was killed in front of her family for not cooperating with the Empire because she refused to be detained.

The *Star Wars* franchise is widely loved, but has long been controversial. In particular, critics contend that both the good and the bad characters routinely use violence to achieve their goals, typically with little or no efforts made toward nonviolent conflict resolution.

Laura L. Finley

See also: Alien Franchise; *Star Trek*; "War of the Worlds"; *X-Files, The*

Further Reading

Chew, J. 2015. "Star Wars Franchise Worth More Than Harry Potter and James Bond, Combined." *Forbes*, December 24. http://fortune.com/2015/12/24/star-wars-value-worth/

Creighton, S. 2015, December 16. "Is Violent New Star Wars Too Disturbing for Under-12s?" *The Daily Mail*, December 16. http://www.dailymail.co.uk/news/article-3363540/Is-violent-new-Star-Wars-disturbing-12s-Parents-urged-consider-children-film-violent-scenes.html

McAloon, J. 2015. "Where's the Gore in Star Wars?" *The Telegraph*, December 15. www.telegraph.co.uk/film/star-wars-the-force-awakens/violence-gore-fight-scenes/.

Rosenberg, A. 2015. "How Violence Sets the 'Star Wars' Movies Apart." *The Washington Post*, October 30. https://www.washingtonpost.com/news/act-four/wp/2015/10/30/how-violence-sets-the-star-wars-movies-apart

Superhero Films

Superhero films tend to have very similar plots. An average person endures something odd or tragic and emerges with super powers that are needed to fight a villain or group of villains. Although the films position superheroes as good and villains as bad, both sides use violence to achieve their desired outcomes.

Critics note that superheroes do nothing to create long-term solutions to crime and violence. They tend to oversimplify the world and its problems. Critics have expressed concern that superhero films depict the world in black and white and emphasize individual over collective action. One exception is in *The Dark Knight* (2008), when Batman realizes Harvey Dent's policies will actually be more helpful to save Gotham than are his individual actions and takes the fall for Dent.

The violence in superhero films has been increasing. Twentieth Century Fox's *Deadpool* (2016), which is based on a series of comic books directed at adults, even aimed for an R-rating in the United States. In *Deadpool*, Ryan Reynolds stars as Wade Wilson, a terminally ill man who is tricked by a criminal mastermind (Ed Skrein) into undergoing a lifesaving procedure, which activates his latent healing power. The experiment works but leaves Wilson horribly disfigured. He sets out on a campaign of revenge, which is exacerbated when the bad guys kidnap the love of his life, Vanessa (Morena Baccarin). His revenge is particularly bloody, featuring several close-ups of gun violence. This coupled with the nudity in the film resulted in it being denied release in China.

Likewise, David Ayer's *Suicide Squad* (2016) was dark and gratuitously violent, although it received a PG-13 rating in the United States. *Suicide Squad* features a roundup of villains who are employed to help save the world. The crew includes an elite hitman, a former psychiatrist who is struggling with her own sanity, and a specialty assassin. Harley Quinn (Margot Robbie), the psychiatrist, is the girlfriend of the Joker (Jared Leto), who commits other acts of violent mayhem. Critics also pointed out that Quinn's relationship with the Joker is dangerously abusive. It received a 15 certificate in the UK, which means it is only suitable for persons ages 15 and above. Like *Suicide Squad* and *Deadpool*, a trend in superhero films is for viewers to identify with the more violent, even sometimes villainous, characters. *The Dark Knight* features a terrifying Joker (Heath Ledger). It starts with men, including the Joker, in clown masks robbing a bank and then killing the bank employees. The violence escalates thereafter, with scenes depicting a man being carved up with a knife, another having his face partially burned off, and yet another's eye slammed into a pencil. Children are held at gunpoint, and men are bound to chairs and burned. Because the Joker is such a dominant figure, and because Ledger played him with such intensity, many have alleged that the heroism of Batman is overshadowed.

Fox Pictures came under fire for a billboard advertising its *X-Men* (2016) film that depicted the character Mystique (Jennifer Lawrence) being choked. Fox later apologized for the use of this violent image.

Sharon Lamb, a professor of mental health at University of Massachusetts-Boston, and her colleagues surveyed 674 boys between the ages of 4 and 18 and analyzed the marketing of action figures from superhero movies. They concluded that violence is targeted at young boys through characters that are emotionally aloof and hypermasculine. The original comic book characters were better role models than today's bigger, badder, and more violent versions. Although superheroes are marketed most often to boys, there are some notable exceptions. In 2015, in advance of the 2017 release of the new *Wonder Woman* film, Mattel and DC announced plans to reveal teen versions of several female superheroes and to integrate them into comic books, action figures, toys, and apparel. Long accused of sexism, the move is intended to counter those claims as well as to broaden the company's fan bases.

Proponents maintain that superhero films give us hope. They help us believe we can do anything. Superheroes can also inspire us to be caring, smart, kind, and fearless. In the 1970s, psychologist Bruno Bettelheim argued that fairytales and fantasy stories help children understand and confront their fears. Some superheroes exemplify positive characteristics. Peter Parker from *Spider-Man* shows his sensitive side in a scene where he decides to devote himself to the life of an evil-defeating superhero, instead of living happily ever after with Mary Jane. *The Incredibles* (2004) is by all definitions an action superhero movie, but one that is centered on family values.

Further, proponents maintain that the rating systems used in the United States, UK, and other countries can help parents ensure that children who are too young to see such violence do not. Critics complain about the subjectivity of the rating system used by the Motion Picture Association of America, pointing out that films depicting adults smoking pot sometimes are designated with an R-rating but those featuring machine gun violence and bombings can be labeled PG-13. A 2013 study showed that there is, on average, more gun violence in PG-13 movies than in R-rated movies.

Laura L. Finley

See also: Blaxploitation Films; *Mad Max* Films; *Rambo* Films

Further Reading

Abad-Santos, A. 2013. "Marvel's Latest Movie Hero, Ant-Man, Abused His Wife." *The Atlantic,* August 26. http://www.theatlantic.com/entertainment/archive/2013/08/will-anyone-care-if-marvels-new-hero-hit-his-wife/311781/

Campbell, T. 2013. "The Morals We Should But Don't Take from Superhero Movies." *Huffington Post*, June 11. http://www.huffingtonpost.com/troy-campbell/the-questionable-morality_b_3421503.html

Dockterman, E. 2015. "DC and Mattel Team Up to Create Superhero Action Figures and Comics for Girls." *Time*, April 23. http://time.com/3833320/dc-mattel-superhero-action-figures-comics-girls

Guerasio, J. 2016. "The 'Suicide Squad' PG-13 Exposes What's Really Twisted about Movie Ratings." *Business Insider,* August 4. http://www.businessinsider.com/why-suicide-squad-got-pg-13-rating-2016-8

Hawkes, R. 2016. "When Did Superhero Movies Stop Being for Kids?" *The Telegraph,* July 20. http://www.telegraph.co.uk/films/2016/07/20/suicide-squads-15-certificate-when-did-superhero-movies-stop-bei/

McCartney, J. 2008. "Our Attitude to Violence Is Beyond a Joke as New Batman Film, The Dark Knight, Shows." *The Telegraph,* July 28. http://www.telegraph.co.uk/news/celebritynews/2461820/Our-attitude-to-violence-is-beyond-a-joke-as-new-Batman-film-The-Dark-Knight-shows.html

Orcutt, M. 2010. "Are Modern Superheroes Bad Role Models?" *Popular Mechanics,* August 15. http://www.popularmechanics.com/culture/a6033/superheroes-and-role-models/

Williams, M. 2016. "'X-Men's' Shameful Marketing Fail: Don't Glamorize Violence Against Women to Sell Tickets." *Salon,* June 3. http://www.salon.com/2016/06/03/x_mens_shameful_marketing_fail_dont_glamorize_violence_against_women_to_sell_tickets/

Tarantino, Quentin

Quentin Tarantino (1963–) is as controversial a director as are the topics of his films. Quentin Tarantino comes from a middle-class American upbringing. His childhood wasn't too different from most middle-class immigrants in California. His parents divorced when he was young, and during this split, Tarantino spent much of his time learning about cinema, which his mother especially fostered and supported. The multiaward-winning, now globally recognized, director was as fascinated with the aesthetics of the nature of violence then as he is today. According to interviews, Quentin Tarantino has publicly denounced over and over for the past 20 years the accusation that his movies directly promote violence (Mohammad & Greene, 2007).

In his movies, Tarantino chooses to illustrate the beauty of violence, just as love is explored through movies like *Romeo and Juliet.* To understand Quentin Tarantino's films there are several prerequisites to acknowledge. First, violence to Tarantino is simply "just fun," as he has grudgingly repeated over the last 20 years. Second, revenge is featured in the majority of his storylines. Third, he focuses on sharing the experience of the scene with his audience, sometimes a bit too generously on his part.

This third point is vital to understanding the timings of his shots, the settings, and especially the dialogue between the characters. Many of his movies are filmed out of sequence, bringing the audience to an "in the moment" type of mentality, focused on the seemingly trivial aspects of the daily grind of different walks of life. Tarantino complicates the labels of specific characters as "the bad guy," "the good guy," and "the criminal." These characteristics are part of the significant value Tarantino places on originality. His view on originality hinges heavily on being "different." To be different means that everything occurring outside of the movie has to find itself in the movie; it is not suppressed but instead channeled into the artwork in some form; otherwise, it is not authentic.

Tarantino spends a great deal of effort exploring the irrationality of human logic as well as competing motivations in his first box office hit, *Reservoir Dogs* (1992). From the plot, this movie could be interchangeable with dozens of others, but the focus makes the heist nothing more than a sales meeting in the life of a marketing director. This movie starts out with the crew talking about a moral interpretation, which leads to the morality of tipping, which they all adhere to even though they are not in accordance with it, demonstrating the civility of these supposed "monsters." This scene in itself says a lot of the light Tarantino wishes to shine upon humanity. It humanizes the doers of such "unimaginable" acts. Tarantino likes to use the screen to help humanize these individuals such that at the end of the movie, the audience feels personally vested in a character whom they would not dare be associated with in "real" life.

In *Reservoir Dogs*, Tarantino uses violence to connect. Pain is one of the few things in life that connects all humans. Humans cringe at the sight of violence because we can place ourselves in the shoes of others. In *Reservoir Dogs*, the director uses violence in two ways specifically. There is a particularly disturbing scene where a man is torturing a police officer simply for the sake of torture. Additionally, multiple levels of morality are shown, as the criminals aren't just "criminals" but they are individuals the same way Mr. Joe could live next door, so could Mr. Blonde and you would never even suspect at thing, until it's possibly too late (Mohammad & Greene, 2007).

In *Pulp Fiction* (1994), one of the movies that really cemented the legacy of Quentin Tarantino, violence is used in a more compensatory manner to rebalance the scales. *Pulp Fiction* revolves around two hit men who murder from various moral stances. *Pulp Fiction* transcends the importance of social class in favor of "right" and "wrong." In this movie, social classes are flipped on their heads and spun into a joke. Principled hit men, unprincipled computer nerds, a betraying boxer, and a sociopathic kingpin are all reduced to the same blip of insignificance though violence. *Pulp Fiction* focuses on the logical retort of violence through ironically similar issues "normal" people got through. In one scene, the hit men get to their target's home a bit earlier than contracted, so as a regular office worker would, they stepped to the side to continue their personal conversation, which "coincidentally" dealt with not only the moral righteousness of violence, but based on what degree, by posing the question of the act of massaging a married woman's feet. Apart from the known foot fetish of director Tarantino, the two characters first had to define the definition of a foot massage, then decipher the meaning behind it, and then the intention or possible awareness of retribution or the consequences based on who said woman was (wife of violent hit squad leader in this case). After considering all these mitigating and aggravating factors, they come to a truce. This is a joke on the audience who must juxtapose the hit men going from home to home murdering for hire with the stark reality of the "daily grind," which is shown through emotional toil, dark-humored self-depreciation (shooting Marvin in the face), and having to wear "costumes" just as goofy as hand-knitted Christmas sweaters worn at corporate holiday parties.

Kill Bill: Volume I (2003) and *Kill Bill: Volume II* (2004) exuberantly express Quentin Tarantino's style. The *Kill Bill* series is as much a revenge-quencher as there is. In these movies the vengeance is portrayed in a multilayered fashion. For example, vengeance is against "Bill," who is assumed to be the leader of an assassin hit squad who has betrayed one of his agents. The moral code of all the assassins is portrayed as tangible as any physical barrier. Despite having the opportunity to murder their target, if certain debts are not cleared or other "standards" met, the act cannot continue based on their moral code. This is interesting, as it begs the question of what revenge actually consists of, in contrast to most movies, where what is referred to as revenge is getting their way at any cost, including deception and taking "advantage" of unjust situations. For example, in the first *Kill Bill* film, a dead-set assassin is literally seconds away from ending her unknowing victim, but since she was not able to defend herself, she is unable to complete the task. In the *Kill Bill* series, Quentin Tarantino also refreshes the audiences' need for vengeance by portraying the karma against a man who sexually assaults an assumed-paralyzed woman. His head gets "caught" on a door multiple times, until his gratifying and "rightful" demise.

Inglorious Basterds (2009) is Quentin Tarantino's satirical-comical imaginative spin on a very real and terrible time period. This movie takes place in mid-1940s Germany during the Third Reich's reign of the Nazi regime. The movie highlighted the disturbing capacity of humans to destroy their own kind with surprisingly little resistance. To counter this hideous face of the human race, he demonstrates that no matter how controlling and influential a regime is laid upon people, the human spirit will never cease to be completely suppressed. In this case, Tarantino chooses to portray violence as a tool as viable as any other to the oppressed. This opportunity is demonstrated through the small group of "Naatzii killers," through their savagely comic acts of violence, such as a scene where Nazi generals were captured and a stereotype-defying giant of a Jew smashed his head in with a baseball bat, upon the foreseen noncooperation of the soldiers. This power of the small "man" is actually portrayed by the gentlest flower of a girl, who, through imposed dedication and an unweathering will brought onto her through the traumatizing execution of her entire family, is patient and maintains her untethered determination to gain a true victory to avenge her family Despite being tempted with small victories, she maintains a strong posture long enough to carry out her ultimate deed of burning down a chunk of high-ranking officers alive in a theater turned kettle at the very end, reaping the fully ripe and thirst-quenching fruit of vengeance.

More recently, Quentin Tarantino took on a film featuring a host of hateful and despicable characters. The *Hateful Eight* (2015) is full of violence of many sorts. This movie demonstrates the human depths of grudges and bottled pain.

Naren Navarro

See also: Blaxploitation Films; Coen Brothers Films; *Dexter*; *Fight Club*; Hitchcock, Alfred; Holocaust Films; Italian Films; Kubrick, Stanley; Lee, Spike; Western Films

Further Reading

Curran, D. 2011. "Tarantino, Quentin." In *Movies in American History: An Encyclopedia*, edited by P. C. DiMare, Vol. 3, 821–22. Santa Barbara, CA: ABC-CLIO.

Davis, T. F., & Womack, K. 1998. "Shepherding the Weak: The Ethics of Redemption in Quentin Tarantino's Pulp Fiction." *Literature/Film Quarterly, 26*(1): 60–66.

Gormley, P. 2005. *The New Brutality Film: Race and Affect in Contemporary Hollywood Cinema.* Bristol, UK: Intellect.

Mohammad, K. S., & Greene, R. 2007. *Quentin Tarantino and Philosophy: How to Philosophize with a Pair of Pliers and a Blowtorch.* Chicago: Open Court.

Ross, D. R., & Favero, M. 2002. "The Experience of Borderline Phenomena through Cinema: Quentin Tarantino's Reservoir Dogs, True Romance, and Pulp Fiction." *Journal of the American Academy of Psychoanalysis, 30*(3): 489.

Tapley, K. 2015. "Grateful Mates: Quentin Tarantino and Samuel L. Jackson Are Happy to Be in Each Other's Company Again in Controversial and Timely Western 'The Hateful Eight.'" *Variety*, December 8. http://variety.storied.co/the-hateful-eight/the-hateful-eight

Twilight Saga, The

The *Twilight* series, by Stephenie Meyer, includes four vampire-fantasy novels released between 2005 and 2008. The books were then made into five films, as the fourth book was broken into two parts. The films, released between 2008 and 2012, are *Twilight, The Twilight Saga: New Moon, The Twilight Saga: Eclipse, The Twilight Saga: Breaking Dawn—Part One,* and *The Twilight Saga: Breaking Dawn—Part Two.* The books and films were tremendously popular, especially with young girls but even with adults. In 2009, sales from the series was 16 percent of all book sales for the year. When *Breaking Dawn* was released in 2008, it was the biggest first-day release for the publisher, with some 1.3 million copies purchased. Books and academic articles have been devoted to analyzing the series, and various apparel, jewelry, and other products have been created around the characters (Oakley, 2012).

Twilight tells the story of Bella Swan (Kristen Stewart), who moves to a small town in Washington and falls in love with Edward Cullen (Robert Pattinson), who is a member of the Cullen vampire family. The vampires are in conflict with a team of werewolves, and Bella becomes friends with one of them, Jacob Black (Taylor Lautner), who is also romantically interested in her. There are other threats to the vampires, so the books and films feature a great deal of fighting and bloodshed. Bella nearly dies in the first book/movie. Fans tended to separate into "teams," depending on which of Bella's pursuers they preferred, and "Team Edward" or "Team Jacob" signs, clothing, and other paraphernalia were widely marketed. Bella and Edward have a complicated relationship, with some critics calling it abusive. In the second book/movie, she attempts suicide because Edward has broken things off, claiming that he cannot live with the fact that their being together threatens her life. The two end up married and have a child together.

Despite the commercial success of the series, critics have complained that it glorifies abusive relationships. Edward is depicted as a troubled soul and Bella his personal savior. She has low self-esteem, and is constantly telling herself how unattractive and awkward she is. Edward's interest boosts her esteem, and she becomes dangerously dependent on him. Edward tries, like all abusers, to isolate Bella from others. He pulls her away from her father, with whom she is close, and forbids her from seeing Jacob, even sabotaging her car at one point. He stalks her and insists on spending nearly all their time together once they are officially a couple. Edward even uses his vampire abilities to enter Bella's bedroom and watch her sleep. Yet due to their romantic relationship and her alleged "need" for protection, Edward's stalking behavior is depicted as a sign of love. Edward coerces Bella into various activities, even marriage, despite Bella's protestations that she is not ready. Additionally, Edward is very jealous and possessive. Finally, Bella is often bruised and injured from Edward's vampire strength, but she sees this as representative of their love, not as a problem. Bella is not the only character who threatens suicide, as Jacob does as well when she rejects him for Edward.

Bella's actions routinely upset Edward to the point of nearly uncontrolled rage. He is only able to control himself, it seems, due to his vampire powers. Critics contend that this depiction makes it seem as though aggressive feelings are normal in a relationship and that the average male might not be able to control his violence because he lacks vampire superpowers. Unwanted sexual overtures, both by Edward and Jacob, are not only depicted as normal but are applauded and commended by characters in the books and movies.

Gigi Meenakshi Durham, an author of many books on gender inequality and popular culture, studied the series. She found that the *Twilight* saga presents women as helpless and in need of protection, a dangerous stereotype. She identified five major themes related to gender inequality. First, the series depicts violence as an inevitable component of masculinity. Second, Bella accepts various forms of violence as normal in her relationship with Edward. Third, the series shows the "good" male characters as being able to suppress their violent feelings but the "bad" male characters cannot. Fourth, as the female protagonist, Bella is repeatedly placed in dangerous situations. And fifth, the male characters dominate her decision making (Durham, 2011).

One study examined the romantic beliefs held by 18- to 20-year-old fans of the *Twilight* series. One hundred ninety-four women participated in the study, which found that those who identified most with the Bella-Edward relationship held less healthy attitudes about relationships and less realistic expectations of them (Jacobstein, 2016). Similar studies have been conducted about the *Fifty Shades of Grey* series.

Another criticism is that the series reinforces racial prejudice. The Cullens are the good vampires, and they are so white and impossibly beautiful that their skin sparkles. The werewolves are depicted as darker skinned, and Jacob is Native American.

Laura L. Finley

See also: *Buffy the Vampire Slayer*; Dystopian Young Adult Literature and Film; *Family Guy*; *Harry Potter* Films; Nollywood; *South Park*

Further Reading

Durham, G. 2011. "Blood, Lust and Love: Interrogating Gender Violence in the Twilight Phenomenon." *The Journal of Children and Media, 6*(3), 281–99.

Fetters, A. 2012. "At Its Core, the Twilight Saga Is About." *The Atlantic,* November 15. https://www.theatlantic.com/entertainment/archive/2012/11/at-its-core-the-twilight -saga-is-a-story-about/265328/

Goodfriend, W. 2011. "Relationship Violence in 'Twilight.'" *Psychology Today,* November 9. https://www.psychologytoday.com/blog/psychologist-the-movies/201111 /relationship-violence-in-twilight

Jacobstein, A. 2016. "Till (Un)Death Do Us Part: Exploring the Romanticization of Adolescent Dating Violence in the Twilight Saga and the Romantic Relationship Beliefs Held by Female Fans." (MA thesis). Northampton, MA: Smith College. https:// scholarworks.smith.edu/cgi/viewcontent.cgi?referer=https://www.google.com /&httpsredir=1&article=2798&context=theses

Oakley, S. 2012. "'I Could Kill You Quite Easily, Bella, Simply by Accident': Violence and Romance in Stephenie Meyers's 'Twilight' Saga." (MA thesis). Mankato, MN: University of Minnesota at Mankato. https://cornerstone.lib.mnsu.edu/cgi /viewcontent.cgi?referer=https://www.google.com/&httpsredir=1&article=1125 &context=etds

War Films

Whether war films are useful teaching tools to educate the populace about the horrors of war or simply gratuitous displays of violence under the guise of a history lesson is a matter of some debate. Some war movies are indeed more gory than others, although defenders often claim that such depictions are just realistic and that the difficult parts of war should not be hidden or sanitized.

The Civil War has been the subject of numerous films. One of the first was D. W. Griffith's *The Fugitive* (1910), a silent film. *The Birth of a Nation* (1915) follows two rival families during the Civil War and Reconstruction. In doing so, it furthered racist stereotypes of black men and glorified the actions of the KKK. *Glory* (1989) told the story of the first formal unit of the Union Army made up entirely of black men, paying tribute to the 37,000 black soldiers who were killed in the war.

Gettysburg (1993) focuses on just that battle in a four-hour epic. Although there have been many documentaries about war, Ken Burns's *The Civil War* is the most watched on *PBS*.

William A. Wellman's *Wings* (1927) was the first and only silent film to win a Best Picture Oscar. Set in World War I, the script was rewritten to have a romantic spin as a way to appease Hollywood leading lady Clara Bow. It featured hundreds of extras in aerial battle scenes. *All Quiet on the Western Front* (1930) used little dialogue but moving cinematography and acting to show the horrors of the Great War. Winner of two Oscars in 1930, allegedly Nazis in Germany interrupted the screenings with chants and released rats into the audience. Stanley Kubrick's *Paths of Glory* (1957) is considered to be one of the darkest war films. It is set during World War I and depicts a failed attack for which commanders demanded there be scapegoats. Colonel Dax (Kirk Douglas), who led the attack, is charged with picking three victims who will be subject to court-martial and firing squad.

World War II is the most popular subject of war films. During the war, the War Department commissioned propaganda films, as did the Germans, Russians, and Japanese. More than 200 war films were produced in both the 1950s and 1960s. Set in World War II, *Saving Private Ryan* (1998) depicts soldiers enduring the violence of war to rescue others. It was nominated for 11 Academy Awards and won for Best Director, Best Cinematography, Best Film Editing, Best Sound Editing, and Best Sound Mixing. Less graphically violent is *Schindler's List* (1993), which tells the true story of Oskar Schindler, who saved 1,200 Jews from the Plasnow Concentration Camp in Poland. It won seven Oscars, including Best Director and Best Picture. Mel Gibson's *Hacksaw Ridge* (2016) tells the story of WWII conscientious objector Desmond Doss, a Seventh-day Adventist who won a Medal of Honor for his role as a medic with the 307th Regiment, 77th. Despite the fact that Doss (Andrew Garfield) never picks up a weapon, the film is full of gory, bloody battles. Gibson used the dramatic and ubiquitous violence as a way for viewers to better understand the actions of Doss.

The Deer Hunter (1978) tells the story of Michael, Steven, and Nick (Robert De Niro, John Savage, and Christopher Walken, respectively), who are forced by their Vietcong captors to play a nightmare version of Russian roulette after they are captured in a firefight. They escape, but find life at home more challenging than they thought. The Russian roulette aspect was criticized as unrealistic. The film is credited with raising awareness about how war affects the lives of small-town soldiers. It won five Academy Awards and was named by the American Film Institute as the 53rd greatest American film of all time. *Apocalypse Now* (1979) is a retelling of Joseph Conrad's *Heart of Darkness*, also set during the Vietnam War. It is one of the most famous war films and an indictment of the madness of war. It won the Palme d'Or at Cannes and paved the way for a succession of Vietnam War stories in the 1980s. Oliver Stone's *Platoon* (1986) won four Oscars and a total of 18 awards. One year later, Stanley Kubrick's *Full Metal Jacket* (1987) showed the horrific way in which recruits are treated as they are readied for war. Private Pyle ends up murdering the staff sergeant before killing himself.

Three Kings (1999) is set in the aftermath of the Persian Gulf War, where four soldiers set out to steal gold that had been stolen from Kuwait. A rare comedy-action-war film, it featured a host of stars, including George Clooney, Mark Wahlberg, and Ice Cube. It is said to be a criticism of American practices in the war and media coverage of it. Also about the Gulf War, *Jarhead* (2005) focuses on how soldiers occupy themselves during the boring times in between intense battles. The main character, Anthony Swofford (Jake Gyllenhaal), wrote in his 2003 memoir that he never took a shot during the war. Clint Eastwood's *American Sniper* (2015) is based on the story of Navy SEAL Chris Kyle. Whereas some applauded the film, other critics contended that the movie was horrible, sanitizing the atrocities of the war in Iraq and disregarding the dubious evidence for the invasion.

Black Hawk Down (2001) showcases American soldiers on a rescue mission in Somalia during the civil war of 1993. It is known for its drawn-out but realistic battle scenes.

Laura L. Finley

See also: Catch-22; *China Beach*; Disney Films; Holocaust Films; Islam, Depictions of; *M*A*S*H*; North Korean Films; *Rambo* Films; Vonnegut, Kurt

Further Reading

Anonymous. 2016. "From All Quiet on the Western Front to Hacksaw Ridge: The 25 Best War Films Ever Made." *The Telegraph*, November 4. http://www.telegraph.co.uk/films/0/the-best-war-movies-ever-made/

Dalton, S. 2016. "Critic's Picks: The Ten Best Civil War Films." *Hollywood Reporter*, June 23. http://www.hollywoodreporter.com/lists/critics-picks-10-best-civil-905713/item/birth-a-nation-best-civil-905689

Lane, A. 2016. "The Madness and Majesty of *Hacksaw Ridge*." *The New Yorker*, November 7. http://www.newyorker.com/magazine/2016/11/07/the-madness-and-majesty-of-hacksaw-ridge

Taibbi, M. 2015. "*American Sniper* Is Almost Too Dumb to Criticize." *Rolling Stone*, January 21. http://www.rollingstone.com/politics/news/american-sniper-is-almost-too-dumb-to-criticize-20150121

Western Films

"The western has always been the American epic. It's exciting and violent and huge. We don't have a single text like *The Iliad* or *The Odyssey* but the western is our story," said Robert Thompson, director of Syracuse University's Bleier Center for Television & Popular Culture (Miller, 2016).

Westerns were very popular, starting with the 1903 film *The Great Train Robbery*. After World War II it was the dominant genre in the United States, with the country in love with the rugged manliness and self-reliance of stars like John Wayne. They were a celebration of American exceptionalism. Nearly one-quarter of all films made between 1910 and 1960 were Westerns. These films typically featured a moral struggle between good and bad, and the violence perpetrated by "good guys" was merely in response to that done by the "bad guys." The better films were always a bit more nuanced, showing the protagonists as racists, as in John Ford's *The Searchers* (1956).

The genre faded in the 1960s and even more between 1980 and 2003. The generation who opposed the Vietnam War and was critical of governmental lying was bothered by the notion of the macho white savior and the glorification of Manifest Destiny against "savages." This new generation was less concerned with historical views and more with science fiction and technology. A new kind of Western emerged showing less morally righteous protagonists, like the doomed robbers played by Robert Redford and Paul Newman in *Butch Cassidy and the Sundance Kid* (1969).

Sam Peckinpah's *The Wild Bunch* (1969) is widely credited with shifting the genre to one that is more active and violent. Peckinpah was tremendously influenced by Arthur Penn's *Bonnie and Clyde* (1967), with its ultraviolent ending and slow-motion filming. His film is considered shocking not just for the violence that was far more than in typical Westerns but also for the choreography and repetition of the action scenes, all shot at different speeds. Additionally, and pretty new to Westerns, was the idea that the bad guys were the heroes. *The Wild Bunch* is the story of five ruffians who are in U.S. cavalrymen gear in a small town on the Texas border. It is 1913, and the men, led by Pike Bishop (William Holden), are working for railroad executive Pat Horrigan (Albert Dekker) and his lieutenant, Deke Thornton (Robert Ryan). As they enter the railroad building a ring of gunmen perched on the rooftop appears ready to shoot. Realizing that they are surrounded, a gunfight ensues, and Pike and most of his men end up leaving town with what they believe to be the railroad company's bags of money. They seek refuge at an old ranch and find that the bags are filled with worthless washers, yet they still have bounty hunters chasing them. The group hooks up with Mapache (Emilio Fernandez), a bandit who has stolen Pike's man Angel's (Jaime Sanchez) girlfriend. After a scuffle Mapache offers Pike and his men a job: hijacking a munitions train for the gold. They are successful despite being pursued by Thornton. When Mapache double-crosses them, the film concludes with a huge slaughter. Thornton rides in to collect the bodies and the gold. During the filming, Peckinpah grew angry with the special effects crew, as he wanted more and more realistic-sounding and -looking guns. There were also controversies with the filming, as many of the Mexican extras were in the army and brought real bullets to the set, and the actors complained of being spooked because they were staying in an allegedly haunted area. Several members of the cast were hurt while filming to the precision required by Peckinpah. But it was the final scene that is considered to be the game-changer. Reportedly special effects specialist Phil Ankrum used some 90,000 rounds of blank ammunition—more than in the Mexican revolution of 1913. Film historian Laurent Bouzereau wrote, "When the smoke clears, it seems we can almost smell the blood" (Bouzereau, 2000, p. 20). During test showings audiences expressed disgust at the violence, which infuriated Peckinpah, who had made seven visits to the Motion Picture Board to convince it to assign the film an R-rating rather than an X. It was not a box office success, prompting Warner Brothers to cut an additional seven minutes. It is clear that the ultraviolence influenced directors like Martin Scorsese, Oliver Stone, Francis Ford Coppola, Walter Hill, and Quentin Tarantino.

In the 1980s and 1990s, Westerns were typically slick action films, like *Young Guns* (1988), *Tombstone* (1993), *Maverick* (1994), and *Wyatt Earp* (1994), or they were comedies like *Three Amigos* (1986) and *City Slickers* (1991). There were a few exceptions between 1989 and 1992: *Lonesome Dove* miniseries (1989), the hit films *Dances with Wolves* (1990) and *Thunderheart* (1992), and Clint Eastwood's *Unforgiven* (1992).

Unforgiven took Eastwood back to the genre that made him famous as an actor. It is the story of an aging gunslinger who comes out of retirement to hunt down a group of cowboys who have hurt one of the town's prostitutes. He couples with an old friend, and both grapple with their task. As such, the film was applauded for showing the psychological impact of killing in a way different from most Westerns.

After the terror attack of September 11 and the wars in Iraq and Afghanistan, there was a resurgence in the making and popularity of Westerns, according to Richard Aquila, author of *Wanted Dead or Alive: The American West in Popular Culture.* "It was a time that sent people into shock and America was longing for a way to figure out what went wrong, who we are, what are values are and where we go in [the] future" (Aquila, 1998).

More recent Westerns have changed the focus some, featuring more complex protagonists and more graphic violence. Films like *The Hateful Eight* (2015), as well as TV shows like *Westworld* (2016–) and *Deadwood* (2004–2006), mix genres, coupling traditional Western elements with action films. They are no longer focused on life in small-town America. Aquila asserts that the reason the Western still exists is due to its flexibility as a genre. "It's like an inkblot test and every generation uses it for its own purposes." The Coen brothers' *No Country for Old Men* (2007) was "a morality play with an ending that shows good doesn't necessarily triumph over evil," according to Aquila. Quentin Tarantino's *Django Unchained* (2012), released during the presidency of Barack Obama, the first black president of the United States, showed a black man as the gunslinger hero, theretofore unheard of. Critic David Denby wrote in *The New Yorker*: "Some of it, particularly in the first half, is excruciatingly funny, and all of it has been brought off in a spirit of burlesque merriment—violent absurdity pushed to the level of flagrancy and beyond," whereas other critics called the film racist and did not see the humor.

Critics have contended that Westerns, even more recent ones, are still sexist. Female characters are props or love interests of the men, and even those like Calamity Jane are rarely depicted as wielding guns.

Laura L. Finley

See also: Dukes of Hazzard; Lonesome Dove; Natural Born Killers; Tarantino, Quentin

Further Reading
Aquila, R. 1998. *Wanted Dead or Alive: The American West in Popular Culture.* Chicago: University of Illinois Press.

Bakare, L. 2017. "My Favorite Best Picture Oscar Winner: Unforgiven." *The Guardian,* February 21. https://www.theguardian.com/film/2017/feb/21/best-picture-oscar-winners-unforgiven-clint-eastwood-1993

Bouzereau, L. 2000. *Ultra Violent Movies.* New York: Kensington Publishing.

Denby, D. 2013. "'Django Unchained': Put-on, Revenge, and the Aesthetics of Trash." *The New Yorker,* January 22. http://www.newyorker.com/culture/culture-desk/django-unchained-put-on-revenge-and-the-aesthetics-of-trash

Miller, S. 2016. "'The American Epic': Hollywood's Love for the Western." *The Guardian*, October 21. https://www.theguardian.com/film/2016/oct/21/western-films-hollywood-enduring-genre

Zombie Films

Zombie films come in a variety of genres, including horror/slasher, action, and campy comedy. Although more recent films in the zombie genre tend to show a great deal of graphic violence, earlier films more frequently showed violent situations but little actual violence. One exception to that was George A. Romero's *Night of the Living Dead* (1968).

Night of the Living Dead was made on a very limited budget and was like nothing ever filmed before. The black and white look made it even more scary, giving it a Gothic feel. The film tells the story of a young woman, Barbara (Judith O'Dea), and her brother, who are attacked by a stranger while visiting their father's tomb. Barbara flees, seeking refuge at a nearby farmhouse, which is crawling with ghouls. Another character, Ben (Duane Jones), battles the zombies to get into the house, where it is revealed that a molecular mutation created living-dead zombies who can only be killed when someone smashes their brains out. A wound from the zombies means that they will be inflicted with the flesh-eating disease. Ben and others try to fight the creatures, but only Ben survives. In the end, he is mistaken as a zombie by a team of rescuers and killed. It was a huge success, due in part to the marketing of a fake $50,000 life insurance policy if someone died of fear while watching.

Film scholar R.H.W. Dillard described it, noting, "The film's horrific specifics are remarkably detailed. Walking corpses fighting over and eating the intestines of the film's young lovers, a close shot of one of them eating her hand, a child's stabbing of her mother on camera fourteen times or gnawing on her father's severed arm, to say nothing of the countless rekillings of the living dead, the bashing in of their skulls" (Bouzereau, 2000, p. 210). Many were appalled and cautioned parents not to bring their children to see it. *Variety* referred to it as a type of pornography of violence. It was remade in 1990, and a sequel, *Dawn of the Dead,* was released in 1979. *Day of the Dead* was yet another sequel in 1985, and all three have attained cult classic status.

28 Days Later (2002) tells the story of an incurable virus that strikes the United Kingdom. The rage-inducing virus spreads after a group of animal rights activists break into a lab and one is bitten by a chimpanzee that has it. Twenty-eight days later, a man wakes up to find a deserted London. In his wanderings he finds a few others, and a small group of survivors struggle to find safety and to stay alive. Director Danny Boyle shot it so the film has a documentary feel. The fights between the survivor crew, various infected zombies, and soldiers are quite graphic. Roger Ebert wrote this about it: "'28 Days Later' is a tough, smart, ingenious movie that leads its characters into situations where everything depends on their (and our) understanding of human nature" (Ebert, 2013). Boyle co-produced the sequel, *28 Weeks Later*, in 2007. It shows a ravaged London and features a zombie attack within the first five minutes. After that sequence viewers are told that the virus ran its course and that the American army has come to help in the rebuilding. The challenges are not entirely over, and the film follows two kids and an American doctor as they navigate their way across the city. Phillip French, a reviewer for *The Guardian*, wrote "the movie is ruthless and not only in the way it spares no one from plague and bullet. The chilling theme is that the road to hell on earth is paved with good intentions, starting with the well-meaning scientists and the animal activists who light the fuse, and continuing with those inspired by compassion and moral decency" (French, 2007).

Other zombie films are more gory, like Sam Raimi's *Evil Dead* series (1981, 1987, 1992, and 2013) and Peter Jackson's *Dead Alive* (1993), which set new standards for graphic violence. The zombies in these films are far more voracious than in *Night of the Living Dead*, although these films also bring some comedic levity to the situations. The *Evil Dead* series stars Bruce Campbell as Ashley "Ash" Williams, who with a series of friends and allies, fights zombies who are both terrifying and ridiculous. It is a cult classic that spawned a television show, *Ash vs. Evil Dead* in 2015.

The success of these films spawned a variety of zombie television shows, including the wildly popular *The Walking Dead* (2010–). Video games also reignited interest in zombies in the 2000s. *Zombieland* (2009) was the first zombie film to break $100 million at the box office. In *Zombieland*, a virus has turned most everyone into zombies, who battle the few surviving humans. Four survivors, led by Tallahassee (Woody Harrelson), attempt to survive as they make their way to a supposed safe ground in Los Angeles. Critics found it funny and lighthearted despite the violence. *World War Z* (2013) starring Brad Pitt played similarly well at the box office. *Shaun of the Dead* (2004) was also popular for its likeable nerd of a protagonist and its humorous presentation of his fight to show his masculinity to his girlfriend by fighting zombies. George Romero has criticized *The Walking Dead* as a soap opera with the occasional zombie. Many agree, preferring the classic style of the zombie film.

Laura L. Finley

See also: Dystopian Young Adult Literature and Film; Italian Films; *Mad Max* Films; *Walking Dead, The*

Further Reading

Bouzereau, L. 2000. *Ultra Violent Movies.* New York: Kensington Publishing.

Ebert, R. 2013. "28 Days Later." *Rogerebert.com*, June 7. https://www.rogerebert.com/reviews/28-days-later-2003

French, P. 2007. "28 Weeks Later." *The Guardian*, May 13. https://www.theguardian.com/film/2007/may/13/features.review17

Hoover, S. 2014. *Undead Cinema: The Essential Zombie Films.* Stephen Hoover Self-Publishing.

Robey, T. 2013. "George A. Romero: Why I Don't Like The Walking Dead." *The Telegraph*, November 8. http://www.telegraph.co.uk/culture/film/10436738/George-A-Romero-Why-I-dont-like-The-Walking-Dead.html

Silver, A., & Ursini, J. 2014. *The Zombie Film: From White Zombie to World War Z.* Self-published: Applause Theater and Cinema.

3

Violence in Television

Introduction

In 2013, Americans spent an average of 4 hours and 31 minutes per day watching television, with U.S. adults spending almost 12 hours each day using some form of media (Delo, 2013). Children in the United States between ages 8 and 18 spend, on average, 40 hours behind a screen (Grossman & DeGaetano, 2014). In addition to the issue of how so much screen time makes people sedentary, there have long been concerns about the content of television programming. More than violence, historically the concern about television programming came from those who asserted that young people should not be exposed to anything "indecent." For decades, the law was not clear about what precisely constituted indecent or obscene programming. In 1973, Pacifica Radio's New York affiliate WBAI ran comedian George Carlin's 12-minute "Filthy Words" monologue. Six weeks later, John Douglas, a member of the pro-censorship group Morality in Media, complained that he had heard the broadcast while driving with his young son, which was a time when the Federal Communications Commission (FCC) was under pressure to do something about children's exposure to media's effect on children. Reports by the U.S. Surgeon General and the National Institute of Mental Health in 1972 discussed the negative effects of violent media, and Congress had threatened to cut off funding to the FCC if it didn't take action. The Supreme Court finally weighed in in 1978, with its ruling in *FCC v. Pacifica*. The decision was that patently offensive material is not protected by the First Amendment and therefore can be censored. Although critics expressed concern that the decision would result in a tidal wave of media indecency cases, the FCC did not find a single indecency violation between 1978 and 1987. Many still subscribed to the philosophy, articulated by Reagan's FCC-appointee Mark Fowler, that "[i]f you don't like it, just don't let your kids watch it" (Heins, 2001, p. 109).

It is not so simple as just tuning out, however. Even programming that is supposedly benign often features violence, as do programs marketed to children. The

National Television Violence Study (NTVS) provided an in-depth look at violence on television. This study looked at violent content over a three-year period (1996–1998), finding that approximately 60 percent of shows on television contained some type of violence. On average, these programs had about six instances of violence per hour (University of California, 1998). Although much of the mediated violence is perpetrated by adult characters, an article published from the NTVS specifically examined the age of perpetrators and found that about 7 percent of perpetrators of violence on television (excluding programming such as news and game shows) were teens; of those teens, 81 percent were male and 60 percent committed violence against another teen (Wilson, Colvin, & Smith, 2002). Although there was an overall low percentage of teen perpetrators, teens were the most likely characters to be portrayed in violent activities that were classified as "high risk" for viewers learning aggression based on a combination of factors. A study by the Kaiser Foundation found more violence in children's television programming than in any other category (Durham, 2008). In the time that children watch television, they observe at least 40,000 simulated murders and 200,000 acts of violence (Grossman & DeGaetano, 2014).

One of the concerns about violence in television is not just what is depicted, but how. Much of the violence depicted in children's programming is what communications scholar George Gerbner called "happy violence." This kind of violence is presented as though it is cute, funny, and without consequence. The danger is that young people, whose brains are not fully formed, may believe that real-life violence is not as damaging as it is, believing that, as in TV shows like *Tom and Jerry*, people will bounce back from horrendous assaults.

Also of concern is that violence is used by both "good" and "bad" characters. For instance, professional wrestling, which has been and remains very popular among young men, shows both the "heels," or bad characters, and the "faces," or good characters, using violence and degrading taunts to best their opponents. Increasingly the storylines of these shows are intended to make viewers even identify with the heels and to see the faces as weaker or less impressive. Crime dramas often show police, investigators, private detectives, and others using illegal or controversial tactics if they can help crack the case.

Some of the most violent shows on television are on cable channels, where the regulations are much looser. *The Sopranos, Breaking Bad, Game of Thrones,* and others are widely popular and involve a great deal of violence—some say, too much, although fans love these shows.

Television programs have long been accused of depicting domestic violence and sexual assault problematically. Myths and misconceptions suggest that only women are victims; that victims precipitate abuse and assault through their looks, clothing and behavior; that strangers are the biggest fear; and that false accusations are common. Shows like *Law & Order: SVU*, which purportedly come from a victim's perspective, often reinforce such beliefs.

Even comedic shows often make jokes about abuse and assault. Adult comedies like *South Park* and *Family Guy* joke about virtually everything, but some have found that their rape jokes are less than amusing.

Further, research has shown that television over-represents the amount of violent crime, which may lead viewers to be more concerned or fearful than is necessary. People respond to that fear in different ways, but one of the ways is to purchase security for their homes, weapons, and other devices they believe will keep them safe.

Defenders maintain that violent television is far from the most important influence on a child's or teenager's behavior.

> Adolescents are sexually charged, skeptical of authority, and hungry for experience. They hardly need television or the internet to give them sexual ideas; as Victor Strasburger has written, this is a large part of what makes adults so nervous about them. From a purely pedagogical viewpoint, disempowering teenagers through censorship of the information or entertainment they receive is not likely to resolve the emotional and social problems of an age group that in our modern era is already kept in dependency too long. (Heins, 2001, p. 259)

Efforts have been made to help parents control the sexual and violent content that their children may see on TV. In 1996, new legislation was enacted to require all TV sets with screens larger than 13 inches that were manufactured after February 1998 to contain a new blocking feature called the V-chip. Congress also required the television industry to develop a new rating system to work alongside the chip. The goal was to allow parents better control over what type of programming their children were able to view. The TV industry had lobbied hard against the V-chip, but once the law was passed quickly formed a committee to develop the required labeling plan. It proposed six age-based categories, from TV-Y, which was appropriate for all children, to TV-M, which contained mature themes, profanity, graphic violence, and explicit sexual content. Comments were solicited from the public, and the Senate held hearings to debate the proposal. Almost no one seemed pleased, as some asserted it went too far and others not far enough. After much publicity, the committee announced a new plan, with a V label for violence, S for sex, L for "coarse language," and D for "suggestive dialogue. This was combined with the other labels, so a show with "crude indecent language" would receive a rating of TV-MA-L, but if it featured "strong, coarse language" it would be rated TV-14-L, or suitable for ages 14 and up (Heins, 2001, p. 196). News and sports television were exempt from the labeling.

Many argue that ratings will have little effect.

> TV ratings, like movie ratings, will push programming in two oddly contrary directions. On the one hand, ratings have a 'forbidden fruit' effect. The quest for adventuresome (especially teenage) audiences will cause some producers to *add* sexual or violent content, for what self-respecting adolescent wants to watch a TV-Y-rated show? On the other hand, advertisers will be reluctant to support programs with TV-M, V, S, L, or D labels. Less advertising means less revenue, which in turn means less likelihood that the show will survive—unless, of course, its content is changed. (Heins, 2001, p. 197)

Data show that the effects of consuming violent television are both short and long term. A longitudinal study followed up on 557 youth ages six to nine from a 1977 Chicago study in an attempt to ascertain the long-term effects of exposure to violent media. They reinterviewed 329 of the participants who were then in their mid-twenties. They found a clear connection between childhood viewing of violent media and aggressive adult behavior, in particular against women. Men who were "high TV violence viewers" as children were more likely to have pushed, grabbed, or shoved their spouses; to have responded to an insult with physical aggression; to have had a traffic violation; and to have been arrested—more than three times more often than those who were not heavy viewers. Similarly, women who were high TV violence viewers were more likely to have thrown something at their spouse; to have pushed, shoved, beaten, or choked someone in anger; to have a traffic violation; and to have committed a criminal act. The reported rate of punching, choking, or beating another adult was four times higher among high-TV-violence-viewing women than other women—a startling statistic (Huesmann, Titus, Podolski, & Eron, 2003).

Further Reading

Delo, C. 2013. "U.S. Adults Now Spending More Time on Digital Devices Than Watching TV." *Adage*, August 1. http://adage.com/article/digital/americans-spend-time-digital-devices-tv/243414/

Durham. M. G. 2008. *The Lolita Effect*. Woodstock, NY: Overlook Press.

Grossman, D., & DeGaetano, G. 2014. *Stop Teaching Our Kids to Kill: A Call to Action against TV, Movie, & Video Game Violence*. New York: Harmony.

Heins, M. 2001. *Not in Front of the Children: "Indecency," Censorship, and the Innocence of Youth*. New York: Hill & Wang.

Huesmann, L., Titus, J., Podolski, C., & Eron, L. 2003. "Longitudinal Relations between Children's Exposure to TV Violence and Their Aggressive and Violent Behavior in Young Adulthood: 1977–1992." *Developmental Psychology, 39*(2): 201–21.

Orr, C. 2015. "Why Does *Game of Thrones* Feature So Much Sexual Violence?" *The Atlantic*, June 17. https://www.theatlantic.com/entertainment/archive/2015/06/game-of-thrones-sexual-violence/396191

Rosenberg, A. 2016. "How Much Violence Is Too Much on 'Game of Thrones?'" *The Washington Post*, May 3. https://www.washingtonpost.com/news/act-four/wp/2016/05/03/how-much-violence-is-too-much-on-game-of-thrones/?utm_term=.19712209d08f

University of California. (1998). National Television Violence Study Volume Three, Executive Summary. Retrieved August 1, 2018 from www.academia.edu/944389/National_Television_Violence_Study_Executive_Summary_Editor_University_Of-California_Santa_Barbara_

Wilson, B., Colvin, C., & Smith, S. 2002. "Engaging in Violence on American Television: A Comparison of Child, Teen and Adult Perpetrators." *Journal of Communication, 52*(1), 36–60.

American Horror Story

American Horror Story (AHS) (2011–) is the widely successful anthology series featured on the FX network created by directors Brad Falchuk and Ryan Murphy. *AHS* has catalogued all of the horror genre's classic aspects and added some of its own. The show incorporates many sexual, dark, and at times humorous tones featuring mysterious twists and psychopathic characters. *AHS* has become increasingly popular with its gothic undertones and violent plotlines, bringing unprecedented ratings for the FX network.

The first season, *Murder House*, chronicles the life of the Harmon family, Ben (Dylan McDermott), Vivian (Connie Britton), and Violet (Taissa Farmiga). Upon the patriarch's discovered affair with a student and his wife's untimely miscarriage, the family moves across the country in search of a fresh start. The Harmons choose a pre-war gothic-style mansion in the valley of Los Angeles. Deeper in the season, they discover that the house is haunted by the souls of the previous owners, all of whom died inside its walls, trapped in the house for eternity. Violet, Vivian and Ben's daughter, falls into a relationship with one of the deceased denizens of the house, Tate (Evan Peters). Later in the show it becomes known that he was killed 20 years prior by police after committing a school shooting. Violet eventually dies from an overdose of prescription medicine, leaving viewers unaware until at least three episodes after, with her parents being murdered by ghosts shortly thereafter.

The following seasons include *Asylum, Coven, Freak Show, Hotel,* and the most recent season, *Roanoke. Asylum* follows the story of a journalist in 1960s Massachusetts who is admitted into a hospital for the criminally insane. Two of the major plotlines involve a serial killer who skins his female victims and an ex-Nazi doctor who performs gruesome scientific experiments on humans. *Coven* chronicles a group of young witches in modern-day New Orleans. This series incorporates actual historical characters such as Delphine LaLaurie (1780–1849), the 19th-century New Orleans socialite known for her grisly murders of multiple slaves. The next season, *Freak Show,* takes place in Florida in 1952 and features characters based on actual, historical performers in freak shows. This season follows the trials of each performer working in the show as well as a side story involving a murderous clown. *Hotel*, the fifth installment in the anthology, was intended to be the most sinister chapter of the show by Murphy and Falchuk. The inspiration came from actual hotels in the Los Angeles area where eerie events are reported to have taken place. This season comes with two murderous plotlines in the guise of a killer who chooses victims based on biblical passages and another who stalks the hotel with a drill bit sex toy. The most recent season, *Roanoke,* is presented in the form of a documentary, telling the fictional story of a couple who moved to the notoriously mysterious island of Roanoke. One plotline with historical reference in the latest season is that of two killer nurses. The characters are based on real murders committed by two caretakers who were also lovers in the Alpine Manor Nursing home during the late 1980s. This season kept up with the show's legacy of high ratings, with a total of 5.14 million viewers on the season premiere. *Roanoke* also follows in the violent footsteps of previous seasons with the first episode depicting a ritualistic murder in the woods and an angry mob wielding knives and torches.

The show is known is for its boundary-pushing gore and psychosexual subject matter. The show's critics center their complaints around the idea that it relies too heavily on shock value. One of the most frequent complaints from viewers is the renewed presence of sexual assault in every season to date. Each anthology involves either rape or some kind of sexual assault woven into the plotline. The first instance of rape appears in *Murder House*, with a scene in which Vivien believes she is having sex with her husband in a masked suit but it is later revealed it was the ghost of Tate Langdon. *Asylum* also revives the subject with Lana Winters (Sarah Paulson) becoming pregnant through rape after she is held captive by the serial killer Bloody Face (Dylan McDermott). The following season details a more realistic and frequently seen form of sexual assault. In the first episode of *Coven*, multiple men at a fraternity party rape Madison (Emma Roberts).

With episodes that are consistently gory, many have questioned the show's place on cable television. Even one of the show's reigning stars, Evan Peters, has admitted to becoming upset by the violent subject matter. Ryan Murphy has responded that not all of the content is senseless violence but that there are underlying themes to most of it. For example, the rape scene in season 5 that many voiced their disturbance over was a metaphor for the violent handle addiction has on a person's life. Each season has its own overarching theme that goes beyond serial killers and witches. *Murder House* touches on infidelity and betrayal. *Asylum* explores the theme of sanity and mental illness. The theme of *Coven* is oppression, often coinciding with race. *Freak Show* is about physical appearance and deception.

Despite any negative opinions of the show, its success since premiering is undeniable. The show has been nominated for over 200 awards and has won 59. The premiere of *American Horror Story* brought FX its highest viewer ratings for any show premiere in the history of the network. After five seasons of tremendous success, the show struck a deal with Universal Studio's *Halloween Horror Nights* to include an exhibit based on multiple seasons of the show.

As with *AHS,* cable television shows like *The Walking Dead* and *True Blood* are taking TV violence to new limits. Although many of these shows receive negative feedback for their frequent use of violence, this genre of cinematic gore and horror continues to gain viewers at staggering rates. With media companies earning the most profit off of this violent entertainment, it is no surprise that America continues to see more programs like this being produced and marketed. The biggest concern about shows like *American Horror Story* is the effect and possible desensitization of the subject matter to children and teens. The show has a target audience of people aged 18 to 25, but the fan base has proven to include viewers as young as 14. Throughout all of the reviews, negative and positive, *American Horror Story* has served as a landmark for the horror genre by delivering it to cable television. Despite any public opinion, ratings indicate that neither the show nor its violent content will be leaving America's televisions anytime in the near future.

Laura L. Finley

See also: Buffy the Vampire Slayer; *Dexter*; *Law & Order*; Nollywood; Rape Films; *Walking Dead, The*

Further Reading

Boboltz, S. 2016. "The Real Horror Story Behind Those 'American Horror Story' Killer Nurses." *The Huffington Post*, September 22. https://www.huffingtonpost.com/entry /alpine-manor-murders-american-horror-story-nurses_us_57e34623e4b0e28b 2b5246aa

Myrick, T. 2014. "The Horror of Sexual Violence: The Representations of Rape in American Horror Story." (Master's thesis). Salt Lake City: The University of Utah.

Snetiker, M. 2016. "'American Horror Story': Inside the New Maze at Universal Halloween Horror Nights." *Entertainment Weekly*, September 14. http://ew.com/article/2016 /09/14/american-horror-story-maze-universal-halloween-horror-nights/

Anime

Anime, a cartoonish style of popular culture that originated in Japan, often features sex, violence, and death. It has become a global phenomenon, despite criticism of its violence and sexism, and it became popular in the United States in the 1980s. The United Nations even proposed bans on Japanese media in 2016, including anime, manga, and video games, which it says depicts sexual violence against women.

Anime television shows feature significant amounts violence, as described by a *New York Times* contributor: "A pug-nosed thug kicks in an elderly storekeeper's face. Then he punches a young heroine in the eye and cracks her in the small of the back with a heavy bar stool. Her limp frame collapses to the ground as he stands over her with his gun drawn and pointed at her head" (Rutenberg, 2001). Shows featuring this kind of violence have aired on the WB, Fox, and the Cartoon Channel. Proponents maintain that because Japan, where many of these ideas originate, has little violent crime, there is no problem with airing such shows, even on channels marketed to young people.

Critics have contended that the depiction of women in anime is not without female representation, and to ban it would do great harm to women who work in the field. As one female artist explained,

> There is nothing to be gained from regulating fictional sexual violence. However, while you're trying to fix the rights of fictional characters, you're leaving the human rights of real women in the real world left to rot. As well, in Japan, the entire reason we have a media genre such as manga that developed to take on themes such as the sexual exploitation of women came from an attitude to tolerate "drinking the pure and the dirty without prejudice." It's because we had the freedom to express our views and with that to express the view of a world of humans that live and die, that there are pure and wonderful things and dirty and nasty things mixed with each other. (Barder, 2016)

Anime has influenced many films that are popular in the United States, including *Ghost in the Shell* (2017), which starred Scarlett Johansson. Critics expressed concern not just at the violence of the story but that a white woman was cast as the lead.

In 2016, Pokémon Go, a game based on an anime show, swept the nation, as users sought to collect virtual items. Although many had a good time doing so, it was not without problems, as at least one player found a dead body and others were targeted for armed robberies. It was not the first time that the craze resulted in violence, as a girl was allegedly stabbed to death in New York in 1999 over Pokémon trading cards. Principals in some schools banned the trading of Pokémon cards, as they inevitably left out some students and resulted in verbal or physical altercations. Additionally, the animal rights group People for the Ethical Treatment of Animals (PETA) argues that Pokémon glorifies fights against animals.

In 2015, China's Ministry of Culture announced that it would be punishing Japanese firms that hosted anime, calling it vulgar and denouncing it for promoting terrorism. In particular, the ministry noted *Blood-C,* a series that featured a beheading scene, as well as *High School of the Dead,* a show about teens surviving a zombie apocalypse (Kelion, 2015).

Laura L. Finley

See also: Japanese Films; *Ren & Stimpy Show, The*; *South Park*

Further Reading

Barder, O. 2016. "Japanese Response to UN Proposed Ban for Media Depicting Sexual Violence Is Cogent and Sane." *Forbes*, March 3. https://www.forbes.com/sites/olliebarder/2016/03/03/japanese-response-to-un-proposed-ban-for-media-depicting-sexual-violence-is-cogent-and-sane/#1b497af05b3e

Borrelli, C. 2002. "Everything Anime—Slowly But Surely, the Japanese Style of Animation Is Gaining a Foothold in America." *The Blade*, October 13, p. B6.

Brenner, E. 2007. *Understanding Manga and Anime.* Westport, CT: Libraries Unlimited.

Chambers, S. 2012. "Anime: From Cult Following to Pop Culture Phenomenon." *The Elon Journal of Undergraduate Research in Communications, 3*(2): 94–101.

Kelion, L. 2015. "China Cracks Down on Violent Anime Online Cartoons." *BBC,* April 1. http://www.bbc.com/news/technology-32149754

Rothman, L. 2016. "Parents Have Long Feared that Pokémon Is Bad for Kids." *Time,* July 11. http://time.com/4401041/pokemon-1999-time-magazine-cover

Rudell, C. 2013. "Cutting Edge: Violence and Body Horror in Anime." In *Controversial Images: Media Representations on the Edge,* edited by F. Attwood, V. Campbell, I. Hunter, & S. Lockyer, 157–69. London: Palgrave Macmillan.

Rutenberg, J. 2001. "Violence Finds a Niche in Children's Cartoons." *The New York Times,* January 21. http://www.nytimes.com/2001/01/28/us/violence-finds-a-niche-in-children-s-cartoons.html

Truong, A. 2016. "You Realize Pokémon Is Basically Animal Cruelty, Right?" *Quartz,* July 20. https://qz.com/736945/you-realize-pokemon-is-basically-animal-cruelty-right

Breaking Bad

Breaking Bad (2008–2013) first aired on *AMC* in September 2008. It is a crime drama television series created and produced by Vince Gilligan. The title of the series comes from a Southern colloquialism meaning to raise hell. Gilligan's intention with the series was that the hero would become the villain. He claimed that "[t]elevision is historically good at keeping its characters in a self-imposed stasis so that shows can go on for years or even decades" (Nelson, 2012). He aimed to change the main character, Walter White (Bryan Cranston), from a soft, goofy character to someone well respected like Scarface. Depicting White as relatable to almost every individual who longs to attain the American Dream has made the series of great interest to viewers. It was among the most popular cable shows on American television and has received numerous awards. Bryan Cranston won the Primetime Emmy Award for Outstanding Lead Actor in a Drama Series four times. In 2013, *Breaking Bad* entered the Guinness World Records as the most critically acclaimed show of all time.

Walter White is a middle-aged high school chemistry teacher who has been diagnosed with inoperable lung cancer. A graduate of the California Institute of Technology, Walt was once a promising chemist who co-owned the company Gray Matter Technologies with his close friend Elliot Schwartz (Adam Godley) and Walt's then-girlfriend Gretchen (Jessica Hecht). Walt left Gray Matter not long after its opening, selling his shares for $5,000. He then moved to Albuquerque, New Mexico, where he became a high school chemistry teacher. Soon after, the company made a fortune from research that he had contributed to and became a billion-dollar entity. The series begins on White's 50th birthday when he is diagnosed with stage IIIA lung cancer. Walt is angry about both things.

Walter has a nuclear family, consisting of his wife, Skyler (Anna Gunn), and two children, Walter Jr. (R. J. Mitte) and Holly (Elanor Anne Wenrich). Walter Jr. has cerebral palsy. In an effort to secure his family's financial future, Walter begins producing and selling crystallized methamphetamine, with the help of one of his former students, Jesse Pinkman (Aaron Paul). Also featured in the show is Skyler's sister, Marie Schrader (Betsy Brandt), and her husband Hank (Dean Norris), who is a Drug Enforcement Administration (DEA) agent. Walter hires a lawyer, Saul Goodman (Bob Odenkirk), who turns him onto private investigator and fixer Mike Ehrmantraut (Jonathan Banks), and later drug kingpin Gus Fring (Giancarlo Esposito).

Vince Gilligan has said that he intended to show that there are repercussions for our actions. An individual who starts off simply becomes a drug lord. What unfolds are the problems that come along with the dangerous path Walter has chosen. He makes many choices that affect not only him, but his loved ones as well. This is displayed very graphically in the show. *Breaking Bad* shows characters who are very aware of the consequences of their actions as they weigh the cost versus benefits. Gilligan said that the underlying humanity is very present, even when the protagonist is making the most devious and terrible decisions. He claims that humanity is something that must be shown in order to make the show relatable. Proponents say that, instead of glamorizing violence, *Breaking Bad* very much shows its short- and long-term effects.

In the pilot episode, Walter murders a man and then comes up with a plan to get rid of the body with hydrochloric acid. In Episode Six of Season One, Jesse gets beaten by Tuco Salamanca (Raymond Cruz). Walter tracks down Salamanca and blows up his home. He later watches Jesse's girlfriend Jane (Krysten Ritter) die horribly of an overdose and does nothing to help in season two. Also in season two, viewers see a tortoise walking with a man's severed head on it. Minutes later, the head explodes, sending body parts flying across the screen and killing two DEA agents. These are just a few of the violent scenes depicted throughout the show.

Walter acts violently toward Skyler in several episodes. In season two, he yanks down her underwear and slams her into the refrigerator. Walter Jr. comes home to find a smear of makeup on the refrigerator and the kitchen in disarray, implying that Walter raped his wife. Skyler says that Walter should not take his anger out on her, but nothing else is said and Walter never apologizes. In season five, he poisons Lydia (Laura Fraser) with ricin.

Although Walter is the primary perpetrator, occasionally the other characters use violence as well. Jesse ends up killing a chemist in season three so that he can prevent the man from murdering Walter. In season two, Jesse's friend Combo (Rodney Rush) gets killed by an 11-year-old on a bike as part of a turf war.

Criticism of the show grew when they began making action figures that portrayed Walter with a gun in his hand and selling them in *Toys R' Us*. The mothers who protested against it also claimed that the figures had detachable sacks of fake meth. This was seen as a dangerous deviation from the store's family-friendly values. Oscar-winning director Oliver Stone denounced the violence in *Breaking Bad* and said that if it had been a movie it would have been laughable. He said it was not realistic and claimed that such fantastical depictions of violence serve to normalize it for viewers.

Chelsea Wagner

See also: Hill Street Blues; Mad Men; Mexican Crime Novels; *Miami Vice;* Narcocorridos; *Sopranos, The; 21 Jump Street; Walking Dead, The*

Further Reading

Anonymous. 2013. "The 30 Most Jaw-Droppingly Shocking Moments from Every Season of 'Breaking Bad.'" *Business Insider,* September 20. http://www.businessinsider .com/most-shocking-breaking-bad-moments-2013-9#20-walts-need-for-speed -killing-spree-11

Gilligan, V. 2013. "'Breaking Bad' Illustrates the Consequences of Violence." *Variety,* January 18. http://variety.com/2013/voices/opinion/gilligan-2444

Nelson, E. 2012. "Vince Gilligan: I've Never Googled 'Breaking Bad.'" *Salon*, July 23. https://www.salon.com/2012/07/23/vince_gilligan_ive_never_googled_breaking _bad

O' Brien, L. 2013. "Oliver Stone Slams Breaking Bad's 'Ridiculous' Violence and Labels the Series Finale a 'Joke.'" *The Independent,* October 9. http://www.independent .co.uk/arts-entertainment/tv/news/oliver-stone-slams-breaking-bads-ridiculous -violence-and-labels-the-series-finale-a-joke-8868968.html

Wilder, A. 2013. "The Forgotten Rape of Skyler White." *Huffington Post,* September 20. http://www.huffingtonpost.com/alice-wilder/the-forgotten-rape-of-sky_b_4013 319.html

British Television

British media is known to be somewhat more open to sexuality than that in the United States; British television tends to show less violence but perhaps more sexuality than U.S. television.

A controversial BBC1 drama series, *Ripper Street,* is a re-imagination of the serial killings by the person known as Jack the Ripper in the late 1880s. An Inspector, Edmund Reid, and his two friends seek the killer, who is after largely female characters who are prostitutes. The opening episode featured the apprehension of a killer who was essentially making a snuff film about his work. Some say this is an indication that the BBC is open to more violence in television dramas. They also cite an episode on BBC2's drama *Line of Duty* in which a 13-year-old is tortured. Research by Ofcom found that a third of British television viewers believe that there is too much violence and cursing on television programs. Yet such violence is not entirely new, as 10 years prior BBC1 showed an episode of *Spooks* in which a woman's head was dunked into a sizzling hot fryer. Despite complaints, the show went on to be one of the most successful drama series in BBC history. *Hunted,* a follow-up to *Spooks,* about a private investigator, featured shootings, fighting, and gory killings, including one scene in which a character is murdered by having a syringe stabbed into his eyeball.

BBC1 also airs the show *Apple Tree Yard,* which features a scientist, Yvonne, who is involved in a steamy affair that is fairly graphically depicted. She is also raped by a colleague at a work party. Another show, *Call the Midwife,* featured a pregnant woman being pinned against a wall, pushed to the floor, and having a cigarette stubbed out on her chest by her husband. The series *Sherlock* showed a character being shot, a secret agent being tortured, and a plot to drown a child.

Game of Thrones, the popular HBO series, is also one of the most widely viewed in Great Britain.

A series on ITV, *Liar*, focuses on rape and addresses real issues faced by victims, according to Katie Russell, a spokesperson for Rape Crisis England and Wales. After initially being concerned that the show would reinforce myths about rape, she said the show was well researched and praised the depiction of the two police characters who treat the victim, Laura, with empathy and respect. Others expressed concern that it is "turning real-life horror into a cheap thrill." Fay Maxted, CEO of The Survivors Trust, said "There is a real risk the programme will deter victims from coming forward." The show's writers, Harry and Jack Williams, have said they are attempting to take on stereotypes about rape and that they did extensive research (Saunders, 2017).

Critics also contend that, like in the United States, television programs in Great Britain overrepresent the amount of murder. The concern is that shows like *Midsomer Murders*, which show an estimated murder rate of 32 per million, far higher than that of England and Wales, create dangerous stereotypes among viewers (Townsend, 2013).

The BBC's controller of dramatic programming, Ben Stephenson, said that the shows are not shocking and are carefully produced to be emotionally impactful, not gratuitous. He said, "I think that conflict and correcting life's wrongs are at the heart of drama. Different dramas require different levels of violence." And although these series are popular, they are not usually ranked in the top 10 in terms of viewership (Dowell, 2012).

Surveys show that British viewers are somewhat concerned about the amount of sex and violence in television programming. The survey found 20 percent had been offended by something they had watched the previous year, with older adults expressing more concerns about sex, bad language, and violence. Men were more supportive of both violent and sexually explicit material. In all, 80 percent supported some type of regulation (Four in Ten Adults . . . , 2015).

Laura L. Finley

See also: Charlie's Angels; Cop Films; *Dexter*; *Game of Thrones*; *Hill Street Blues*; *Law & Order*; Soccer/Football Hooligans; Sports on Television; *21 Jump Street*

Further Reading

Anonymous. 2015. "Four in Ten Adults Say 'Too Much' Violence on TV." *BBC*, May 19. http://www.bbc.com/news/entertainment-arts-32802268

Dowell, B. 2012. "Violence in TV Drama: The Brutal Truth." *The Guardian*, December 31. https://www.theguardian.com/tv-and-radio/tvandradioblog/2012/dec/31/violence -tv-drama-ripper-street

Lambert, L. 2017. "Whatever Happened to Cosy Sunday Nights on the BBC? Domestic Violence, Rape, and Adultery Punctuate Call the Midwife and Apple Tree Yard." *Daily Mail*, January 22. http://www.dailymail.co.uk/tvshowbiz/article-4146164 /Domestic-violence-rape-adultery-BBC.html

Saunders, T. 2017. "Liar: Is the ITV Drama's Handling of Rape Damaging to Victims?" *The Telegraph*, September 22. http://www.telegraph.co.uk/tv/0/liar-itv-dramas -handling-rape-damaging-victims

Townsend, L. 2013. "How Unrealistic Is Murder on Television?" *BBC*, January 16. http://www.bbc.com/news/magazine-20910859

Buffy the Vampire Slayer

Buffy the Vampire Slayer ran on the WB for seven seasons with 144 episodes between 1997 and 2003. It featured Sarah Michelle Gellar as Buffy, an average teenage girl who by night fights the monsters that have invaded her town, Sunnydale, California. The town has a "hellmouth" which attracts supernatural villains (such as vampires, demons, and monsters). Director Joss Whedon has said he created *Buffy* to be an icon, not just a television show, and that the main character was to be a model of female empowerment. It was ranked by Rob Sheffield of *Rolling Stone* as the 38th best show of all-time. *Buffy*, along with other critically acclaimed series like *The X-Files*, *Twin Peaks*, and later, *The Sopranos*, has been examined from numerous scholarly traditions. Academics have found the series, which is a cult classic, to be replete with allegory and to offer important examination into various social issues. Hundreds of books and articles have been written about *Buffy*, and the series has spawned an academic journal and a conference called Slayage. The show won two Emmy Awards in 1998 for Outstanding Makeup and Outstanding Music Composition.

Douglas Kellner, a professor at UCLA, has argued that popular television is useful for expressing the subconscious fears and fantasies of a society. Kellner has said that *Buffy* is an especially good example in that its fantasy elements provide "access to social problems and issues and hopes and anxieties that are often not articulated in more 'realist' cultural forms," like sitcoms or police dramas (Kellner, n.d.). In *Buffy*, monsters represent societal differences and threats. Vampires are sexual predators, werewolves represent bodily forces out of control, and witches are used to address female power and critique how sexuality is viewed as threatening. Buffy and her friends fight the oppression we face in real life. Each season there was a new primary villain, referred to as "The Big Bad." The show is also known for its plot twists that helped viewers better understand the main characters. They make bad choices, have difficult relationships, and even turn evil when they have suffered harm, rather than other fantasy shows that depict evil as being due to magic spells. Despite the dark themes, fans loved its humor. In the episode "Seeing Red," Warren, a tech-geek, chooses to become a villain because he is a disgruntled loner. He forms "The Trio," a group intent on killing Buffy and allowing the dark forces to take over Sunnydale. Unlike the other villains in the show, the members of this group are all human. When Warren gets a gun and shows up to murder Buffy, he fails but ends up murdering another young woman.

One controversy about the show involved the pulling of a season finale that was scheduled to air on May 25, 1999. The WB pulled the show, which was about a mayor who turned into a giant serpent and attacked students at the fictitious Sunnydale High commencement ceremony, because of high school shootings that occurred just before that in Colorado and Georgia. Another episode, "Earshot," depicts a teen named Jonathon assembling a rifle in the clock tower of his school, and Buffy can hear him proclaiming that he will kill everyone. She manages to talk him into handing over the gun. Critics have noted that whereas in some episodes *Buffy* critiqued rape culture, in other episodes it normalized nonconsensual and coercive sexual interactions. Further, critics note that many of the relationships depicted in the show are dangerously abusive. In an episode called "Dead Things," The Trio create a magical equivalent of a date-rape drug and they intend to use their "Cerebral Dampener" to, as Warren explains, "make any woman we desire our willing sex slave" (Lenk & Lynch, 2015, p. 4). It also depicts the sexual assault of two male characters, which is quite unusual in popular culture.

Psychologist Christopher Ferguson found that capable female role models like Buffy help reduce the negative effects of sexually violent media, which he calls "The Buffy Effect." Ferguson asked 150 college students to watch one of three types of television shows. One featured slasher-type sexual violence against weak female characters; one showed sexual violence against strong, independent female characters like Buffy; and the third did not include sexual violence. Ferguson found that men who watched the slasher film reported more sexist beliefs than did those who watched *Buffy* or a similar type of show. The men who watched the sexual violence in *Buffy*-type shows registered higher levels of anxiety, and the women in the study registered the highest anxiety levels when they were watching this type of sexual violence. Ferguson did not measure the students' pre-existing sexist attitudes, however.

Laura L. Finley

See also: American Horror Story; Broadway Musicals; *Charlie's Angels*; *Crucible, The*; Nollywood; *Twilight* Saga, The

Further Reading

Buffy World. http://www.buffyworld.com

Carman, J. 1999. "'Buffy the Vampire Slayer' Finale Postponed Because of School Violence." *SFGate,* May 25. http://www.sfgate.com/entertainment/article/Buffy-the-Vampire-Slayer-Finale-Postponed-2929133.php

Ginn, S. 2012. *Power and Control in the Television Worlds of Joss Whedon.* Jefferson, NC: McFarland.

Hess, A. 2012. "Is Sexual Violence on TV OK If the Heroine Is Tough?" *Slate,* August 21. http://www.slate.com/blogs/xx_factor/2012/08/31/sex_and_violence_on_tv_does_buffy_the_vampire_slayer_solve_the_problem_.html

Kellner, D. n.d. "Buffy the Vampire Slayer as Allegory: A Diagnostic Critique." Faculty paper. Los Angeles: UCLA.

Lenk, L., & Lynch, D. 2015. "'Yes Men?' Rape Myths and Gender Stereotypes in Buffy the Vampire Slayer and Marvel's Agents of S.H.I.E.L.D." *Watcher Junior, 8*(2), 1–15.

Schwab, K. 2015. "The Rise of Buffy Studies." *The Atlantic,* October 1. https://www.theatlantic.com/entertainment/archive/2015/10/the-rise-of-buffy-studies/407020

Sheffield, R. 2016. "100 Greatest TV Shows of All Time." *Rolling Stone,* September 21. http://www.rollingstone.com/tv/lists/100-greatest-tv-shows-of-all-time-w439520/buffy-the-vampire-slayer-w439599

Charlie's Angels

Charlie's Angels is an American crime television series written by Ivan Goff and Ben Roberts and produced by Aaron Spelling and Leonard Goldberg. The original series aired on ABC from September 22, 1976, to June 24, 1981, producing a total of five seasons containing 110 episodes. The plot of this crime-fighting series highlights the lives of three beautiful women working in a private detective agency in Los Angeles, California. Kate Jackson, Farrah Fawcett-Majors, and Jaclyn Smith star as the three women: Sabrina Duncan, Jill Munroe, and Kelly Garrett, respectively. John Bosley (David Doyle) arranges their investigations and provides support. Cheryl Ladd joined the cast in season two as Kris Munroe, another Angel. Having the female sex-symbol of that era, Farah Fawcett, as the lead role, as well as a cast of beautiful women, resulted in feminist critics labelling the series "Jiggle TV" (Capretto, 2016). Despite mixed reviews from critics and a reputation for emphasizing the sex appeal of the female leads *Charlie's Angels* continues to maintain its pop-culture fan base through television series and film remakes. Although the women investigated violent crimes in many episodes, the series did not really show the violence or its effects.

Leonard Goldberg began to manifest the idea for the series three years previously. His idea was for a show that would be a cross between *The Avengers* and *Honey West*, a brief drama from the 1960s about a female private eye detective. Goff and Roberts had first titled the series *The Alley Cats* in which the three females would live among the alleys and wear whips and chains. After much debate about the representation of the females, the title was changed from "Cats" to "Angels" and the series was then renamed *Harry's Angels*. However, the title was dropped when ABC did not want to create conflict with the series *Harry O,* which was airing at the time, and was thus changed to its renowned title *Charlie's Angels.*

The show was popular for its fashion and for taking on issues important in the 1970s. In one episode, Jill joins a roller derby team to investigate a suspicious death that occurred during a match. Roller derby was very popular at that time. Also popular was Icecapades, an ice-skating show, and in one episode Kelly and Kris become skaters to investigate a plot to kill some Arab dignitaries. Another episode shows Jill and Kelly posing as nurses to investigate a string of sexual assaults of nurses at a hospital. They pose as cheerleaders in another episode in order to root out what is happening with two cheerleaders who have gone missing.

Due to the fact that the series aired during the feminist movement in the 1970s, there was much controversy about whether it promoted female exploitation and about its depiction of female sexuality in the media. These images began to have a negative effect on adolescent girls' outlook on their body and sexuality, with an increase in aggressiveness. Research has shown that female criminal justice professionals tend to be portrayed as young, white, single, nurturing, affectionate, and sexually attractive (DeTardo-Bora, 2009).

Ladd responded to these criticisms: "Nobody thinks it's Shakespeare, [but] at the same time, we were very inspirational to a lot of young women. . . . Young women . . . would write in and say, 'I want to be like you. I'm going to be a cop when I grow up'—taking chances to be something else other than the 'acceptable' schoolteacher or secretary" (Capretto, 2016). Jaclyn Smith agrees, arguing that it was progressive at the time to show three financially independent, career women. Further, she maintains that the women all developed deep friendships that were obvious in the closeness of their characters (Gomez & Stone, 2016).

A 2000 movie of the same name featured Drew Barrymore, Cameron Diaz, and Lucy Liu as the Angels. Roger Ebert (2000) referred to it as "eye candy for the blind."

A reboot of the movie began shooting in winter 2018 and is supposed to air in 2019. It stars Kristen Stewart and Lupita Nyong'o. Elizabeth Banks is set to direct the series (Guthrie, 2017).

Laura L. Finley

See also: British Television; *Buffy the Vampire Slayer*; Cop Films; *Law & Order*

Further Reading

Capretto, L. 2016. "The Criticism that 'Irritated the Crap' Out of This 'Charlie's Angels Star.'" *Huffington Post,* September 22. https://www.huffingtonpost.com/entry /charlies-angels-criticism_us_57e2f904e4b08d73b82f5914

DeTardo-Bora, K. 2009. "Criminal Justice 'Hollywood Style': How Women in Criminal Justice Professions Are Depicted in Prime-Time Crime Dramas." *Women and Criminal Justice, 19*(2), 153–68.

Ebert, R. 2000. "Charlie's Angels." Roger Ebert, November 3. https://www.rogerebert.com /reviews/charlies-angels-2000

Gomez, P., & Stone, N. 2016. "Charlie's Angels Turns 40: Jaclyn Smith Reflects on the 'Groundbreaking' Series that Had a $20,000 per Episode Wardrobe Budget." *People,* September 22. http://people.com/tv/charlies-angels-turns-40-jaclyn-smith -reflects-on-groundbreaking-series

Guthrie, S. 2017. "Charlie's Angels Movie to Be Rebooted with Big Names." *The New Daily,* October 3. https://thenewdaily.com.au/entertainment/movies/2017/10/03 /charlies-angels-reboot-cast

Murray, N. 2012. "What Was the Quintessential Charlie's Angels Undercover Guise?" *AV Club*, October 3. https://tv.avclub.com/what-was-the-quintessential-charlie-s-angels -undercover-1798234314

China Beach

China Beach is a dramatic series that ran on ABC for four seasons, from 1988 to 1991. It is set at an evacuation hospital during the Vietnam War and follows a largely female cast of medics, soldiers, Red Cross volunteers, and civilians. It is based on the book *Home Before Morning,* written in 1983 by a former U.S. Army Nurse, Lynda Van Devanter. Like the book, the TV show follows the main characters when they return to the United States. *China Beach* is one of only two television series set in the Vietnam War.

The base provides triage and emergency surgery for wounded American soldiers who were recently evacuated from Vietnam. As such, *China Beach* shows the atrocities of war. At the same time, the show also documented the personal lives of the main characters and frequently showed them enjoying their rest and recreation (R & R) time. Although it depicted the carnage of war, *China Beach* was also funny, and critics loved its character development. In that way it drew many comparisons to *M*A*S*H*. Importantly, the writers and producers did their research on the Vietnam War and accurately depicted the struggles faced by soldiers and others who returned to a United States that was not always supportive. One of the co-creators, William Broyles, Jr., was himself a Vietnam War veteran. Before each episode the writers, directors, and producers spoke with Vietnam veterans. In particular, the final episode, titled "Hello Goodbye," was intended, according to show representatives, to pay tribute to veterans. Set in 1988 at a 20-year reunion of veterans, it shows the main characters reflecting on their time in the war. Throughout its run, *China Beach* drew attention to issues that affected many soldiers, like post-traumatic stress disorder and the rampant drug and alcohol abuse among those serving in Vietnam (Froula & Takacs, 2016).

Dana Delany, who played the main character, army nurse Lieutenant Colleen McMurphy, was widely lauded for her portrayal of the heavy-drinking "girl next door." Delany won two Emmy awards for her role, which showed her as a dedicated medic who was devastated by the physical and emotional toll of the war. In the final episode, she vividly recalls one soldier who dies, explaining that "there's always one" who stays with you (Froula & Takacs, 2016). Marg Helgenberger, who played K. C. Kolowski, a prostitute serving military leaders, also won an Emmy. Major Lila Garreau, played by Concetta Tomei, is the stern yet caring commanding officer. Although the show was applauded for focusing on females in the war, there were several important male characters. Dr. Dick Richards, played by Robert Picardo, was a wealthy gynecologist who had been drafted into the war, and Private Samuel Beckett, played by Michael Boatman, was the undertaker for the base.

In an interview about the show, Delaney said, "I thought it was quite true to the experience of nurses in Vietnam. I know when we first came out the [real life] nurses were really concerned that they were going to be portrayed as sex bombs in service of the doctors, because honestly, up until that point, nurses often were portrayed that way. I think they were relieved that we took great pains to get it right and listen to their stories, going as far as having real nurses in an episode called *Vets*. . . . Eventually I was part of the whole movement to get The [Vietnam] Women's Memorial up in D.C., because I became close to a lot of the nurses" (Weiner, 2013). Delany also studied the war, and her role inspired her to speak out about some controversial issues, including the United States' usage of Agent Orange, a defoliant that is toxic and has been tied to numerous health effects, including birth defects. She commented, "I think the show did heal some wounds from Vietnam, having it on TV every week. I'm mostly pleased about the vets who came up and said it allowed them to cry and talk about what it meant to be there. I think the series took a lot of chances, and I'm proud of it" (Du Brow, 1991).

Critics noted that advertisements for the show emphasized the attractiveness of the primary characters, arguing that this was not true for shows about males during war. For instance, on the day the show premiered, an advertisement in *The New York Times* depicted Delaney and her love interest, Boonie Lanier, played by Brian Wimmer, with their arms around one another, seemingly enjoying a day at the beach rather than suffering the devastation of war. Sexuality, critics say, was the real emphasis of the show, as depicted not only in the various storylines but also in the filming, which tended to emphasize the women's bodies. Further, critics argue that rather than a progressive, feminist depiction, Delaney's McMurphy reinforced traditional gender role stereotypes (Vuic, 2010).

Laura L. Finley

See also: *M*A*S*H*; North Korean Films; *Rambo* Films; War Films

Further Reading

Burst-Lazarus, R. 2013. "'China Beach': An Appreciation of a Forgotten Quality War Drama Finally Available on DVD.*" Indiewire*, May 23. http://www.indiewire.com /2013/05/china-beach-an-appreciation-of-a-forgotten-quality-war-drama-finally -available-on-dvd-38144

Du Brow, R. 1991. "'China Beach' Puts Star on New Paths." *Los Angeles Times,* May 28. http://articles.latimes.com/1991-05-28/entertainment/ca-2602_1_china-beach

Froula, A., & Takacs, S. 2016. *American Militarism on the Small Screen.* New York: Routledge.

Goodykoontz, B. 2013. "25 Years Later, 'China Beach' Earns Your Respect." *USA Today,* May 28. https://www.usatoday.com/story/news/2013/05/28/television-china-beach /2367887

Vuic, K. 2010. *Officer, Nurse, Woman: The Army Nurse Corps in the Vietnam War.* Baltimore: The Johns Hopkins University Press.

Weiner, D. 2013. "Dana Delaney Looks Back at 'China Beach.'" *ET Online,* May 29. http:// www.etonline.com/tv/134516_Dana_Delany_Looks_Back_at_China_Beach

Dexter

Dexter Morgan is a fictional character that was developed by writer Jeff Lindsey. He was first introduced to people in *Darkly Dreaming Dexter* (2004), a novel about a serial killer who works for the Miami Police Department as a blood analyst. Jeff Lindsey has written eight Dexter novels, the last published in 2015. They are *Darkly Dreaming Dexter, Dearly Devoted Dexter* (2005)*, Dexter in the Dark* (2007)*, Dexter by Design* (2009)*, Dexter Is Delicious* (2010)*, Double Dexter* (2011)*, Dexter's Final Cut* (2013)*,* and *Dexter Is Dead* (2015). Shortly after the first few novels, Dexter Morgan became a household name when millions of people tuned into Showtime's hit series *Dexter* (2006–2013). *Dexter* was based on the original novel and later diverted into its own story. Showtime's *Dexter* features a hero who struggles between his belief system and his pleasure in killing people. He works for law enforcement by day and kills those who escape the law by night. Showtime describes him as a smart, good-looking man with a great sense of humor who is everyone's favorite serial killer. He is the antihero serial killer that viewers want to see succeed.

In the first episode of *Dexter,* the viewer is introduced to a man driving through the streets of Miami on his way to kidnap and murder his next victim. The man driving is Dexter Morgan (Michael C. Hall), and the soon-to-be victim is a pedophile who killed and buried young boys. The next scene cuts to a man walking into his car where Dexter is lying in wait. It is clear to the viewer that this has been methodically planned out when Dexter pulls out a garrote and wraps it around the man's neck, telling him to drive to a secluded area. Once they arrive, they enter a room filled with dead bodies that Dexter excavated. They were the man's victims. Dexter makes his victim admit to his crimes as the man pleas for forgiveness. The man is then seen, naked and wrapped in Saran Wrap, on a table where Dexter slices his face to get a blood sample. After getting the blood sample, Dexter is seen cutting the man's throat with a mini electric saw. Within the first five minutes of the first episode, all of this transpired, leaving the audience knowing that *Dexter* was going to be a violent show where viewers root for a killer.

Throughout the series, the viewer gains much insight into the mind of Dexter. He narrates the story in every episode, confessing to the viewer his deep dark thoughts. Viewers witness him killing rapists, murderers, pedophiles, and other violent criminals who have slipped through the cracks of the criminal justice system.

Dexter imposes his unofficial death sentence upon perpetrators of various social crimes, including a pederast, human traffickers, drug traffickers, arsonists, a neo-Nazi, and corrupt Assistant District Attorney Miguel Prado (played by Jimmy Smits), who seeks to use Dexter to wield greater power. Only in season four does Dexter finally make a mistake, killing a photographer who turns out to be innocent of the murder of his young models.

Aside from watching the serial killer hunt and kill, viewers are also given some understanding as to why Dexter is a killer. At three years old Dexter was found crying in a pool of blood next to his mother's dead body by Officer Harry Morgan (James Remar). Harry decided to adopt Dexter and raise him as his own. Dexter had somewhat of a normal childhood. He was raised by two parents and had a sister, Deborah Morgan (Jennifer Carpenter). Deborah and Dexter have a strong relationship. Not only do they work together (Deborah is police officer), but she truly loves and looks up to Dexter. Throughout the series, she constantly seeks Dexter's advice in every aspect of her life. Dexter knows that Deborah loves him as if they were "real" siblings. He states in season one, episode two that Deborah is the only person who really loves him and that he'd love her too if he was capable of loving. The viewer is never formally introduced to his mother, Doris, as she is deceased (she's only seen in a few flashbacks depicting family outings), but we are introduced to his deceased father through scenes depicting the past and hallucinations Dexter has. These hallucinations typically depict Dexter speaking to his father about the code in killing others. "'The 'Code of Harry' mandates a specific formula for killing people who deserve to die, and its elaborate details also help Dexter avoid detection. The code posits that by eliminating evildoers, Dexter is protecting innocent people and thereby making the world a better and safer place" (Pittman, 2015, p. 174). Harry realized that Dexter was different after discovering dead animals buried in their yard. As a cop, he knew who Dexter was and what he was going to become. In season one, episode three you hear Dexter say that without the Code of Harry, he would've killed innocent people "just to watch the blood flow." One of Harry's conversations with Dexter, while in the hospital, was about remembering the lessons (Code of Harry), as he wasn't going to be able to stop the inevitable (Dexter committing murder). It was in the hospital where Harry and Dexter found his first victim. Harry's nurse was killing her patients, and Harry figured it out. Harry was able to guide Dexter during his first kill, making sure the last lesson was given. Dexter showed up to the nurse's home, covered her entire living room in plastic, and when she walked in he attacked her. He laid her on a table, naked and wrapped in Saran Wrap, and he stabbed her repeatedly, killing her for her sins. Harry was able to live for about a year longer, giving him more time to perfect Dexter's skills.

Dexter describes himself as one who has to fake human interaction and who is hollow inside when it comes to any human emotions. He states that he is a "very neat monster" who uses an intoxicating ritual to kill criminals ("Dexter," 1:1). He names the monster the Dark Passenger that he cannot rid himself of. The only excitement you see from him is when he speaks about the crimes he commits and the crimes he investigates. It is easy to find yourself rooting for Dexter once you realize that he is using his psychopathy to avenge the victims of many criminals. One can't help but feel sorry for Dexter as well, as his disconnect from society could be attributed to witnessing his mother's murder at the age of three.

> Viewers watch the scope and deftness of Dexter's control in the same way audiences would watch a superhero movie. For Dexter—like most screen superheroes of social rescue narratives—carries a wound, a childhood trauma that gives him special powers, at least within the bounds of his own fantasy world, transforming the mild-mannered brother . . . into Miami's dark avenger with a fantasy pseudonym of his very own, the "Dark Defender" (2:5). (Green, 2011, p. 26)

Showtime's *Dexter* has had its fair share of controversy due to the violence it portrays and the fact that several murderers have specifically said that Dexter Morgan has inspired them to kill. In 2008, Mark Twitchell lured two men into his studio under the guise of being part of a movie about a serial killer. He ended up killing one of the men, while the other one escaped. "Twitchell had adopted the persona 'Dexter Morgan' on his Facebook page and made a movie similar to how Dexter operates on the TV show" (Ramsland, 2014). In 2009, Andrew Conley admitted that the show had inspired him to strangle his brother (Ramsland, 2014). He later placed a plastic bag over his brother's head so as to mimic Dexter's ritual. In 2012, Mark Howe stabbed his mother over 53 times with a 12-inch knife. "In court, Howe was described as a recluse who was obsessed with *Dexter*. His profile photo on Facebook was the blood-spattered face of the series character and he'd told a friend he wished he *was* Dexter." Also in 2012, Jessica Lopez strangled a woman "saying that it was as if 'Dexter had spoken directly to me'" (Ramsland, 2014). She had tried to cut the bodies into pieces, mimicking Dexter's ritual, but realized it was harder than she thought and she was afraid that the power tools would make too much noise.

Richard Cibran

See also: American Horror Story; British Television; *Law & Order*; Murder Ballads; Tarantino, Quentin

Further Reading

Anderson, C. A. 2016. "Media Violence Effects on Children, Adolescents and Young Adults." *Health Progress*, 97(4), 59–62.

Bishop, Denis (Producer). 2006–2013. *Dexter*. Hollywood, CA & Miami, FL: Showtime.

Donnelly, Ashley M. 2012. "The New American Hero: Dexter, Serial Killer for the Masses." *Journal of Popular Culture, 45*(1), 15–26.

Green, S. 2011. "Dexter Morgan's Monstrous Origins." *Critical Studies in Television*, 6(1), 22–35.

Lasswell, M. 2009. "Such a Nice Boy Serial Killer: How the TV Series Dexter Glorifies a Murderer." *Commentary, 4*, 77–80.

Pittman, M. 2015. "Thou Shalt Kill . . . Carefully: Secular Religion, the Immanent Frame, and Showtime's Dexter." *Journal of Religion & Popular Culture*, 27(3), 171–85.

Ramsland, Katherine. 2014. "The 'Dexter' Murders." *Psychology Today*, January 18. https://www.psychologytoday.com/blog/shadow-boxing/201401/the-dexter-murders

Showtime. 2016. "Dexter." http://www.sho.com/dexter

Dukes of Hazzard

Dukes of Hazzard is a television action-comedy that aired on CBS from 1979 to 1985. It was inspired by a 1975 movie, *Moonrunners*. Set in the South, in fictional Hazzard County, Georgia, it told the story of cousins Bo and Luke Duke (John Schneider and Tom Wopat, respectively); their cousin, Daisy (Catherine Bach); and their uncle, Jesse (Denver Pyle). The Dukes are "good old boys" who engage in minor mischief but always manage to evade the law, and in particular, the corrupt county commissioner, Boss Hogg (Sorrell Booke), and his inept sheriff, Rosco P. Coltrane (James Best). The Dukes had been in trouble for illegally transporting moonshine and are on probation, which Boss Hogg oversees. Hogg is always upset with the Dukes, who manage to get in the way of his crooked plans to get rich quick. He often tries to frame the Dukes, but because they are essentially happy-go-lucky, the cousins typically end up helping out Boss Hogg. A 2005 film with the same name was released by Warner Brothers but was a box office flop. Different actors (not the originals) played all the main characters, and critics referred to it as "silly, loud and dumb" (Vice, 2005).

The good-natured Dukes do use violence with some regularity and enjoyed frequently blowing things up. Their probation status prohibited them from owning guns, but the two are often depicted with bows and arrows. In 1980, *Dukes of Hazzard* was considered one of the five most violent shows on television by the National Coalition on Television Violence (Fowles, 1999). Producer Gy Waldron said he was inspired to take on the show because at the time, country music represented one sixth of all music record sales but no television programs were aimed at that market. Yet no one really gets hurt in the show, which never depicted blood or death, and most of the violence is toward objects like cars.

Critics expressed concern about the depiction of Daisy Duke, who was usually seen wearing very short blue jean shorts, which came to be known as "Daisy Dukes." Southern white women were often sexualized but were nonsexual, as was Daisy. Although she was to be an object of desire, the show did not depict her as overtly sexual.

One of the controversies about the show was the Dukes' car, which they called "General Lee." The Dukes raced around Hazzard County in the iconic car, and some 150 different models were used over the stunts that were involved. The 1969 Dodge Charger had a Confederate flag emblazoned on the roof. In 2015, TV Land pulled reruns of the show after teenager Dylann Roof killed nine Black people who were worshipping in a church in Charleston, South Carolina. Schneider defended the show, saying, "Labeling anyone who has the flag a 'racist' seems unfair to those who are clearly 'never meanin' no harm" (Stanhope, 2015). Schneider's comments echoed the theme song for the show, which was written and sung by Waylon Jennings. In the same year, Warner Brothers announced that it would stop making toy cars modeled after the General Lee. Critics pointed out that the show's cast was virtually all white and that it had always glorified the "Southern lifestyle," which many saw as racist.

In 2017, Wopat was arrested and charged with groping a 16-year-old castmate in a musical he was appearing in (Anderson, 2017).

Laura L. Finley

See also: Bonnie and Clyde; Lonesome Dove; Western Films

Further Reading

Anderson, T. 2017. "'Dukes of Hazzard' Star Arraigned on Charges of Indecently Assaulting a Teenager." *Boston Globe,* November 10. https://www.bostonglobe.com/metro/2017/11/10/dukes-hazzard-star-arraigned-charges-indecently-assaulting-teenager/GQ0gclyTOzYbqdoFchMegP/story.html

Ennis, J. 2016. "Is 'Dukes of Hazzard' Really Racist?" *Huffington Post*, July 3. https://www.huffingtonpost.com/john-wellington-ennis/is-dukes-of-hazzard-reall_b_7725078.html

Fowles, J. 1999. *The Case for Television Violence.* Thousand Oaks, CA: Sage.

Hofstede, D. 1998. *The Dukes of Hazzard: The Unofficial Companion.* Los Angeles: Renaissance Books.

Jones, G. 2002. *Killing Monsters: Why Children Need Fantasy, Superheroes, and Make-Believe Violence.* New York: Perseus.

Stanhope, K. 2015. "TV Land Pulls Dukes of Hazzard Episodes Amid Confederate Flag Uproar." *Hollywood Reporter,* July 1. http://www.hollywoodreporter.com/news/tv-land-pulls-dukes-hazzard-806265

Vice, J. 2005. "Film Review: Dukes Is Silly, Loud, Dumb, Fun." *Deseret News,* August 5. https://www.deseretnews.com/article/700003917/Dukes-is-silly-loud-dumb-fun.html

Family Guy

The American sitcom *Family Guy* has been one of the most successful television shows, airing since 1999, with a break between 2002 and 2004. The main characters in this sitcom are the Griffins. Peter Griffin, known as the "family guy," is crude, disgusting, and ignorant. Lois Griffin is the stay-at-home wife who cooks, cleans, and attempts to keep the family sane whenever Peter decides to do something he should not be doing. They live in the town of Quahog, Rhode Island, and have three children: Meg Griffin, Chris Griffin, and Stewie Griffin. Meg, who is the oldest, is a complete outcast and gets bullied throughout the show, whether at school or at home by her own family members. Chris is completely lost when it comes to dealing with the opposite sex, awkward and clueless the majority of the time. Stewie, although a baby, speaks the most intellectually of them all but still acts like a baby in certain situations. He plots to kill his mother and take over the world. The last member of the Griffin family is the family dog, Brian. Brian is a talking dog, and his role is important because he happens to be the most reasonable and rational member of the family. However, he also acts like a dog and makes mistakes as well.

A few other characters who seem to be important because of their frequent appearances on the show are Peter's friends: Joe, Quagmire, and Cleveland. Joe is a disabled police officer who is confined to a wheelchair, yet has more physical strength than anyone else on the show. Quagmire has an unhealthy sexual life and treats women as objects instead of actual human beings. Cleveland, Peter's only African American friend, appears a few times in the show as the more or less quiet friend.

Family Guy is also known for its catchy and easy to sing-a-long theme song that contradicts the whole purpose of the show. The theme song begins by musing that the only things you see on television and film are sex and violence. It then asks, "but where are those good old-fashioned values, on which we used to rely?" Apart from the humor *Family Guy* attempts to portray, it is a show that is known for its unapologetic insults, violence, sex, racism, and fighting. The main forms of violence that are depicted in *Family Guy* are domestic violence, fighting, sexual abuse (including pedophilia), rape, gun violence (including intraracial violence), and bullying.

As mentioned, domestic violence is one of the major forms of violence on the show. In fact, it dedicated a whole episode to domestic violence, which aired on October 30, 2011. Season 10, Episode 3 was named "Screams of Silence: The Story of Brenda Q." Brenda is Quagmire's little sister who had been dating a man named Jeff for years. He was continuously beating her. In this episode, Lois mentions how she is in disbelief that Brenda continues to be in a relationship with Jeff when he beats her, while Peter replies, "Yeah, but *she's* gotten a lot better" (Jefferson, 2011). Peter is implying that Brenda deserves to be beaten and Jeff is just correcting her behavior. The show also critiques the police response to domestic violence. When Quagmire asks Joe if there is anything he can do, Joe replies "Sorry—police policy is that we can't step in until it's been too late" (Jefferson, 2011). This episode, like many others, sheds light on how domestic violence is portrayed as just another life situation.

Another instance of domestic violence and fighting that was portrayed in *Family Guy* was during Season 4, Episode 16. This episode was named "The Courtship of Stewie's Father." Lois brings to Peter's attention the fact that Stewie has been acting up because he does not see his father often. Peter starts to spend more time with Stewie and notices that pain to Lois makes Stewie laugh. With that information, Peter takes it into his own hands, literally, to hit Lois with cans of food, hose her down with water when she is wearing no pants, push her inside the car and then dumps the car in the lake to let her fend for herself. When Peter realizes what he has done he simply says, "Well, I hope she can get out" (MacFarlane, 1999). Ignorant of his wrongdoings, when Lois arrives back, dripping wet, he says "Hey drippy, you're back! What's for dinner?" (MacFarlane, 1999). Domestic violence is laughed at throughout the show.

Sexual abuse and rape is another very common topic that is made fun of frequently on *Family Guy*. According to the Parents Television Council (PTC), "79% of all the sexual violence scenes that aired on *Family Guy* from 2012–2015 has been perpetrated on children and teens" (Oliver, 2015). Also, "every instance of sexual violence that aired on *Family Guy* was delivered in the form of a joke or humorous depiction of rape, statutory rape, molestation or pedophilia" (Oliver, 2015). Examples of this have been found in Seasons 2, 4, and 5. In Season 2, Episode 8, Peter is charged with sexual harassment because of an inappropriate joke he made toward a female co-worker. When accused of sexual harassment his comment was that, "Women are not people, they are devices built by the Lord Jesus Christ for our entertainment" (MacFarlane, 1999). This episode made numerous jokes about women. Also, Season 4, Episode 16 centered on a perverted elderly man, Herbert, who happens to be the Griffins' neighbor. Herbert has a sick, pedophilia crush on Chris Griffin and finds any way to see Chris shirtless or sweaty. Herbert fantasizes about Chris and what his life would be if they were together. This is a classic example of pedophilia in the show. According to *CNSNews*, "Media makers may call what they make 'entertainment', but everything a child sees is actually 'education'. For better or for worse. If they [children] hear jokes about sexual violence, they 'learn' that sexual violence is not much of a problem, not much of a crime, and doesn't really hurt anyone" (Brown, 2015). Another scene from Season 5, Episode 6 focused on abstinence. Lois does not like the fact that Peter has taken a vow to be abstinent, and Lois forces herself onto Peter, raping him. The dialogue between Lois and Peter says it all. Lois begins by saying, "I'm going to have regular sex with you, whether you like it or not!" Peter responds with, "No!" In return, Lois replies, "I wasn't asking for your permission!" (MacFarlane, 1999). These are only a few examples of the sexual abuse and violence that is portrayed in the show.

While domestic violence and sexual violence are critical parts of the show, so are the gun violence and intraracial violence depicted on *Family Guy*. One of the episodes "A Shot in the Dark" from Season 14, Episode 9 shows how the media is a significant motivator of crimes related to race and guns. In this episode, Peter decides to start a community watch and, in sum, accidently shoots Cleveland's son, Cleveland Brown Jr., in the arm. The episode addresses race, rights, and how the media dictates the way the public will take sides. At the beginning of the episode everyone in the black community is shaming Peter for shooting a black unarmed boy. Halfway through, sides are swapped and now Peter is no longer looked at as a suspect. Now the media has portrayed Cleveland Brown Jr. as a street thug, even though he was not. At the end of the episode Cleveland and Peter are able to reconcile their differences when Cleveland takes blame for the crime and the media moves on to other issues. Cleveland says, "You want to make the media go away? Just mention black on black crime," and Brian responds by saying "Boy, the world we live in, huh?" (Soderstrom, 2015). Season 6, Episode 5 encourages the use of weapons of mass destruction. In this episode, Stewie creates a simulation of how killing his mother Lois would occur. Stewie shoots his mother on a cruise ship at least 12 times, causing her to fall into the ocean, which he believes is the end of her fate. He also successfully shoots Cleveland to his death inside the Griffin home and attempts to take over the world by taking over the world's power supply. Lois finds Stewie's secret room filled with weapons, including handguns, semi-automatics, missiles, grenades, and other flashy gadgets. Lois uses these devices and weapons in order to blindly attack Stewie in the White House, but ultimately freezes when it comes to killing her evil child. Peter, on the other hand, for the sake of his wife and her safety, pulls the trigger for her, killing their Stewie.

Another topic of interest for *Family Guy* is bullying. One of the characters in the show who is constantly being bullied is Meg. The popular kids bully Meg at school, and her father bullies her at home. "Television and movie comedies occasionally portray adults as bullies. Television reality shows are rife with using similar bullying and mean girl methods as adolescents" (Oppliger, 2013). In Season 3, Episode 5, Meg gets bullied by the popular kids at school on the first day she becomes a Flag Girl. Peter decides to laugh at her and bullies her at home just as much. In other episodes Peter trips her, degrades her, and constantly jokes about her "ugly" looks. In Season 3, Episode 8, Stewie loses his tricycle to a bully and doesn't know how to deal with the situation at first. Stewie did not realize that he was being bullied, but then realizes that in order to take care of a bully, he has to become the bully. Stewie's way of bullying is by being violent and aggressive.

Jazmin Medina-Morales

See also: Disney Films; *Ren & Stimpy Show, The*; *South Park*; *Twilight* Saga, The

Further Reading

Brown, K. 2015. "TV Watchdog: 91% of Sexually Violent 'Jokes' on Family Guy Involved Children." *CNS News*, May 22. http://www.cnsnews.com/news/article/kathleen-brown/tv-watchdog-91-sexually-violent-jokes-family-guy-involved-children

Jefferson, W. 2011. "Family Guy Hits Horrible New Low with Domestic Abuse Episode." *Jezebel*, October 21. http://jezebel.com/5854810/family-guy-hits-horrible-new-lows-with-domestic-abuse-episode

MacFarlane, S. 1999, January 31. "Family Guy [Television Series]." FOX.

Oliver, K. 2015. "Sexual Violence against Children as a Joke on Family Guy." http://w2.parentstv.org/main/Research/Studies/FamilyGuy2015/FGStudy2015.pdf

Oppliger, P. A. 2013. *Bullies and Mean Girls in Popular Culture*. Jefferson, NC & London: McFarland & Company, Inc.

Soderstrom, E. 2015. "Family Guy Shows Exactly How to Make the Media Disappear." *Newsbusters*, December 14. https://www.newsbusters.org/blogs/culture/erik-soderstrom/2015/12/14/family-guy-shows-exactly-how-make-media-disappear

Game of Thrones

The hit HBO series *Game of Thrones* brings to life a mystical world of magic and monsters but at the same time it features brutal fights for power. It first aired in April 2011 and is the adaptation of a book series by George R. R. Martin called *A Song of Ice and Fire*. *A Game of Thrones* is the first book in the series. The show is very popular with viewers and critics. It has received 38 Emmy Awards, including 2 for Outstanding Drama Series in 2015 and 2016, and many other awards. It is considered the world's most popular show (Kelly, 2017).

The series focuses largely on two powerful families fighting for control of the Seven Kingdoms of Westeros. It features a host of flamboyant, controversial, conniving, and violent characters. Although fans love the series, many have criticized it for showing gratuitous nudity, for being excessively violent, and in particular, for its depictions of sexual violence.

Defenders assert that the show is merely based on the books, which feature a great deal of violence, and which Martin says is intended to depict the reality of the medieval world. Film writer Alyssa Rosenberg (2016) explains, "[A] willingness to depict extreme violence or the after-effects of a wound or torture is of direct service in overturning our gilded dreams about golden ages past." Further, some note that HBO has long pushed those boundaries, and of course, one can simply tune out if the violence is too much.

Yet although the show's directors have pared down some of the violence from the books, in other cases they have added to it. They have created new characters simply to be victims, and some of the acts of sexual violence are more extreme than the books indicated. For instance, in Season 3, a character named Ros, a prostitute, is given to the sadistic King Joffrey, who strips her naked, ties her up, and shoots her full of crossbow bolts, including two to her groin and one to her breasts. In another episode in season two, Joffrey had Sansa Stark stripped and beaten. Another character, Talisa Maegyr, is repeatedly stabbed while pregnant. Myranda is another character who does not exist in the books. Film writer Christopher Orr (2015) described her role this way: "Myranda's role is essentially limited to a) having rough sex with Ramsay; b) assisting Ramsay in his violent depredations; c) being threatened by Ramsay when she suggested that she, like he, might marry; and d) making graphic promises of sexual torture and mutilation toward Sansa, the latter of which got her pushed off the Winterfell ramparts to her death." Although it is included in the books, the wedding-night rape of Sansa Stark is visually very disturbing (Orr, 2015).

Further, some believe that there is too much violence that does not need to be depicted to move the plot along. Rosenberg (2016) wrote that the outcomes of violent incidents can easily be made clear without some of the gory visuals and terrifying sounds that are part of the show. For example, Daenerys Targaryen vows to "see" every one of the 160 miles of dead girls who were crucified, but critics say that viewers gain little by seeing that gruesome imagery.

Carrie Wittmer (2017) of *Business Insider* ranked the 20 most gruesome murders in the show's history. It includes incidents when characters are strangled, stabbed in the throat or eyes, burned alive, have their heads smashed against a wall, their heads ripped off, killed by then becoming zombies, their bodies ripped apart by rioters, have their throat ripped out with someone's bare hands, being eaten by hounds, their necks sliced open, molten gold poured over their heads, being stabbed in the stomach, eaten by rats, having their eyes gouged out, and being beheaded. Ranking number one was the murder of Oberyn Martell, whose head is smashed by another character during a trial by combat.

Critics have also expressed concern about mistreatment of animals in *Game of Thrones*. In 2017, the activist group People for the Ethical Treatment of Animals (PETA) filed a complaint with the U.S. Department of Agriculture alleging that the company Birds & Animals Unlimited, which supplies animals for *Game of Thrones* and many other shows, had violated the Animal Welfare Act at their shelters. The complaint alleges that various animals were deprived of food for training purposes, that they were left outside overnight in cold temperatures with no bedding, and that some animals had untreated injuries (Baum, 2017).

Laura L. Finley

See also: Ancient Greek Literature and Culture; British Television; *Law & Order*; Rape Films; Shakespeare, William; *Walking Dead, The*; *X-Files, The*

Further Reading

Baum. G. 2017. "A Dead Kangaroo, a Bleeding Pig: Hollywood's Top Animal Training Firm Hit with PETA Abuse Claims." *Hollywood Reporter*, January 11. https://www .hollywoodreporter.com/news/animal-abuse-claims-brought-hollywoods-top -training-firm-963331

Kelly, L. 2017. "Here's Why 'Game of Thrones' Has Exploded in Popularity in Asia." *Forbes,* August 25. https://www.forbes.com/sites/ljkelly/2017/08/25/heres-why -game-of-thrones-has-exploded-in-popularity-across-asia/#6d70c0b9467f

Okundaye, O. 2014. "Why I Can't Watch 'Game of Thrones.'" *Huffington Post,* April 9. https://www.huffingtonpost.com/osahon-okundaye/why-i-cant-watch-game-of -thrones_b_5120281.html

Orr, C. 2015. "Why Does *Game of Thrones* Feature So Much Sexual Violence?" *The Atlantic,* June 17. https://www.theatlantic.com/entertainment/archive/2015/06/game-of -thrones-sexual-violence/396191

Rosenberg, A. 2016. "How Much Violence Is Too Much on 'Game of Thrones?'" *The Washington Post,* May 3. https://www.washingtonpost.com/news/act-four/wp/2016/05 /03/how-much-violence-is-too-much-on-game-of-thrones/?utm_term=.19712 209d08f

Wittmer, C. 2017. "The Twenty Most Gruesome 'Game of Thrones' Deaths, Ranked." *Business Insider*, May 14. http://www.businessinsider.com/most-gruesome-game-of -thrones-deaths-ranked-2017-5

Hill Street Blues

Hill Street Blues was a popular police drama that ran on NBC from 1981 to 1987. It focused on a police station in a fictional city, Hill Street. The title referred both to the color of the police officer's uniforms and the drama of their lives. Its 146 episodes received critical acclaim, earning the show a record eight Emmy Awards in its first season, a record that was broken by *The West Wing* in 2000. In all it received 98 Emmy nominations. *Rolling Stone* listed it as the 59th best TV show ever.

Steven Bochco and Michael Kozoll were the show's writers, and each episode featured several intertwined storylines. Some carried over to other episodes. The two had said they did not really want to write another cop show, but the network insisted. *Hill Street Blues* was innovative in the way that it focused not just on the work lives of the officers but on their personal lives as well. Bochco and Kozoll wanted to emphasize the emotional toll of police work. Most episodes began with a briefing and roll call that served as a teaser for what was to happen, and many ended with two of the primary characters, Captain Frank Furillo, played by Daniel J. Travanti, and public defender Joyce Davenport, played by Veronica Hamel, discussing and even disagreeing about their work. The two were in a long-term relationship, which was also unique on TV. It received great critical reviews in the beginning but poor Nielsen ratings, in large part due to its time slot. NBC deemed it too grim, too violent, and too sexy for primetime. It finally did find its place and became a public favorite as well, due largely to its blend of drama and comedy.

Hill Street Blues also used innovative filming techniques involving handheld cameras and rapid cutting between stories so that it had more of a documentary feel. Further, the show was one of the first to include Black Americans as core characters, and it often grappled with interracial relationships and tensions. The writers also took on controversial subjects, including police corruption, racism, gang violence, and alcoholism. Officers are depicted as troubled when things go awry, for instance, when a man they've arrested commits suicide in his jail cell. It also made it clear that policing can be both mundane and dangerous, showing lots of time completing paperwork coupled with intense moments, like when Officers Hill and Renko are shot when they accidentally break up a drug deal. Although it showed violence and violent criminals, as well as occasionally police violence, it was never gratuitous. "*Hill Street Blues* revolutionized the TV 'cop show,' combining with it elements from the sitcom, soap opera, and cinema verite-style documentary. In the process, it established the paradigm for the hour-long ensemble drama: intense, fast-paced, and hyper-realistic, set in a densely populated urban workplace, and distinctly 'Dickensian' in terms of character and plot development" (Schatz, n.d.).

Critics contend that some of the portrayals of minority characters relied heavily on stereotypes and that its rapid movement between storylines prohibited a more contextual look at social problems. Further, the police officers may have grappled with difficult choices, but they are all essentially depicted as heroic. In 1982, the Coalition for Better Television listed *Hill Street Blues* as one of the most violent shows on television.

Bochco went on to even more success with *LA. Law. Hill Street Blues* is credited with paving the way for later hits, including *The Sopranos, Mad Men,* and *Breaking Bad*, as well as other police shows like *The Shield* and *NYPD Blue*.

Laura L. Finley

See also: *Breaking Bad*; British Television; Cop Films; *Law & Order*; *Mad Men*; *Miami Vice*; *Sopranos, The*; *21 Jump Street*

Further Reading

Deming, C. 1985. "Hill Street Blues as Narrative." *Critical Studies in Mass Communication, 2*(1), 1–22.

Leopold, T. 2014. "Hill Street Blues: The Most Influential TV Show Ever." *CNN*, May 1. http://www.cnn.com/2014/04/29/showbiz/tv/hill-street-blues-oral-history/index.html

Murray, N. 2013. "NYPD Blue and Hill Street Blues' Pilots Hooked Viewers with Sex, Violence, and Depth." *AV Club,* January 10. https://tv.avclub.com/nypd-blue-and-hill-street-blues-pilots-hooked-viewers-1798235641

Sabin, R. 2015. *Cop Shows: A Critical History of Police Dramas on TV.* Jefferson, NC: McFarland and Co.

Schatz, T. n.d. "Hill Street Blues." *Museum of TV.* http://www.museum.tv/eotv/hillstreetb.htm

Thompson, R. 1997. *Television's Second Golden Age: From Hill Street Blues to ER.* Syracuse, NY: Syracuse University Press.

Law & Order

NBC's *Law & Order*, a television crime drama series that was established in 1990, focuses on many sectors in the police and procedural (legal) system. It is most notable for depicting how police and lawyers take steps to investigate violent crimes and legal cases that are typically seen in today's society. The most successful of the *Law & Order* series is the Emmy award–winning *Special Victims Unit*, now in its 17th season. It is focused on the investigation of sexually based crimes. The popularity of these shows and the ways they seem to realistically depict crime investigation and prosecution shape public thought about those issues. Many studies have analyzed *Law & Order* regarding whether it affects the social perspective on crime and the legal system itself. For having such an active and successful run as a primetime show, there is concern that the way that crimes are portrayed in these shows may not be entirely accurate or may be an exaggeration (Parker, 2013).

It is important to note that the audience themselves have rarely experienced the crimes that are being depicted in the show, and it creates a type of window for the viewer to look at the criminal world. Studies have found that these shows create a potential moral attitude, or the "existence of a relationship between viewing crime dramas and attitudes towards crime" (Rader & Rhineberger-Dunn, 2010, p. 232). One positive effect is that shows like *SVU* can "enhance viewers' understanding of victimization more generally by providing information about their likelihood of victimization, ways to prevent victimization, and victim culpability" (Rader & Rhineberger-Dunn, 2010, p. 233). At the same time, critics contend that such shows may increase the fear of crime in ways that can be troublesome.

Rader and Rhineberger-Dunn's analysis of the representation of the victims in *Law & Order* focused on the demographics of the characters. Personalizing the victims and creating a sense of direct focus on the victim help the audience relate to and sympathize with the victims. Yet in many episodes victims still face stigma and are treated poorly, as they are in the society in general, and critics contend that such depictions, albeit realistic, may reinforce that stigmatization. This is exemplified in how women are portrayed as victims within the crimes of rape and sexual assault, intimate partner abuse/family violence, stalking, and sexual harassment (Rader & Rhineberger-Dunn, 2010). Viewers may get the impression that only women can be victims of these crimes, which is not accurate.

Andrew G. Selepak and Jason Cain (2015) argue that television dramas like *Law & Order* help draw attention to race differentials in criminal activity, which shape the views that minorities (nonwhites) have on Caucasians themselves. The way that violent crime is portrayed in *Law & Order* may contribute to the growing distrust and fear in society. This is expressed in Jamieson and Romer's analysis as well (2014), where they found that the violent crime that viewers observe begins to shape the way that viewers see their reality around them. Both of these analyses are based on the "cultivation theory," which was first proposed in light of how the society takes the popular media culture and builds it into its framework on "gender, age, education, environment, socioeconomic status, and previous experience with violence" (Selepak & Cain, 2015).

Law & Order shows more whites as the offenders of the show's crimes, which is actually true despite the more common television portrayal involving disproportionately people of color as offenders (Selepak & Cain, 2015).

Although *Law & Order* is no longer a running show, *Law & Order: SVU* is, so it is important to examine how the crimes seen in headlines today are incorporated into it. Research does show that in light of looking at the police investigation and legal procedures shown, the inaccuracy is there, and that it is dramatized, so the concern for viewers and their influence based on this popular series can be detrimental if it is taken seriously drop to an extent.

To conclude, NBC's *Law & Order*, a television crime drama series that had been established in 1990, has been a success in the rating of its own genre, depicting violent crimes, most notably today in the most prevalent branch of *Law & Order: SVU*, and portraying characters that are relatable in the sense of demographics. There is much reason to argue that a generalization of the accuracy of how well these are represented can be disputed and whether the depiction of such crimes can truly foster strong perceptions of the viewers; however, this is largely based on the media influence that the viewer has. It is important to note that *Law & Order* does its work as a dramatization of the crimes being depicted, expressing awareness in the hopes of fostering attitudes toward crime in general.

Laura L. Finley

See also: *American Horror Story*; Bollywood; British Television; *Charlie's Angels*; Cop Films; *Dexter*; *Game of Thrones*; *Hill Street Blues*; *Miami Vice*; *21 Jump Street*

Further Reading

Jamieson, P. E., & Romer, D. 2014, June 17. "Violence in Popular U.S. Prime Time TV Dramas and the Cultivation of Fear: A Time Series Analysis." *Cogitatio: Media and Communication, 2*(2), 31–41. http://repository.upenn.edu/cgi/viewcontent.cgi ?article=1365&context=asc_papers

Parker, S. 2013. "The Portrayal of the American Legal System in Prime Time Television Crime Dramas." *The Elon Journal of Undergraduate Research in Communications, 4*(1), 108–15.

Rader, N. E., & Rhineberger-Dunn, G. M. 2010. "A Typology of Victim Characterization in Television Crime Dramas." *Journal of Criminal Justice and Popular Culture, 17*(1), 231–63. http://www.albany.edu/scj/jcjpc/vol17is1/Rader7_7.pdf

Selepak, A. G., & Cain, J. 2015. "Manufacturing White Criminals: Depictions of Criminality and Violence on Law & Order." *Cogent Social Sciences, 1*(1). doi:10.1080/23311886.2 015.1104977

Lonesome Dove

The *Lonesome Dove* miniseries, which aired on CBS in 1989 from February 5 to February 8, was based on a 1985 Larry McMurtry novel portraying a great Western adventure taking place during the 1870s. The story follows a group of former Texas Rangers as the journey from the small, dusty southern Texas town of Lonesome Dove, all the way to Montana, where leaders Captain Augustus "Gus" McCrae (Robert Duvall) and Captain Woodrow Call (Tommy Lee Jones) hope to be the first cattle ranchers to settle in the state's territory.

The theme of violence reflected throughout the miniseries could often fall under the context of *retributive justice*. Retributive justice, according to the *Stanford Encyclopedia of Philosophy*, follows three basic principles:

> (1) that those who commit certain kinds of wrongful acts, paradigmatically serious crimes, morally deserve to suffer a proportionate punishment; (2) that it is intrinsically morally good—good without reference to any other goods that might arise—if some legitimate punisher gives them the punishment they deserve; and (3) that it is morally impermissible intentionally to punish the innocent or to inflict disproportionately large punishments on wrongdoers. ("Retributive Justice," 2014)

These principles provide support for nearly all of the violent acts portrayed in each 90-minute episode, and naturally, suggestive and violent language followed as these deadly crimes were a part of everyday life in the aptly named "Wild West." Conflicts between the whites and Native Americans accounted for much of the violent conflict the former Rangers encountered on the trails from Texas to Montana—specifically with old enemy of Woodrow and Gus, Blue Duck (Frederic Forrest)—but fighting between cowboys and outlaws was just as routine.

In *Part I: Leaving*, Jake Spoon (Robert Urich), a former Texas Ranger and friend of Gus and Call, returns to Lonesome Dove, fleeing Fort Smith, Arkansas, after accidentally killing the mayor. When Spoon speaks of the incident, he does so in a casual air, chuckling at the fact he had killed an innocent man. This was the first sign in the series that violent acts were tolerated and seen as normal behavior. Neither Gus nor Call bat an eye when Spoon speaks of the account, or when he recklessly shoots near a Mexican cook in the bar they were sitting in just moments later. The act of shooting a gun indoors, or even killing a man on the street, did not make any of the people in Lonesome Dove flinch. True to not only the people of south Texas, the first episode also follows a whiskey boat in Arkansas where a man is quickly killed for irritating another passenger and his body hoisted into the river without a thought, men laughing all the while. Those same male passengers also make relentless threats of sexual assault to the only female passenger, even after she made known she was married.

Rambling man Spoon spoke highly of the untouched land of Montana, inspiring his former comrades to journey north before their old age disallows them. Gus and Call gather a group that includes two other former Texas Rangers, Deets (Danny Glover) and Parker (Tim Scott). Spoon trails behind en route to San Francisco with Lonesome Dove prostitute Lorie Wood (Diane Lane) as his companion. Further displaying casual acts of violence, Spoon shoots his gun dangerously close to Lorie as a prank while she washes in a river, and later hits her across the face when she refuses to detour to San Antonio for his gambling. Such actions made it clear that domestic abuse was routine and that women in prostitution were seen as a possessions and often only valued for their services.

Similarly, in *Part II: On the Trails,* an older man living in east Texas beats a young girl in front of a visitor passing through, justifying his actions by exclaiming she was his wife, "bought and paid for." The girl flees the abusive home with the help of the visitor after breaking her husband's knees with a kitchen pan so he could not come after her, knowing he would kill her for leaving. In this episode, Blue Duck kidnaps Lorie and proclaims he would cut her stomach open and let coyotes eat her alive if she tried to run away. Blue Duck kicks Lorie for no apparent reason while she lies on the ground, held hostage by the Natives who bicker over who can "use" her first. Blue Duck proposes a sort of gambling game to determine whether the others could "poke" Lorie and kills one of the men for holding up the game. In one of Part II's final moments, a prostitute shoots and kills a male customer for wanting his money back. This shows that although most discrimination is aimed toward women by men, the norms of violence ran along a two-way street.

Part III: The Plains contains both senseless and retributive justice–motivated murders. Spoon and three men he met playing poker approach two working "sodbusters" who were minding their own business. One of the men shoots them dead, then hangs and burns their dead bodies with a smile. The Rangers find the bodies, and their eye-for-an-eye mentality motivated them to hang the four men, including Spoon, because they had slain the innocent farmers. Knowing Spoon as an old friend and a "good guy" did not make him exempt from this form of justice. Gus mentions the men were "a pleasure to hang."

In *Part IV: Return,* Deets is killed with a spear while comforting a blind Native American infant in the wake of violence and confusion. Later, Blue Duck is incarcerated and proudly confesses he has raped, kidnapped, and murdered. As a final act of violent vengeance, he throws himself and a police officer out of a second story window before his scheduled hanging.

Lonesome Dove told a tale that showed incidents of violence, both senseless and purposeful, were a common part of everyday life in America's Old West.

Brendan Newman

See also: Dukes of Hazzard; Gang Films; Western Films

Further Reading

Aquila, R. 1998. *Wanted Dead or Alive: The American West in Popular Culture.* Chicago: University of Illinois Press.

Lemann, N. 1985. "Tall in the Saddle." *The New York Times,* June 9. http://www.nytimes.com/books/99/01/10/specials/mcmurtry-dove.html

Madsen, D. 2009. "Discourses of Frontier Violence and the Trauma of National Emergence in Larry McMurtry's *Lonesome Dove* Quartet." *Canadian Review of American Studies, 39*(2), 185–204.

"Retributive Justice." 2014. *Stanford Encyclopedia of Philosophy,* June 18. https://plato.stanford.edu/entries/justice-retributive/

M*A*S*H

M*A*S*H was a popular television series that ran on CBS from 1972 until 1983. Based on a novel and then a feature film with the same title, the series follows the 4077th Mobile Army Surgical Hospital in South Korea during the Korean War. It is considered by many to be among the best television shows ever, with *Rolling Stone* listing it as number 16 in its 100 best. It was largely a comedy but had many dramatic moments. It often critiqued war, which was somewhat controversial, in that when it began the Vietnam War was still going on. In all, it won eight Golden Globes, six People's Choice Awards, and 14 Emmy Awards. Its final show, which aired on February 28, 1983, set a record for being the most-watched television show, which stood until the airing of the 2010 Super Bowl (Abbey, 2013). In it, the main character, Hawkeye Pierce, played by Alan Alda, wakes up in a mental hospital and recalls a woman smothering her child so as to avoid detection by the enemy. *M*A*S*H* is credited with introducing the concept of the "dramedy," although that word was not used at the time.

Many of the episodes were narrated by main characters as letters home. Along with Hawkeye Pierce, the other major characters, Trapper John, B. J. Hunnicutt, Colonel Potter, Margaret "Hot Lips" Houlihan, Colonel Black, Major Winchester, Radar O'Reilly, and Corporal Clinger, used humor to survive the war and the horrors they faced tending to the wounded. Brian Lowry, a critic for *Variety*, has called the cast the best in TV history (Lowry, 2012).

Hawkeye Pierce was based on a real person, H. Richard Hornberger, who wrote the novel on which the show was based. Hornberger liked Alda's interpretation of Pierce, in that he was wise-cracking, but he did not like the show very well. Not only did Hornberger get paid poorly for it, just $500 per episode, which is not typical, but he did not appreciate the show's criticism of war. Hornberger wanted to be a thoracic surgeon but was sent to the war in Korea in 1951, disrupting his effort to attend medical school. His accounts of the war were grueling, as the stress of the war, long hours in surgery, and then having to move with the mobile unit took its toll. Hornberger is credited with using surgery techniques that at the time were prohibited but that clearly saved lives. He and others repaired arteries when they were supposed to only close off blood vessels. The book was his effort to heal. Hornberger claims that the depiction of the mobile unit "tramples on my memories" (Blakemore, 2017). Other critics felt as though the show made the generals look like buffoons and overly glamorized communists.

The final episode of season three shocked viewers and even some of the cast, as Henry Blake received his discharge papers but is later killed when his plane is shot down. Some of the cast said they barely heard about it before the taping.

A criticism of the show is the sexist fashion in which the largely male cast treats the head nurse, "Hot Lips" Houlihan, played by Loretta Swit. They often make sexual remarks to her, come on to her, and in one episode, Hawkeye and others jimmy-rig the makeshift shower so that it falls down, exposing her in front of everyone. Alda has said he dislikes the show's treatment of the Houlihan character. He is a long-time feminist and an early campaigner for the Equal Rights Amendment (ERA).

Laura L. Finley

See also: China Beach; North Korean Films; *Rambo* Films; War Films

Further Reading
Abbey, J. 2013. "M*A*S*H: Where Are They Now?" *ABC News,* February 28. http://abcnews.go.com/Entertainment/mash-now/story?id=18612687
Blakemore, E. 2017. "Why the Real-Life Hawkeye Pierce Hated M*A*S*H." *History.com,* August 28. http://www.history.com/news/why-the-real-life-hawkeye-pierce-hated-mash
Kalter, S., & Gelber, L. 1988. *The Complete Book of M*A*S*H.* New York: Harry N. Abrams.
Lowry, B. 2012. "Critics Say MASH Top Show of Character." *Variety,* September 21. http://variety.com/2012/tv/awards/critic-says-mash-top-show-of-character-1118059360
Reiss, D. 1993. *M*A*S*H: The Exclusive Insider Story of TV's Most Popular Show.* New York: Macmillan.
Sheffield, R. 2016. "100 Greatest TV Shows of All Time." *Rolling Stone,* September 21. https://www.rollingstone.com/tv/lists/100-greatest-tv-shows-of-all-time-w439520/mash-w439624

Mad Men

Mad Men is a TV drama that premiered in 2007 on AMC. It ran until 2015 with seven seasons and 92 episodes. Set in the 1960s, *Mad Men* told the story of Don Draper, an advertising executive played by Jon Hamm, and the people in his personal and professional life. It won 16 Emmy Awards, five Golden Globe Awards, and numerous other accolades. *Mad Men* was the first cable series to win the Emmy Award for Outstanding Drama. It was not only a fan and critic's favorite, but it also inspired commercial success, with Banana Republic offering a Don Draper–inspired line of suits. *Mad Men* is credited with essentially launching Hamm's career. Creator Matthew Weiner had written for HBO's *The Sopranos*, making him the most well-known of anyone associated with *Mad Men* when it premiered.

Although it was not necessarily known for bloody violence, the show was controversial in some of its depictions. One of the bloodiest scenes was in Episode Six, Season Three when a secretary runs over someone's foot with a lawnmower after they had all been drinking at an office party. In another episode a character is accidentally shot in the face during a hunting trip. Although no one generally used guns or other weapons in the show, characters died with some frequency. A small character, Don's half-brother, hangs himself in season one, and another small character dies in a plane crash in season two. But a major character dies in seasons three and four, and another commits suicide in season five. Some also assert that *Mad Men* was racist, depicting a largely white 1960s. In episode three, fellow advertising executive Roger Sterling sings in blackface to his new wife.

Don Draper is a sexist who makes many comments about female clients, colleagues, and his wife. In season two he rapes Bobbie Barrett, the wife of a man hired to create TV spots for the advertising company. Many were disturbed at this depiction, which made the act look more consensual, reinforcing the stereotype that there are often "blurred lines" in sexual encounters. In an episode called "The Mountain King," Joan Harris, played by Christina Hendricks, is raped by her husband. She said, "When Joan's new husband raped her in the office, that was pretty shocking to read and do, and I think to watch. It was a doozy moment. . . . The biggest shock came after it aired, that people said, 'Remember when Joan sort of got raped?' And my heart just started beating faster and my hands clenched up because, to me, it's so absurd. But I think it was really smart how Matt portrayed it, because of that conversation, because of how controversial rape is and the way people talk about it, and the blame game that is still happening when people tell these stories. Matt said a lot of people, when they described the situation that happened to them, would call it a 'bad date'" (Rosen, 2015). In episode four, season five, Don has a dream about an old lover and then proceeds to choke her to death and kick her lifeless body.

One of the show's controversies was actually about a poster promoting its fifth season. It depicted the black shadow of a man falling against a white background and hung in Manhattan. Critics argued that it too closely mirrored images of the September 11, 2001, terror attack and was offensive to families who lost someone that day. Weiner argued that such an accusation was ridiculous and that the image predated the attack. AMC defended the advertisement, saying it was a metaphor for the turmoil experienced by Don Draper (Bates, 2012).

Critics have argued that *Mad Men* was far less accurate in its depiction of the social, political, or cultural vibe of the 1960s. They assert that the show makes only token nods to major events and that the characters do not engage with things like the civil rights movement, which viewers only know "happens." "Instead, *Mad Men* bathes the period in a meticulously glamorized light. Watch impossibly magnetic Don, quiet bombshell Betty, sexy yet classy Joan, or superbly confident Roger sip scotch or smoke cigars or hold beautiful handbags, and it's clear that what Weiner is selling an image of a glowing past—a prettier, simpler time when people knew their social roles and played them perfectly. It's ideally pitched to stir nostalgia among viewers dealing with a diverse, pluralistic present" (Wolfson, 2014).

The success of *Mad Men* is said to have paved the way for subsequent AMC shows, including *Breaking Bad*, *The Walking Dead*, and *Better Call Saul*.

Laura L. Finley

See also: Breaking Bad; Hill Street Blues; Sopranos, The; Walking Dead, The

Further Reading

Bates, D. 2012. "Falling Man Image Is NOT Insensitive to 9/11 Victims: Mad Men Creator Weiner Hits Back in Row over Poster." *Daily Mail*, March 20. http://www.dailymail.co.uk/news/article-2117175/Mad-Men-creator-Matthew-Weiner-hits-9-11-Falling-Man-poster-row.html

Booker, M., & Batchelor, B. 2016. *Mad Men: A Cultural History.* Lanham, MD: Rowman & Littlefield.

Carveth, R., South, J., & Irwin, W. 2010. *Mad Men and Philosophy: Nothing Is as It Seems.* New York: Wiley.

Peterson, L. 2009. "On Mad Men, When Is It Rape?" *Jezebel,* October 5. https://jezebel.com/5374654/on-mad-men-when-is-it-rape

Rosen, L. 2015. "'Mad Men' Stars Remember Biggest Bombshells Hurled at Them on the Show." *L.A. Times,* May 28. http://www.latimes.com/entertainment/envelope/emmys/la-en-st-mad-men-20150528-story.html

Thompson, A. 2013. "Sneak Peek: Banana Republic's New 'Mad Men' Collection." *USA Today,* February 26. https://www.usatoday.com/story/life/style/2013/02/25/banana-republic-mad-men-collection/1946703

Whittmer, C. 2017. "Why Ten-Year-Old 'Mad Men' Is Still the Best Show to Come Out of Television's Golden Age." *Business Insider*, July 19. http://nordic.businessinsider.com/mad-men-is-the-best-television-show-ever-heres-why-2017-7?r=US&IR=T

Wolfson, M. 2014. "How 'Mad Men' Became the Most Controversial Show on TV." *Salon*, April 27. https://www.salon.com/2014/04/27/how_mad_men_became_the_most_controversial_show_on_tv

Mexican Wrestling

Mexican wrestling, often known as *lucha libre*, is similar in some ways to the professional wrestling of World Wrestling Entertainment (WWE) in the United States, although it has far deeper cultural roots. It is more violent, although the fighters disavow violence in real life. Lucha libre translates to "free fight," which is a good word to describe this form of wrestling. Wrestlers typically wear colorful masks, which they never appear in public without, and engage in athletic and acrobatic maneuvers. Matches often involve tag teams or even trios. It is said to date back to 1863 and to have become popular in the early 1900s. The advent and distribution of television in the 1950s helped popularize it.

Luchadores, as the wrestlers are known, are usually part of a family that wrestles. Similar to wrestling in the United States, wrestlers can win by pinning their opponent for a count of three, knocking him out of the ring for 20 seconds, or forcing him to submit. Some moves are illegal (such as the piledriver), as are weapons, hitting the opponent in the groin, using outside interference, removing the opponent's mask, or attacking the referee. Luchadores compete in several different weight classes. Like American professional wrestling's heels and faces, luchadores are divided into rudos, the bad guys, and tecnicos, the good guys. Some luchadores also wrestle in drag. Lucha libre has been described as a combination of violence, sport, theater, and dance.

One of the most popular luchadores was known as El Santo, or "The Saint," whose career began in 1942 and spanned almost five decades. Another popular luchadore, Gory Guerrero, is credited with developing many of the moves still used today. The greats were popular culture icons, appearing in hundreds of B movies and product advertisements. There are also female luchadoras, although they are less popular than their male counterparts, and a division for very short luchadores. Lucha libre has gained some following in the United States since a television promotion in 1994. It airs weekly via a program called *Lucha Underground* on El Ray Network and in Spanish on UniMas. Although there is much violence and bloodshed in lucha libre, it is popular with families.

One company, which used to be called Total Ultra-Violent Disaster but is now known as DTU Mexican Professional Wrestling, aims to offer fans an even more extreme version of lucha libre. Six wrestlers enter the wring at the same time, and pretty much anything goes, as they bash each other with their bodies and anything else they can find. Many wear masks, and fans scream and yell at the bloodied fighters to carry on. The fight goes on for 15 minutes, and a pair of winners is announced. Although the losers initially vow revenge and hurl insults, that is all part of the show, and they ultimately praise one another and hug before leaving.

Laura L. Finley

See also: Professional Wrestling; Sports on Television

Further Reading

Aguilar, R. 2016. "Mexican Wrestling Fans Demand Blood in Extreme 'Lucha Libre.'" *Reuters*, November 18. https://www.reuters.com/article/us-mexico-wrestling /mexican-wrestling-fans-demand-blood-in-extreme-lucha-libre-idUSKBN13 D1ZD

Bull, A. 2008. "Spandex, Flying Dwarves and Transvestites: Mexican Wrestling Comes to Town." *The Guardian*, December 10. https://www.theguardian.com/sport/blog /2008/dec/10/mexican-wrestling-lucha-libre-andy-bull

Levi, H. 2008. *The World of Lucha Libre: Secrets, Revelations, and Mexican National Identity.* Durham, NC: Duke University Press.

Venville, M. 2012. *Lucha Loco: The Free Wrestlers of Mexico.* New York: Rizzoli Universe Promotional Books.

Miami Vice

Miami Vice was a crime drama set in Miami during the 1980s, what has been referred to as the "Cocaine Cowboys" era. Produced by Michael Mann, the show aired on NBC from 1984 to 1989 and starred Don Johnson as James "Sonny" Crockett and Philip Michael Thomas as Ricardo "Rico" Tubbs, two Miami-Dade undercover police detectives working largely on narcotics. It was innovative for the way that it glamorized Miami, its music, and dress. The show's producers consulted with fashion designers like Gianni Versace and Hugo Boss, and the pastels, white suits, and unshaven faces were a hit with the public. It received a record 15 Emmy Award nominations in its first season. The show's creator, Anthony Yerkovic, said his inspiration for it came when he read a *Wall Street Journal* article in 1982 that said that 20 percent of all unreported income in the United States came from Miami-Dade County. He wanted to write a show about police who have access to the fruits of all this unreported income, most of which came from illegal drugs, hence the fancy cars, boats, watches, and other items (Cohen, 2014).

The show frequently depicted violence, as many episodes ended in gun battles between the detectives and drug traffickers. Episodes were loosely based on actual crime incidents in Miami and with a Miami connection. It took on politically charged topics like organized crime, crime by Cuban migrants from the Mariel Boatlift, the drug war in South America, and the conflict in Northern Ireland, among others. It got darker as the seasons went on.

It popularized a variety of guns, including the Glock 17 pistol, which had never before been depicted on television. Automobiles were also featured prominently, and the Ferrari Daytona and Testarossa were popularized by the show, as were a variety of boats and the stylish clothing worn by the main characters. It made celebrities of the actors. Executive producer Michael Mann told of being pulled over by a police officer who was so enamored with hearing the stories from the show that he forgot to write Mann a ticket.

More than just a police drama, the show also addressed the personal lives of the main characters. Crockett is divorced, and his second wife is killed by an enemy, while Tubbs had an ongoing conflict with the Calderone organized crime family. Mann also used an innovative filming style, with aggressive angles, and the music of Jan Hammer was not the typical crime drama trope but rather funky synthesizer-heavy popular tunes of the era. Some considered Mann a dictator because he insisted on being personally involved in virtually every part of the filming, but he was liked by his very loyal cast and crew. All spoke highly about their experience, and Johnson once described his *Miami Vice* colleagues as, "the most unselfish group of actors I've ever worked with" (Benedek, 1985).

The show's production team consulted with Metro Dade police, including two technical advisors, Sergeant Bob Hoelscher and Commander Nelson Oramas. Hoelscher was a weapons expert and a regional training coordinator for Metro Dade. He helped address traffic and security problems on location, advised as to the realism of plots, and was even seen in many episodes, as were many other officers. He cited the fact that the show identified with a specific police agency as one factor that made it especially unique, as most police shows prior, like *Hill Street Blues*, were set in fictional areas. Broadcast Standards often criticized the show for being too violent and even cut shots, but Johnson and others involved claimed that none of the violence depicted was ever gratuitous; rather, it was intended to show the real threats faced by police in urban areas like Miami. Further, they pushed back, arguing that shows such as *The A-Team* feature as much, if not more, violence but faced less scrutiny because it is depicted in a more cartoonish fashion (Benedek, 1985).

Yerkovich argued that the show changed Miami. He says that law enforcement and criminals began behaving differently, and the public gained a new appreciation for the work of police in the era of Cocaine Cowboys. Even the drug dealers began to dress better, he said (Cohen, 2014).

In 2006, Mann directed the $135 million film of the same name, which starred Colin Farrell as Crockett and Jamie Foxx as Tubbs. It was considered to be darker and more violent than the show. Some officers in Miami claim that the television show inspired them to take up law enforcement. Public Information Officer Roy Rutland, who was the technical advisor for the film, said, "I spent my career in narcotics, working undercover, and I think the reason I worked narcotics was *Miami Vice* in the '80s. As a kid I loved it so much it drew me to working undercover, and it came full circle" (Cohen, 2014).

Laura L. Finley

See also: *Breaking Bad*; Cop Films; *Hill Street Blues*; *Law & Order*; Mexican Crime Novels; *Murder, She Wrote*; Narcocorridos

Further Reading

Armstrong, N., & Tennenhouse, L. 1989. *The Violence of Representation: Literature and the History of Violence.* New York: Routledge.

Benedek, E. 1985. "Inside Miami Vice." *Rolling Stone,* March 28. https://www.rollingstone .com/tv/features/inside-miami-vice-19850328

Cohen, H. 2014. "How 'Miami Vice' Changed TV." *Miami Herald,* September 29. http:// www.miamiherald.com/entertainment/tv/article2261012.html

Murder, She Wrote

Murder, She Wrote is a television series focusing on a mystery writer and amateur detective, Jessica Fletcher, played by Angela Lansbury. It aired from 1984 until 1996 on CBS with a total of 264 episodes. Four TV films and a short-lived spin-off series followed. It was widely popular in its Sunday evening spot, average nearly 26 million viewers each week. Lansbury was applauded for her depiction of Fletcher and received 10 Golden Globe and 12 Emmy Award nominations. She is the record-holder for the most Golden Globe nominations for Best Actress in a television drama series and for Emmy Award nominations for Outstanding Lead Actress in a Drama Series. She won four of the Golden Globes. Lansbury already had a successful acting career, having appeared in many films and on Broadway, but the show rocketed her into stardom.

Lansbury's Jessica Fletcher is a widowed, retired English teacher who has become a successful mystery writer. She lives alone in small-town Cabot Cove, Maine, and is well liked in the community, although not always by law enforcement. In each episode, Jessica is more dedicated to cracking a case than are the local police, who are depicted as wanting to arrest the first person they suspect and closing the case. She works tirelessly to piece together various clues. Critics noted that murder occurred far more frequently in Cabot Cove than would be expected in a small, coastal town; in fact, if Cabot Cove was real it would have been considered the murder capital of the world.

Because she is so devoted to tracking down every clue and her cracking of cases often makes them look bad, Jessica has a complex relationship with the police. While most do not really want her interfering, they respect her abilities and often listen to her. Throughout the series she ends up making friends with some officers and even a British officer with Scotland Yard, and in season eight she moves part-time into an apartment in New York City to teach criminology and so works with even more murders, and more police, there. Toward the end of the series, as Lansbury began to express that she was ready to leave the show, the writers added new characters and increased their depictions of others, like Private Investigator Harry McGraw.

The show was not innovative in the way that others in the era were. It lacked the flash of *Miami Vice*, for instance. But it was loved because of Lansbury's acting, the plots and narratives that read like mystery novels, and was one of only a few shows in the time period to star an older woman who was not representative of sex appeal. Rather than a traditional police show, with screeching tires, chases of suspects, and shoot-outs, *Murder, She Wrote* is more cerebral. Rarely was the actual body of the murdered individual shown, and the show rarely depicted overt violence.

In 2011, Lansbury said she might like to make a comeback appearance as Jessica Fletcher, but in 2015 she changed her mind, then in 2017 appeared to change it again. In 2014 there was talk of a reboot of *Murder, She Wrote*, which was going to feature Octavia Spencer as Jessica Fletcher. Lansbury criticized the idea publicly, saying, "Octavia Spencer is a superb actress. She had no business being put into a situation that she couldn't win" (Flint, 2014). The popular Lansbury faced criticism in 2017 when she made comments that indicated her belief that women face sexual harassment due to the clothes they wear. These comments came amidst a flurry of sexual harassment allegations against Hollywood executives in fall 2017 (Seeraj & Zdanowicz, 2017).

Laura L. Finley

See also: King, Stephen; *Miami Vice*; Poe, Edgar Allan; Scandinavian Crime Novels; *Serial*

Further Reading

Atkin, D. J., Moorman, J., & Lin, C. A. 1991. "Ready for Prime Time: Network Series Devoted to Working Women in the 1980s." *Sex Roles, 25*, 677–85.

Davis, D. 1990. "Portrayals of Women in Prime-Time Network Television: Some Demographic Characteristics." *Sex Roles, 23*, 325–32.

Flint, H. 2014. "'I Knew It Was a Terrible Mistake': Dame Angela Lansbury Overjoyed the Murder, She Wrote Reboot Is Cancelled." *Daily Mail,* January 24. http://www.dailymail.co.uk/tvshowbiz/article-2545132/Dame-Angela-Lansbury-overjoyed-Murder-She-Wrote-remake-cancelled.html

O'Connor, J. 1986. "TV View: It's Fun and It's Not Violence." *The New York Times,* February 16. http://www.nytimes.com/1986/02/16/arts/tv-view-it-s-fun-and-it-s-not-violent.html

Seeraj, I., & Zdanowicz, C. 2017. "Angela Lansbury Says Women Must 'Sometime Take the Blame' for Sexual Harassment." *CNN,* November 30. http://edition.cnn.com/2017/11/28/entertainment/angela-lansbury-sexual-harassment-comments-trnd/index.html

Professional Wrestling

Professional wrestling, in particular, World Wrestling Entertainment (WWE), has been tremendously popular for decades, but its popularity soared in the 1980s and 1990s. It is broadcast in 12 languages to over 130 countries, was viewed at its peak by some 34 million people in the United States, and generated more than $1 billion in revenue annually across the globe. Key to its success has been targeted marketing to 18- to 34-year-old males. Critics contend that the increasingly violent and sexualized content was the key to attracting this demographic. Industry leaders like WWE owner Vince McMahon utilized faux violence and problematic storylines to create allegiance to various characters. Further, critics maintain that the WWE markets to children, as it sells toys and video games and partners with companies like Chef-Boy-R-Dee. Much of the violence is presented in a sexually provocative fashion. For instance, the WWE women, known as divas, often wrestle in "bra and panties" matches where the first to strip her opponent of undergarments wins.

Further, the storylines that accompany the introduction of the female characters often imply or even state that any abuse they endure is deserved. The documentary *Wrestling with Manhood* by the Media Education Foundation provides countless examples of how female characters are said to be lying and conniving and therefore deserving of any verbal or physical abuse. Such depictions may be linked to abusive behavior in dating relationships, according to researchers at Wake Forest University. One of the study's authors, Dr. Robert Durant, noted that as the participants were exposed to more wrestling, their abusive dating behavior intensified. This included verbal and physical fighting as well as drinking and drug use. Durant was cautious, however, in determining the exact relationship between the two, noting that youth who were more prone to engage in violent behavior may also be more likely to watch professional wrestling. Interestingly, the same increase in violent behavior was observed among teenage female viewers of professional wrestling. Durant's recommendation is that parents must monitor their children's viewing behaviors. WWE refuted the study, asserting that it did not show a direct causal relationship and that it ignored other factors that might be related to the observed behaviors. It noted that most viewers and attendees at WWE events see it as a positive experience and that teens say it helps them with confidence and self-esteem.

Similarly, *Wrestling with Manhood* draws attention to the bullying behavior exhibited by professional wrestlers in the ring, especially against those who are perceived to be gay. Those characters face additional taunts and homoerotic physical attacks in the ring. Some assert that this reinforces to viewers that gay men are not to be accepted and that it normalizes violence against that population.

Critics also point to the number of professional wrestlers who have been accused and even convicted of domestic and other forms of violence. "Stone Cold" Steve Austin allegedly attacked his former wife, Debra Williams, in 2002 and 2004. In June 2007, the bodies of wrestler Chris Benoit, his wife Nancy-Daus Benoit, and his seven-year-old son Daniel were found in Fayetteville, Georgia. It is believed that Benoit strangled his wife then suffocated his son before hanging himself. Investigators found drugs and anabolic steroids in the home, raising attention to the role that performance-enhancing drugs (PEDs) may have in stimulating violent behavior. Debra Williams also said that Austin was abusive due to drugs. Mrs. Benoit had sought a divorce from Chris Benoit in 2003 and then applied for a restraining order; similarly, Williams applied for a restraining order against Austin. She claims that he, like Chris Benoit, essentially forced her to tell authorities that the complaint was a mistake. Austin was sentenced to one year of probation, but Williams was placed under a gag order that prohibited her from talking about the situation or about what she says was widespread drug use, alcoholism, and abuse within the WWE. Jerry Lawler, long-time announcer for the WWE, and his girlfriend were both accused of domestic violence in June 2016. Lawler, 66 at the time, and Lauryn McBride, 27, were arrested after police were called to their East Memphis home. Both claimed the other was the assailant. Lawler was suspended from the WWE after his arrest.

In 2014, as a result of a scandal involving Minnesota Viking football player Ray Rice, the WWE announced a new zero-tolerance policy regarding domestic violence. It includes a provision that allows for the organization to terminate employees even when they have not been convicted.

Professional wrestling has inspired a host of copycats. Some of the notorious are backyard wrestlers, who emulate the moves they see on WWE but without the same training and equipment. "Hardcore" wrestlers take it a step further, using tables, chairs, ladders, barbed wire, glass, and other implements to attack their opponents. Although it has been around in other countries for some time, hardcore wrestling only gained popularity in the United States in the 1990s. In some cases, the losers of these matches face additional sanction, like being thrown into a pool filled with salt and lemon juice that burns their wounds.

There have been other instances in which individuals have copycatted WWE, to horrific result. Lionel Tate, at the time 12 years old, smashed the skull of his cousin, Tiffany Eunick, while practicing wrestling moves he saw on WWE. Three other deaths in 1999 were attributed to youth practicing wrestling moves. WWE filed a suit asserting that the allegations were libelous. At the time of the incident, Tate weighed 170 pounds and had the intelligence of an eight-year-old. His attorneys maintained that he did not have the capacity to understand the consequences of his actions. Studies have shown that televised violence does affect youth who are heavy viewers, although at the time few had addressed professional wrestling.

Some years later, several professional wrestlers filed a lawsuit against the WWE, alleging that it sold violence while neglecting the health of its athletes. Former WWE wrestlers Vito LoGrasso and Evan Singleton alleged that the WWE knew or should have known that it was subjecting its athletes to potentially lethal danger, including brain damage. LoGrasso claimed that he suffered from neurological damage, including depression, anxiety, and memory loss. Singleton alleges that the WWE was the source of his tremors, convulsions, and impaired reasoning capacity. Even more, the data show that professional wrestlers are at risk for heart attacks. Between 1997 and 2004, the rate of professional wrestlers dying from heart attacks surpassed by far the average for people in the same age range. Drug use, including cocaine, painkillers, steroids, and other drugs, was a factor in some 20 percent of the cases.

Laura L. Finley

See also: Mexican Wrestling; Soccer/Football Hooligans; Sports on Television

Further Reading

ABC News. 2006. "Watching Wrestling Linked to Teen Dating Violence." *ABC News,* August 7. http://abcnews.go.com/Health/story?id=2274722

Almond, K. 2015. "The Art of the 'Death Match.'" *CNN,* August 6. http://www.cnn.com /2015/08/06/us/cnnphotos-hardcore-wrestling-death-matches

Bernthal, M. 2008. "How Viewing Professional Wrestling May Affect Children." *The Sport Journal,* February 22. http://thesportjournal.org/article/how-viewing-professional -wrestling-may-affect-children

Fox News. 2007. "Pro Wrestling Wife Claims Drug Abuse, Domestic Violence 'Out of Hand in the WWE.'" *Fox News,* June 7. http://www.foxnews.com/story/2007/06/27 /pro-wrestling-wife-claims-drug-abuse-domestic-violence-out-hand-in-wwe.html

Jhally, Sut (Director). 2010. *Wrestling with Manhood.* Documentary available for purchase from Media Education Foundation at http://shop.mediaed.org/wrestling-with -manhood-p170.aspx

Rhodes, D. 2015. "Why Do Wrestlers So Often Die Young?" *BBC News,* August 8. http://www.bbc.com/news/magazine-33817959

Tamborini, R., Skalski, P., Lachlan, K., Westerman, D., Davis, J., & Smith, S. "The Raw Nature of Televised Professional Wrestling: Is the Violence a Cause for Concern?" *Journal of Broadcasting and Electronic Media, 49*(2), 202–20.

Ren & Stimpy Show, The

The Ren & Stimpy Show is an animated series that aired on Nickelodeon from 1991 until 1995, running five seasons and 52 episodes. Created by John Kricfalusi, its main characters are a chihuahua, Ren, and a cat, Stimpy. Ren is emotionally unstable, and Stimpy is his good-natured but dim-witted counterpart. *The Ren & Stimpy Show* was controversial for its sexual innuendos, adult jokes, dark humor, and violence, in particular because it aired on a channel that is widely viewed by children. It was tremendously popular, however, and has retained a cult following. Many attribute *The Ren & Stimpy Show* as paving the way for other adult-oriented cartoons, including *Beavis and Butt-Head* and *South Park*. MTV later picked up the rights to the show. Spike TV offered a spin-off, *Ren & Stimpy "Adult Party Cartoon."*

Throughout the show, Ren and Stimpy get into various adventures, often set in history. Kricfalusi said he had no intent on creating an educational series nor on anything beyond entertaining, so jokes were made at the expense of all types of people. Some episodes were changed to exclude the topics of religion and politics. Many featured slapstick humor, while others involved violent and even gruesome deaths, some of which were removed. One episode, titled "Man's Best Friend" shows Ren brutally beating a character with a canoe oar. Nickelodeon refused to show it so it remained unseen until it aired on *Adult Party*. Kricfalusi was fired after the controversy over that episode, along with most of the production team. He has said he was in near-constant battle with executives at Nickelodeon, as even at the beginning they wanted him to change the way the characters looked. He has been a vocal critic of the corporate culture at the network. "The biggest motivating factor for me is that I think authority is funny. I'm always trying to buck it," Kricfalusi said. When the network objected to rude gags, Kricfalusi argued, "I thought to myself, 'Have you ever met a kid?' Who doesn't know that kids think rude things are funny?"(Duca, 2014).

Ren looks demented, with crooked teeth, pink eyes, and a very short temper. Kricfalusi was inspired to create him when he once saw a chihuahua wearing a sweater. Ren is also greedy and is always scheming to get rich. Stimpy is pudgy, eats disgusting things including his own kitty litter, and watches too much television. The two are constantly bickering in the trailer they share, often when Stimpy does something to wake Ren up. Their ill-advised plans always go awry, and when they get upset or angry their already ugly features worsen. Ren's eyeballs get so big they are larger than his head and his skin peels. In one episode, "Black Hole," the two implode, and in "Marooned" they are eaten by a monster. Like most cartoon characters, they always survive (Schoemer, 1992).

Fans of the show have created a list of censored or controversial episodes. One scene that was censored was in the episode "Out West." Two characters, Abner and

Ewalt, are seen tying nooses around their necks, and Ewalt says "Ya'll bring the kids now, ya hear?" The scene does appear in the Spike TV version of the show. An episode called "Powdered Toast Man Versus Waffle Woman" was pulled after the terrorist attacks on September 11, 2001, as it featured the Twin Towers in New York being destroyed. Some episodes were cut only in certain countries. "Stimpy's Fan Club" was banned in the UK because Ren threatens to kill Stimpy (List of Banned/Censored Episodes, 2016).

Laura L. Finley

See also: Anime; *Family Guy*; *South Park*

Further Reading

Duca, L. 2014. "How the Creator of 'Ren and Stimpy' Changed the Face of Cartoons, Then Got Fired." *Huffington Post,* August 27. https://www.huffingtonpost.com/2014/08/27/ren-and-stimpy_n_5647944.html

List of Banned/Censored Episodes. 2016. *Fandom by Wikipedia.* http://renandstimpy.wikia.com/wiki/List_of_banned/censored_episodes

Schoemer, K. 1992. "Review/Television: Twisted View of Children's Cartoon Gains a Cult." *The New York Times,* March 12. http://www.nytimes.com/1992/03/12/movies/review-television-twisted-humor-of-children-s-cartoon-gains-a-cult.html

Soccer/Football Hooligans

Hooligans are violent and destructive fans. The sport of soccer, known outside the United States as football, is most known for inspiring hooligans. Team rivalries have often incited hooliganism before games, during them, and after them as well. Hooligans may taunt opposing players, but are often involved in spitting, fighting, throwing objects, and using weapons against their opponents. The first hooliganism is traced to 14th-century England, and King Edward II even banned football because of the surrounding disorder. The 1880s in England saw widespread hooliganism at football matches. Media began paying attention to the issue in the 1950s, both in England and in Latin America. Over time, many countries have enacted laws, and sporting organizations have created policies, designed to reduce hooliganism. These include the banning of weapons in stadiums, banning persons who have previously engaged in hooliganism, segregating opposing fans, and more.

Some of the most notorious hooligans include the group Hooligans gegen Salafisten in Germany, which sports more than 3,000 members, many of whom are neo-Nazis and nationalists. In the 2010s, they have routinely targeted Islam and have joined right-wing groups, which concerns authorities. In 2012, "Ultra" hooligan groups were also generally influenced by right-wing politics ad were active in Hungary and Romania. In Brazil, 2013 saw a record number of deaths due to hooliganism. In Croatia, the situation became so bad that a truce was declared between the two main hooligan groups, the Dinamo and the Hajduk. Italy has also seen a number of hooligan attacks on players and fans in advance of the 2018 World Cup. Russian officials enacted legislation to create harsher penalties for disturbing the public order, which includes a seven-year ban for persons who are convicted. Hooliganism in Africa, meanwhile, is more spontaneous and less planned.

Popular culture has tended to glorify hooliganism. Films, books, and television shows portray these fans as merely passionate. Critics maintain that security measures merely displace hooligans' activity to spots outside of stadiums. Further, critics note that media attention increases the likelihood that hooligans will engage in extreme behavior. Hooligans are often fueled by alcohol and drugs, and enthusiastic support for teams tends to be passed down over generations.

Law enforcement efforts today emphasize online hooliganism, as fans who abuse players or supporters may be subject to arrest and prosecution. Advocacy groups have applauded the initiative, arguing that some fans, including those who identify as LGBTQ, might be hesitant to attend matches when hooliganism is allowed or tolerated.

A number of films have been made about hooligans, and many songs are written for and used by hooligans. Critics contend that these glorify hooligan culture, whereas proponents explain that they are merely a reflection of pride.

Laura L. Finley

See also: British Television; Islam, Depictions of; Professional Wrestling; Sports on Television

Further Reading

Brewen, J. 2015. "Hooliganism in England: The Enduring Cultural Legacy of Football Violence." *ESPN-FC*, February 4. http://www.espnfc.us/blog/espn-fc-united-blog/68/post/2193850/hooliganism-in-england-the-enduring-cultural-legacy-of-football-violenace

Duarte, F., Wilson, J., Walker, S., Bandini, P., & Doyle, P. 2013. "Football Violence: A View from around the World." *The Guardian*, December 19. https://www.theguardian.com/football/2013/dec/19/football-violence-view-around-world

Press Association. 2013. "Football Fans Face Prosecution for 'Online Hooliganism.'" *The Guardian*, August 23. https://www.theguardian.com/football/2013/aug/23/football-fans-prosecution-online-hooliganism

Spiegel Staff. 2014. "The Unholy Alliance of Neo-Nazis and Football Hooligans." *Spiegel*, November 4. http://www.spiegel.de/international/germany/new-right-wing-alliance-of-neo-nazis-and-hooligans-appears-in-germany-a-1000953.html

Sopranos, The

The Sopranos was a tremendously popular cable television series focusing on a modern-day mobster, Tony Soprano (James Gandolfini), suffering from a midlife crisis. The major networks turned down the pilot, calling it too dark and violent. Only *HBO* would take the chance, and premiered the show on January 10, 1999. It ran until June 10, 2007. Fans saw the show as realistic, and critics assert that it was a masterpiece of popular culture that forever transformed television. Audiences fell in love with the characters and laughed at the comical way much of the violence was depicted. It earned 121 Emmy nominations and won 21. It also won awards from the Screen Actors Guild and Peabody Awards. Several of the actors won Golden Globe Awards. In 2016, Rob Sheffield of *Rolling Stone* called it the best of 100 television shows in history, noting that it paved the way for *The*

Wire, Mad Men, Breaking Bad, and other cable shows (Sheffield, 2016). Initially, the violence depicted was part of Tony's job and thus only targeted against rivals. Although the show was critically acclaimed, many expressed concern that the levels of violence depicted grew each season and that it was increasingly committed against women and innocent characters.

Tony is first depicted as killing someone, a snitch, in the fourth episode. The show's writers and directors grappled with whether showing him commit a murder would decrease the audience's love of the character or whether it was essential to remain realistic. In the scene, Tony kills the man with his bare hands; the show's directors won Emmy Awards for it.

The third season featured violence involving the main characters as well as guest characters. Silvio (Steven Van Zandt) slaps a stripper who is working for him at the Bada Bing Club, and then Ralph (Joe Pantoliano) beats her to death when he learns she is pregnant. Jennifer Melfi (Lorraine Bracco), Tony's psychiatrist, is raped and beaten in the stairwell of a parking garage, which was depicted in a long and graphic scene. It largely focuses on Melfi's screams and sobs. Critics assert that this prolonged scene took it too far, as her assailant was a neighborhood punk who had nothing to do with the mob. Melfi identified her assailant, but as is so often true in real life, he was released on a technicality. She considers but decides not to ask Tony to seek revenge. Bracco, who reportedly injured her arm filming the scene, defended it, saying, "We've been very courageous in showing the violence for what it is and not glorifying it in any way," she says. "It is the life of the Mob. It is despicable, and as much as we do love this family and these characters, I find it brave of David not to be afraid to show you what horrible people they really are" (Cruz, 2001).

When his girlfriend Gloria (Annabella Sciorra) threatened to reveal their affair, Tony throws her around, slams her into the floor, and holds his hands around her neck. Although he does not kill her, it is clear he considered it. Tony also tells Gloria that he had beaten a former girlfriend. Gloria had been stalking Tony, calling the Soprano home, and immediately before his attack she had been smashing dishes and throwing a burnt dinner at Tony's head. This type of violence is rare, as typically the hero of a show does not exhibit such an extreme attack.

Guest character violence included a man getting his head beaten in with a golf club, an older man killing his godson, and a young man dying in a gory heap of blood in his own kitchen. Caryn James of *The New York Times* argued that this was a good move because it showed the consequences of mob life and allowed viewers to remain uncomfortable with it. Further, James wrote that the violence against women is a logical spillover of mob life. Viewers did not seem opposed to the added violence, as 5.5 million people tuned in each week.

In 2001, a group of New York politicians reportedly boycotted a press conference for the New York State Assembly's film fund initiative because the actor who plays Ralphie, Joe Pantoliano, attended. Italian American New York State senator Serphin R. Maltese, a Republican from Queens, encouraged his constituents to cancel HBO in protest of the show's violence. *Sopranos* creator David Chase responded to the critics, "Of course, it was graphic and hard to take—that's the purpose of it" (Cruz, 2001).

The final episode implies that Tony has been killed, although some criticized it for being ambiguous. David Chase defended it, asserting that it was obvious but later made statements to suggest it was not.

Laura L. Finley

See also: Breaking Bad; Hill Street Blues; Mad Men; Mafia Films; Walking Dead, The

Further Reading

Biskind, P. 2007. "An American Family." *Vanity Fair,* April 4. http://www.vanityfair.com /news/2007/04/sopranos200704

Cruz, C. 2001. "Behind 'The Sopranos' Violent Tendencies." *Entertainment Weekly,* April 25. http://ew.com/article/2001/04/25/behind-sopranos-violent-tendencies

James, C. 2001. "Critic's Notebook: 'The Sopranos:' Brutally Honest." *The New York Times,* May 22. http://www.nytimes.com/2001/05/22/arts/critic-s-notebook-the-sopranos -brutally-honest.html

Leibowitz, A., & Kashner, S. 2012. "The Family Hour: An Oral History of *The Sopranos.*" *Vanity Fair,* March 15. http://www.vanityfair.com/hollywood/2012/04/sopranos -oral-history

Sheffield, R. 2016. "100 Greatest TV Shows of All Time." *Rolling Stone*, September 21. https://www.rollingstone.com/tv/lists/100-greatest-tv-shows-of-all-time-w439520 /the-sopranos-w439641

South Park

South Park (1997–) is an American animated sitcom that is intended for adults. It was created by Matt Stone and Trey Parker, and has aired solely on Comedy Central television network. *South Park* grew out of a short film that Stone and Parker made called *The Spirit of Christmas* in which they used construction cut-outs with stop motion. This short film then gained popularity and developed into the internationally recognized sitcom. It became a national sensation and is one of the most-watched cartoons in cable history. The show is about four boys and their adventures that take place in a small town in Colorado. The first boy is Eric Cartman, known for being the "fat kid" with a racist, rude, and obnoxious attitude. Cartman is the show's star, and perhaps the most influential character in the sitcom's history. The second boy is Stan Marsh, known as the quiet kid who has a crush on Wendy Testaberger. Stan is one of the main protagonists of the series, and is a symbol of the "good" character. The third boy is Kyle Brofloski, the Jewish kid who gets bullied by Cartman. He is also Stan's best friend and a co-protagonist. Lastly, there is Kenny, the kid who always wears an orange hoodie and dies in nearly every episode. The show is known for its harsh language, violent humor, and controversial topics. Episodes take on politicians, celebrities, and whatever is popular in the world that they can ridicule. The show remains very popular and is known for its irreverent humor and violence. In 1999, during the show's height in popularity, the movie *South Park: Bigger, Longer & Uncut* was released. The movie, full of violence and gore, went on to earn $83 million in ticket sales.

South Park has concerned parents and is criticized for how it might influence younger children. It attracts kids due to its cartoon format, which is a significant concern because of its crude humor. It even criticizes taboo topics such as religion and race. *South Park* pushes the limits of what can be televised, and was the first weekly program to be assigned the TV-MA rating, which was assigned because of the excessive violence, gore, and profanity that could be found in any given episode. However, the show attempts to redeem itself by showing intolerance to cruel behavior. Kyle and Stan often stand up to Cartman's intolerant behavior, although it still depicts a lot of abuse, both verbal and physical. Regardless of the controversy, *South Park* is one of the highest-rated series in Comedy Central's history.

South Park has also been criticized for its portrayal of different taboo issues, its lack of sensitivity, religious violence, and crude humor. Many religious figures have condemned the show, as episodes frequently mock religion. At the height of its fame, some schools went as far as banning students from wearing any *South Park*–related clothing. Ironically, the most popular character—Cartman—is the character that is responsible for the most racism, profanity, and violence. Many viewers, however, are in allegiance with him, as they typically side with his unethical behaviors, thereby glorifying his controversial ways. VH1's list "Greatest Icons of Pop Culture," lists Eric Cartman as one of the 50 greatest cartoon characters. In 2005, he was listed on Bravo's "One Hundred Greatest TV Characters." Cartman immediately became a star in the first season, and his popularity only continues to rise with time, despite the fact that he is the show's only antihero. He constantly picks on and harasses Kyle because of his Jewish background, and his self-professed idol is Adolf Hitler.

One of the most consistent predecessors to Cartman's strings of violence is his hate speech. In the episode "Ginger Kids," Cartman bullies and harasses kinds with orange hair and freckles. He ridicules them constantly and singles them out for being different, or "gingers." This led to a rise of attacks against actual red-headed children at school, notably in England, where they were subject to physical violence following the release of this episode. Cartman also utters hate speech in other episodes to gays, lesbians, Mormons, Muslims, and Jews. Because Cartman ridicules people who he perceives to be different, critics have contended that he is an idol to children who bully their peers.

One of the most obvious and consistent patterns of violence in the show is the plight of Kenny. Kenny, whose speech is impaired due to his orange hood, is killed via various methods on virtually every episode. The manner in which he is killed usually results in excessive bloodshed and extreme gore. For example, he has been crushed by a train, trampled by a theater crowd, trampled in a mosh pit, and has committed suicide. The fact that the speech-impaired Kenny is the most consistent victim of violence can potentially cause viewers to become desensitized to violence against persons with disabilities.

South Park also portrays violence as "cute" and "funny." This type of violence is also known as "happy violence." Happy violence influences children the most, as it glorifies violent situations and displays them as humorous and without consequence. Children are led to believe that violence and bullying are justifiable due to their constant presence in media. Viewers are left sitting on the edge of their seats in anticipation of discovering the next way that Kenny dies, which is depicted in an unorthodox and very humorous manner. This is especially apparent in episode

807, where Michael Jackson kills Kenny. The fact that a superstar and media icon kills Kenny with his own hands brings humor and absurdity to the act. *South Park* has even attempted to add humor to the taboo subject of rape, as Donald Trump was raped and killed by the school teacher Mr. Garrison in one episode.

South Park also brings to light current issues such as militarism, as police violence against minorities is one of the most addressed issues. The town's officer, Officer Bradley, shoots a six-year-old Latino child in the beginning of the "Naughty Ninjas" episode. That episode depicted most police officers as being racist and trigger-happy. After the shooting, the town fights back, similar to the nationwide protests that took place in 2015 and 2016 in many different major cities across the United States. The episode ends with the town realizing that they need their police force due to the chaos that took place while the police force was run out of town.

Despite the show's endemic violence, Stan and Kyle seem to be the voices of reason in many episodes. Stan and Kyle always seem to find a way to fix the destruction and mayhem that is caused by Cartman and other antagonistic characters. Often when the town would be on the brink of mayhem, these two boys would always figure out a way to save the day. Despite their good actions, however, Cartman has continued to be the most-popular character, with the other main characters becoming secondary characters when it comes to popularity.

South Park continues to be one of the most influential cartoons in the history of modern cable television. The show tackles controversial issues in our society, while using violence as the primary way to amuse and captivate its viewers. This show has influenced both adults and children to commit acts of verbal and physical violence, and has glorified the violence that takes place in everyday life. The fact that the ratings continue to climb season by season shows the hunger for and desire for it that our country has.

Dina Odeh

See also: Anime; Disney Films; *Family Guy*; Islam, Depictions of; *Ren & Stimpy Show, The*; *Twilight* Saga, The

Further Reading

Delingpole, J. 2010. "South Park: The Most Dangerous Show on Television?" *The Telegraph*, May 3. http://www.telegraph.co.uk/culture/tvandradio/7671750/South-Park -The-most-dangerous-show-on-television.html

Ida, E. (n.d.). "Violence and Jokes in 'South Park.'" *Academia.edu.* http://www.academia .edu/1857233/Violence_and_Jokes_in_South_Park_

Pilkington, E. 2010. "South Park Censored after Threat of Fatwa over Muhammad Episode." *The Guardian*, April 22. https://www.theguardian.com/tv-and-radio/2010/apr /22/south-park-censored-fatwa-muhammad

Spanish-Language Television

Television became massively popular in Latin America in the 1950s and 1960s, and as it did, it disseminated images of various sorts, including crime victims, perpetrators, and those who bring justice. Television programs in Spanish-speaking Latin America are full of violent programming, ranging from domestic violence to sexual assault, to police corruption and abuse, and more. *Ugly Betty* is considered one of the first telenovelas to reach American popular-culture status.

Domestic violence is the most common storyline in Spanish dramas, called telenovelas. Telenovelas are among the most popular types of shows in many Latin American countries and even in parts of the United States. Although telenovelas are successful for many reasons, a primary factor is that the characters generally resolve their problems, which makes audiences feel empowered to do the same. This "emotional realism" explains how the characters and plots are credible to the audience based in their own experiences. Critics contend that telenovelas are chauvinistic and that they depict women by using dangerous stereotypes.

Mexican talk shows also address the topic of violence. *Laura,* which aired on Televisa, the biggest channel in Latin America, features a psychologist who helps families address issues like domestic violence. The show was cancelled after less than a year on air because Mexican officials claimed it invaded the privacy of teenagers.

Queen of the South is a popular telenovela, which stars Alicia Braga as Teresa Mendoza. A tough woman, she is kidnapped, beaten, and sexually assaulted, and then goes on the run from drug cartels who are pursuing her because she dated a drug dealer who was killed. It was well received both in and out of Latin America (Marshall, 2016). Critics have said that the show is dominated by explosions, yet is unique for showcasing a female "narca," or drug dealer. Writing for *Variety*, Sonia Soraiya (2016) commented, "[M]uch of the appeal of *Queen of the South* is the romantic thrill of seeing the world of guns and gore run by an immaculately dressed fashion plate in gold stilettos, glamorous sunglasses, and a crisp white blazer, so carefully put-together she could be a traficante Barbie."

Spanish-language TV has also been criticized for failing to depict LGBTQ characters. A 2015 study of characters in Univision, Telemundo, and MundoMax found that only 3 percent were identifiable as LGBTQ, and most were not primary characters. LGBTQ characters tended to be stereotypical "gossipy best friends." The bisexual characters were sexually voracious (Littleton, 2016).

Whereas most see telenovelas as simply soap operas with an occasional realistic storyline, some have argued that they are responsible for high crime rates in countries like Venezuela. In 2014, President Nicolas Maduro accused soap operas of glamorizing drugs, violence, and guns, after Miss Venezuela Monica Spear and her ex-husband were shot to death by robbers, with their five-year-old daughter looking on. After the attack, President Nicolas Maduro noted the soap opera *De todas Maneras Rosa*, and accused the nation's biggest broadcaster of profiteering from violence.

Isabel Rapisardo-Calvo

See also: Breaking Bad; Mexican Crime Novels; *Miami Vice*; Narcocorridos

Further Reading

Associated Press. 2014. "Venezuela's President Blames Telenovelas for High Crime, Murder of Former Miss Venezuela." *New York Daily News*, January 21. http://www.nydailynews.com/news/world/venezuelan-president-blames-telenovelas-high-crime-murder-beauty-queen-article-1.1586867

Littleton, C. 2016. "GLAAD Study: Few LGBTQ Characters On U.S. Spanish-Language TV." *Variety*, November 17. http://variety.com/2016/tv/news/lgbtq-telemundo-univi sion-spanish-language-tv-1201920527

Marshall, S. 2016. "The Rise of the Telenovela." *New Republic*, December 26. https:// newrepublic.com/article/138918/rise-telenovela

Soraiya, S. 2016. "TV Review: 'Queen of the South.'" *Variety,* June 21. http://variety.com /2016/tv/reviews/queen-of-the-south-tv-review-1201797493

Sports on Television

Violence in sport has long been a spectacle. From the days of Roman gladiators, when prestige grew with the number of men a fighter slew, to modern-day boxing, professional wrestling, mixed martial arts, and football, hyperviolence seems to be a consistent part of certain sports and, as a result, the media coverage of them. Famed author George Orwell, writing as his pen name Eric Arthur Blair, even called sport "war minus the shooting" in 1945.

One of the earliest violent sport spectacles to be captured by media was the July 4, 1910, fight between black heavyweight champion Jack Johnson and his challenger, Jim Jeffries, who was white. Johnson beat Jeffries "to a bloody pulp," and when the result was telegraphed across the nation, people responded violently. There were reported murders in Pueblo, Little Rock, Shreveport, New Orleans, Norfolk, Washington, D.C., Wilmington, New York, and other cities (Guttman, 1998, p. 17).

Boxing remains a very violent sport, yet coverage of high-profile matches brings in billions of dollars. Many fans hold viewing parties and wager bets on who will win, and violence is sometimes the result of lost bets and excessive drinking. Popular culture has criticized boxing on many occasions. Bob Dylan's 1963 song "Who Killed Davey Moore" addressed the violence in boxing, and although it was not a commercial success it was popular during his live performances. Davey Moore was an American boxer known as "The Little Giant," due to his height of just five feet, two inches. He began boxing in 1953, and on March 18, 1959, won the World Featherweight Title. He held the title for more than four years, then lost to Cuban Sugar Ramos on March 21, 1963. Moore was beaten badly during that fight and ended up losing by technical knockout during the 10th round. After pledging to reporters that he would fight Ramos again and regain his title, he complained of headaches and fell unconscious. He was taken to White Memorial Hospital where he was diagnosed with inoperable brain damage. Never regaining consciousness, Moore died on March 25, 1963. Critics contended that boxing was far too dangerous, and Dylan's song echoed that of folk singer Phil Ochs, although Ochs was more critical of the sport. In his song, Dylan takes turns taking the perspective of various players, from the referee, the crowd, the manager, the gambler, the boxing reporter, and then Sugar Ramos, all of who deny responsibility. This is alternated with the chorus, "Who killed Davey Moore, Why and what's the reason for?" Today, many have expressed concern about violence in boxing and its link to brain injuries.

One sport that has generated violent responses with more frequency is soccer, or football as it is referred to outside the United States. Hooligans who attend games and cause trouble have received much attention. For instance, in 1964 in Lima, Peru, the crowd rushed and broke through a barbed wire fence after an official disallowed a goal that would have equalized the score between Peru and Argentina. They set fire to the stadium, and police responded with tear gas. Hundreds of people were crushed to death as they tried to leave the stadium. Most of the violence by hooligans occurs in or around stadiums, but some fans watching from public locations like bars or pubs have also responded to the coverage with various acts of violence. Many of the football leagues in Europe have made great strides in reducing the access known hooligans have to attend games and have placed other restrictions that have decreased hooliganism.

Some have argued that people enjoy violent sport for the cathartic effect. That is, it is allegedly a way to channel our natural aggressiveness, especially for men, who are theorized to be more naturally aggressive than women. Studies do not support catharsis, however, as they have repeatedly found that persons who spectate violent sporting events (whether live or in the media) are more aggressive after viewing, not less. The most violent sports are most popular with males, and thus much concern has been generated about the effect of participation and viewing on young men.

Ice hockey has long been criticized for its often excessive violence. It "has been called the only all-human sport in which physical intimidation outside the rules is encouraged as a customary tactic: very nearly a blood sport, in fact" (Jewell, Moti & Coates, 2011, p. 11). Academic research suggests that more violence increases attendance at National Hockey League (NHL) games and among television viewers, so it is not likely that the league, the teams, or the players feel incentivized to curtail it.

Mixed martial arts (MMA) is also very popular, again largely among young men. MMA combines wrestling, boxing, kickboxing, and jiu-jitsu. The biggest promoter of MMA is the Ultimate Fighting Championship (UFC). After its premier in 1993, Arizona Senator John McCain called it "human cock fighting" because of its brutality (Szczerba, 2014). Although participants are not killed, MMA is known to be particularly brutal. At the time, the rules of the match allowed for anything except for eye gouging and biting. Fights only ended when an opponent was knocked out or by a judge's decision. Due to its brutal violence, the competition was banned from all but three states. The UFC instituted more regulations, including more than 31 fouls and eight ways to end a bout, which resulted in a return for the pay-per-view televised audiences. In 2008, *Forbes* magazine reported that the UFC promotion company was worth close to $1 billion.

American football has taken some heat in recent years, due to two major issues. One involves the high rates of concussions among former players, and the other involves the number of players involved with sexual assault and domestic violence scandals. ESPN came under fire for its coverage of domestic violence when video footage was released by *TMZ* showing Baltimore Ravens player Ray Rice punching his then-fiancé Janay Palmer and knocking her out in an elevator. The network's largely male commentators made remarks that many females took issue with, such as that there was something wrong with Palmer for staying with and later marrying Rice. NFL Commissioner Roger Goodell was criticized for doing too little about the problem of players abusing women and for having to be told he needed to allow a woman, Jane McManus, into his special announcements. McManus had written extensively about domestic violence in her column for espnW, the network's website that's focused on female fans, and she was quick to criticize the NFL when it initially suspended Ray Rice for just two games. Her ESPN colleague Hannah Storm, CNN's Rachel Nichols, and CBS's Jericka Duncan and many other female sports reporters were also vocal critics of the league's handling of the Rice case and the issue in general.

Like boxing, American football has been accused of being too dangerous for players. Between 2012 and 2015, there were 967 documented player concussions in either the preseason or regular season. But as far back as 1994, NFL Commissioner Paul Tagliabue identified that the NFL might have a problem and created a committee, the Mild Traumatic Injury Committee, to study brain injuries. He appointed Dr. Elliott Perlman to head it, despite the fact that Perlman has no particular experience in that area. In 2002, Dr. Bennett Omalu was the first to identify chronic traumatic encephalopathy (CTE) in the brain of former Pittsburgh Steelers' center Mike Webster, age 50, who committed suicide. He argued that repeated concussions were the problem. Yet in 2005 the Mild Traumatic Injury Committee found that the sport "does not involve significant risk of a second injury either in the same game or during the season." In 2011, former Chicago Bears defensive back Dave Duerson, age 50, committed suicide but shot himself in the chest rather than the head so his brain could be researched for CTE, which was found by Boston University researchers. After several other suicides and homicides perpetrated by players with CTE, players filed more than 80 concussion-related lawsuits in a unified suit on behalf of more than 2,000 players. A settlement was proposed in August 2013, but the players association declined to accept it because they did not believe it was enough. In July 2016, the NFL and the NFL Players' Association set new policies regarding concussions, including discipline for teams who allow players to take the field with concussions. In 2015, the film *Concussion* starring Will Smith told the story of Dr. Omalu.

Many have also critiqued the violence in World Wrestling Entertainment (WWE), what is sometimes called a "soap opera for men." The storylines feature bullying, abuse, sexual harassment, and homophobia. Female characters undergo horrific abuse, and the storylines often imply or even state that "she deserved it." The documentary *Wrestling with Manhood* by Media Education Foundation provides countless examples of this, showing how the female characters are allegedly lying, conniving flirts who deserve any verbal or physical abuse. Studies have found that such depictions may be linked to abusive behavior in dating relationships. In one study, Dr. Robert Durant and colleagues found that as the participants were exposed to more wrestling, their verbally and physically abusive dating behavior intensified, as did their drinking and drug use. The authors did note that youth who were more prone to engage in violent behavior may also be more likely to watch professional wrestling. Interestingly, the same increase in violent behavior was observed among teenage female viewers of professional wrestling, who make up a considerable minority. Officials with the WWE critiqued the study, asserting that it did not show a direct causal relationship and that it ignored other factors that might be related to the increased abuse, drinking, and drug use.

Wrestling with Manhood also draws attention to the bullying behavior exhibited by professional wrestlers in the ring, especially against those who are perceived to be gay. Those characters face additional taunts and homoerotic physical abuse as a way to show the masculinity of their opponents. Some assert that this reinforces to viewers that gay men are not to be accepted and that it normalizes violence against that population.

Critics also point out that a number of professional wrestlers have been accused and even convicted of domestic and other forms of violence. "Stone Cold" Steve Austin allegedly attacked his former wife, Debra Williams, in 2002 and 2004. In June 2007, the bodies of wrestler Chris Benoit, his wife Nancy-Daus Benoit, and his seven-year-old son Daniel were found in Fayetteville, Georgia. It is believed that Benoit strangled his wife and then suffocated his son before hanging himself. Investigators found drugs and anabolic steroids in the home, which drew attention to the role that performance-enhancing drugs (PEDs) may have in stimulating violent behavior. Debra Williams also said that Austin was abusive due to drugs. Mrs. Benoit had sought a divorce from Chris Benoit in 2003 and then applied for a restraining order, and Williams had previously applied for a restraining order against Austin. She claims that he, like Chris Benoit, essentially forced her to tell authorities that the complaint was a mistake and to withdraw the order. Austin was sentenced to one year of probation, but Williams was placed under a gag order that prohibited her from talking about the situation or about what she says was widespread drug use, alcoholism, and abuse within the WWE. Jerry Lawler, long-time announcer for the WWE, and his girlfriend were both accused of domestic violence in June 2016. Lawler, 66 at the time, and Lauryn McBride, 27, were arrested after police were called to their East Memphis home. Both claimed the other was the assailant. Lawler was suspended from the WWE after his arrest. In 2014, as a result of the NFL scandal involving Minnesota Viking Ray Rice, the WWE announced a new zero-tolerance policy regarding domestic violence. It includes a provision that allows for the organization to terminate employees even when they have not been convicted.

Like the NFL, several professional wrestlers have filed a lawsuit against the WWE, alleging that it sold violence while neglecting the health of its athletes. Former WWE wrestlers Vito LoGrasso and Evan Singleton alleged that the WWE knew or should have known that it was subjecting its athletes to potentially lethal danger, including brain damage. LoGrasso claimed that he suffered from neurological damage, including depression, anxiety, and memory loss. Singleton alleges that the WWE was the source of his tremors, convulsions, and impaired reasoning capacity. Data show that professional wrestlers are at greater risk for heart attacks. Between 1997 and 2004, the rate of professional wrestlers dying from heart attacks surpassed by far the average for people in the same age range. Drug use, including cocaine, painkillers, steroids, and other drugs, was a factor in some 20 percent of the cases.

Laura L. Finley

See also: British Television; Mexican Wrestling; National Anthem, The; Professional Wrestling; Soccer/Football Hooligans

Further Reading

ABC News. 2006. "Watching Wrestling Linked to Teen Dating Violence." *ABC News,* August 7. http://abcnews.go.com/Health/story?id=2274722

Almond, K. 2015. "The Art of the 'Death Match.'" *CNN,* August 6. http://www.cnn.com /2015/08/06/us/cnnphotos-hardcore-wrestling-death-matches

Bernthal, M. 2008. "How Viewing Professional Wrestling May Affect Children." *The Sport Journal.* http://thesportjournal.org/article/how-viewing-professional-wrestling-may -affect-children

Fox News. 2007. "Pro Wrestling Wife Claims Drug Abuse, Domestic Violence 'Out of Hand in the WWE.'" *Fox News,* June 7. http://www.foxnews.com/story/2007/06 /27/pro-wrestling-wife-claims-drug-abuse-domestic-violence-out-hand-in-wwe .html

Guttman, A. 1998. "The Appeal of Violent Sports." In *Why We Watch: The Attractions of Violent Entertainment,* edited by J. Goldstein, 7–26. New York: Oxford.

Jewell, R., Moti, A., & Coates, D. 2011. "A Brief History of Violence and Aggression in Professional Sports." In *Violence and Aggression in Sporting Contests. Sports Economics, Management and Policy,* edited by R. Jewell, Vol. 4, 11–26. New York: Springer.

Jhally, Sut (Director). 2010. *Wrestling with Manhood.* Documentary available for purchase from Media Education Foundation at http://shop.mediaed.org/wrestling-with-man hood-p170.aspx

"NFL Concussion Fast Facts." 2016. *CNN,* August 1. http://edition.cnn.com/2013/08/30/us /nfl-concussions-fast-facts/index.html

Rhodes, D. 2015. "Why Do Wrestlers So Often Die Young?" *BBC News,* August 8. http:// www.bbc.com/news/magazine-33817959

Rose, J. 2014. "For Women in Sports TV, a Seat at the Table." *NPR*, September 26. http:// www.npr.org/2014/09/26/351678310/domestic-violence-is-the-central-sports-story -espn-reporter-says

Szczerba, R. 2014. "Mixed Martial Arts and the Evolution of John McCain." *Forbes*, April 3. https://www.forbes.com/sites/robertszczerba/2014/04/03/mixed-martial -arts-and-the-evolution-of-john-mccain/#24e6fe092d59

Tamborini, R., Skalski, P., Lachlan, K., Westerman, D., Davis, J., & Smith, S. "The Raw Nature of Televised Professional Wrestling: Is the Violence a Cause for Concern?" *Journal of Broadcasting and Electronic Media, 49*(2), 202–20.

Star Trek

Star Trek is a science fiction television series and media franchise that debuted in 1966. In addition to the original series, there are animated series, spin-off television series, films, and other manifestations of *Star Trek*. The franchise has been a cult phenomenon since it began, and fans, often called "Trekkies," attend events, purchase products, and adore it. It has generated more than $10 billion in revenue, making it the highest-grossing media franchise in U.S. history. The original series follows Captain James T. Kirk (William Shatner) and his colleagues on the starship *Enterprise* as they explore outer space and occasionally grapple with extraterrestrial life.

The *Original Series*, as it is known, ran from 1966 to 1969. In addition to Shatner, it starred Leonard Nimoy as Spock, George Takei as Sulu, and a host of others as regular cast members. *Star Trek: The Next Generation* ran from 1987 until 1994. The Enterprise-D was led by Captain Jean-Luc Picard (Patrick Stewart) and Commander William Riker (Jonathan Frakes). It was the highest-rated *Star Trek* show. *Star Trek: Deep Space Nine* ran from 1993 to 1999. It aired for seven seasons and starred Avery Brooks as Captain Benjamin Sisko. *Star Trek: Voyager* ran from 1995 until 2001, starring Kate Mulgrew as Captain Kathryn Janeway, the first female commanding officer in the series. Science fiction star Scott Bakula starred as Captain Jonathan Archer in *Voyager*. *Star Trek: Discovery*, the latest version, began in 2017 and stars Sonequa Martin-Greenplays as Lieutenant Commander Michael Burnham. It is a prequel to the Original Series.

The *Star Trek* franchise has been applauded for showcasing a racially diverse cast. It is recognized as having featured the first interracial kiss on television, in 1968. Fans see it as among the most progressive show ever on American television. In 2016, *New Yorker* commentator Manu Saadia wrote,

> Each successive "Star Trek" cast has been like a model United Nations. Nichols' black communications specialist worked alongside George Takei's Japanese helmsman and Walter Koenig's (admittedly campy) Russian navigator. Leonard Nimoy's Spock was half-human, half-Vulcan, and he bore traces of the actor's own upbringing in a poor Jewish neighborhood in Boston. The Vulcan hand greeting, for instance, which Nimoy invented, is the Hebrew letter shin, the symbol for the Shekhinah, a feminine aspect of the divine. The original series aired only a few years after the Cuban missile crisis, at the height of the Vietnam War and the space race, and its vision of a reconciled humanity was bold. Nichols, who considered leaving the show after the first season, has said that she was persuaded to stay on by Martin Luther King, Jr., who told her that he watched "Star Trek" with his wife and daughters.

It is also credited as the first television series to feature an openly gay character. Yet *Star Trek* has also been criticized for its historic emphasis on "alpha males" and faced a backlash of negative comments regarding its female stars.

Although the violence in the show was not controversial in the United States, it was seen as such in other countries. The BBC did not air four episodes of the *Original Series* because it addressed topics like torture, sadism, and disease. Proponents maintain that the bad guys are far more interesting than are those in other science fiction series, such as *Star Wars*. They are more political in their motivations yet also more complex.

Laura L. Finley

See also: Alien Franchise; *Star Wars* Franchise; "War of the Worlds"; X-*Files, The*

Further Reading

Andrews, T. 2017, June 23. "'Star Trek' Fans Anger at Remake's Diversity Proves They Don't Understand 'Star Trek.'" *Chicago Tribune,* June 23. http://www.chicagotribune.com/entertainment/tv/ct-star-trek-discovery-diversity-20170623-story.html

Brode, D. & Brode, S. 2015. *The Star Trek Universe: Franchising the Final Frontier.* Lanham, MD: Rowman & Littlefield.

Ryan, M. 2017. "TV Review: 'Star Trek: Discovery' on CBS and CBS Access." *Variety,* September 24. http://variety.com/2017/tv/reviews/star-trek-discovery-cbs-all-access-review-sonequa-martin-green-1202569322

Saadia, M. 2016. "10 Reasons 'Star Trek' Is Better than 'Star Wars.'" *Business Insider*, June 2. http://www.businessinsider.com/10-reasons-star-trek-is-better-than-star -wars-2016-5?r=US&IR=T&IR=T/#1-star-trek-is-tv-star-wars-is-primarily-feature -films-1

21 Jump Street

The television series *21 Jump Street* is a police drama that aired from April 1987 until April 1991 for a total of 103 episodes. It featured a squad of young-looking police officers who go undercover to investigate crime in high schools, colleges, and other locations where teens congregate. It was created by Patrick Hasburgh and Stephen J. Cannell, and was one of the early hits for the fledgling station Fox. It starred Johnny Depp as Officer Tom Hanson, Dustin Nguyen as Officer Ioki, Peter DeLuise as Officer Penhall, and Holly Robinson as Sergeant Judy Hoffs, the undercover officers. The officers investigate a variety of offenses, including drug abuse, child abuse, gang rape, and hate crimes. Part of the reason it was popular among younger viewers is that it took on issues that were really happening. Many actors who appeared as guests on the show went on to stardom, including Jason Priestly, Brad Pitt, and Bridget Fonda. Many episodes ended with public service announcements featuring the show's actors or other famous people cautioning viewers against drugs or other ills.

One episode, "Swallowed Alive," featured the officers infiltrating a juvenile prison to find out how heroin is being trafficked from it. Officer Hanson ends up on his own, as two of the others are transferred, and Officer Penhall, who ended up in solitary confinement, can't take it and is pulled from the operation. The episode depicts the brutality of the guards and how easy it is to become worse, not better, when locked up. "Blinded by the Thousand Points of Light" is about a serial killer who preys on homeless youth. Hanson poses as a prostitute so that they can draw in the killer.

Another somewhat controversial episode drew attention to U.S. policy in El Salvador and the plight of refugees from the violent civil war there in the late 1980s. Executive producer Bill Nuss said, "It's a challenging thing to deal with such a heavy social issue within the context of a high school show about social issues. We think that the refugee issue is an ongoing and important problem. We won't back off of issues just because they are not real hot in the news right now. This is a problem we think our audience should be aware of. They should know what's going on down there." The artist Peter Gabriel filmed a public service announcement that aired after the episode and shed light on the human rights group Amnesty International, which had been openly critical of the United States' role in El Salvador (Weinstein, 1989).

The producers have said they were proud to have offered a show that tackled important issues in a way that appealed to teens. They also believed the show helped young people. For instance, after one episode that featured a father sexually abusing his daughter, they cited 4,000 calls to a hotline that night. The hotline normally received approximately 900 calls per night. They also claim that an episode about busting up a pornography ring was being used to train real police officers (Brennan, 1987).

In the 2012 film *21 Jump Street*, directed by Phil Lord and Chris Miller, two young men, Morton Schmidt (Jonah Hill) and Greg Jenko (Channing Tatum) join the police academy and are asked to undergo a top-secret assignment as undercover cops. They are required go back to their old high school to find the main drug supplier. Both Schmidt and Jenko are living at Schmidt's parents' house and refer to themselves as "brothers" throughout the movie. Schmidt and Jenko soon realize that their high school has changed since the last time they were there. They both also find out the lead dealer is a popular kid in the high school, Eric (Dave Franco). After figuring out who was dealing the drugs, they went to the dealing room, where Eric made them take the drug right then and there to prove they were legitimate. While Schmidt is busy becoming friends with the dealer, Jenko realizes his chemistry friends can hack into phones.

Schmidt decides to have a party at his parents' house to gain Eric's complete trust, while Jenko takes the opportunity during the house party to tap into Eric's phone. As soon as Schmidt gains Eric's full trust he pretends to sell the drug for Eric, but rather gives it to Captain Dickson, his boss (Ice Cube). As the movie progresses, Schmidt and Jenko figure out that Eric is making a big deal soon. Jenko leaves to follow Eric, taking Schmidt with him as well, but they are both compelled to run away when they get caught. Schmidt and Jenko get into an argument and get kicked out of high school for fighting. Later on, Eric tells Schmidt and Jenko that he wants to bring them on a deal as security. Eric tells Schmidt and Jenko about what's going to go down on the night of prom, where they are going to meet the supplier. On the night of prom all the guys are shocked to see that their supplier is a teacher at their school, Mr. Walters, who realizes that Schmidt and Jenko are police officers and tells two of his guys to kill them. Yet the two men who were asked to kill Schmidt and Jenko are Drug Enforcement Agency (DEA) agents who were a part of the Jump Street program as well. A gunfight breaks out between all the guys in the room, causing them to flee the scene in limos. Inside of Schmidt and Jenko's limo, Jenko creates a homemade chemical bomb from his experience in AP Chemistry. Schmidt and Jenko confront Mr. Walters, who then shoots at Schmidt, dodging Schmidt and hitting Jenko because Jenko jumped in front of Schmidt to save his life. Schmidt and Jenko successfully arrest Mr. Walters and Eric and make amends with each other. After Schmidt and Jenko complete their job, Captain Dickson assigns them another job in a college setting instead of high school this time. Johnny Depp made a cameo appearance in the film, as did Holly Robinson Peete. In his review, Roger Ebert expressed that he surprisingly enjoyed the film (Ebert, 2012). It was followed in 2014 by a sequel, *22 Jump Street*.

Laura L. Finley

See also: Breaking Bad; British Television; *Hill Street Blues*; *Law & Order*

Further Reading

Brennan, P. 1987. "21 Jump Street." *The Washington Post*, December 13. https://www
.washingtonpost.com/archive/lifestyle/tv/1987/12/13/21-jump-street/b0cc270a
-cb2b-454c-af66-22c5ef402359/?utm_term=.d849b5d05259

Ebert, R. 2012. "21 Jump Street." *Roger Ebert*, March 14. https://www.rogerebert.com
/reviews/21-jump-street-2012

Ihnat, G. 2017. "21 Jump Street Did More than Just Make Johnny Depp Famous." *AV Club*, April 10. https://tv.avclub.com/21-jump-street-did-more-than-just-make-johnny -depp-famo-1798260689

Weinstein, S. 1989. "'Jump Street' Tackles Plight of the Poor in El Salvador." *LA Times*, October 9. http://articles.latimes.com/1989-10-09/entertainment/ca-173_1_jump -street

Walking Dead, The

The Walking Dead is a critically acclaimed drama series based on the comic book series of the same name written by Robert Kirkman. The first episode aired on October 31, 2010, and the show has had a large following ever since. The series follows police officer Rick Grimes (Andrew Lincoln), who is shot in the line of duty and then ends up in a hospital to recover. He awakens in the hospital, only to find it deserted and then sees that the outside world has been overrun by zombies. He eventually is able to find a group of survivors of which he becomes the de facto leader, and the story follows him and his group as they try to survive the violent and savage world they live in. They learn quite quickly that as scary and violent as the zombies are, the people who have survived are perhaps even more dangerous. One thing that sets this show apart from other media where zombies are the central plot element is the fact that the interactions between the characters in the show are the main emphasis, rather than the zombies themselves.

From the pilot episode of *The Walking Dead*, it was clear that violence was going to be integral to the show. The very first scene in *The Walking Dead* depicts Rick shooting a zombie child in order to defend himself. From there, the violence escalates rapidly. Within the course of the series, we see multiple characters shoot, stab, murder, and get eaten. More often than not, these instances are portrayed in very realistic detail, as opposed to being implied. The show constantly places characters in peril where the only course of action is for them to use violence to escape from a particular predicament.

Despite the gratuitous use of violence, the show has maintained a devoted following. On October 23, 2016, the premiere episode of the seventh season of the series brought close to 17 million viewers, even overshadowing the Sunday Night Football game that was playing the same day. The series is also always at least in the discussion for the television Emmy awards. The series boasts a total of 15 Emmy nominations (mostly for categories related to makeup and design) and was the winner of awards for Outstanding Prosthetic Makeup in a Series, Miniseries, Movie, or Special in 2011 and 2012.

For all of its awards and accolades, the show does have its fair share of critics. *The Walking Dead* has a very engaging main story, but oftentimes, at least to critics, it seems that the graphic violence is the main attraction of the series, rather than the story. Many feel that the series is glorifying and normalizing graphic displays of violence. For example, on the premiere episode of the seventh season, which aired October 23, 2016, viewers watched as the current antagonist Negan (Jeffrey Dean Morgan) attacked two characters with his signature barbed-wire wrapped baseball bat. Negan repeatedly bashed one of the victim's heads with the bat, in realistic detail. This display resulted in multiple groups upset with the amount and depiction of violence in the series. The Parent Television Council feels that "[w]ith *The Walking Dead*, the creative team has resorted to the graphic violence as a crutch for what used to be better storytelling. When you can't figure out what lines to write, you put something in easier, which is a graphic depiction. To me, it's too much" (Deerwester, 2016).

The actor who plays Rick Grimes, Andrew Lincoln, has also voiced his apparent apprehension about some of the events that unfold in the series, specifically the season six finale. In this episode, "Negan makes a weird threat, that if anybody moves, he'll cut out Carl's eye and feed it to his father [Rick]" (Vigna, 2016). While this is going on, Rick and his group are all forced to kneel before Negan and his men, completely at the mercy to his menace. Lincoln was reported to have said this concerning season six's finale: "I felt sick to my stomach when I read the script. It was the first day in the whole six years of working on *'The Walking Dead'* that I was late for work because I woke up in the middle of the night and I couldn't get back to sleep. I was so angry and frustrated and I felt sick. And that was just after reading it" (Saclao, 2016).

Supporters of *The Walking Dead* are quick to point out that most things that happen in the TV series are because the directors are following its source material, the comics. Critics of the violence, however, argue that although it is necessary to be true to the source material, oftentimes now, it seems as if the TV series is content to linger on the instances of violence, further making it a spectacle. In response to the episode regarding Negan's beat-down of his victims, media critic Matthew Zoller Seitz wrote: "The brutality was nearly eroticized, with loving inserts of the villain's bloody weapon, lingering images of hostages' tearful, terrified faces and low-angled shots that made Negan loom like a conquering badass hero" (Seitz, 2016). Seitz goes on to argue that violence in other shows is usually used as a tool to ask moral questions about the characters in those shows, but in *The Walking Dead*, "[t]he longer this series goes on, the more obvious it becomes that the violence is the point, and everything else is an intellectual fig leaf."

The Walking Dead, despite the controversy it generates, continues to be one of the most popular TV shows on primetime television.

Jhaland Francois

See also: American Horror Story; *Breaking Bad*; Broadway Musicals; *Fight Club*; *Game of Thrones*; *Mad Men*; *Sopranos, The*; Zombie Films

Further Reading

Deerwester, J. 2016. "Parents Television Council Slams 'Walking Dead' Violence." *USA Today*, October 25. http://www.usatoday.com/story/life/tv/2016/10/25/parents-television-council-slams-walking-dead-violence/92715428

Pattern, D. 2016. "'Walking Dead' Ratings Near All-Time High with Season 7 Debut & Thrashes NFL." *Deadline*, October 25. http://deadline.com/2016/10/walking-dead-ratings-season-7-premiere-nfl-1201842022

Saclao, C. 2016. "'The Walking Dead': Andrew Lincoln Says He Felt 'Sick' after Reading Season 6 Finale Script." *Design Trend*, February 13. http://www.designntrend.com/articles/70200/20160213/the-walking-dead-andrew-lincoln-says-he-felt-sick-after-reading-season-6-finale-script.htm

Seitz, M. Z. 2016. "The Empty Violence of The Walking Dead." *Vulture*, October 24. http://www.vulture.com/2016/10/walking-dead-empty-violence.html

Vigna, P. 2016. "'The Walking Dead' Season 6 Finale Recap." *The Wall Street Journal*, April 4. http://blogs.wsj.com/speakeasy/2016/04/04/the-walking-dead-season-6-finale-recap

X-Files, The

The X-Files is a science fiction drama created by Chris Carter in 1993. The television series aired from September 1993 to May 2002, running for nine seasons and featuring 202 episodes. After the end of *The X-Files* in 2002, Chris Carter wrote a second feature film in 2008, *The X-Files: I Want to Believe*, which led to a tenth season of *The X-Files*. The tenth season aired six episodes in January 2016. An eleventh season aired on Fox in January 2018.

Carter, the show's creator, executive producer, and one of the writers, based the series on two FBI specialists who examined unexplained, weird, and confusing cases known as "X-Files." In the story, the government believes that these reports are absolutely false; however, Fox Mulder and Dana Scully (the FBI specialists), for the greater part of the television series, would go to the ends of the earth to find "the truth" they sought. Scully, played by Gillian Anderson, is the more skeptical one, as opposed to Mulder, played by David Duchovny, who is much more of a conspiracy theorist. When creating these characters, Carter wanted to switch the stereotypical "female and male role" by making the male the "believer" in most situations. Gender is the basis of many controversies surrounding this television series.

Perhaps one of the most controversial episodes of *The X-Files* was "Home." This episode was about a deformed family, the Peacock Family. The Peacocks Family are violent murderers in a country town called Mayberry. There are three males, all brothers, one having fathered the other two with his mother, who had sex with all three of her male sons. This disturbing episode disrupted television screens nationwide. The episode aired in 1994 and was banned soon after, only reappearing in 1999 for a Halloween special. The producer and crew members felt that this episode went way too far (Bassett, 2016).

Episode 14 of *The X-Files* is about a creature that changes gender in order to kill its victims during sex. This episode caused a lot of controversy because fans felt that it was too "black and white." That is, the fans saw issues emerge right off the bat, when Scully adjusts Mulder's supposition that the killer is male on the grounds that there are casualties of both genders. They did not even try to acknowledge bisexuality; they only saw this "monster" as either gay or straight. Another controversial aspect to this episode is how the monster kills. The facts that it has to change its gender in order to sleep with someone raised a few flags for viewers. Seeing that violence against transgender individuals typically happens after sex occurs with cisgender people, this episode is particularly insensitive. Viewers state that throughout the television series, not just in this one episode, transgender people are looked at as "other," instead of equally (Harnick, 2017).

In Season 5, there was controversy about who is to blame in rape cases. In the episode "Post-Modern Prometheus," Scully basically blames the victim for what happens, discredits her argument, and states that she's just in it for the fame. This is a dangerous way to show how law enforcement handles rape cases. It gives the impression that the victim is always to blame and that the perpetrator can get away with anything. It is interesting that in this case Scully, the female agent, has no problem seeing this as a cry for fame, whereas Mulder, the male agent, seems to be the only one who actually seems to care about the facts of the case at hand. Even after finding out that the victim was telling the truth, agents Mulder and Scully listened to the rapist's reasoning, sympathized with him, and instead of taking him to jail, they rewarded him with a concert. Viewers did not like that he was "rewarded" for such a heinous crime.

In another episode, "Irresistible," Scully is abducted by a woman-hating monster named Donnie Pfaster, who kidnaps and murders women and then desecrates their bodies. "Irresistible" was followed by "Die Hand Die Verletzt" in Season 2, which features a girl recounting being assaulted by her stepfather.

Later, it was discovered that only 2 of the 207 episodes were directed by women. As of August 2017, Chris Carter had hired two female directors and two female writers. The new writers include Karen Nielson, and Kristen Cloke. Carter expects that the new women will add something extra to the show (Harnick, 2017).

Laura L. Finley

See also: Alien Franchise; *Game of Thrones*; Rape Films; *Star Trek*; *Star Wars* Franchise; "War of the Worlds"

Further Reading

Ashurst, S., & Jeffery, M. 2017. "The X-Files Season 11: Release Date, News, Comic, Cast and Everything You Need to Know." *Digital Spy*, October 23. http://www.digitalspy .com/tv/the-x-files/feature/a830297/the-x-files-season-11-release-date-news-cast -plot

Bassett, J. 2016. "This X Files Episode Is So Scary It Was Banned from Television." *NME*, January 8. http://www.nme.com/blogs/nme-blogs/as-the-iconic-show-returns-we -remember-the-x-files-episode-so-scary-it-was-banned-from-television-768041

Graham, S. 2018. "Scully, the Victim: The Legacy of Gendered Violence on The X-Files." *Bitch Magazine*, January 29. https://www.bitchmedia.org/article/gendered-violence -on-the-x-files

Harnick, C. 2017. "The X-Files Gets Female Writers and Directors in Wake of Controversy." *E! Online*, August 8. http://www.eonline.com/news/871995/the-x-files-gets-2 -female-writers-and-directors-in-wake-of-controversy

Mason, H. 2017. "Problematic Faves: The X-Files." *SyFy Wire*, January 13. http://www.syfy .com/syfywire/problematic-faves-x-files

4

Music and Violence

Introduction

Music has always had the ability to inform and inspire, both in positive and negative ways. Violence is a common topic for song lyrics across all genres. National anthems, for instance, often glamorize militarism as a tool for independence, as does the U.S. national anthem, "The Star Spangled Banner." Songs were used by slaves before and during the Civil War to protest their conditions and to provide a sense of solidarity. When radio became more widely broadcast in the 1920s, music began to reach a far broader audience, giving rise to concerns that some lyrics would promote bad behavior.

These concerns hit a new high in the 1950s, during the height of popularity of rock and roll. Critics contended that the music of popular artists like Elvis Presley, with his hip-shaking moves on stage, were too much for young people to handle. The focus was less on violence, which did not feature prominently in Presley's music, and more on his sexuality. Presley's 1956 performance of "Hound Dog" on *The Milton Berle Show* was dubbed "vulgar" and critiqued for its "animalism," prompting the Catholic Church to issue a caution to families about the so-called danger of the artist's music. He has also been critiqued for co-opting Black music despite being a racist who once said, "The only thing black people can do for me is shine my shoes and buy my music" (Kolawole, 2002).

The civil rights movement of the 1950s and 1960s also used music to garner support. Many of the popular songs used during the movement came from slave songs, like "We Shall Be Free." "We Shall Overcome" was used by protestors and performed by a number of artists. Nina Simone's "Mississippi Goddamn" was written in response to the murder of four Black girls in a Mississippi Church in 1964 (Lynskey, 2011). Similarly, music was key to the anti–Vietnam War movement. Songs like Bob Dylan's (1963) "Blowin' in the Wind"; Phil Ochs's (1964) "What Are You Fighting For?" and (1965) "I Ain't Marching Anymore"; Barry McGuire's "Eve of Destruction"; Tom Paxton's (1965) "Lyndon Told the Nation"; Pete Seeger's

(1966) "Bring 'Em Home," (1967) "Waist Deep in the Big Muddy," and (1968) "2 + 2+?"; Arlo Guthrie's (1967) "Alice's Restaurant Massacre"; Nina Simone's (1967) "Backlash Blues"; Joan Baez's (1967) "Saigon Bride"; Country Joe and the Fish's (1967) "Feel Like I'm Fixin' to Die Rag"; Richie Havens's (1967) "Handsome Johnny"; Creedence Clearwater Revival's (1969) "Fortunate Son"; John Lennon's (1969) "Give Peace a Chance" and (1971) "Imagine"; Jimmy Cliffs's (1969) "Vietnam"; Crosby, Stills, Nash and Young's (1970) "Ohio"; Edwin Star's (1970) "War"; and Marvin Gaye's (1971) "What's Going On" are listed among the top antiwar protest songs of the era (Lindsay, 2015). Bob Dylan's "Masters of War" (1963), one of his most snarling, angry tunes, is a powerful indictment of the government's authorization of other people's children to fight in dangerous wars. Decades later, the band Pearl Jam performed the song as a critique of the U.S. invasions of Iraq and Afghanistan.

Black artists gained attention in the 1960s and 1970s for their critique of racism and police abuse. James Brown had been facing criticism for being an "Uncle Tom" who cozied up to the White establishment while other Black people, like the members of Black Panther Party, were doing something to fight it when he began performing "Say It Loud—I'm Black and I'm Proud." Evidently the Panthers had been putting pressure on Brown to take a more aggressive stance and were critical of an earlier tune by the artist, the patriotic "America Is My Home." The song sold 750,000 copies in its first two weeks and seemed to be a catalyst for other Black artists to issue more scathing critiques. These included Sly and the Family Stone's "Don't Call Me N****r, Whitey," Curtis Mayfield's "Mighty Mighty (Spade and Whitey)," "Miss Black America," and "We the People Who Are Darker than Blue" (Lynskey, 2011). Mayfield went on to write the soundtrack for *Super Fly*, one of the early Blaxsploitation films that further drew attention to the conditions of life for Black Americans. The 1970s saw many Black artists raising awareness about the daily violence of the ghettoes in which many lived.

The 1980s ushered in a new time of musical controversy. On one hand, the rise of rap music, especially what was called gangsta rap, brought new critics of Black artists' attempts to problematize life in urban ghettoes. On the other, heavy metal music, including what is often called "hair" or "glam" metal, featured largely White artists discussing drugs, booze, sex, and violence. Perhaps the first commercially successful gangsta rap group was N.W.A., with its (1988) album *Straight Outta Compton*. That album featured the controversial "F**k tha Police," which begins with a spoken introduction in which "Judge" Dr. Dre is asking MC Ren, Ice Cube, and Eazy E for testimony against the police department. The artists go on to discuss police harassment, unlawful searches, and being targeted for being Black. The song is full of curse words and repeatedly refers to the police as thugs. The honest yet abrasive lyrics and tones to this and other hit gangsta rap songs caused tremendous backlash, as parents and pundits criticized it for inciting violence. Yet others noted that the music was simply depicting reality in certain communities and that it was being targeted because it was made by Black artists who refused to be quieted.

Heavy metal artists also faced criticism and calls for censorship. For instance, in 1980, Ozzy Osbourne's song "Suicide Solution" allegedly encouraged suicide, and Osbourne faced a lawsuit six years after it was released by the family of a teen who had committed suicide. The suit went nowhere. Often, such criticisms merely served to increase interest in the music, album purchases, and ticket sales to concerts.

Critics have long-contended that kids who listen to a lot of music and frequently watch music videos are at increased risk for engaging in violent behavior or risk-taking behavior, like early sexual activity and substance abuse. Yet data are not entirely clear that listening to music or watching music videos has this effect. Efforts have been made to identify music that might have this effect and to issue warning labels on albums or songs that feature graphic lyrics or adult content. Tipper Gore and three other women founded the Parents Music Resource Center (PMRC) in 1985, which would establish guidelines for regulating music deemed sexual or violent. The group also testified before the Senate about the danger of the so-called "Filthy 15," 15 songs that they deemed were the most offensive. The Filthy 15 included Prince's "Darling Nikki" and Cyndi Lauper's "She Bop" for references to sex and masturbation; Sheena Easton's "Sugar Walls," Judas Priest's "Eat Me Alive," Vanity's "Strap on Robbie Baby," ACDC's "Let Me Put My Love into You," Madonna's "Dress You Up," W.A.S.P.'s "Animal (F**k Like a Beast), and Mary Jane Girls' "In My House" for sexual material; Def Leppard's "High and Dry" and Black Sabbath's "Trashed" for references to drug and alcohol use; Venom's "Possessed" and Merciful Fate's "Into the Coven" for promoting the occult; and Motley Crue's "Bastard" and Twisted Sister's "We're Not Gonna Take It" for references to violence. During the hearings, which repeatedly made reference to this music as "porn rock," Ms. Gore and others testified about the alleged dangers of listening to such music, while many artists, including Twister Sister front man Dee Snider, country singer John Denver, and Frank and Dweezil Zappa, argued that the PRMC's efforts were misguided and dangerous (Schonfeld, 2015).

The Recording Industry Association of America says that the labels work well, despite being voluntary. Others note that warning labels actually increase record sales. For instance, N.W.A.'s *Straight Outta Compton*, featuring the controversial hit "F**k tha Police," sold 750,000 copies before the band toured the record (Grow, 2015). Critics have also noted that efforts like those of the PRMC focus on certain genres of music more than others. Country music, for instance, features a great deal of violence, sex, and alcohol abuse, but has not generally faced such calls for censorship. Many country music songs talk about domestic violence, as well, with some seeming to promote revenge themes.

Further, critics contend that calls for censorship are ill informed. For instance, Dee Snider has said that Twisted Sister's "We're Not Gonna Take It" was wrongly cited as promoting violence, given that it actually made no references to violent behavior, while Nirvana's (1993) "Rape Me" is an antirape song but has been said to promote sexual assault.

Music continues to be at the forefront of efforts to draw attention to societal problems. The 2014 shooting of Black teen Michael Brown by White police officer Darren Wilson, and the subsequent failure to indict Wilson for excessive force, resulted in a number of protest songs. Ezra Furman's "Ferguson's Burning" was an ode to Brown's mother and an indictment of the world for paying too little attention to police brutality. Lauryn Hill penned "Black Rage" to detail why Black people were so upset at the situation in Ferguson. From being considered three-fifths of a person in the U.S. Constitution, to slavery, to modern-day racism, Hill's powerful song, to the tune of "Favorite Things" from the musical *Sound of Music*, stresses that Black rage is the result of wounded souls.

The 2016 election of Donald Trump to the presidency has resulted in a number of parodies and protest songs. One of the notable songs is "The Party's Over" by Prophets of Rage. Prophets of Rage is a supergroup that includes Chuck D of Public Enemy, B Real of Cypress Hill, and several members, including Tom Morello, of Rage Against the Machine. The track features B Real in a scathing indictment of Trump. The band sold merchandise at their concerts featuring the tagline "Make America Rage Again," a take on Donald Trump's campaign slogan "Make America Great Again."

In 2014, the National Coalition Against Censorship released a list of the 40 most banned and censored songs. Many were censored due to references for drugs. Among those included for violent lyrics were Red Nation's (2011) "The Game," which was banned by MTV, BET, and many radio stations for allegedly glorifying gang life; Billie Holiday's (1939) "Strange Fruit," which describes the bodies of lynched men as dead fruit hanging in the South; Robin Thicke's (2013) "Blurred Lines," which is said to promote unwanted sexual behavior; the Notorious B.I.G.'s (1994) "Juicy," which was banned from many radio stations after the September 11, 2001, terrorist attack due to the line "time to get paid, blow up like the World Trade"; John Lennon's (1971) "Imagine," banned by Clear Channel after the 9/11 attack and by the BBC during the Gulf War in 1991, despite being perhaps the most widely known peace song; and Body Count's (1992) "Cop Killer," which artist Ice-T says is about police brutality (Morrison, 2015).

Laura L. Finley

Further Reading

Armstrong, E. 1993. "The Rhetoric of Violence in Rap and Country Music." *Sociological Inquiry, 63*(1): 64–78.

Donkin, J. 2008. "Heavy Metal and Violence: More than a Myth?" *CNN,* May 12. http://edition.cnn.com/2008/SHOWBIZ/Music/05/09/metal.violence/index.html

Grow, K. 2015. "PMRC's 'Filthy 15': Where Are They Now?" *Rolling Stone,* September 17. https://www.rollingstone.com/music/lists/pmrcs-filthy-15-where-are-they-now-20150917

Kolawole, H. 2002. "He Wasn't My King." *The Guardian,* August 14. https://www.theguardian.com/music/2002/aug/15/elvis25yearson.elvispresley

Lindsay, J. 2015. "The Twenty Best Vietnam Protest Songs." Council on Foreign Relations, March 5. https://www.cfr.org/blog/twenty-best-vietnam-protest-songs

Lynskey, D. 2011. *33 Revolutions Per Minute: A History of Protest Songs, from Billie Holiday to Green Day.* New York: HarperCollins.

Morrison, O. 2015. "Turn that Down! 40 Banned and Censored Songs." *National Coalition Against Censorship,* March 3. http://ncac.org/blog/turn-that-down-40-banned-and-censored-songs

Schonfeld, Z. 2015. "Parental Advisory Forever: An Oral History of the PMRC's War on Dirty Lyrics." *Newsweek,* September 19. http://www.newsweek.com/2015/10/09 /oral-history-tipper-gores-war-explicit-rock-lyrics-dee-snider-373103.html

"Sex and Violence . . . And It's on the Radio." *Today,* February 3. http://www.today.com /id/6901467/ns/today-parenting_and_family/t/sex-violence-its-radio/#.WBEPr SRUXeI

African Gangsta Rap

Since the 1980s, hip-hop has been popular in Africa, in part due to the influence of America as well as to the African tradition of griots, or storytellers. Senegal, in particular, was influenced by American artists. Popular rappers, including M.C. Solaar, Positive Black Soul, and M.C. Lida, infused West African styles with hip-hop. South Africa and Tanzania have shown similar trends. The spread of American-style hip-hop was largely the result of technology and globalization.

In some African countries, hip-hop and gangsta rap helped to fuel revolutions, as is the case in Sierra Leone after that country's civil war of 1991–2002. Critics have expressed concern, however, that the music has been co-opted by politicians and that piracy of CDs destroyed the profitability and thus led to its decline. In 2013, authorities banned a concert by hip-hop star Kao Denero, which resulted in riots.

Yet, critics note, hip-hop and gangsta rap has not always been connected to positive social change. Rather, civil wars and conflicts in Sierra Leone and other countries have been glorified and perhaps even fueled by gangsta rap, via icons depicted in the uniforms of child soldiers and lyrics suggesting that violence might be the only solution.

Reports show that gangsta "swagger" is popular among male youth in South Africa. While much of it involves posturing and imitation, there is also a significant hip-hop culture that is largely underground that raps about social issues, including poverty, hunger, discrimination, police abuse, and resilience. South African rappers often evoke historical heroes, like Steve Biko, who criticized apartheid. Artist XNasty said South Africa still struggles from segregation and the internalization of hopelessness. Rapper Zion Eyes describes the difficulties of living in poverty. Other artists, like Azlan, implore listeners to see former prisoners as human beings (Schoon, 2016).

In Kenya, hip-hop has played a significant role in giving voice to youth, in particular after the disputed 2007 election that led to 1,400 people killed and some 350,000 internally displaced (Howden, 2007). The Hip Hop Parliament bore witness to the atrocities and demanded that the government address the issues of racism, sexism, and violence. Likewise, in Burkina Faso, rapper Smockey (real name, Serge Bambara) helped lead the movement that toppled dictator Blaise Compaoré in 2014. Rapper El Haqed, or "The Enraged" (real name Mouad Belghouat), helped lead pro-democracy protests in Morocco 2011, and was even jailed for his activism.

In Angola, a rapper named MCK (real name Katrogi Nhanga) protested against the authoritarian regime headed by long-ruling president José Eduardo dos Santos.

MCK is so popular that he was invited to attend a rap festival in Brazil, but authorities seized his passport and prevented him from leaving the country. Another Angolan rapper Ikonoklasta (real name Luaty Beirao), who is often featured on MCK's albums, has been detained several times by the police for criticizing politicians and was among 17 activists arrested in June when their book club dared to discuss a book that focused on the success of nonviolent resistance. He went on a 36-day hunger strike to protest his imprisonment (York, 2015).

The collective of Senegalese rappers and journalists called Y'en a Marre ("We're Fed Up") helped youth get out to vote so as to defeat Senegal president Abdoulaye Wade in 2012. Members of the group helped register 300,000 young Senegalese voters, even though three of the group's founders were arrested during their efforts. After defeating the president, they went on to help democratic movements in Burkina Faso and Congo (York, 2015).

In Mauritania, rap is one of the few ways that young people can express their political positions and rally support. Antigovernment positions predominate. "When a rapper supports the government, he is immediately abandoned by his fans," says one of Mauritania's first rappers, 39-year-old Mister X (real name Cheikh Diagne). He said, "Rap isn't just an American kind of music—it's a way for us to tell our stories and our issues. It's the best way for us to send a message (York, 2015).

Hip-hop is also credited with helping reconstruct Rwanda after its 1994 genocide, which killed some 800,000 people in just 100 days. Today, approximately 80 percent of the population is under the age of 25, making hip-hop music all the more influential. Rapper Bac-T idolizes American rappers who emphasize social justice, like KRS-One, and seeks to use his music to bring people together, even though political music is heavily censored in Rwanda. Instead of criticizing, artists like Bac-T focus their work more positively (Dreisinger, 2013).

In Mauritania, N'dat Bouwaner is the only female rapper, but she is not allowed to address politics, despite her desperate urge to address racism, police brutality, and other issues.

Laura L. Finley

See also: Dancehall Music; Gangsta Rap; Hip-Hop; Jamaican Reggae Music; Protest Music Worldwide; Protest Songs

Further Reading

Dreisinger, B. 2013. "Two Decades Out of Ghastly Violence, Rwanda Sings of Love." *NPR*, December 15. https://www.npr.org/templates/story/story.php?storyId=251281776

Howden, D. 2009. "Kenya's Hip-Hop Parliament: Where the MCs Challenge MPs." *The Independent.* https://www.independent.co.uk/news/world/africa/kenyas-hip-hop-parliament-where-the-mcs-challenge-mps-1625529.html

Marsh, C., & Petty, S. 2013. "Globalization, Youth Identity and Resistance: Kenya's Hip Hop Parliament." *MUSICultures, 38*: 132–43.

Schoon, A. 2016. "The Town Where Hip-Hop Is Healing South Africa's Broken Youth." *The Conversation*, April 4. https://theconversation.com/the-town-where-hip-hop-is-healing-south-africas-broken-youth-56943

Tucker, B. 2013. "Musical Violence: Gangsta Rap and Politics in Sierra Leone." *Current African Issues No. 52.* http://www.diva-portal.org/smash/get/diva2:618529/FULLTEXT01.pdf

York, G. 2015. "Hip-Hop Music Speaking for Africa's Disenfranchised Youth." *The Globe and Mail,* December 23. https://www.theglobeandmail.com/arts/music/hip-hop-music-speaking-for-africas-disenfranchised-youth/article27922096/

Blues Music

Blues music, historically associated with Black artists and a largely Black audience, often focuses on violence of various sorts. From racism, to lynching, to domestic violence, these songs offer both commentary and a call to action.

One of the most widely known blues songs is "Strange Fruit," a song that describes the lynchings that occurred throughout the South until the 1930s, largely of Black men. It is most associated with Billie Holiday, who performed it frequently, but the song was actually written by Abel Meeropol, a Jewish communist. Dozens of others have performed it, but Holiday's rendition is most renowned. In 1999, *Time* named her studio performance of "Strange Fruit" the song of the century. Although it wasn't the first protest song, it was the first song that made such a strong statement of resistance that was performed in popular clubs and venues. The only hit song prior to "Strange Fruit" to deal with race was Andy Razaf and Fats Waller's "Black and Blue," which was included in the 1929 musical *Hot Chocolates.* It was often a show-stopper, as not just the violence described in it but also the tune elicited deep emotion. Meeropol was inspired to write the song after seeing a photograph of a double lynching in Indiana in 1930. It was first published as a poem in the *New York Teacher.* Another famous blues artist, Nina Simone, once said that "Strange Fruit" "is about the ugliest song I have ever heard. Ugly in the sense that it is violence and tears at the guts of what White people have done to my people in this country" (Lynskey, 2011, p. 5). It was not universally applauded, as many radio stations banned or ignored the song.

Another blues song that addressed racism is Nina Simone's "Mississippi Goddam." She wrote the song when she heard the news that a bomb had exploded at the Sixteenth Street Baptist Church in Birmingham, Alabama, killing four Black girls who were in Bible study class. The attack followed others on Black people in the South, and was just months after civil rights leader Medgar Evers was murdered in Mississippi. Simone's husband and manager, Andrew Stroud, found her on the apartment floor that day, ranting hysterically and attempting to fashion some kind of firearm out of scrap metal. She was so infuriated that she says she was not above violence, but Stroud talked her out of it and instead she wrote "Mississippi Goddam." It became one of the two most influential Black protest songs in 1964, with Sam Cooke's "A Change Is Gonna Come." Cooke's song was hopeful, whereas Simone's was more angry and demanding (Lynskey, 2011). Simone was also known to perform "Strange Fruit" during this period.

Domestic violence was a primary theme in the songs of Ma Rainey and Bessie Smith, two popular blues artists. They rarely use those words specifically, instead referring to someone as "wronging" the female narrator or as a "mistreater" who is physically or mentally abusive. Some are more brutal in their description of the abuse, such as the lines in Rainey's "Sweet Rough Man." She wrote in the song about waking up with a sore head, as "My man beat me last night with five feet of copper coil." Songs like "Sweet Rough Man" often emphasize that the abuse has occurred over years but that the narrators stay with their men because they love them. Interestingly, many of these songs were actually written by men. Another of Rainey's songs, "Outside of That," also details physical abuse, including black eyes and knocked-out teeth, but still she feels love and attraction for her abuser. Smith's "Empty Bed Blues, Part I" tells of a woman who is beaten, cheated on, and left, but still misses her man.

In other blues songs, the female narrators threaten revenge against their abusers. This revenge narrative set the stage for later films referred to as rape-revenge films. The female narrators may make threats of violence, such as in Rainey's "Sleep Talking Blues," where she threatens her man that if he lets slip a sign that he has another woman, "your friends will hear about being dead." Yet in blues songs, they rarely follow through on the threats. One exception is Smith's "Sing Sing Prison Blues," which discusses a woman who has killed her lover during a fight and is sent to Sing Sing Prison, where she accepts her punishment. Rainey's "Cell Bound Blues" features a woman lamenting about killing her husband and landing in prison.

Laura L. Finley

See also: Arab Media; Bollywood; Country Music; Folk Music; Hip-Hop; Murder Ballads; Protest Music Worldwide; Protest Songs; Rape Films; South Korean K-Pop

Further Reading

Gussow, A. 2002. *Seems Like Murder Here: Southern Violence and the Blues Tradition.* Chicago: University of Chicago Press.

Lovket, D. n.d. "The Lynching Blues: Metaphors of Racial Violence in Early Blues Music. *Academia.* http://www.academia.edu/31367357/The_Lynching_Blues_Metaphors _of_Racial_Violence_in_Early_Blues_Music

Lynskey, D. 2011. *33 Revolutions Per Minute: A History of Protest Songs from Billie Holiday to Green Day.* New York: Harper Collins.

Whipple, S. 2006. "'Prove It on Me': Topics in the Blues Music of Gertrude 'Ma' Rainey and Bessie Smith." *Transcending Silence.* http://www.albany.edu/womensstudies /journal/2006/whipple.html#returnsweet

Broadway Musicals

Although Broadway doesn't often come up in conversations about popular culture and violence, many shows and their musical scores involve various types of violence. Violence is central to the plot of classic shows like *West Side Story* and *Chicago*, while in others such as *Hamilton* and *The Phantom of the Opera*, it is peripheral but important. Some studies seem to indicate that Broadway and off-Broadway shows are increasingly violent. One analysis found that 43 percent of Broadway productions on stage in July 2014 featured themes and content involving crime and violence. Prior to these shows, others featuring significant violence played on Broadway and in off-Broadway venues, although many were short-lived.

West Side Story is a retelling of Shakespeare's *Romeo and Juliet*. It focuses on the relationship between Maria, whose brother Bernando is the leader of a gang called the Sharks, and Tony, a former member of the Sharks' rival, the Jets. It first appeared on Broadway in 1957, then returned in 1960, 1980, and 2009. It was the Broadway debut for composer Stephen Sondheim and was nominated for six Tony Awards. The dramatic musical numbers focus on fights between the gangs.

Chicago is one of the longest-running musicals in Broadway history. It won six Tony Awards in 1997. It tells the story of Velma Kelly and other women who have been imprisoned for killing their husbands. Roxie Hart faces charges and, like Kelly before her, enjoys the notoriety that comes with her case.

In 1979, *Sweeney Todd*, the story of a vengeful barber who kills the people who took his daughter, appeared on Broadway. It was revived in 1989 and 2005, and again played off-Broadway on March 1, 2017. *Carrie: The Musical* is the gory story, based on a Stephen King novel, of a prom queen who seeks revenge on her high school bullies. Despite sold-out performances, it closed after five performances in May 1988. *Heathers: The Musical* played off-Broadway in 2014 and received good reviews, but never made it to Broadway. It is based on the cult classic film featuring Winona Ryder and Christian Slater. *Heathers* is the story of a group of popular but mean girls and the revenge that Vanessa (Winona Ryder) and her angst-ridden boyfriend J.D. seek on them and the jocks in their school. *American Psycho*, adapted from the novel by Bret Easton Ellis, came to Broadway a decade and a half after the hyperviolent film adaptation reached the silver screen. It is the story of a handsome and clever businessman who is also a serial killer. It has been referred to as "torture porn," given the degree to which the main character, Patrick Bateman, sadistically abuses his victims. *Assassins* is a musical about the nation's most notorious presidential assassins. It opened off-Broadway in 1990 and was revived in 2004, when it won five Tony Awards.

The 2015–2016 Broadway season featured several shows that depicted sexual violence from various perspectives. In *Waitress*, the main character Jenna (Jessie Mueller) desperately wants to leave her abusive husband Earl (Nick Cordero) but isn't sure she can. When she finds out she is pregnant, things get even more complicated. Writer Jessie Nelson says she wanted to explore the dynamics of abusive relationships and depict characters that went beyond simple stereotypes. "I wanted to understand why Jenna initially loved Earl, when it turned, why she wasn't able to extricate herself from it and for people to feel compassion for that rather than judgement" (Weiner, 2016). Nelson also wanted to show that Earl wasn't always abusive. "People need to see who he was when Jenna met him, who he became, why he became that" (Weiner, 2016). She worked with psychologists and experts at a sexual assault intervention program to create the story. At one point Earl almost hits Jenna, but he stops short when she tells him she is pregnant.

Danai Gurira's *Eclipsed* also focuses on abuse, but from a different perspective. Set in the second Liberian civil war, it shows how women cope afterward. In contrast to Nelson's choices with *Waitress*, she preferred not to focus on the relationship between women and their abusers, but instead on how women survive after being sexually assaulted. She purposely took men out of the narrative so as to focus on the women's loss of innocence. Saycon Sengbloh plays Helena, or Wife Number One. She researched the ways that women handled abuse so that she could bring an appropriate sense of humor to the character. Although there are difficult moments, like *Waitress*, Gurira purposely avoided having a man physically assault a woman on stage.

The Color Purple debuted on Broadway in 2015. It is the musical retelling of Alice Walker's story of abused yet strong women. It is largely the story of Celie, a young African American girl who is twice impregnated by her abusive father. She tries to protect her prettier sister, Nettie, from their father and from other men who are interested in her. Eventually Nettie goes off to Africa with another family while Celie is selected to marry "Mister." Mister is horribly abusive to Celie as well, but other characters throughout the story help her remain strong, including her friend, Sophia, who is also abused but fights back. It is through writing letters to Nettie, however, that we learn the most about Celie. Unbeknownst to her, Nettie has written her for years but Mister hid the letters. Eventually, Celie stands up to Mister and the sisters are reunited. Isaiah Johnson, who plays Mister, said, "There's never a bad time to talk about violence against women and address it" (Weiner, 2016).

Laura L. Finley

See also: *Buffy the Vampire Slayer*; Gang Films; *Walking Dead, The*

Further Reading

Hoffman, D. 2014. "Broadway Starring Crime and Violence." *Huffington Post,* September 27. http://www.huffingtonpost.com/davian-hoffman/broadway-starring-crime-a_b_5627187.html

Pincus-Roth, Z. 2006. "The Case for Onstage Violence." *Slate,* May 3. http://www.slate.com/articles/news_and_politics/theater/2006/05/break_a_leg.html

Wiener, I. 2016. "The Onstage Issue No One Is Talking About, But Should Be." *Playbill,* June 30. http://www.playbill.com/article/the-onstage-issue-no-one-is-talking-about-but-should-be

Wolcott, J. 2016. "Is American Psycho Too Bloody for Broadway?" *Vanity Fair,* March 4. http://www.vanityfair.com/culture/2016/03/american-psycho-broadway

Classic Rock

Classic rock refers to a genre of rock music that includes generally commercially successful bands from the mid-1960s through the late 1980s. Some radio stations are devoted specifically to classic rock. Artists typically associated with the genre include the Beatles, Led Zeppelin, Eric Clapton, the Rolling Stones, Pink Floyd, Rod Stewart, The Who, and Neil Young.

Many classic rock songs are said to glorify sexual assault and abuse and to demean women. Stewart's "Tonight's the Night" is controversial for its lyrics that seem to promote sexual assault: In the song, he tells his love interest, who he refers to as an angel, that she'd be foolish to deny his male desire. He then says, "you'd be a fool to stop this tide / spread your wings and let me come inside." The Beatles "Getting Better" has also been criticized for violence against women: "I used to be cruel to my woman / I beat her and kept her apart from the things that she loved." The singer then reflects on how mean he was and that he's changing his ways.

The Rolling Stones' "Brown Sugar" was controversial for its references to slavery and rape. It was the first single released from the album *Sticky Fingers* in 1971, and it shot to number one on the U.S. Billboard charts on May 7 of that year. The Rolling Stones' live debut of the song, which was written by lead singer Mick Jagger, was at a concert at Altamont Speedway in California on December 6, 1969. Jagger has said he would probably censor himself more if he wrote the song today. The song features the refrain, "Brown Sugar, how come you taste so good, Brown Sugar, just like a young girl should" and refers to Black women being whipped by slave owners. The debut of the song at Altamont is also controversial because the concert, conceived as a festival similar to Woodstock, erupted in violence. Fans drank excessively, and rather than hire a private security company, the organizers paid a local chapter of the motorcycle gang the Hells Angels to provide security. The Angels were paid in beer, so well before the Stones took the stage there had been a variety of altercations. The worst incident of the night occurred during another controversial Rolling Stones song, "Under My Thumb." Eighteen-year-old attendee Meredith Hunter attempted to get on the stage and was pushed back by one of the Hells Angels. Hunter pulled out a gun, and Angels member Alan Passaro pushed the gun out of his hand and stabbed and killed Hunter. Three other fans died that night. Passaro was charged for the killing but was acquitted.

"Under My Thumb" has been widely criticized for promoting men's control of women. It includes the chorus, "It's down to me, the way she does just what she's told. / Down to me, the change has come." Jagger goes on to say that under his control, she will keep her eyes to herself, but he can look at whoever he desires to. Jagger has said the song is not antifeminist and is instead about "pushy women" (Adams, 2015).

Although the Beatles were often considered to be squeaky clean, that is not necessarily the case, nor did the band want that image. For instance, the 1966 U.S. album *Yesterday . . . and Today* featured images of the four in white smocks, posing with dismembered baby dolls and raw meat. The band said it was intended to be a critique of the Vietnam War. Capitol Records replaced the images with something more mundane. The band's song "Revolution" was also controversial in that some believed it would incite people to do just that. After the band broke up, John Lennon went on to pen many songs critical of capitalism, greed, and violence. Perhaps his most famous is "Imagine," which asks listeners to think about a world free of greed, possessions, and hatred. He and his wife, performance artist Yoko Ono, staged two different "bed-ins" for peace, one in Amsterdam and another in Montreal, where they invited the press to see the honeymooning duo surrounded by posters and peace signs talking about peace. Lennon and Ono also sang "Give Peace a Chance," and "Happy X-Mas (War Is Over)." In his "Attica State," Lennon called for more humane treatment of prisoners and argued to "free the prisoners, jail the judges." His "Woman Is the N***** of the World" criticized patriarchal society for oppressing women. The song was banned from many radio stations. Lennon borrowed the slogan "Power to the People" from the Black Panthers in his song of that name. "Working Class Hero" is a commentary on the treatment of workers from a Marxist perspective.

Neil Young penned several songs, which he sang solo as well as with Crosby, Stills, and Nash, that were critical of militaristic violence. "Ohio" is about the shooting of four Kent State University students who were protesting the Vietnam War by members of the National Guard. Crosby, Stills, Nash, and Young performed the song just 17 days after the shooting on May 4, 1970. That same year Young engaged in a rock war with the band Alabama, as his "Southern Man" spoke about burning crosses and his "Alabama" critiqued the state for its slow entry into the Civil War. The classic rock band Lynyrd Skynrd responded in their song "Sweet Home Alabama," claiming that "Southern man don't need him around, anyhow." "Stand and Be Counted" is about the protests of Chinese repression at Tiananmen Square in the late 1980s. In 2006, Young called on people to "impeach the president," due to George W. Bush authorizing the United States to engage in war against Iraq and Afghanistan after the terrorist attack of September 11, 2001. Young also wrote and performed several songs critical of environmental destruction, especially by chemical companies like Monsanto.

Laura L. Finley

See also: Country Music; Folk Music; Goth and Industrial Music; Hair Metal; Heavy Metal; Protest Music Worldwide; Protest Songs

Further Reading

Adams, C. 2015. "The Most Politically Incorrect Lyrics in Classic Hit Songs that You Would Never Get Away with These Days. *The News*, July 30. http://www.news.com.au /entertainment/music/the-most-politically-incorrect-lyrics-in-classic-hit-songs -that-you-would-never-get-away-with-these-days/news-story/6deb1645a8c29ec75 48e9a1c784b178a

Della Cava, M. 2014. "Missing a Few Beats: Five Beatles Controversies." *USA Today,* February 9. https://www.usatoday.com/story/life/music/2014/02/09/five-beatles-myths -hoaxes-controversies/5271607/

Deriso, N. n.d. "Top Ten John Lennon Solo Political Songs." *Ultimate Classic Rock.* http:// ultimateclassicrock.com/john-lennon-solo-political-songs/

"The 50 Greatest Protest Songs." n.d. *Radio X.* http://www.radiox.co.uk/features/x-lists /music-changed-world-50-best-protest-songs/

Lepore, S. 2015. "On Neil Young's Birthday, His Most Famous Protest Songs." *Daily News,* November 12. http://www.nydailynews.com/entertainment/neil-young-famous -protest-songs-article-1.2432475

Mastropolo, F. n.d. "The Story of the Rolling Stones Controversial 'Brown Sugar.'" *Ultimate Classic Rock.* http://ultimateclassicrock.com/rolling-stones-release-brown -sugar/

Whitaker, S. 2015. "Ultimate Classic Rock. The Story of the Rolling Stones' Altamont Concert." http://ultimateclassicrock.com/rolling-stones-altamont/

Country Music

From interpersonal violence to domestic violence and even, occasionally, criticisms of war, country music has been a powerful platform to discuss a variety of social issues.

Garth Brooks and Pat Alger's "Thunder Rolls" is about domestic violence. It depicts a woman waiting for her man, who has been out cheating on her. She smells the other woman's perfume and then retrieves a pistol, saying, "Cause tonight's the last night she'll wonder where he's been." Cable stations TNN and CMT pulled the video of the song, but it remained popular. It was number one on the country music charts, and the video won Music Video of the Year at the Country Music Association awards.

Martina McBride's "Independence Day" is also about domestic violence. It is an up-tempo song told from the eyes of a young girl who witnessed the abuse. It is a powerful commentary on how people notice the signs of abuse yet still ignore it, saying, "Some folks whispered and some folks talked / But everybody looked the other way" (Mark27, 2011). The battered woman waits for her child to leave then burns the house down. Its popularity helped turn McBride into an activist against domestic violence. "I have always believed what she did (in *Independence Day*) was an act of self-defense and a matter of life or death. And, yes, when I sing it, it's a victory cry for so many women and children who have been abused and hurt" (Watts & Rau, 2013).

The Dixie Chicks' "Goodbye Earl" is a controversial tune that describes the abuse of a woman by her new husband. She turns to a friend for help, and they concoct a plan to kill the abuser, Earl, and dispose of his body. Earl assaulted his wife, ignoring a restraining order and landing her in intensive care. The women poison his black-eyed peas, and the song ends saying that they don't feel bad about it. Set to an upbeat sound, many criticized it for promoting killing an abuser as the answer. Rita Smith, executive director of the National Coalition Against Domestic Violence, said the group approved of radio play for the song, saying, "Many battered women feel trapped and feel that violence is their only option to get away from the abuser. We don't want them feeling that way. We want them to know there are resources available to them. . . . We want stations who play the record to tell their listeners that there is a hotline number they can call if they've been a victim of violence" (Lewis, 2000).

Carrie Underwood's "Church Bells" was her 24th career number-one *Rolling Stone* song, and it, too, featured a domestic violence-revenge theme. In the song, "Jenny" poisons her alcoholic and abusive husband's whisky, killing him. It wasn't the first time Underwood sang about abuse or about violent revenge. In "Little Toy Guns" she sang about a girl "caught in the crossfire" of her fighting parents, and in "Two Black Cadillacs" she described a wife and a mistress conspiring to murder their two-timing lover. "Blown Away" features a little girl who fails to wake her "mean old mister" father during a tornado. The song implies she does so on purpose as "sweet revenge" for his abuse. In "Before He Cheats" Underwood describes a woman who vandalizes her boyfriend's truck after learning he cheated on her. She won her second Grammy Award for Best Female Country Vocal Performance for it.

Tyler Farr's "Redneck Crazy" also addresses abuse, although in this case it focuses on the side of the abuser, who goes "redneck crazy" on his girlfriend's front lawn because he believes she cheated on him. The song reached number one on the country charts but generated a great deal of controversy for lyrics like, "I didn't come here to start a fight, but I'm up for anything tonight." Farr said he meant the song to be edgy but not to condone abuse or stalking behaviors. Martina McBride criticized it, saying that the man was acting immature and was a bully, rather than a legitimate victim like the one she described in "Independence Day" (Watts & Rau, 2013).

While country music and country artists have long been associated with a pro-America patriotic view that supports soldiers and war, occasionally some have taken antiwar positions. The Dixie Chicks saw their careers plummet after they spoke out against the war in Iraq. Lead singer Natalie Maines said that she was ashamed President Bush was from Texas. Many stations refused to play the band's music after her comments. More recently, country artists, including Maren Morris, Rose-anne Cash, Sheryl Crow, Brothers Osborne, and Eric Church, have denounced gun violence and called for people to resist the influence of the National Rifle Association.

Laura L. Finley

See also: Blues Music; Classic Rock; Folk Music; Murder Ballads; Protest Music Worldwide; Protest Songs

Further Reading

Armstrong, E. 1993. "The Rhetoric of Violence in Rap and Country Music." *Sociological Inquiry, 63*(1): 64–78.

Aroesti, R. 2018. "Maren Morris and the Country Singers Attacking Gun Violence at the Grammys." *The Guardian,* January 26. https://www.theguardian.com/music/2018/jan/26/grammys-2018-country-music-gun-control-violence-maren-morris

Hodak, B. 2016. "Carrie Underwood Takes Another Domestic Violence Song to Number 1." *Forbes,* July 18. https://www.forbes.com/sites/brittanyhodak/2016/07/18/carrie-underwood-takes-another-domestic-violence-song-to-number-1/

Lewis, R. 2000. "'Earl' Creates Heat, and Heated Debate." *LA Times,* April 1. http://articles.latimes.com/2000/apr/01/entertainment/ca-14748

Mark27. 2011. "The 10 Darkest Country Songs of All Time." *Daily Kos,* January 2. https://www.dailykos.com/stories/2011/1/2/933029/-

NCS Staff. 2017. "The 10 Most Controversial Songs in Country Music History." *Nash Country Daily,* January 27. http://www.nashcountrydaily.com/2017/01/27/the-10-most-controversial-songs-in-country-music-history/

Watts, C., & Rau, N. 2013. "'Redneck Crazy' Country Song Divides Listeners." *USA Today,* October 28. https://www.usatoday.com/story/life/music/2013/10/28/redneck-crazy-music-violence/3291955/

Dancehall Music

Dancehall music has always been prominent in Jamaican culture. Since the early 1950s it has been intertwined with classical reggae. This genre of music was a historical creation of Afro-Jamaican rituals that incorporated drumming, singing in various languages, and dancing. Dancehall was a form of liberation for African slaves who were exported to Jamaica. It served as a special means of gathering between the slaves. In the 1980s, dancehall music became less like original reggae and more like the genre of American hip hop—"an era dominated by synthesized music production" (Sterling, 2005). Marvin Sterling, an anthropology professor at Indiana University and a Jamaica native, described the transformation of dancehall music stating that:

> While much of root reggae has been lyrically informed by the anti-colonialism of the Rastafarian faith and call for Black spiritual ascendance, dancehall—except where it has periodically tapped into the positivist message of its predecessor—has been steeped in heterosexual machismo, conspicuous consumption, and the fetishization of violence. (p. 200)

Contemporary dancehall music affects the identity of not only Jamaicans, but other Caribbean islands where negative ideologies and images are becoming widely accepted and adopted. This new version of dancehall music has drawn criticism for its frequent description of gun and sexual violence.

Dancehall music slowly worked its way from the Caribbean islands into North America, as Jamaican dancehall artists travelled to perform their lyrical work. During the 1990s, dancehall record sales in the United States increased as this genre of music began to spread globally—reaching over $300 million a year in the market (Morgan, 2012). Not only did sales of dancehall music increase, but also the usage of dancehall music in movies and dance competitions. Although dancehall music became widely accepted into mainstream pop culture, it began to receive disapproval from many upper-class Jamaicans, as well as other Caribbean islands and highly diverse countries such as Britain. They deem dancehall music sexually explicit and extremely violent. In some cases, dancehall artists were banned because of their vulgar use of sexual and violence activities in their lyrics. Other incidents include the hateful attitudes about homosexuality. The Barbadian community and certain European countries have refused to give dancehall artists such as Beenie Man, Buju Banton, Mavado, and Bounty Killer visas or permission to travel to their country because of their homophobic concerns. Other artists have been banned because of the influence they have on violent behavior. The majority of the time, the audiences in clubs break out in fights because of the context of the lyrics and the emotion it brings out. This shows the severity and the encouragement dancehall artists and their music have on their listeners to engage in devious behavior—eventually leading countries to take preventive measures to stop the negativity dancehall music produces.

A study on dancehall music and its correlation with sexual activity and violence among adolescents who live in Jamaica was conducted by various researchers in 2008. They found that "issues relating to sex and violence among adolescents have, in recent times, raised much public health and policy concerns, especially in an era where first sexual debut is at the mean age of 11.4 years for boys and 12.8 years for girls in Jamaica" (Crawford, 2010). Dancehall could have possibly been a cause for such early engagement of sexual intercourse among adolescents due to the exposure of sexual content in the artists' lyrics. The subjects of this study were 50 girls and 50 boys, totaling 100 adolescents. Findings have shown that 40 percent of females and 26 percent of males gravitated to sexually explicit lyrics. On the other hand, 34 percent of males and 24 percent of females were more interested in lyrical content that was conscious of violence. However, 20 percent of both males and females responded similarly to lyrical content of explicit language. Males were less likely to be stimulated emotionally by dancehall music in contrast to their female counterparts—at a percentage of 62 and 82, respectively (Crawford, 2010). The study also concluded that 52 percent and 54 percent of males and females, respectively, indicated that they were sexually active, whereas 19 percent of males and 13 percent of females demonstrated violence in their homes, communities, and school. These statistics are the result of the strong influence dancehall music has on these young adolescents, both at home and in school. The lyrical content of most dancehall music includes messages relating to male-female sexual relationships—messages that are not associated with values, respect, or care for others. In these lyrics, they discuss ways in which a woman should be treated, mostly in a derogatory manner.

Dancehall lyrics also contributed to a homophobic mentality, not only in Caribbean islands, but also in the United States. Masculinity has been embedded in Jamaica's culture, where men are the dominant group and they control most of the social order. In Jamaican culture, it is considered abnormal and disgraceful if a man has sexual relations with another male or if a woman does so with another female. As more male dancehall artists expressed critical attitudes about homosexuality, more people began to act hostile toward gays and lesbians. Dancehall artists normally ridicule or belittle gay men by saying "fire burn batty boi." In order words, they are saying that gays and lesbians deserve to be killed by being burned. Also, it can be translated in terms of a biblical context in which they will be burnt in hell. Buju Banton, one of dancehall's prominent artists, made a song that expressed his opinion about homosexuality called "Boom Bye Bye." In his song, he stresses that any man who caresses another man deserves to be shot and killed with an automatic gun or Uzi gun instead with no remorse. Under the influence of dancehall music, others take matters into their own hands to eliminate gays and lesbians—physically or psychologically abusing them.

In relation to the homophobic culture that has been in existence for decades, artists such as Beenie Man have expressed feelings about homosexual behaviors through their songs. Beenie Man created a song titled "Han Up Deh" which influenced many of his listeners to be antigay. In his lyrics, he talks about his dreams for a so-called new Jamaica, saying "come to execute all the gays. . . . All batty man fi dead." This caused an uproar among those who advocate for the gay community, and they demanded that Beenie Man apologize.

Dancehall music also contributed to the male objectification of women and their appearance. Most lyrical content of dancehall music either identifies women as less than a person or as a person that should live to an unfair standard of beauty—curves, big bosoms and behind, and long hair. The glorification of a woman with an idealized body and complexion has influenced many Caribbean women and American women to bleach their skin.

Dancehall music videos also play an important role in encouraging sexually explicit behaviors against women. "Continuous crotch grabbing by male and some female artistes, for example, as well as the use of expletives and other provocative performance gimmicks to excite audiences (sexually) into desired responses are well documented" (Pinnock, 2007, p. 59). Music videos such as these suggest that it is acceptable for men to touch a woman without her consent. Not only are women's bodies being idolized, but men are also expected to live up to an idealized body standard. They must be muscular with a flat stomach—this defines true masculinity. Pinnock described this as "the subversion of the standard practice of constructing the male body as the canvas against which the exploits of the deified female form is projected, in traditional Dancehall popular culture" (p. 58). As previously mentioned, these types of images not only influence adults, but also children to participate in early sexual behavior and violence.

In addition to some of the prominent dancehall artists mentioned previously, there are other artists who have been a cause of concern for the public regarding this genre of music. One notorious dancehall artist by the name of Vybz Kartel has been known for his strong sexually explicit lyrics, which may have had or still have an influence on adolescents—especially those who engaged in sexual activities at a young age. Some of his well-known songs, including "Virginity" and "Ramping Shop," have storylines that involve women begging for their virginity to be taken away. He also mentioned how sexual intercourse is such a strong addiction that it will encourage women to sneak out of their homes. In addition, there are other songs in which he encourages sexual violence against women. Considering the popularity of his music in Jamaica and the United States, it is possible that his music may contribute to high rates of early sexual activities as well as sexual violence. It is clear how influential dancehall music is in present cultures, on both adults and adolescents.

The transition of classical reggae and dancehall to a synthesized musical production forming contemporary dancehall took a drastic turn. The shift in this genre of music went from a positive liberation movement to a negative contribution, promoting dangerous sexual activity, increasing violent behavior, and degrading women as well as gays and lesbians. Studies have shown that the lyrical content of dancehall music has caused many adolescents especially in Jamaica to engage in early sexual intercourse. The consistent exposure to these sexually explicit lyrics led to the normalization of such behavior. Dancehall music also contributed to consciousness of violence. With regard to individuals living in a homophobic culture, dancehall artists have encouraged their audiences through their lyrics to belittle gays and lesbians—as it is seen to be abnormal and a disgrace. In addition, this genre of music portrays women as sex symbols and objects, especially in music videos, where males are groping the private parts of women. Like other media influences, women are viewed as objects that should uphold to the standards of beauty created by society itself—such as having a curvy body, plumped body parts, "good" hair, and a light complexion. All in all, dancehall has both its positive and negative effects on society globally that can possibly lead to an increase in sexual violence and gun violence.

Kesha Bassue

See also: African Gangsta Rap; Gangsta Rap; Hip-Hop; Music Videos; Protest Songs; Punk Music

Further Reading

Anonymous. 2009. "Beenie Man's Homophobic Lyrics." *ILGA*, October 1. http://ilga.org
/beenie-man-s-homophobic-lyrics/

Crawford, A. 2010. "The Effects of Dancehall Genre on Adolescent Sexual and Violent
Behavior in Jamaica: A Public Health Concern." *North American Journal of Medical Sciences, 2*(3), 143–45. https://www.ncbi.nlm.nih.gov/pmc/articles/PMC
3354427/

Morgan, C. 2012. *Early Globalization and the Roots of Dancehall.* https://sophia.smith.edu
/blog/danceglobalization/2012/04/19/early-globalization-and-the-roots-of
-dancehall-dance/

Pinnock, A.M.N. 2007. "A Ghetto Education Is Basic: (Jamaican) Dancehall Masculinities as Counter-Culture." *Journal of Pan African Studies, 1*(9), 47.

Sterling, M. D. 2005. "Wake the Town and Tell the People: Dancehall Culture in Jamaica."
Canadian Journal of Latin American & Caribbean Studies, 30(59), 200–02.

Folk Music

Folk music has become virtually synonymous with protest music. Many offer criticisms of the government, of war, and of other forms of violence.

In 2009, Folk Alley, the 24-hour online stream of Kent State University's WKSU, compiled a list of the 100 most essential folk songs. Near the top of the list were several songs that either describe or critique violence. Bob Dylan's "Blowin' in the Wind" was listed at number two. "Blowin' in the Wind" quickly became an anthem of the civil rights movement that was then reaching its peak. Dylan sang it himself at a voter registration rally in Greenwood, Mississippi, in the spring of 1963. Peter, Paul and Mary performed it on the steps of the Lincoln Memorial in August of that year, a few hours before Martin Luther King delivered his "I Have a Dream" speech. And Peter Yarrow remembers singing it during the march from Selma to Montgomery. He said, "When we sang it, it was in a field where probably I'd say, oh, 5,000 of the poorest people I'd ever seen, all of them black. And they waited in the rain for a couple of hours 'cause the sound system had gone to the wrong destination. We sang it very slowly, very, very—in a very determined way, but with a sense of the weariness of the people that surrounded us." Peter, Paul and Mary's version of the song became the fastest-selling single in Warner Brothers' history (Naylor, 2000).

Number four on the Top 100 list is "Where Have All the Flowers Gone?," written by Pete Seeger and performed by the Kingston Trio. A popular war critic, Seeger described how he came to write the song, noting that he had been reading about Cossack soldiers in Russia in the czar's army and was struck by three lines, which he quoted in the song. The specific lyrics refer to girls plucking flowers, then getting married, while all the men are in the army. He was on an airplane later when he thought that the line "long time passing," which he had written in one of his notebooks previously, and the refrain "When will we ever learn" went well with the others. He wrote the entire song in 20 minutes and sang it in 1955 at Oberlin College. A student there, Joe Hickerson, took the song to a summer camp, where he was a counselor, and in playing it for the kids, added lines about soldiers going to graveyards, and graveyards being covered by flowers. Seeger gave Hickerson 20 percent of the royalties for the song.

Another Seeger song, "We Shall Overcome," was listed at number eight. It is famous for being a civil rights song, but it was widely sung in the labor movement and is commonly heard at nonviolent protests of a variety of sorts. The song did not originate with Seeger but rather in 18th-century Europe. Later, it was carried to the cotton fields of the U.S. South, where enslaved people sang it. It went through several mutations before Lucille Simmons made it the rallying cry of Black strikers in Charleston, South Carolina, in October 1945 (Lynskey, 2011).

The Kingston Trio's "Tom Dooley" was ranked number 12. It was the band's first hit, about a man named Tom Dula (pronounced Dooley), who was a Confederate soldier in the Civil War, and who was captured and held as a prisoner of war. On the day he was to be married his fiancé, Laura Foster, she disappeared and was found stabbed to death weeks later. Tom knew he would be accused so fled the county, then left for Tennessee. A posse found him and brought him back for trial, where he was found guilty and hanged in Statesville, North Carolina.

Buffy Sainte-Marie's "Universal Soldier" was ranked number 16. It tells the story of a young G.I. in 1967, who wrote in Morse code on the canvas on the bottom of the bunk above him. The song asks the listener to decide who will die and who will live, then says, "You're the one who gives his body as a weapon of the war—And without you all this killing can't go on." It was housed in the Smithsonian and then published in the *Smithsonian* magazine. Then it became known that the "mystery poem" was actually a portion of Buffy Sainte-Marie's song, "Universal Soldier." She wrote it in 1962 and it was released in 1964, quickly becoming an anthem of the antiwar movement. "It's about the personal responsibility of all of us. Because we can't blame just the soldier for the war, or just the career military officer, or just the politician. We have to blame ourselves too since we are living in an era where we actually elect our politicians." "Universal Soldier" was banned by many radio stations in the 1960s ("In Depth," 2010).

Bob Dylan's "Masters of War" came in at 59th on the list. Dylan says he wrote the song in just 10 minutes and set it to the tune of an old emancipation song, "No More Auction Block for Me." He didn't want to come off as "preachy and one-dimensional" (Lynskey, 2011, p. 55). It is an angry and sarcastic song, which ends with the hope that the politicians who send young people to die in wars themselves die. Dylan has said he never wrote anything like that before, but he couldn't help feeling so angry about the Vietnam War. In the song, Dylan denounces those who build the "guns," "death planes," and "bombs," all while hiding behind walls and desks (Lynskey, 2011).

Laura L. Finley

See also: Blues Music; Classic Rock; Country Music; Murder Ballads; Narcocorridos; Protest Music Worldwide; Protest Songs; Punk Music

Further Reading

Folk Alley. 2009. "Folk Alley's 100 Most Essential Folk Songs." *NPR*, June 19. http://www .npr.org/templates/story/story.php?storyId=105677068

"In Depth: Universal Soldier." 2010. *Buffy Sainte-Marie*, October 10. http://buffysainte
-marie.com/?p=809http://www.songfacts.com/detail.php?id=8510

Lynskey, D. 2011. *33 Revolutions Per Minute: A History of Protest Songs from Billie Holiday to Green Day.* New York: Harper Collins.

Naylor, B. 2000. "'Blowin in the Wind' Still Asks the Hard Questions." *NPR,* October 21.
http://www.npr.org/2000/10/21/1112840/blowin-in-the-wind

Gangsta Rap

Gangsta rap is a subgenre of hip-hop music that began to emerge in the later 1980s.
Its lyrics emphasize the so-called "thug life." Because of the lyrical content of the
genre, gangsta rap is not without its share of controversies. Critics have accused
gangsta rap of promoting violence, crime, murder, sex, promiscuity, street gangs,
and more. For many others, however, the music is simply a reflection of society
and deals with topics that are addressed within inner-city Black communities. In
other words, what started out as an underground art form has become a way of
exposing critical issues that no one wished to address in American politics. Among
the most popular and controversial artists are Dr. Dre, Snoop Dogg, Ice Cube,
N.W.A., Tupac Shakur, the Notorious B.I.G., Nas, and Ice-T, all of whom are Black.
There are few White gangsta rappers, although one, Eminem, is popular with fans
and critics.

N.W.A. is credited with being the first commercially successful gangsta rap
group. Their song "F**k tha Police," from the 1988 album *Straight Outta Compton*, expressed hatred of the police and argued that they are all racists. It was intended
to specifically critique the tactics used by Los Angeles Police Department's chief
Daryl Gates. The album has been referred to as "a brutal, bewildering mix of hedo-
nism and rage" (Lynskey, 2011, p. 435). Public Enemy's album *Fear of a Black
Planet* sold a million copies in its first week. Songs critiqued the lack of services
such as 911 in Black communities, police harassment, stereotyping of Blacks in
Hollywood, and institutional racism (Lynskey, 2011). Dr. Dre moved the industry
forward in 1992 when he established the Death Row Records label. Dr. Dre quickly
signed Snoop Dogg. Suge Knight then came on board as executive producer, followed by a series of popular artists. The songs of these artists not only described
police corruption and brutality, but also emphasized the harsh, crime-ridden neighborhoods where many grew up. Further, gangsta rap has long been accused of
being misogynistic, as lyrics are derogatory to women and often glorify domestic
violence and sexual assault.

Rivalries between artists fueled interest in the genre. Eazy E and Dr. Dre often
called each other out in their songs. Tupac Shakur, who signed with Death Row
Records after Suge Knight bailed him out of a New York prison, fought with rivals
on the East Coast of the United States, especially Christopher Wallace, known as
the Notorious B.I.G., or "Biggie." Bad Boy records started on the East Coast, which
Shakur ripped in some of his songs. Both Shakur and Biggie were murdered in
drive-by shootings that many think were related to their rivalry and their associations with gangs. Shakur was shot and killed on September 7, 1996, on the Las
Vegas Strip. He was with Knight at the time, and Knight later claimed that he may

have been the intended target. Biggie was shot in a drive-by in Los Angeles six months later.

In addition to the violent lyrics, gangsta rap has been denounced as derogatory to women. Artists routinely refer to women using epithets and with images suggesting that all women are good for is sex. For instance, in his song "Remember the Times," Nas describes "hooking up with" all kinds of women and in one instance, jamming a Heineken bottle into one's behind. Additionally, Eminem's songs often describe violence against women. In "Stan," the rapper tells the story of an obsessed fan who kills his pregnant wife in a drunken rage. The Geto Boys described killing a teacher, cutting up her body with a chainsaw, and attacking a woman with a machete in "Assassins."

One of the biggest debates about this genre concerns the relationship between gangsta rap and crime. Many believe that gangsta rap glorifies and encourages criminal behavior, but those who are in support of the music argue that the problem of crime has nothing to do with gangsta rap. Rather, they insist that it is the result of poverty and the lack of opportunity in these communities. It is also believed that blaming rap music just stirs up an unwarranted moral panic. This causes people to look at the music through a racially charged lens and further stereotypes young Black males as dangerous criminals. This kind of thinking contributes to conditions that make it hostile for young Black men in America.

When rap first started there was no message, just lyrics and a beat. Then in 1982, Grandmaster Flash and the Furious Five released a song "The Message," which is considered by most to be the first official rap song with a message. The song is also trying to describe the realities of living in the inner city. In the song, he describes his neighborhood as a jungle. Further, the conditions of the ghetto are so bad, that it's pushing him close to the edge. The song marked a turning point for this type of music, causing other artists to follow suit. Rap music started to be the medium that many artists used to get a message across to the people.

Today greed, money, and commercialization have begun to capitalize on the music, making it less political and more damaging to Black communities. Instead of uplifting Black Americans, it is now portraying a negative image, an image of gangsters and drug dealers. Thanks to corporate record labels, the message in the music has been stolen from its very own communities. According to journalist Christopher John Farley, the commodification of rap music has also deprived it as a form of resistance.

Gina Thompson

See also: African Gangsta Rap; Dancehall Music; Hip-Hop; Jamaican Reggae Music; Latin American MCs; Narcocorridos; Punk Music

Further Reading

Farley, C. 1999. "Hip-Hop Nation." *Time*, February 8. http://content.time.com/time /magazine/article/0,9171,19134,00.html

Henderson, E. 1996. "Black Nationalism and Rap Music." *Journal of Black Studies*, *26*(3), 308–39.

Leland, J. 1996. "Criminal Records: Gangsta Rap and the Culture of Violence." *Newsweek*, November 28. http://www.newsweek.com/criminal-records-191496

Lynskey, D. 2011. *33 Revolutions Per Minute: A History of Protest Songs, from Billie Holiday to Green Day*. New York: HarperCollins.

McCann, M. 2013. "The 30 Most Disturbing Songs of All Time." *Dallas Observer*, August 19. http://www.dallasobserver.com/music/the-30-most-disturbing-songs-of-all-time-7057625

Phillips, C. 1993. "Gangsta Rappers' Arrests Spur More Static over Genre." *The Los Angeles Times*, November 7. http://www.latimes.com/local/la-me-tupacsodomycase7nov0793-story.html

Salem, S. 1996. "Rap Music Mirrors Its Environment." *Billboard*, December 28. EBSCO Host. http://connection.ebscohost.com/c/editorials/9404080016/rap-music-mirrors-environment

German Punk Music

Punk music in large part originated in West Germany, before the fall of the Berlin Wall when the country was divided into east and west. It was influenced, however, by British and American punk. In the late 1970s and 1980s, these bands became more political, and their music is credited in helping to break down the wall and unite Germany. Earliest among these were the artists whose work was dubbed Deutschpunk, which featured very fast beats and left-wing lyrics. Slime, a band from Hamburg, proposed violence against the police, who they saw as oppressors. In contrast, because of its heavy censorship, East Germany saw little punk music action until the countries unified.

Being a punk rocker in formerly communist East Germany was hugely risky, as artists were often targeted and interrogated by police, and in some cases, even tortured and abused. Punk artist Michael Boehlke, lead man of a band called Planlos, or Aimless, is today collecting photographs and footage of the East German punk music scene, documenting the challenges these artists faced in bringing their art and their message to a wider audience. He describes how punk musicians in East Germany had to seek refuge in churches, knowing that at any time government spies or sympathizers could turn them over to the Stasi as traitors.

After unification, German punk generally took a different turn, leaning toward anti-immigrant neo-Nazism. The concern about asylees in the 1980s and 1990s generated a wave of punk songs.

Today, punk music is being used to help draw attention to the plight of refugees. Some 800,000 to 1 million refugees enter Germany annually. Bands like Die Ärzte, a punk band formed in west Berlin in 1982, are donating concert proceeds to Pro-Asyl, a German human rights nongovernmental organization (NGO) working with refugees (Le Blond, 2015). In 2015, German punk band Die Aerzte's song "Cry for Love," first released in 1993, saw a resurgence with its antiviolence message.

Yet punk music is not all about social good. In 1995, more than 100 policemen were injured in street battles with German punks during a three-day riot in Hanover. Some 2,000 punk rock fans had assembled for "Chaos Days," and seemingly their purpose was to inflict violence. Some 450 youths were arrested in one night alone. According to authorities, the punks had chains, razor blades, and other weapons, and they looted supermarkets and businesses. Police responded with water cannons and bulldozers. Critics contend, however, that most of those involved were not real punk fans but instead hoodlums interested in perpetrating violence (Bridge, 1995).

Neo-Nazi music, some coming from Germany but more often influenced by the genre as a whole, has been used by right-wing groups in the United States to rally attention to their causes. Many punk groups historically adorned themselves with swastikas and other Nazi insignia as a means of protest, but these groups are using such symbols for different purposes.

Laura L. Finley

See also: Holocaust Films; Protest Music Worldwide; Protest Songs; Punk Music

Further Reading

Andrews, T. 2017. "Yes, Neo-Nazis Have Rock Bands Too. They've Been Around for Decades." *The Washington Post*, August 23. https://www.washingtonpost.com/news/morning-mix/wp/2017/08/23/yes-neo-nazis-have-rock-bands-too-theyve-been-around-for-decades

Associated Press. 2015. "Punk Band's Anti-Nazi Song Reaches Top of German Charts." *Chicago Tribune,* September 8. http://www.chicagotribune.com/entertainment/sns-bc-eu--germany-migrants-anti-nazi-song-20150908-story.html

Bridge, A. 1995. "German Punks Turn 'Chaos Days' into an Orgy of Violence." *The Independent*, August 6. http://www.independent.co.uk/news/world/german-punks-turn-chaos-days-into-an-orgy-of-violence-1595163.html

Le Blond, J. 2015. "German Punk Band Set to Top Charts in Wake of Refugee Arson Attacks." *The Guardian*, September 29. https://www.theguardian.com/world/2015/sep/09/german-punk-band-die-arzte-top-charts-refugee-arson-attacks

Oroschakoff, K. 2011. "Archive Immortalized East German Punk Rock Scene." *Reuters,* July 20. https://www.reuters.com/article/us-germany-punks-archive/archive-immortalizes-east-german-punk-rock-scene-idUSTRE76J2B320110720

Schroter, M. 2015. "80,000,000 Hooligans." *Critical Discourse Studies, 12*(4): 398–425.

Shahan, C. 2013. *Punk Rock and German Crisis: Adaptation and Resistance After 1977.* New York: Palgrave Macmillan.

Goth and Industrial Music

Goth and industrial music, often similar to electronic dance music (EDM) or "emo" music, is a genre that features heavy keyboards, synthesizers, and drum beats along with avant-garde noises that typically sound raw and give the music an angry feel. The genre emerged in the 1970s and has tended to have little commercial appeal but great popularity in clubs and indie circuits. It is often considered a fusion of rock and punk music. Many songs in the genre address controversial topics, including the occult and serial killers.

Three groups that have managed to obtain commercial success are Nine Inch Nails, Ministry, and Marilyn Manson, with the latter being more difficult to classify to one specific musical genre. Trent Reznor is the writer, arranger, producer, and performer of all of Nine Inch Nails' (NIN) work. He assembled a band and released the album *Pretty Hate Machine* in 1989, which was co-produced by several others and resulted in three radio hits. "Head Like a Hole" received the most attention, due in part to the fact that the band promoted it on tours and at festivals like Lollapalooza for several years before the release of the album. Another song on the album, "Sin," was banned from MTV because it showed genital piercings and had gay men smearing blood on each other. The FBI actually investigated Reznor because the images on the video for "Down in It" were so disturbing they thought they must have been taken from a snuff film. Reznor then started his own recording label, Nothing, and released "Happiness in Slavery." The video for the song was controversial, as it showed a man being sexually tortured and then ground into a bloody pulp in a machine. Reznor remained controversial, moving into the Los Angeles house where Charles Manson and his followers killed actress Sharon Tate in 1969 and turning it into a recording studio. After appearing at the Woodstock '94 festival, Reznor put together a live album from that and other performances of "Happiness in Slavery," which won NIN its second Grammy for Best Metal Performance in 1995. In addition to NIN, Reznor produces soundtracks for violent films, including Oliver Stone's *Natural Born Killers* (1994) and David Lynch's *Lost Highway* (1997). *Time* named him one of the 25 most influential people in 1997. In 2005 the band was slated to perform "The Hand that Feeds" at the 2005 MTV Video Music Awards, a song that is critical of former president George W. Bush but refused when the channel prohibited them from performing in front of a large image of the president (Nine Inch Nails bio, n.d.).

NIN has nine studio albums and remains popular today. Reznor also helped give rise to the career of shock-rocker Marilyn Manson, as he co-produced Manson's album *Antichrist Superstar*. Manson, born Brian Hugh Warner, took the stage name from actress Marilyn Monroe and serial killer Charles Manson. He introduced himself as the "antichrist superstar," the name he gave to one of his albums, and from day one generated controversy due to his appearance, his lyrics, his videos, and his stage performances. At one point he said, "My point on Earth is chaos. I'm the third act of every movie you've ever seen. I'm the part where it rains and the part where the person you don't want to die dies" (Grow, 2015). The following is only a partial list of some of Manson's most outrageous antics. In a concert in the early 1990s, Manson had an actress, who appeared to be pregnant, ironing the wrinkles from a Nazi flag on stage. She then spread herself across the ironing board and simulated performing an abortion. During a 1995 concert, Manson cut himself with a pocketknife, and during another show he thrust a broken beer bottle into his own chest, dragging it across his skin and leaving scars across his torso. Manson has said that he went grave digging in New Orleans and that he and some friends chipped off parts of the bones and put them into pipes that they smoked. He claims, "It was terrible. It smelled like burnt hair, gave you a really bad headache and made your eyes red" (Grow, 2015).

Manson's image on the cover of his 1998 album, *Mechanical Animals*, prompted K-Mart, Walmart, and Target to refuse to carry it. It featured Manson with a female, alien-like nude body and red eyes and hair. The album also carried a parental advisory sticker. Yet despite these companies arguing that they are "family stores" and are trying to protect children, it is now available online at all three stores, and the explicit version is cheaper than the clean one (Grow, 2015).

One year later, Manson became the focus of negative media attention when two teens, Eric Harris and Dylan Klebold, shot and killed 13 people and then themselves at Columbine High School in Littleton, Colorado. Early reports suggested that the boys were Manson fans, although later reports indicated they were only occasional listeners. Manson has said he was an easy target and that the attention virtually "killed his career" (Petridis, 2017). Another Manson controversy occurred in 2013, when 15-year-old Paris Jackson, daughter of Michael Jackson, allegedly slit her wrists because she could not attend his concert. The singer responded by simulating cutting his own wrists and dedicating the song "Disposable Teens" to her (Grow, 2015).

Al Jourgensen founded the band Ministry in Chicago in 1981. The band, which featured a revolving door of artists except for Jourgensen, has always been controversial for its critique of America as a land of violence. Most recently Ministry released a song called "Antifa," which is seemingly in support of the violent antifascist groups that have used that name and engaged in a variety of clashes with right-wing demonstrators.

Laura L. Finley

See also: Classic Rock; Hair Metal; Heavy Metal; Punk; *Quake*; South Korean K-Pop

Further Reading

Distefano, A. 2014. "The Ten Best Industrial Bands." *OC Weekly*, August 28. http://www.ocweekly.com/music/the-10-best-industrial-bands-6589779

Grow, K. 2015. "The Golden Age of Grotesque: Marilyn Manson's Most Shocking Moments. *Rolling Stone,* January 6. https://www.rollingstone.com/music/lists/the-golden-age-of-grotesque-marilyn-mansons-most-shocking-moments-20150106

Kaufman, G. 1998. "Marilyn Manson's New LP Banned by Major Chain Stores." *MTV*, August 14. http://www.mtv.com/news/500302/marilyn-mansons-new-lp-banned-by-major-chain-stores/

"Nine Inch Nails Bio." n.d. *Rolling Stone.* https://www.rollingstone.com/music/artists/nine-inch-nails/biography

Petridis, A. 2017. "'Columbine Destroyed My Entire Career': Marilyn Manson on the Perils of Being the Lord of Darkness." *The Guardian*, September 21. https://www.theguardian.com/music/2017/sep/21/columbine-destroyed-my-entire-career-marilyn-manson-on-the-perils-of-being-the-lord-of-darkness

"Trent Reznor." 2016. *Biography*, June 2. https://www.biography.com/people/trent-reznor-051816

Hair Metal

Hair metal refers to a subgenre of heavy metal that was popular in the later 1970s and through the 1980s. The hair reference is to the long locks that were worn by the mostly male artists as well as the few females who played this type of music. It is sometimes referred to as glam metal due to the fashion that was borrowed from glam rock, which featured leather clothing, metal studs, and heavy makeup. Popular hair metal bands included Motley Crue, Quiet Riot, Def Leppard, Bon Jovi, Poison, Skid Row, Ratt, Cinderella, Dokken, Stryper, and Warrant. It still has a cult-like following but generally waned in the 1990s with the rise of grunge music that rejected the flamboyance of hair metal. Like heavy metal, hair metal bands were criticized for their lyrics, for their excesses, and for their performances and music videos. The artists became notorious for their debauchery, flaunting their attendance at late-night parties, their love of strippers, and their frequent use of drugs.

Motley Crue was one of the first hair metal bands to achieve commercial success. But 1983 has been called hair metal's breakout year due to the release of Quiet Riot's album *Mental Health*, the first heavy metal album to reach number one on the *Billboard* charts. Motley Crue released its second album, *Shout at the Devil*, that same year, while Def Leppard released *Pyromania*, Lita Ford released *Out for Blood*, and Kiss released *Lick It Up*. Los Angeles was the epicenter of hair metal, with artists appearing frequently at clubs like the Trip, the Starwood, and Whisky a Go Go. The genre was so popular by the mid-1980s that MTV featured a show called *Headbangers Ball*, which saw more than 1.3 million viewers each week. Another big year was 1986, with Bon Jovi releasing *Slippery When Wet*. That album spent eight weeks at the top of the Billboard album chart and was the first hard rock album to have two singles reach number one and another in the top 10.

Many of the songs by hair metal bands talked about love gone wrong, and the artists were often critiqued for their misogynistic depiction of women. Many made reference to the devil. Some also discussed violence. One of Ratt's most popular songs was "18 and Life," about a young person going to prison for life for murder. Motley Crue's "Bastard" featured the lines "Out go the lights, in goes my knife / Pull out his life, consider that bastard dead."

Largely in response to the popularity of hair metal, Tipper Gore, wife of Senator Al Gore; Susan Baker, wife of Treasury Secretary James Baker; and Pam Hower and Sally Nevius, wives of prominent Washington, D.C., businessmen, formed the Parents Music Resource Council (PMRC) in 1984. The group created a list they called the "Filthy 15," which were the songs they felt were the worst for teen ears. These included tunes by Madonna and Prince, as well as Twisted Sister and other hair metal bands. Judas Priest's "Eat Me Alive" was included on the list due to these lines: "Groan in the pleasure zone, gasping from the heat. . . . I'm gonna force you at gunpoint to eat me alive." The Twisted Sister song that bothered the PMRC was "We're Not Gonna Take It," which actually does not discuss violence in any way (Grow, 2015b).

The group also pushed for some type of ratings system, which resulted in the parental advisory stickers that are now placed on albums or CDs. The work of the PMRC also resulted in hearings before the Senate about violence and sex in music in 1985. The hearings repeatedly referred to the Filthy 15 as "porn rock." In addition to Gore and Baker, many artists whose work was criticized testified, as did some who spoke in solidarity. One of the most scathing criticisms of PRMC's efforts was levied by country musician John Denver, who likened it to Nazi book burnings.

Motley Crue front man Niki Sixx, responding to critics who said their music would warp young people, said "I don't want to tell kids what to do . . . I've always thought of us as the psychiatrists of rock & roll because the kids come to see us, get all this anxiety and pent-up aggression out. That hour and a half is theirs. No one can take it away. No parent can tell them to turn it down" (Schonfeld, 2015). Snider has reflected about that time and believes he was inappropriately made into a public enemy and that he remains proud of how he represented himself and fellow rockers. For instance, he testified, "Ms. Gore claimed that one of my songs, 'Under the Blade,' had lyrics encouraging sadomasochism, bondage, and rape. The lyrics she quoted have absolutely nothing to do with these topics. On the contrary, the words in question are about surgery and the fear that it instills in people. . . . I can say categorically that the only sadomasochism, bondage and rape in this song is in the mind of Ms. Gore" (Grow, 2015a).

Other defenders of hair metal argued that people missed the point of many of these songs, getting too caught up in the appearance of the artists. For instance, Motley Crue's "Shout at the Devil" is speaking out against Satan (Considine, 1984). Interestingly, the parental advisory labels on albums and now on CDs have not necessarily proven to be effective, as artists whose work is so labeled often see increased sales to curious teens seeking the so-called "forbidden fruit." Some bands also poked fun at the advisory system. Judas Priest's 1986 album *Turbo* featured a tune called "Parental Guidance" (Grow, 2015a).

Laura L. Finley

See also: Classic Rock; Goth and Industrial Music; Heavy Metal

Further Reading

Considine, J. 1984. "Motley Crue: Shout at the Devil." *Rolling Stone,* February 16. https://www.rollingstone.com/music/albumreviews/shout-at-the-devil-19840216

Grow, K. 2015a. "Dee Snider on PMRC Hearing: 'I Was a Public Enemy.'" *Rolling Stone,* September 18. https://www.rollingstone.com/music/news/dee-snider-on-pmrc-hearing-i-was-a-public-enemy-20150918

Grow, K. 2015b. "PMRC's 'Filthy 15': Where Are They Now?" *Rolling Stone,* September 17. https://www.rollingstone.com/music/lists/pmrcs-filthy-15-where-are-they-now-20150917

Schonfeld, Z. 2015. "Parental Advisory Forever: An Oral History of the PMRC's War on Dirty Lyrics." *Newsweek,* September 19. http://www.newsweek.com/2015/10/09/oral-history-tipper-gores-war-explicit-rock-lyrics-dee-snider-373103.html

Heavy Metal

Heavy metal is a genre of rock music that is known for driving guitars and controversial lyrics. Some of the most popular heavy metal artists include Alice Cooper, Iron Maiden, Judas Priest, Black Sabbath, Metallica, Ozzy Osbourne, Slayer, and Marilyn Manson, although Manson is sometimes considered an industrial or Goth artist. Critics point to heavy metal lyrics that glorify violence, the devil, and suicide, as well as to bizarre and violent behavior by some of the artists. Occasional violence at heavy metal concerts fueled these critiques.

Iron Maiden was criticized for the title of its 1982 album, *The Number of the Beast* and the repeated use of the so-called "sign of the devil," the number 666, in its title track. Critics denounced the band as devil worshippers. As is often the case, the attention increased the band's visibility and led to packed shows on their tour.

Ozzy Osbourne took heat not just for his music but also for his on-stage antics. He bit the head of a bat during a show with Black Sabbath. Osbourne says he thought it was a rubber rat and only learned it was not when it bit him back. Osbourne also recalls throwing a bucket of water on a bunch of fans who he thought were not adequately interested in his show. It turns out the fans were not "rocking out" because they were deaf. Before Osbourne, Alice Cooper and Kiss were known for their extreme stage behavior. Kiss lead singer Gene Simmons would spit blood and breathe fire at the audience.

Police in the 1980s often made claims that it was heavy metal that influenced young people to commit crimes. In one case known as the West Memphis Three, Damien Echols, Jason Baldwin, and Jessie Misskelley were convicted of murdering three 8-year-old boys in rural Arkansas. Police were quick to believe the three were the perpetrators in part because they listened to Metallica and wore the band's t-shirts. Echols spent 10 years in solitary confinement, and all three were in prison until 2011, when they were released because evidence clearly showed they were not involved.

After the Columbine massacre on April 20, 1999, when Dylan Klebold and Eric Harris shot 12 students, one teacher, and then themselves at Columbine High School in Littleton, Colorado, pundits, politicians, and the public, seeking explanations, turned to the fact that the shooters were fans of Marilyn Manson. Filmmaker Michael Moore discussed the issue with Manson in his 2000 documentary *Bowling for Columbine*, and Manson dismissed his work as having prompted the shooters. It wasn't the first time Manson had been blamed for violence. Schools in Florida had even threatened to expel students who attended his shows, and South Carolina paid the artist not to perform in that state. Manson claims that the constant attacks after Columbine killed his career (Petridis, 2017).

Several other violent offenders are said to have been heavy metal fans. Jared Lee Loughner, who killed 6 and injured 14, including Congresswoman Gabrielle Giffords, on January 8, 2011, was a heavy metal fan. Just months later heavy metal again took the heat after Kyle Smith killed his grandparents and set their house on fire. Smith allegedly had a heavy metal CD and a pentagram in his room.

Metal artists and fans say that the references to blood and destruction and the occasional mockups included in videos and concerts are all just part of the show. Alice Cooper once responded, "There's more blood in 'Macbeth' than in my shows and that's required school reading." Iron Maiden lead singer Bruce Dickinson says he was influenced by the horror movies he liked as a child in the 1970s and that the bands are simply telling a highly dramatic story (Donkin, 2008).

Some research has even found that listening to extreme music like heavy metal can inspire people to feel calm, not angry or violent. A study by a student, Leah Sharman, and Dr. Genevieve Dingle at the University of Queensland included 39 people ages 18 to 34 who regularly listen to heavy metal. They found that "the music regulated sadness and enhanced positive emotions. When experiencing anger, extreme-music fans liked to listen to music that could match their anger." Levels of irritability, stress, and hostility all decreased after the subjects began listening to the music. They also reported feeling more inspired. Listening to the heavy metal music was as relaxing as was sitting in silence (Guardian Music, 2015). Jeffrey

Jensen Arnett, a psychology professor at Clark University and author of *Metalheads: Heavy Metal Music and Adolescent Alienation*, says, "A lot of people think heavy metal inspires violence, because it's violent music. But the surprising truth is that it doesn't make its fans violent, it doesn't even make them angry; it calms them down. They listen to it especially when they're angry or sad, and it helps them empty out those feelings so that they feel better afterward" (Tewksbury, 2011).

See also: Classic Rock; Goth and Industrial Music; Hair Metal

Laura L. Finley

Further Reading

DeSantis, R. 2018. "Ozzy Osbourne Recalls Throwing Buckets of Water on a Deaf Crowd." *AOL*, February 12. https://www.aol.com/article/entertainment/2018/02/12/ozzy -osbourne-recalls-throwing-buckets-of-water-on-a-deaf-crowd/23359596/

Donkin, J. 2008. "Heavy Metal and Violence: More than a Myth?" *CNN*, May 12. http:// edition.cnn.com/2008/SHOWBIZ/Music/05/09/metal.violence/index.html

Guardian Music. 2015. "Listening to 'Extreme' Music Makes You Calmer, Not Angrier, Study Says." *The Guardian*, June 22. https://www.theguardian.com/music/2015 /jun/22/listening-heavy-metal-punk-extreme-music-makes-you-calmer-not-angrier -study

Petridis, A. 2017. "'Columbine Destroyed My Entire Career': Marilyn Manson on the Perils of Being the Lord of Darkness." *Rolling Stone,* September 21. https://www .theguardian.com/music/2017/sep/21/columbine-destroyed-my-entire-career -marilyn-manson-on-the-perils-of-being-the-lord-of-darkness

Severson, K. 2012. "West Memphis Three, a Year out of Prison, Navigate New Paths." *The New York Times,* August 17. http://www.nytimes.com/2012/08/18/us/west-memphis -three-a-year-out-of-prison-navigate-new-paths.html

Tewksbury, D. 2011. "Six Most Idiotic Attempts to Blame Musicians for Violent Events." *LA Weekly*, January 13. http://www.laweekly.com/music/six-most-idiotic-attempts -to-blame-musicians-for-violent-events-or-the-tucson-tragedy-was-caused-by-a -crazy-person-not-by-drowning-pools-bodies-hit-the-floor-2411644

Winegarner, B. 2011. "Metal Monday: When Heavy Metal Becomes Linked with Crime." *USA Today,* September 26. http://content.usatoday.com/communities/popcandy/post /2011/09/metal-monday-when-heavy-metal-becomes-linked-with-crime/1#.Wl0R _DdG02w

Hip-Hop

Hip-hop was mostly unknown outside of the United States prior to the early 1980s. Throughout that decade, it began its spread to every inhabited continent and became a part of the music scene in dozens of countries. The roots of hip-hop are found in Black music and, ultimately, African music. Hip-hop music was initially created in New York City by Black teenagers, and the music was often accompanied by other elements, including breakdancing and graffiti art. Hip-hop artists quickly became icons of fashion, and their styles were emulated by both Black and White youth. The lyrics of hip-hop songs are often about the challenges of urban life. Some hip-hop song lyrics are about gangs, violence, and illegal drugs, which has prompted critics to contend that they glorify these things. Popular hip-hop artists include

Jay-Z, Lil Wayne, Eminem, Kendrick Lamar, Kanye West, Beyoncé, Diddy, and Nicki Minaj.

Jay-Z, born Sean Carter, is one of the best-selling artists of all time. He is worth an estimated $900 million, making him the wealthiest hip-hop artist of 2018 (Mojica, 2018). His music is autobiographical, telling his stories of life on the streets when he was young, selling drugs to get by, and about the violence in his life. At age 12 he shot his older brother during a domestic dispute. Jay-Z himself was shot at close range as a teen but managed to survive. In 2001 he was arrested for criminal possession of a weapon in the third degree when his body-guard was found outside a club with a Glock semi-automatic firearm in his waistband. Later that year Jay-Z was sentenced to three years of probation for stabbing a music executive at a party (Bilmes, 2017). Jay-Z often uses slurs in his songs, which the artist defends as appropriate for his background. He has often been accused of promoting misogyny through derogatory references to women in his music. In a 2010 interview he expressed regret for one of these songs, the very popular "Big Pimpin'." Jay-Z has been married to Beyoncé Knowles, for-mer lead singer of Destiny's Child and herself a widely successful hip-hop art-ist, since April 2008.

Beyoncé's music is less focused on violence, but has been criticized for promot-ing gender stereotypes despite the artist's efforts to promote female empowerment and gender equality. One of her most controversial songs is "Drunk in Love," which she co-wrote and performed with Jay-Z. Jay-Z raps, after stating that he is Ike Turner, "Baby no I don't play / Now eat the cake, Anna Mae." This is a reference to singer Ike Turner's well-documented abuse of his wife, singer Tina Turner, who was born Anna Mae. Critics say this and other lines in the song glorify domestic violence.

Lil Wayne, born Dwayne Michael Carter, Jr., generated controversy in 2013 for a line he rapped as a guest artist for Future's "Karate Chop" remix. The question-able line was "Beat that p**** up like Emmett Till," which is a reference to the 14-year-old Black boy who was lynched in Mississippi in 1955 after he whistled at a White woman. Lil Wayne later apologized and promised never to perform that lyric. The record label Epic also removed the line. In 2015 the artist was again in trouble, this time for trying to fight a referee during a charity basketball game to promote nonviolence. The rapper was coaching one of the teams and grew upset at a call made by the referee. He allegedly spit at the referee then rushed at him (Har-rison, 2015).

Rap artists and their music may discuss violence as part of an exciting and dangerous lifestyle, but some songs also condemn violence and even promote solu-tions. For instance, Jay-Z teamed up with Kanye West for "Murder for Excellence," which condemns "black-on-black" violence, noting "314 soldiers died in Iraq, 509 died in Chicago." Kendrick Lamar's politically charged lyrics may be contro-versial but they also raise awareness about issues like police brutality. Lamar famously performed his song "Alright" on top of a police car during the 2015 BET Awards, prompting Fox News pundit Geraldo Rivera to say, "Hip hop has done more damage to young African Americans than racism in recent years." Not one to back down, Lamar responded by recording his song "DNA" over the top of Rivera's pronouncement. Another song on the album *Damn*, "XXX," criticizes President Donald Trump for wanting "barricades and borders" (Kornhaber, 2017). Emmanuel Jal, a refugee from Sudan, found a sense of peace in music and uses his rap to promote a better world. Rapper Sister Fa uses her music to speak out against genital cutting, which she endured in her home country of Senegal (Frank, 2017).

Laura L. Finley

See also: African Gangsta Rap; Blues Music; Dancehall Music; Gangsta Rap; Jamaican Reggae Music; Latin American MCs; Narcocorridos; Punk Music

Further Reading

Bilmes, A. 2017. "Jay-Z on His Music, Politics and His Violent Past." *GQ*, June 28. http://www.gq-magazine.co.uk/article/jay-z-interview-music-politics-violence

Cubarrubia, R. 2013. "Lil Wayne Apologizes for 'Inappropriate' Emmett Till Lyric." *Rolling Stone*, May 1. https://www.rollingstone.com/music/news/lil-wayne-apologizes-for-inappropriate-emmett-till-lyric-20130501

Frank, P. 2017. "The Hip-Hop Artists Who Use Words to Change the World." *Huffington Post,* January 5. https://www.huffingtonpost.com/entry/photography-hip-hop-acti vists_us_586bd2b9e4b0eb58648a9835

Harrison, L. 2015. "Lil Wayne Starts Fight with Referee during Anti-Violence Charity Basketball Game." *E Online*, June 2. http://www.eonline.com/news/662368/lil-wayne-starts-fight-with-referee-during-anti-violence-charity-basketball-game

Kornhaber, S. 2017. "Kendrick Lamar's Complicated Political Score-Settling." *The Atlantic,* April 14. https://www.theatlantic.com/entertainment/archive/2017/04/kendrick-lamar-damn-politics-fox-trump/523059/

Mojica, N. 2018. "Jay-Z, Diddy and More Among Forbes' Hip-Hop's Wealthiest Acts of 2018." *Forbes*, March 1. http://www.xxlmag.com/news/2018/03/jay-z-diddy-forbes-hip-hops-wealthiest-acts-2018/

Mokoena, T. 2014. "Beyonce's 'Drunk in Love': Should We Have a Problem with It?" *The Guardian*, January 28. https://www.theguardian.com/music/musicblog/2014/jan/28/beyonce-drunk-in-love-problem-lyrics

Indian and Pakistani Pop Music

Although India is most known for its happy, upbeat Bollywood tunes, artists have long used music to express political opinions. Likewise, in Pakistan, a country that has endured decades of fighting and attacks, many musicians use their work to raise awareness and lobby for change.

The Ska Vengers is a ska band devoted to peace and justice. The band's political lyrics focus on controversial topics, including the division of the land of Kashmir, censorship, and human rights abuses. While the sounds and songs were immediately popular, with the rhythms not that different from Bollywood, politicians denounced the music and the Indian media generally ignored the band's politics. The band was even offered a recording contract with a major label but turned it down because they were asked to remove or beep out all references to Kashmir and other contested areas. Instead, they started their own recording label. In 2014, they released a song critiquing Chief Minister Nahendra Modi for allowing the 2002

Gujarat riots that killed some 2,000 people to occur. Media began to pay attention, but not always in a good way, as the band was labeled communist sympathizers, terrorists, and anti-nationalists.

Pop music in India and Pakistan has long been dominated by males. Songs, and the videos that accompany them, often feature sexist and occasionally violent messages. More recently, however, feminist groups have sought to stake out space in the world of pop music. Human rights advocacy group Breakthrough issued a feminist remake of an Indian pop classic "Urvashi Urvashi" that became very popular. In the original video, Indian dance legend Prabhu Deva is dancing while harassing college girls on the bus. The remake shows three women dancing on a roof and urging women to break the glass ceiling. Rather than the refrain "Take it easy Urvashi," the remake features a new mantra, "Don't take it easy Urvashi," and its lyrics address social issues like clothing that supposedly dishonors families, fat shaming, and victim blaming. The women who created it were applauded by many but also received hate mail and were trolled on social media. Breakthrough's primary mission is to end violence against women and girls, and it largely uses popular culture to do so. It was launched in 2000 with an album of music videos, *Mann ke Manjeere*, which features a woman escaping an abusive marriage to become a truck driver. It is based on a real story. It was the first Indian album about a social issue to become a hit.

Similarly, in Pakistan protest music has a long tradition. Artists like Shehzad Roy, Junoon, and Laal are known for their political music. Many of these artists were banned on Pakistani state TV. Satirist and stand-up comic Saad Haroon said, "In the beginning Pakistani bands used music to express dissent because other avenues of communication were closed to them. When you are in a repressive environment you naturally find other ways to communicate and music became that outlet. Nowadays things are much more open, but I think the association between music and free speech remains." Haroon wrote "Burqa Woman," sung to the tune of Roy Orbison's "Pretty Woman," to enter the debate about the wearing of the burqa (Aroral, 2015).

Popular singer Rahim Shah critiques the bloody insurgency in "Shaba Tabahi Oka" ("Come on Destroy Everything"). It was featured in the 2012 film *Ghaddar*, or *Traitor*. Another film, *Da Khkulo Badshahi Da*, or *Beautiful Are Always Crowned*, shows an actress dancing in between a group of armed men, singing about lethal drone strikes. Singer Zafar Iqrar wrote a song in which he implored his lover not to return to the village because it was decimated by the army. Some criticize these artists, suggesting that they are exploiting the bloodshed for fame and fortune. Yet proponents argue that these songs merely reflect the lived experience of many people in the country. Still other singers have written songs about peace. Khattak and female singer Laila Khan wrote a peace song after a deadly Taliban attack that resulted in the massacre of 150 people at an army-run school (AFP, 2015).

Laura L. Finley

See also: Music Videos; Protest Music Worldwide; Protest Songs

Further Reading

AFP. 2015. "Violence and Vulgarity: Pashto Pop Music Reflects Region's War Fixation." *Tribune*, July 6. https://tribune.com.pk/story/915473/violence-and-vulgarity-pashto -pop-music-reflects-regions-war-fixation/

Aroral, T. 2011. "In Pakistan, Protest Music Is a Tradition." *Times of India,* November 1. https://timesofindia.indiatimes.com/india/In-Pakistan-protest-music-is-a-tradition /articleshow/10562389.cms

Bone, A. 2017. "The Power of Pop: This Music Video Is Championing the Rights of Indian Women." *SBS*, May 3. https://www.sbs.com.au/topics/life/culture/article/2017/05/03 /power-pop-music-video-championing-rights-indian-women

Petridis, A. 2017. "The Ska Vengers: 'What's the Worst that Could Happen? We Could Get Lynched.'" *The Guardian,* July 20. https://www.theguardian.com/music/2017/jul/20 /the-ska-vengers-first-india-ska-band-radical-lyrics-lynched

Jamaican Reggae Music

Reggae music was the first genre of music in Jamaica, originating in the 1960s. This genre of music was originally created by the Rastafarians, which is a religious movement with distinctive codes of behavior and appearance. This included wearing dreadlocks, smoking marijuana, rejecting Western medicine, and not eating pork. In addition to this, reggae music was associated with Jamaican culture, which at the time was a ghetto phenomenon associated with gang-style violence. Yet there is also a strong thread of antiviolence and resistance to state violence in reggae music.

Bob Marley was a Jamaican native who lived in one of the poorest neighborhoods, Trench Town, in Kingston, Jamaica. Growing up he struggled in poverty and looked to music as inspiration. Marley was also a part of the Rastafarian movement and became very well known in Jamaica for his music. One of his songs that features violence is "I Shot the Sheriff." The song begins with Marley saying that he did indeed shoot the sheriff, but he did not shoot the sheriff's deputy. The song then continues with him saying that the sheriff always hated him, and refrains that the sheriff will "kill it before it grows," referring to any seed that the civilian tries to plant. That is then followed by the civilian suddenly laying eyes on Sheriff Jon Brown, who is aiming his weapon at him. So, he fires and shoots first, hitting the sheriff. Police abuse was common at the time in Kingston, Jamaica. Bob Marley was arrested for the possession of marijuana and served a month in prison. While in prison he met several prisoners and built relationships with them, and they shared their personal experiences with police brutality. Marley's portrayal of violence was informed by that experience.

Another known reggae artist is Buju Banton, who is also a native-born Jamaican who lived in poverty. He was one of 15 children, and he used music as an escape from the violence he viewed every day. He grew up in conditions conducive to using or selling drugs, which resulted in him being arrested and imprisoned. He is currently serving a 10-year sentence. Buju Banton had a very violent past and holds a deep hatred for gays and lesbians, which is evident in his music. One of his best-known songs is "Boom Bye Bye." The song begins with him saying the world is in trouble. Then, he goes on to say that a "batty bwoy" (gay man) who "caresses" other men should be murdered, no questions asked. This sentiment is repeated several times throughout the song. When he says "boom bye bye in a batty boy head," he is referring to killing gay men by shooting them in the head. That is then followed by lyrics that state that no one should promote same-sex relationships, and if they do, they should also be killed.

This sentiment is not unusual in Jamaica, where same-sex partnerships are looked at negatively, even in the law. The Offences Against Persons Act of 1864 made homosexual acts in Jamaica illegal. Any man who is having sexual relations with another man could be sentenced to a misdemeanor. This act allowed open, legal discrimination toward gays and lesbians, and influenced many people's opinions on the matter. To this day, gays are not welcome in certain areas in the country.

Although there is violence in Jamaican reggae music, the music in this genre also promotes love and unity. The same two artists, Bob Marley and Buju Banton, have created songs that are complete opposites of the violent songs they have already made. In "Positive Vibrations," Marley states that rather than fight and battle every day, promoting darkness and praying to the devil, we should help each other and promote unity and togetherness. He then continues, "Say you just can't live that negative way / make way for the positive day." In "Love Sponge," Banton says "Lord you are lovable, kissable / without you I'm so damn miserable." Here Banton gives a nod to religion, showing how important the Lord's presence is in his life. He goes on to stress the importance of slowing down and listening to people; Banton believes that we shouldn't live life in a rush, but rather live each day slowly. We should take the time to hear what others have to say and enjoy the company of others, as life is not promised.

Laura L. Finley

See also: African Gangsta Rap; Dancehall Music; Gangsta Rap; Hip-Hop

Further Reading

"Bob Marley." 2017. A&E Networks Television. https://www.biography.com/people/bob-marley-9399524

Gaylord, S., & Perez-Santiago, M. 2015. "The World as It Should Be." *Human Rights First,* July. http://www.humanrightsfirst.org/sites/default/files/HRF-Jamaica-Report-final.pdf

Longstaff, Jess. 2011. "Ten Things You Never Knew about Bob Marley." *Clash*, January 4. http://www.clashmusic.com/features/ten-things-you-never-knew-about-bob-marley

"Origins of Reggae" n.d. http://jamaicansmusic.com/learn/origins/reggae

Scaruffi, P. n.d. "A Brief Summary of Jamaican Music." https://www.scaruffi.com/history/reggae.html

Latin American MCs

Latin American MCs are rappers who are increasingly taking on pressing social issues. Influenced by both hip-hop culture in the United States and their own cultures and experiences, many Latin American MCs are denouncing various forms of violence and using their work to make social change.

Long a male-dominated area, there are an increasing number of female MCs. Rima Roja en Venus is a female duo from Quito, Ecuador, and their goal is to reject the objectification that was often part of male hip-hop. In Guatemala City, rapper Rebecca Lane does the same, noting that "[t]he level of gender violence in free-style rhyming battles, and in mainstream rap, can be horrific." Mexican MC Audry Funk is part of a collective called Somos Mujeres Somos Hip-Hop (We Are Women, We Are Hip-Hop), which brings together female MCs to offer support and solidarity. It has released a mixtape featuring female MCs from Mexico, Chile, Colombia, Peru, Ecuador, Bolivia, Costa Rica, Venezuela, and Argentina. The collective pays tribute to Argentina's Actitud Maria Marta, one of the earliest socially conscious female hip-hop groups. These are countries in which simply being female puts one at great risk. For instance, 15 women are killed each day in Brazil. Guatemala saw decades of civil war that led to an estimated 200,000 killed. Hip-hop, according to Lane, "gives young people ways of organizing beyond armed conflict, beyond military or gang violence." Most don't use the word feminist to describe their work, as there's a powerful stigma attached to the term in Latin America (Rigby, 2015).

In the area of Comuna 13, one of the most violent sections in Medellin, Colombia, a city historically associated with brutal gang violence, youth are using hip-hop to change their neighborhood. Many were skeptical, associating hip-hop with gangs and crimes, but things have begun to change, and hip-hop artists are now being seen as helping their communities. Although there are few systemic evaluations of efforts to use hip-hop to keep youth away from gangs and violence, anecdotal evidence seems to suggest it can be effective. This is perhaps due to the fact that its rebellious, anti-establishment tone resonates with young people. In San Salvador, El Salvador, the federal and local government implemented a hip-hop program, which included arts and sports, in some of the most violent neighborhoods. These *raperos conscientes*, which roughly translates to socially aware or "woke" rappers, have been targeted by gangs, with at least a dozen murdered since 2009 (Albaladejo, 2017). Others face government backlash, as was the case in 2010 when rapper Onechot, real name Juan David Chacon, released his video for "Rotten Town," which depicted the immense amount of violence in Caracas, Venezuela. He rapped that a "hundred people die every week" and that Venezuela has "more death than Pakistan, Lebanon, Kosovo, Vietnam and Afghanistan." In 2012, Chacon was carjacked and shot in the head. Although he survived, his career was put on hold for two years. Critics say authorities did little to investigate. Rapper El Prieto, real name Arvei Angulo Rivas, also raps about the violence of his crime-ridden neighborhood in Caracas, saying, "You say we incite violence, but we're not the violent ones. / The street is violent." Venezuela's best-known hip-hop artist is Tyone Jose Gonzalez, known as Canserbero. He died in what authorities say is a murder-suicide with his friend and musician, Carlos Molnar, but many remain skeptical. His signature phrase, borrowed from the Beatles, was "all we need is love," and his music critiqued violence and corruption in the barrios of Venezuela (Otero, 2015).

Not all rappers in Latin America are engaging in such positive work, however. The brutal gang MS13 is known to produce gangsta rap in the style common to the

U.S. West Coast in the 1980s and 1990s, as does their rival, Barrio 18. This has resulted in efforts to repress hip-hop as a way to target the gangs.

Laura L. Finley

See also: Gang Films; Gangsta Rap; Hip-Hop; Mexican Crime Novels; Narcocorridos

Further Reading

Albaladejo, A. 2017. "Can Hip Hop Help Stop Gang Violence in Latin America?" *Insight Crime*, June 9. https://www.insightcrime.org/news/analysis/can-hip-hop-help-stop -gang-violence-latin-america/

Otero, P. 2015. "Venezuelan Hip Hop: The Voice of a Suffering Nation." *Pan Am Post*, October 29. https://panampost.com/pedro-garcia/2015/10/29/venezuelan-hip-hop-the -voice-of-a-suffering-nation/

Rigby, C. 2015. "How Latin American Women Are Changing Hip-Hop." *The Guardian*, August 9. https://www.theguardian.com/music/2015/aug/09/how-latin-american -women-are-changing-hip-hip

Murder Ballads

Murder ballads are songs that tell the details of a particular homicide. Although they can be in any genre, most come from the blues, folk, or country tradition. They are among the most popular tunes in country music history. Domestic violence and revenge are common themes. In 1996, the band Nick Cave and the Bad Seeds released an album in 1996 entitled *Murder Ballads*. It included 65 stabbings, shootings, and stranglings in its nine songs (Christiansen, 2015).

In Lefty Frizzel's "Long Black Veil," the narrator learns that he is accused of a murder 10 years prior because he looks like the perpetrator. He refused to give the judge his alibi when he was accused, as he was at the time in bed with his best friend's wife.

The Dixie Chicks' "Goodbye Earl" is a murder ballad released by the all-female group in 2000. It was immediately controversial, first because it is typically men who sing these songs and because the accompanying video made clear what happened. Wanda is beaten by her husband, Earl, just two weeks after the wedding. She calls a friend, Mary Ann, and they kill Earl by poisoning his black-eyed peas. The two then dispose of the body, and as the song makes clear, do not feel bad about what they have done. They hide his body and then start a lucrative business selling ham and jam. And, most importantly, they "don't lose any sleep at night." The song is as sassy as singer Natalie Maines herself.

In Waylon Jennings's "Cedartown, Georgia," the narrator buys a gun to kill his woman, who he claims has been spending his money and cheating on him. He shoots her and her "dandy" in their hotel room. *Rolling Stone* magazine listed the song as one of the creepiest murder ballads of all time (Crowell, 2014). Another famous murder ballad is Tom Jones's "Delilah," which also discusses a man who finds his girlfriend cheating. His response was to stab her to death. "She stood there laughing / I felt the knife in my hand and she laughed no more." (BBC, 2016). Another revenge song, "Frankie and Johnny," has been covered more than 250 times by various folk and pop artists. It is about a woman who seeks revenge on her unfaithful boyfriend.

Johnny Cash is known for his bloody songs, yet only "I Hung My Head" is considered to be a murder ballad. It tells the story of a senseless murder by a man who borrows a rifle and shoots a rider as he came across the plain. Unlike many murder ballads, the offender expresses remorse. The lyrics state that he knows how it feels to take life and that: "I orphaned his children, I widowed his wife. / I begged their forgiveness, I wish I was dead" (Crowell, 2014).

"The Cruel Mother" is a murder ballad about infanticide. The woman in the song kills her two newborn children with a knife. Afterward, she tries to clean up the weapon but the blade will not wipe clean. She then encounters two babies at a church who are the ghosts of her children and who tell her she's going to hell for their murders.

Bob Dylan wrote and performed several murder ballads. One of them is "The Death of Emmett Till," which is about the murder of the young Black boy in Mississippi in 1955 because he dared to whistle at a White woman at a store. It describes the torture as the men beat him, the way they rolled his battered body into the water and left him to die. The song goes on to discuss the "mockery" that was the trial, as most White people in the town were sympathetic to the perpetrators. In "Hurricane," Dylan tells the true story of the imprisonment of Rubin "Hurricane" Carter, who was wrongly convicted of murder in large part due to racism. Dylan visited Carter at Rahway State Prison in New Jersey.

Laura L. Finley

See also: Blues Music; Country Music; *Dexter*; Folk Music; Narcocorridos

Further Reading

BBC. 2016. "10 of the Most Disturbing Folk Songs in History." *BBC*, April 18. https://www.bbc.co.uk/music/articles/8beeaac5-064c-4406-9e85-d42cebf9a53b

Christiansen, R. 2015. "From Tom Jones to Nick Cave: Music's Macabre Obsession with Murder." *The Telegraph*, November 17. http://www.telegraph.co.uk/music/what-to-listen-to/lulu-a-murder-ballad-music-murder/

Crowell, C. 2014. "Killer Songs: The Ten Creepiest Country Murder Ballads." *Rolling Stone*, October 28. https://www.rollingstone.com/music/lists/creepiest-country-murder-ballads-20141028/lefty-frizzell-long-black-veil-20141028

Dylan, B. n.d. "The Death of Emmett Till." *Bob Dylan.com*. https://bobdylan.com/songs/death-emmett-till/

Underwood, R. 2016. *Crimesong: True Crime Stories from Southern Murder Ballads*. Lexington, KY: Shadelandhouse Modern Press.

Music Videos

Although most people consider the August 1, 1981, launch of MTV to be the origin of music videos, their roots go back to the late 19th century. In 1895, William Dickson used his Kinetophone, a device he had developed in Thomas Edison's lab, to make the first film with music. It featured two men dancing to the sound of a popular violin operetta. In the early 20th century, photographic images were projected from glass slides and played at vaudeville houses and nickelodeons. In April 1923, New York City's Rivoli Theater presented the first motion pictures with sound-on-film. These were often shorts that featured popular musicians and played before feature films into the 1940s. Between 1940 and 1946, soundies were popular three-minute films featuring music and dance performances, designed to display on jukebox-like projection machines in bars, restaurants, and other public spaces. In 1959, singer and songwriter Jiles Perry Richardson, known as the Big Bopper, becomes the first person to use the term "music video" in an interview with a British magazine. It was the Beatles in the 1960s, however, who are credited with introducing music videos to the world. The band starred in several full-length feature films but also issued a series of short promotional clips. Rock bands of the 1960s and 1970s followed their lead. In 1974, Australia paved the way for MTV with the introduction of two weekly music video shows aimed at teens. Three years before MTV hit the airwaves, in 1978, *Video Concert Hall* on the USA Network featured music videos.

Since becoming so popular, many music videos have been banned, not just in the United States but in Britain and other countries. Most of the bans are related to sexually provocative material, although some are due to excessive violence.

Domestic violence is often the subject of songs and music videos, and critics note that the depictions often portray abuse as romantic or normal in relationships. In 1991, Garth Brooks's video for "The Thunder Rolls," in which he depicted a violent, cheating husband, was banned by The Nashville Network and Country Music Television. The Dixie Chicks' "Goodbye Earl" in 1999 featured a woman seeking revenge on an abusive husband. Hosier's "Cherry Wine," which the artist says he intended to show the cycle of violence, portrays the abuse among soft lighting and beautiful birds, sending a mixed message. Shock-rocker Marilyn Manson's 2009 video for "Running to the Edge of the World" showed him beating up on a bloodied female who resembled his then-ex-fiancée, Evan Rachel Wood. The video ends with the woman dead in a bathtub. The 2010 video for Rihanna and Eminem's "Love the Way You Lie" generated both applause and concern, as some said it realistically documented abusive relationships while others critiqued it for making abuse appear mutual. In his 2015 video for "Take Your Time," country artist Sam Hunt is a barroom vigilante who goes after a man he witnesses abusing a woman.

Other videos are said to trivialize or even glorify sexual violence. In 2013, Robin Thicke's song and video "Blurred Lines" generated huge controversy, as they were seen by many to glorify sexual exploitation with the refrain "you know you want it." Maroon 5's video for "Animals" in 2014 was criticized by sexual assault advocates for offering a dangerous glorification of stalking and sexual assault. In contrast, Lady Gaga's video for "Til It Happens to You" shows the difficulties endured by sexual assault survivors and was used in the documentary *The Hunting Ground*.

Since the 2000s, a popular trope for music videos was to feature females rejecting victimization and fighting back. In 2001, Madonna's video for "What It Feels Like for a Girl," produced by her then-husband Guy Ritchie, was banned by MTV and VH1 because it depicts the artist on a crime spree that ends in suicide. Critics today have suggested that the ban was really because it was a woman perpetrating the violence. Disclosure's "Magnets" ends with singer Lorde tying a man to a chair, pushing the chair into a pool, then lighting the pool on fire. She pronounced on Twitter, "[O]ne of my life goals has always been 'to one day play a hitgirl who pretends to seduce then burns alive douchey boyfriends,'" which was positively received by many of her fans (Kornhaber, 2015). A year earlier, Taylor Swift's video for "Bad Blood" featured a mob of revenging women. Lana Del Ray blasts paparazzi with a huge gun in her video "High by the Beach," while Rihanna's "B*tch Better Have My Money" shows torture and dismemberment. Three Lady Gaga videos show the poisoning or burning of men ("Paparazzi," "Telephone," and "Bad Romance"). In 2011, Rihanna's video for "Man Down" was banned because she fired a gun at her rapist. The Parents Television Council condemned it as "an inexcusable, shock-only, shoot-and-kill theme song" (Kornhaber, 2015).

Other banned videos feature excessively gory or senseless violence. In 1988, Motorhead's video for "Killed by Death" was banned from airing on MTV due to its excessive and senseless violence, including a scene where the lead singer is electrocuted. Despite generating huge controversy, Nirvana's video for "Heart-Shaped Box" (1994) won the 1994 MTV Music Video Award. The video features a little girl dressed in KKK robes picking fetuses from a tree and an old man wearing a Santa hat climbing a crucifix. In 2010, M.I.A.'s "Born Free" video was banned from YouTube. The video depicted the genocide of redheaded individuals, showing one young man getting blown up and another shot in the head.

Laura L. Finley

See also: Dancehall Music; Indian and Pakistani Pop Music; Punk Music

Further Reading

Begley, S. 2015. "Lady Gaga's Latest Music Video Is a Sexual Assault PSA." *Time,* September 18. http://time.com/4040143/lady-gaga-til-it-happens-to-you/

Kaufman, G. 2010. "Eminem's 'Love the Way You Lie' Isn't First Video to Deal with Domestic Abuse." *MTV,* August 6. http://www.mtv.com/news/1645288/eminems-love-the-way-you-lie-isnt-first-video-to-deal-with-domestic-abuse/

Kornhaber, S. 2015. "A History of Violence (by Women in Music Videos)." *The Atlantic,* October 1. http://www.theatlantic.com/entertainment/archive/2015/10/hot-new-music-video-trend-murderous-women/408295/

Pemberton, P. 2013. "10 Banned Music Videos." *Rolling Stone,* May 9. http://www.rollingstone.com/music/news/10-banned-music-videos-20130509

Ranscombe, S. 2015. "The Ten Most Controversial Music Videos." *The Telegraph,* May 10. http://www.telegraph.co.uk/culture/music/rockandpopfeatures/11585580/The-10-most-controversial-music-videos.html

Rosa, C. 2015. "We Can't Believe These Music Videos Were Once Banned." *VH1,* October 27. www.vh1.com/news/218298/banned-music-videos/

Staff, History Channel. 2011. "The Music Video Before Music Television." *History Channel,* August 2. http://www.history.com/news/the-music-video-before-music-television

Waite, P. 2016. "4 Music Videos that Make Domestic Violence Look Very Pretty." *Salon,* June 19. http://www.salon.com/2016/06/19/4_music_videos_that_make_domestic_violence_look_very_pretty/

Narcocorridos

Narcocorridos are Mexican ballads that focus on the drug trade. The first narcocorridos emerged in the early 1930s and were influenced by the popular folk tales, *corridos*, which often told the stories of revolutionary fighters. Governments and companies have sought to ban narcocorridos, contending that they glorify drug smuggling and violence by drug cartels. Yet they remain widely popular in Mexico.

Songs in this genre tell the stories of drug lords who are killed and who kill. Given that more than 40,000 people have been killed from the Mexican drug wars since 2006, many assert that these songs simply describe life as it is. One composer, Reynaldo "El Gallero" Martinez, says, "The kids of Reynosa and Matamoros and many parts of Mexico learn the words to a *corrido* before they learn the National Anthem" (Arsenault, 2012).

In addition to telling stories about violence, narcocorrido musicians are often targeted for violence. Some of the most popular artists, including Valentin Elizalde and Sergio Gomez, were murdered between 2006 and 2008. Rarely is someone held accountable for these murders, and some even contend that the government and media have exaggerated the number so as to discourage artists from making this type of music. Others maintain that it is references to particular cartels or traffickers that lead these artists to be targeted. Critics contend that many of the balladeers are actually employed by the cartels to tell their stories in a friendly fashion, which is why few offer the perspective of victims. One artist, Edgar Quintero, admitted that wealthy patrons ask him to write the songs but claimed not to know if his patrons were cartel members. The going rate is $7,000 to $15,000 a song, and songwriters must include what the patron wants in the lyrics (Denselow, 2012). A few artists, however, do criticize the cartels, which might explain why those artists were targeted.

Only a few hours after El Chapo, the head of the Sinaloa cartel, was caught, narcocorridos about his capture were released. They are tremendously popular in Sinaloa, whereas in other parts of Mexico they are listened to by only a small fringe population because they are considered crass.

Narcocorridos have grown in popularity in the United States, largely due to Mexican immigration. In Edinburg, Texas, a radio program called *Killer Corridos* airs every afternoon. It plays narcocorridos, although it is careful in selecting its programming, as references to specific cartels or traffickers might upset rivals. Los Angeles, home to some 6 million Mexicans, is in some ways now the home of narcocorridos.

YouTube is increasingly being used by cartels to brag about their work and to recruit and, in doing so, often uses the music of narcocorridos. Police and other law enforcement bodies are aware of this trend and are gathering intelligence from YouTube, but caution that it can be used for disinformation as well.

Laura L. Finley

See also: Breaking Bad; Folk Music; Gangsta Rap; Hip-Hop; Latin American MCs; Mexican Crime Novels; *Miami Vice*; Murder Ballads; National Anthem, The; Spanish-Language Television

Further Reading

Arsenault, C. 2012. "Narcocorridos: Mexico's 'Gangsta Rap.'" *Al Jazeera,* August 21. http://www.aljazeera.com/indepth/features/2012/08/201281912842770626.html

Burnett, J. 2009. "Narcocorridos: Ballads of the Mexican Cartels." *NPR*, October 10. https://www.npr.org/2009/10/10/113664067/narcocorridos-ballads-of-the-mexican-cartels

Denselow, R. 2012. "Narcocorrido, the Sound of Los Angeles." *The Guardian*, March 28. https://www.theguardian.com/music/2012/mar/28/narcocorrido-sound-los-angeles

Garsd, J. 2015. "Narcocorridos: Telling Truths or Glorifying an Escaped Drug Lord?" *NPR*, July 16. https://www.npr.org/sections/altlatino/2015/07/16/423198482/narco-ballads-praising-el-chapo-or-portraying-the-corrupt-truth

So, J. 2013. "Are Narcocorrido Mexican Drug Ballads Really that Bad?" *The Daily Beast*, November 24. https://www.thedailybeast.com/are-narcocorrido-mexican-drug-ballads-really-that-bad

National Anthem, The

Francis Scott Key wrote "The Star-Spangled Banner" in 1814 during the War of 1812. In September, Key, a lawyer, entered a British ship hoping to negotiate for the freedom of a friend who had been arrested. Although successful in his mission, the British did not allow them to leave because of a planned attack on Baltimore. On September 13, Key watched through the night as Fort McHenry was attacked and did not know who won. Due to the strength of the British forces and enormity of the attack, he believed the British had won. However, when dawn arrived the next morning, he saw an American flag. He wrote a poem while still on the ship, set to the tune of a popular British song of how he witnessed America's victory at the Battle of Baltimore. The original version is four stanzas, though most Americans only recognize the first verse that is traditionally sung.

"The Star-Spangled Banner" did not become the U.S. national anthem until 1931. However, the decision was controversial even back then. It was criticized for its foreign origins, its difficult melody, and its ties to drinking. Many believe the tune was based on a drinking song, and at the time, the United States was in the midst of Prohibition. However, the song it was based on, "To Anacreon in Heaven," was sung at upper-class gentlemen's clubs and was used as a call-and-response competition to show off the best vocalist's range. The tune had been used in campaigns for John Adams and Thomas Jefferson.

In addition, many believed "The Star-Spangled Banner" was too violent and militaristic. The poem was written during war and includes lyrics like "the bombs bursting in air." Some argued that although the song features war and violence, it is inspirational in that Key was worried whether or not the United States would stay a nation, and not whether others would be crushed. However, the violent imagery was against a country that is now our ally. There are many patriotic songs that are less violent, such as "God Bless America," "America the Beautiful," "God Bless the USA," "This Land Is Your Land," and "Lift Every Voice and Sing."

The United States is not unique in having an anthem that is rather violent. The Italian national anthem celebrates burning the heart out of Austria. Vietnam's song features the words "the path to glory is built by the bodies of our foes." In fact, an analysis of the anthems of the 20 most populated countries found that 14 of them had at least somewhat militant lyrics. Consequently, over half the world sings a national anthem featuring violence. The anthem of China, the most populous nation, contains the words "with our flesh and blood, let us build our new Great Wall."

In addition, "The Star-Spangled Banner" has been criticized as being racist. Although some Americans know the story behind the song, few know anything about Francis Scott Key beyond his poem and story during the Battle of Baltimore. In the 1930s, Key served as district attorney under Andrew Jackson. Overall, he made many legal decisions that hurt African Americans and abolitionists. Key once referred to Africans in America as a "distinct and inferior race of people, which all experience proves to be the greatest evil that afflicts a community."

In the third stanza of "The Star-Spangled Banner," Key wrote, "No refuge could save the hireling and slave / From the terror of flight or the gloom of the grave." Key never specified exactly what he meant by this statement. However, many historians believe this was about the British hiring Colonial Marines, former slaves in British territories who the British encouraged to escape or promised freedom to in exchange for their military service. The Colonial Marines were part of the British forces who helped to torch the White House after the Battle of Bladensberg, just weeks before the Battle of Baltimore. Many question why the United States should have a song whose full version contains a line about escaped slaves fleeing and dying in war and written by a man who actively and strongly supported slavery.

The lyrics of "The Star-Spangled Banner" have not been its only source of controversy. Many have used the playing of the national anthem in protests, most famously in the 1968 Olympics when U.S. athletes gave the "Black-power" salute as the anthem played and they stood on the medal stand. During the Vietnam War, some sports fans would continue sitting during the anthem. Mahmoud Abdul-Rauf, a Muslim NBA player, refused to stand and support a nationalistic ideology. More recently, controversy has erupted in the NFL as players refused to stand or took a knee during the national anthem. In 2016, quarterback Colin Kaepernick refused to stand during the national anthem and continued to do so; he was not re-signed by his team. He said his kneeling was in protest of racial injustice in America, partly due to police brutality in America that lead to the deaths of many young Black men. In 2017, more NFL players began sitting or kneeling during the national anthem for various reasons. When President Donald Trump harshly criticized the players as disrespecting the flag, even more players and coaches kneeled together. All of these protests conveyed frustration that the freedom and equality the flag and anthem are supposed to stand for do not exist.

Many Americans do not see a problem with "The Star-Spangled Banner," and it is unlikely that it will change.

Katelyn Scheive

See also: Narcocorridos; Protest Music Worldwide; Protest Songs

Further Reading

Chang, E. 2016. "War or Peace? With Anthems, Violence Wins." *The Washington Post*, November 9. https://www.washingtonpost.com/apps/g/page/lifestyle/war-or-peace -with-anthems-violence-wins/2132/

Jacobson, L. 2017. "A Short History of the National Anthem, Protests and the NFL." *Politifact,* September 25. http://www.politifact.com/truth-ometer/article/2017/sep/25/short -history-national-anthem-and-sports/

Lineberry, C. 2007. "The Story Behind the Star Spangled Banner." *Smithsonian*, March 1. https://www.smithsonianmag.com/history/the-story-behind-the-star-spangled -banner-149220970/

Morley, J., & Schwarz, J. 2016. "More Proof the U.S. National Anthem Has Always Been Tainted with Racism." *The Intercept*, September 13. https://theintercept.com/2016 /09/13/more-proof-the-u-s-national-anthem-has-always-been-tainted-with -racism/

Ng, D. 2016. "How 'The Star-Spangled Banner,' Racist or Not, Became Our National Anthem." *Los Angeles Times*, September 6. http://www.latimes.com/entertainment /arts/la-et-cm-star-spangled-banner-racism-20160823-snap-story.html

Willingham, A. J. 2017. "The Unexpected Connection between Slavery, NFL Protests and the National Anthem." *CNN*, August 22. http://www.cnn.com/2016/08/29/sport /colin-kaepernick-flag-protest-has-history-trnd/index.html

Wilson, C. 2014. "Four Reasons 'The Star-Spangled Banner' Shouldn't Be the National Anthem (But Always Will Be)." *Slate*, July 3. http://www.slate.com/articles/arts /music_box/2014/07/the_star_spangled_banner_four_reasons_it_shouldn_t_be _the_national_anthem.html

Protest Music Worldwide

Around the world, music has been a powerful tool to raise awareness about injustices and to call for social change. Individual artists and groups have made a tremendous impact, as have events and telethons devoted to specific purposes.

One of the first musical benefit events was Live Aid, organized by Bob Geldoff and Midge Ure in 1985. It raised $245 million for famine relief in Ethiopia and was seen by an estimated 1.9 billion people in 150 countries. Before Live Aid, however, former Beatles lead guitarist George Harrison and musician Ravi Shankar held concerts for Bangladesh to raise awareness about refugees from the war there. Some 40,000 people attended. In 2004, a benefit concert for victims of the tsunami in the Indian Ocean, the result of an earthquake, was held and included performances by Madonna, Eric Clapton, Sheryl Crow, and Roger Waters. An estimated $5 million was raised. A global telethon featuring famous musicians, including Madonna, Shakira, and Coldplay, raised funds to help Haiti after a disastrous earthquake struck on January 22, 2010. Some 83 million viewers watched and $58 million was raised. Bono and The Edge (of U2), along with Jay-Z and Rihanna, performed an original song, "Stranded (Haiti Mon Amour)." Farm Aid concerts have been held since 1985, designed to support local farmers. Some $45 million has been raised to date through the efforts of artists including Neil Young, Willie Nelson, John Mellencamp, and Dave Matthews (Nunez, 2015).

Known by some as the "voice of the third world," Jamaican Bob Marley was another artist who used his music to address social and political issues. With the Wailers, Marley criticized poverty and hunger in the 1975 song "Them Belly Full (But We Hungry)." In his "Get Up, Stand Up" of 1973, Marley implored people to stand up for their rights, while "I Shot the Sheriff," of the same year, drew attention to the issue of police corruption. "Revolution" in 1974 features the line, "It takes a revolution to make a solution." "The Redemption Song" of 1980 borrows the famous line from Marcus Garvey, "Emancipate yourselves from mental slavery. / None but ourselves can free our minds."

Africa has been the site of and source of much protest music. In 1985, musician Steven Van Zandt and record producer Arthur Baker formed a collective called "Artists United Against Apartheid" to protest South African policy. They wrote a protest song, "Sun City," and enlisted the help of other well-known artists, including Bruce Springsteen and Miles Davis. In 2003, Nelson Mandela hosted the first 4664 Concert in Cape Town, South Africa. The name comes from the prison number worn by Mandela for the 25 years he was incarcerated. It was intended to raise awareness about HIV/AIDS in that country, and many famous artists, including Beyoncé, Queen, and Youssou N'Door, were in attendance. Many songs have been devoted to Mandela. For instance, Sipho "Hotstix" Mabuse's (1994) song "Nelson Mandela" was commissioned by the African National Congress as a means to support Mandela's campaign. American musician Stevie Wonder penned "It's Wrong" in 1985 to expose the problem of apartheid; Wonder was a Mandela supporter. He was arrested during an anti-apartheid rally that same year and dedicated his Oscar for the song "I Just Called to Say I Love You" to Nelson Mandela. Wonder's songs were subsequently banned in South Africa. Johnny Clegg and his band Sayuka's "Asimbonanga" (We Haven't Seen Him) is one of the most iconic anti-apartheid, Mandela-supporting songs. Peter Gabriel's "Biko" (1980) is about Mandela's peer, Stephen Biko, who founded the Black Consciousness Movement and died while in police custody in 1977. The Special A.K.A. song "Free Nelson Mandela" (1984) repeats that refrain in a virtually joyous melody (Roberts, 2013).

Keinan Abdi Warsame, known by his stage name K'naan, is a native of Somalia who fled with his family at the start of the civil war in that country. His hit song "Wavin' Flag," which talks about the struggles faced by displaced refugees, was the 2010 Soccer World Cup anthem (Nunez, 2015).

The country of Estonia has used music as a means to contest occupation by Germany, Denmark, Sweden, and the Soviet Union. Its history of hosting massive song festivals dates back to 1869, and the events feature up to 30,000 singers and some 100,000 attendees, which is roughly one-tenth of the population. This form of nonviolent social action was a major reason why Estonia split from the Soviet Union in the late 1980s, as 100,000 Estonians gathered for five nights tossing nonstop in what has been called the "Singing Revolution." Every five years the country still gathers for the singing festival (Schwab, 2015).

In this sense, tossing refers to the populace singing for days on end.

Laura L. Finley

See also: African Gangsta Rap; Blues Music; Classic Rock; Country Music; Folk Music; German Punk Music; Indian and Pakistani Pop Music; National Anthem, The; Protest Songs; Punk Music

Further Reading

Nunez, C. 2015. "Music that Has Changed the World." *Global Citizen*, July 27. https://www .globalcitizen.org/en/content/music-that-has-changed-the-world/

Roberts, R. 2013. "Nelson Mandela and Music: 10 Essential Anti-Apartheid Songs." *LA Times,* December 5. http://articles.latimes.com/2013/dec/05/entertainment/la-et-ms -nelson-mandela-dies-music-ten-essential-antiapartheid-songs-20130627

Schwab, K. 2015. "A Country Created through Music." *The Atlantic,* November 12. https:// www.theatlantic.com/international/archive/2015/11/estonia-music-singing -revolution/415464/

Protest Songs

Protest songs can be found in all genres, although are most common in folk, rap, and punk. They are viewed by many as a tool for educating the populace about social issues and inspiring action. They can also create solidarity among marginalized groups and their allies.

Slaves used songs as a form of solidarity and as a way to communicate with one another prior to and during the Civil War. Many of these songs were spiritual ballads that encouraged slaves to have faith. Popular tunes were "Go Down Moses (Let My People Go)," "Steal Away," "We Shall Be Free," and "Run to Jesus." "Get Off the Track," popularized by the most famous group of the 1840s, the Hutchinson Family Singers, is considered to be the ode of the movement, much like "We Shall Overcome" in the 1960s. The Hutchinson Family Singers toured with the church-based American Anti-Slavery Society, and they made money by selling their sheet music. They were arguably the first group to realize that protest music can make money. "Follow the Drinking Gourd" offered a guide for slaves escaping along the Underground Railroad.

One of the most profoundly disturbing songs to call attention to violence was "Strange Fruit," especially as performed by Billie Holiday starting in 1939. The haunting song, which depicts the lynched bodies of Black men hanging from trees as if they are "strange fruit," was written by Jewish Communist Abel Meeropol. In 1999, *Time* magazine named Holiday's first studio version of the song as the "song of the century." Holiday's mother worried about her when she began performing the song live, fearing that there would be a backlash against the song's indictment of the mob mentality involved in lynchings. Holiday remained hopeful, however, that the song could help improve things.

Protest music played a significant role in the U.S. civil rights movement of the 1950s and 1960s. One of the most widely known was "We Shall Overcome," which was utilized in many marches and still is today. It was popularized by many folk performers of the era, including Pete Seeger and Mahalia Jackson. Seeger was subpoenaed in 1955 to testify before the House Un-American Activities Committee (HUAC), one of the many artists to get caught up in the red scare witch hunts.

Nina Simone's "Mississippi Goddamn" (1964) was a reaction to the bombing at Sixteenth Street Baptist Church in Birmingham, Alabama, in 1963, which killed four Black girls. The bombing was one of many atrocities in that year, as the nation mourned the assassination of activist Medgar Evers in Mississippi, and President Kennedy had to intervene to allow the integration of state universities. Simone's husband and manager, Andrew Stoud, found her hysterical in her apartment and convinced her to use her music to soothe herself. Along with Sam Cooke's "A Change Is Gonna Come," "Mississippi Goddamn" became one of the iconic protest songs of 1964.

Country Joe and the Fish issued a fun yet important cry about the Vietnam War in its "I Feel Like I'm Fixin' to Die Rag" of 1965. When it was first released in a Berkeley, California book store, the United States had only been engaged in the Vietnam conflict for six months, and 60 percent of Americans supported the war. By the time the band performed the song at Woodstock in 1969, more than 40,000 U.S. service personnel had died and the song was an ode to the antiwar protestors. Before Woodstock, however, folk artists had critiqued the war in Vietnam. Phil Ochs, for example, as early as 1962, critiqued U.S. involvement in South Asia. Ochs, too, was under investigation from the FBI for his album *I Ain't Marching Anymore*. Jimi Hendrix also performed a protest song at Woodstock, although the lyrics would not suggest so. His electronic interpretation of "The Star Spangled Banner" was considered by many as a "napalm" version, and his rendition was widely banned throughout the United States.

James Brown issued a call for Black pride in his song, "Say It Loud, I'm Black and I'm Proud" in 1968. Brown had been called an "Uncle Tom" by Black artists and fans, who saw his calls for Black pride as just another establishment co-optation of Black music. Like it or not, because of his previous successes Brown was a spokesman for Black pride. And his iconic song demonstrated the potential for funk music to encourage protest. The song sold 750,000 copies in just two weeks, a testament to the timeliness of its lyrics and the power of its beat.

The movement against the war in Vietnam in the 1960s and 1970s saw widespread use of protest songs. Bob Dylan burst onto the scene as a 22-year-old at the Newport Folk Festival and has been perhaps the most widely known protest musician for each decade since. Dylan was actually critical of protest songs, concerned that they came off as "preachy and one-dimensional" (Lynskey, 2011, p. 55). Bob Dylan's "Blowin' in the Wind" captured many of the questions Americans were asking about the war with its poetic vagueness. Dylan's "Masters of War" was an indictment of those in power, who send other peoples' children to wars. By no means a pacifist song, its raging lyrics wish for the death of the responsible parties.

In the later 1960s, former Beatle John Lennon became the musical face of the peace movement. "Give Peace a Chance," recorded with his partner Yoko Ono and the Plastic Ono Band, makes fun of politics, religion, media, and a variety of other issues and institutions. Lennon and Ono engaged in a variety of actions to promote peace, including their "bed-in," in which they committed to staying in bed for a week after they married in March 1969 as a means of protesting "all the suffering and violence in the world" (Lynskey, 2011, p. 134). Lennon's 1971 "Imagine" was his best-selling single as a solo artist. The song was a radical critique of capitalism and religion. On May 4, 1970, when the Ohio National Guard shot and killed four student antiwar protestors at Kent State University, the movement strengthened. Neil Young, having seen photographs of the shootings in *Life* magazine, penned "Ohio" and recorded it with Stephen Stills, Graham Nash, and David

Crosby. Some consider it to be the last protest song of the era, as the unity and hopefulness of many antiwar protestors had begun to turn to rage and divisiveness.

Punk rock became one of the leaders in protest music in the 1980s. The Dead Kennedys were critical of the government for overcontrolling while at the same time undersupporting. "Kill the Poor" was a sarcastic take on the failed promises of the Reagan administration. Alternatively, bands in the 1980s united to raise awareness about and funds for a variety of issues. Lionel Richie and Michael Jackson wrote "We Are the World," which was recorded by a supergroup United Support of Artists (USA) for Africa. The effort followed a similar one in the UK, Band Aid, which raised funds to benefit famine relief in Africa. After the devastating earthquake in Haiti in 2010, artists came together to re-record the song and to raise funds to rebuild the country.

The 1980s also saw the rise in hip-hop and the entry of gangsta rap as tools for protest. Public Enemy's album *Fear of a Black Planet* took on police harassment and brutality, institutional racism, and inadequate emergency services in poor communities, among other issues. Other popular artists who issued similar critiques include but are not limited to Ice-T, N.W.A., Ice Cube, and Easy E. Different from other protest music in style and in its use of curse words, hip-hop reached new audiences but was criticized for promoting violence.

1990s rock/metal band Rage Against the Machine took on a variety of issues, but was particularly critical of the excessive greed of a capitalist society. The group also protested the war in Iraq, the excessive incarceration and racial profiling of people of color, social inequality, media propaganda, and more.

The 2000s also saw a surge in protest songs, as many artists expressed dissatisfaction with the policies of the George W. Bush administration and, in particular, the wars waged after the September 11, 2001, terrorist attack. Green Day's "Wake Me Up When September Ends" (2004), on its *American Idiot* album, was a critique of American foreign policy, and in particular, the Iraq and Afghanistan wars. Also in 2004, gravel-voiced singer Tom Waits released an antiwar album, *Real Gone*, with the powerful single "The Day After Tomorrow." In 2006, Neil Young released "Let's Impeach the President" on his *Living with War* album. The song begins with the first few notes of "Taps," then lists all the reasons why the United States should have impeached George W. Bush. The country band The Dixie Chicks faced criticism and even death threats for their antiwar stance.

In 2006, Bruce Springsteen released "How Can a Poor Man Stand Such Times to Live," a re-recording of the original song from 1929, to confront the poor government treatment of victims of Hurricane Katrina. The entire album, *We Shall Overcome: The Seeger Session,* was protest songs.

Laura L. Finley

See also: African Gangsta Rap; Blues Music; Classic Rock; Country Music; Folk Music; German Punk Music; Indian and Pakistani Pop Music; National Anthem, The; Protest Music Worldwide; Punk Music

Further Reading
Lynskey, D. 2011. *33 Revolutions Per Minute: A History of Protest Songs, from Billie Holiday to Green Day.* New York: HarperCollins.

Margolick, D. 2001. *Strange Fruit: The Biography of a Song*. New York: Ecco Press.

Weissman, D. 2010. *Talkin' 'Bout a Revolution: Music and Social Change in America*. London: Backbeat Books.

Punk Music

Punk music emerged in the late 1960s and was widely popular in the United States and the UK in the 1980s. It typically features very short songs with angry lyrics, often screamed by the band's vocalists, and fans loved it because it brought a sense of danger that was missing from much of the popular music in the 1960s. Many punk songs are politically charged, and some are violent. Another hallmark of punk music is the fashion that is associated with it, which typically included purposely torn garments, jeans, and combat boots. Bands and fans often sported wild hairstyles like mohawks and multiple colors. Critics said it promoted violence, sex, and destruction. Some neo-Nazi skinhead groups adopted punk music as part of their identities, and a new form of White supremacist punk was created.

In the United States punk rock started in the late 1960s in Detroit, with bands like MC5 and Iggy & The Stooges. But it gained popularity largely in New York, especially at the night club CBGB, which often hosted bands like Television, Dead Boys, Talking Heads, and Blondie. Perhaps the most quintessentially punk band that came out of CBGB was the Ramones. The Ramones began playing shows in 1974 and in 1976 debuted its album, *Ramones*, which is considered a pioneer of punk rock. The Ramones managed to pack 14 songs into a 30-minute record, in stark contrast to other 1970s bands like Led Zeppelin and Pink Floyd, who were pumping out long tunes with lengthy guitar solos.

Another popular punk band in both the United States and the UK was the Dead Kennedys. The band came from California and was headed by Jello Biafra, whose style was influenced by punk but also by poetry, jazz, and surf guitar. Its first number-one song, "California uber Alles," was an attack on the policies of Governor Jerry Brown, in particular as they relate to poverty. One year later the Dead Kennedys released "Holiday in Cambodia," which packs in a tremendous amount of social commentary in under four minutes. Some of their more violent lyrics can be found in "The Prey," which focuses on an assault, and "Nazi Punks," which is a critique of neo-Nazism.

A similar scene was taking place in London, especially on King's Road, which had been a popular gathering place for the counterculture in the 1960s. The following decade saw the area flooded with punk rockers, with some of the most popular bands being the Sex Pistols and The Clash. It was the British bands that started the more political messages of punk, and the songs were replete with references to "anarchy" and "violence." The music became the voice of working-class youth, many of whom were disaffected due to the lack of jobs and opportunities they saw. The Sex Pistols' "Anarchy in the U.K." and "God Save the Queen" became punk anthems. The Sex Pistols were also known for their wild behavior; they cursed routinely, and the press saw them as threatening. They appeared on a popular British talk show in December 1976, with some sporting swastika armbands and the guitarist Steve Jones cursing frequently. To some, it really did seem like it was "Anarchy in the UK," the title of their debut hit single. The band broke up in January 1978, after having recorded just one studio album.

The Clash was the world's most influential punk band by the end of the 1970s, perhaps because although in the same basic style, their songs were less menacing and more about violence as a problem, rather than the answer. Some have criticized such bands for being hypocritical. While denouncing the government and white-collar workers, the bands themselves often became wealthy and professionalized.

Punk concerts were often violent places, as this genre popularized the mosh pit. Mosh pits are essentially crowds of people slamming violently into one another, sometimes to the beat and often not. In the UK, some of the violence spilled over from football hooligans who were anxious to assert themselves against rivals. Pubs where punk bands performed came to expect at least some level of violence. In fact, one reason for punk's decline was the development of more professional security arrangements.

Punk lives on today, in two dramatically different forms. One is still the tool of angry, White men, but rather than reflecting working-class woes, it is used to disseminate racism and anti-Semitism. The other version is far less White. For instance, Haram, which means forbidden in Arabic, is a Yonkers-based band that writes dystopian-style music. Moor Mother performs futuristic-sounding punk in the Philadelphia area. Awaaz Do is a South Asian group from Boston.

Neo-Nazi skinheads have adopted punk rock for its hardcore look and style. Some of the earliest groups to use punk music as a recruiting tool were Screwdriver, No Remorse, and Skullhead. In Britain, neo-Nazi groups held "Rock Against Communism" concerts as early as 1978, featuring largely punk bands. The 1992 Russell Crowe film *Romper Stomper*, albeit set in Australia, documents this culture, as does the U.S. film *American History X*. Yet many punk groups disavow any connections to these hate groups. Jello Biafra has repeatedly expressed disdain for hate groups who claim punk music as their own.

Laura L. Finley

See also: Dancehall Music; Folk Music; Gangsta Rap; German Punk Music; Goth and Industrial Music; Hip-Hop; Music Videos; Protest Music Worldwide; Protest Songs

Further Reading

Bergeron, R. 2015. "Punk Shocks the World." *CNN*, August 6. http://www.cnn.com/2015/08/06/entertainment/the-seventies-punk-rock-shocks-the-world/

Cardew, B. 2016. "Dead Kennedys: Ten of the Best." *The Guardian,* November 16. https://www.theguardian.com/music/musicblog/2016/nov/16/dead-kennedys-10-of-the-best

"Racist Skinheads: Understanding the Threat." 2012. *Southern Poverty Law Center*, June 25. https://www.splcenter.org/20100126/racist-skinheads-understanding-threat#music

Simonelli, D. 2010. "Anarchy, Pop and Violence: Punk Rock Subculture and the Rhetoric of Class, 1976–1978." *Contemporary British History, 2,* 121–44.

Usmani, R. 2016. "Because Punk Still Rocks." *The New York Times,* September 18. https://www.nytimes.com/2016/09/18/opinion/sunday/because-punk-still-rocks.html?mcubz=2&_r=0

South Korean K-Pop

K-Pop is a tremendously popular style of music in South Korea that emerged in the early 1990s and has since spread around the world. Although the music is generally upbeat and light-hearted, it has also been used to create awareness about violence and to prompt nonviolent campaigns.

K-Pop artists have drawn attention to domestic violence. Artist Juniel's video for her song "Last Carnival" begins with her slowly opening her bruised and swollen eyes, and is intended to be intense, as the artist had a similar experience and thus "decided to express the dangers of date violence through music" (Min-sik, 2017).

Another issue that K-Pop artists have grappled with is suicide. In 2017 even more attention was paid to that issue, given the suicide of popular K-Pop artist Kim Jonghyun. Suicide rates are very high in South Korea, and are the highest among 35 industrialized nations according to the Organisation for Economic Co-operation and Development. Suicide is the number-one cause of death for people ages 10 to 39 in South Korea, due largely, critics contend, to the immense pressure to be successful. "Our society pressures us too much," said a 23-year-old Yonsei University student who asked to be identified only by her family name, Shin. "When I think about studying in high school, I don't wish that kind of pressure on anyone" (Stiles, 2017).

Bullying is a common accusation in South Korean popular culture, especially among girl groups. Because agencies orchestrate these groups, critics contend that fighting is inevitable because performers are not bonded by common interests or talents. Further, K-Pop artists are often sent to rigorous training "camps," which are intense and by many definitions, abusive. Suicides are all too common among K-Pop artists, including the 2017 suicide of Jonghyun. In his suicide note he described the intense pressure of South Korean K-Pop. Others who committed suicide, like actress Jang Ja-yeon, said they were forced to perform sexual favors in exchange for roles (Kil, 2017).

K-Pop has also been criticized for negatively depicting women. Even though Korean women are among the world's most educated, K-Pop is said to objectify and vilify women. Artists say they are pressured to have plastic surgery and to sign restrictive contracts that limit their movement, dress, and other activity. Artists are essentially slaves, and these contracts can last for more than a decade. One artist explained, K-Pop "shapes not only what music you should listen to but what you should look like while listening to it." Some 50 percent of South Korean women in their twenties have had cosmetic surgery (Volodzko, 2016). Yet although women are criticized for being hypersexualized, TV and other popular culture in South Korea emphasize such depictions. Women face a double standard, as they are to be seen as sex objects while also expected to adhere to conservative Confucian sexual norms.

The Korean boy group Bangtan Sonyeondan (BTS) partnered with the United Nations Children's Fund (UNICEF) to launch an antiviolence campaign, #ENDviolence, which emphasizes self-respect and empowerment. Proceeds from the initiative are to be donated to child and teen victims of domestic violence, school violence, and sexual assault around the world. BTS won a Billboard Music Award in 2017 for Top Social Artist, beating Justin Bieber and Selena Gomez.

Laura L. Finley

See also: Blues Music; Dystopian Young Adult Literature and Film; Goth and Industrial Music; North Korean Films

Further Reading

ABS-CBN News. 2017. "K-Pop Group BTS Launches Anti-Violence Campaign with UNI-CEF." *ABS-CBN News*, November 21. http://news.abs-cbn.com/entertainment/11/01/17/k-pop-group-bts-launches-anti-violence-campaign-with-unicef

Kil, S. 2017. "Jonghyun Suicide Note Points to Brutal Pressure of Korean Spotlight." *Variety*, December 19. http://variety.com/2017/music/asia/shinee-jonghyun-dies-dead-suicide-note-k-pop-pressure-1202644698/

Lee, R. 2012. "Bullying Scandals Hit K-Pop Groups." *Korea Times*, August. http://www.koreatimes.co.kr/www/news/art/2012/08/143_116402.html

Min-sik, Y. 2017. "K-Pop Singer Depicts Being Victimized by Date Abuse." *Korea Herald*, August 5. http://www.koreaherald.com/view.php?ud=2017080400071

Stiles, M. 2017. "Death of K-Pop Superstar Shines a Spotlight on South Korea's Suicide Problem." *Los Angeles Times*, December 19. http://www.latimes.com/world/asia/la-fg-south-korea-suicide-20171219-story.html

Volodzko, D. 2016. "K-Pop's Gross Double Standard for Women." *PRI*, April 25. https://www.pri.org/stories/2016-04-25/k-pop-s-gross-double-standard-women

5

Violence in Literature

Introduction

Since the first written stories and books, literature has been associated with the telling of violent tales. Religious texts tell stories of war, violent assault, rape, and other forms of violence. Greek mythology is full of violence, as are the plays of Shakespeare. Every culture produces literature with violent themes and imagery, committed often out of sheer brutality, the quest for power or greed, but sometimes in self-defense.

Edgar Allan Poe is considered the father of the horror story and of the detective story. His poetry and short stories were typically dark tales that reflected the time period and the author's life. His *Murders in the Rue Morgue* (1841) is considered the first detective story in America. Although probably baseless, his violent tales have been blamed for inspiring Jack the Ripper.

In the United States, many renowned books by exemplary authors have been banned due to their violent themes. One of the earliest novels to face such controversy was Harriet Beecher Stowe's *Uncle Tom's Cabin*, which is credited by many for ushering in the Civil War and the end of slavery. Published in 1852, the novel showcases the violence of slavery but does not fail to depict the violence used by many in the abolitionist movement as well. It is said to have helped popularize the abolition movement in the North, which was previously weak, and to have paved the way for a presidential candidate like Abraham Lincoln.

Turn-of-the-century classics like those of Jack London faced similar allegations of excessive violence. London's (1903) *Call of the Wild* is the epic tale of animal versus nature. Written after the author's time spent in the Yukon, the protagonist, Buck, saves his human master and encounters many threats that require a violent response. Another of London's most popular books, *White Fang* (1906), also features a canine protagonist. Considered too radical, *Call of the Wild* was banned in Italy and Yugoslavia and was burned en masse in Nazi Germany. It has regularly faced criticism from American parents, who believe the book is too violent and bloody for the teens to whom it appeals.

The calls for censorship have extended to other genres of writing. The 1930s and 1940s saw widespread calls for banning comic books that were popular with juveniles. The *Chicago Tribune* ran a column in 1940 that denounced comic books as "[b]adly drawn, badly written and badly printed—a strain on young eyes and young nervous systems. . . . Their crude blacks and reds spoil the child's natural sense of color; their hypodermic injection of sex and murder make the child impatient with better, though quieter, stories" (History of Comics Censorship, n.d.). Public burnings occurred across America, and the movement to ban comics gained speed and credibility after psychologist Fredric Wertham published *Seduction of the Innocent* (1954), in which he blamed comic books for increases in juvenile delinquency and a host of other problems. The Senate Judiciary Committee's Subcommittee to Investigate Juvenile Delinquency held two days of hearings on the issue in 1954, with Dr. Wertham presenting on the dangers of comic books, even those featuring superheroes. The industry responded by establishing the Comic Magazine Association of America, which instituted the Comics Code Authority, a censorship code that thoroughly sanitized the content of comics for years to come. Among other limitations, it included the following:

> Crimes shall never be presented in such a way as to create sympathy for the criminal, to promote distrust of the forces of law and justice, or to inspire others with a desire to imitate criminals; [p]olicemen, judges, government officials, and respected institutions shall never be presented in such a way as to create disrespect for established authority; [i]n every instance good shall triumph over evil and the criminal punished for his misdeeds; [s]cenes of excessive violence shall be prohibited. Scenes of brutal torture, excessive and unnecessary knife and gunplay, physical agony, gory and gruesome crime shall be eliminated; [n]o comic magazine shall use the word horror or terror in its title; and [a]ll scenes of horror, excessive bloodshed, gory or gruesome crimes, depravity, lust, sadism, masochism shall not be permitted. (History of Comics Censorship, n.d.)

These restrictions lasted for several decades. Another hit to the industry came with the 1973 Supreme Court decision in *Miller v. California*, which developed a three-pronged test to determine whether something was obscene. Yet comic book makers and sellers persisted, and despite more current attempts to deem manga and horror-focused comic books obscene or inappropriate, that genre remains popular among both youth and adults.

Although they feature generally antiwar themes, some classic books by renowned authors have also been considered controversial. Kurt Vonnegut's *Slaughterhouse-Five*, inspired by his witnessing of the World War II attacks on Dresden, inspired antiwar activists during the Vietnam War and has long faced bans in public schools. Similarly, Joseph Heller's *Catch-22*, published in 1961, is a reflection on the challenges of war and the unjustness of orders into battle. Interesting, however, is that Heller, who also served in World War II, felt much differently about his service than does his main character, Yossarian. Heller says he found the experience to be largely an exciting adventure (Bates, 2011).

Many novels have grappled with racial violence. Among the most notable of these are Richard Wright's *Native Son* (1940) and Harper Lee's *To Kill a Mockingbird* (1960). Wright's *Native Son*, set in Chicago in the 1930s, tells the story of a Black man, Bigger Thomas, who is eventually convicted of rape and murder and sentenced to death. The novel highlights the plight of Black males in that time period and remains relevant, as too often they are believed to be hyperviolent. The book contextualizes Black male violence within broader societal oppression and violence against Black men.

Harper Lee's *To Kill a Mockingbird* is a story about racial hate, resilience, and redemption. It is told through the eyes of a little girl, Scout, who like the rest of her peers, is afraid of the stories that are told about reclusive Boo Radley. It also relates her father, Atticus's, defense of a Black man, Tom, who is accused of raping a White woman. The book shows how often Blacks were accused of such crimes and the largely inadequate legal protections they were afforded, Atticus's work aside.

Other books provide important insight into violence against women. Alice Walker's *The Color Purple* (1982), Toni Morrison's *Beloved* (1987), and Arthur Miller's play *The Crucible* (1953) all focus on this topic. Walker's novel, set in the Depression era, tells the story of Celie, a Black woman who is abused by her father, raped twice, and has the babies born from the assault taken from her, and then is married to "Mister" who continues to physically and sexually assault her. Yet the story is also one of power and strength, as Celie endures, and eventually befriends two women, Shug Avery and Sofia, wife of her husband's son, Harpo, who are models for strong women. But it is through Celie's writing to her sister Nettie, who escaped to Africa, that she finds hope, even though she learns later that Mister has kept from her Nettie's letters in response. *Beloved*, along with several other novels by award-winning author Morrison, showcase the extent to which Black mothers will go to protect their daughters from violence. Somewhat different, *The Crucible* is a parable about the McCarthy hearings in the 1950s, where authors, actors, scholars, and activists were widely accused of sympathizing with communism. It is a largely true depiction of the Salem witch trials, where women and girls who believed differently than the norm were accused of witchcraft. Many were murdered in an attempt to root out their devilry.

Another focus of popular novels is violence as a tool of control. Books like *Lord of the Flies* (1954), *1984* (1949), *Brave New World* (1932), and *Fahrenheit 451* (1953) emphasize the problems associated with government control and out-of-control subjects. *Lord of the Flies* is the story of a group of adolescents who are stranded on a deserted island. As they struggle to survive, different groups battle for power and influence, and ultimately, the more controlling and violent pervade. George Orwell's *1984* is a scary commentary on the power governments can have to distort truth and to commit violence against the public in the name of safety. In contrast, *Brave New World* documents how it is apathy that will result in mass violence, as it depicts a future world in which people are too numbed to care about anything. *Fahrenheit 451* picks up on that theme, with its storyline about how people are so disinterested in their history that they burn all the books they deem to be controversial.

Literature is a powerful way for people to understand the violence that happens outside of their home countries. Books like *Things Fall Apart* (1958) offer a critical examination of the violence that occurs in many African countries, while Mexican narcoliterature and Scandinavian crime novels, although fictional, shed light on the violence associated with drug cartels, organized crime, and government corruption. Native American authors, including Sherman Alexie and Louise Erdrich, offer insight into both historical and current violences against Native peoples.

Books aimed at teen audiences are not exempt from controversy. Among the most controversial are the *Harry Potter* series, the dystopian series *The Hunger Games*, and the vampire-focused *Twilight* series. J. K. Rowling's *Harry Potter* series is perhaps the best-selling series ever. The books were adapted into widely popular films, and *Harry Potter* products, games, and amusement parks remain popular today. The novels tell the story of Harry Potter, who learns that he is a wizard and is sent to Hogwarts School of Witchcraft and Wizardry. The series shows that Harry has a special capacity to fight the evil that is trying to take over, headed by Lord Voldemort. This is due to the love that his mother, Lily, and his father James, gave him as they died during an attack by Voldemort. While readers (and viewers) are definitely supposed to relate to Harry and his peers, Ron Weasley and Hermione Granger, most notably, the series shows that these protagonists also use violence, which is demonstrated as the only way to defeat the evil of Voldemort.

Similarly, *The Hunger Games* trilogy tells the story of Katniss Everdeen, who volunteers to replace her younger sister in the draft to enter the Hunger Games. Set in a world devastated by apocalypse, each region must allow two individuals to fight in the Hunger Games, a brutal and violent battle to determine which region receives additional food and supplies in a devastated time. Orchestrated by the opulent Capitol, the opponents in the Hunger Games battle natural, animal, and human-made disasters, all while fighting to attract the financial support of sponsors. Katniss and her friend/boyfriend Peta Mellark defy the odds by co-winning the competition, spawning aggression from both the Capitol and its opposition.

A slightly different teen-focused series, the *Twilight* saga, by Stephenie Meyer, depicts the fights between vampires and werewolves, and the efforts of a teen girl, Bella, to fight off her sexual attraction to the primary vampire, Edward. Bella is, in many expert assessments, in an abusive and controlling relationship (Goodfriend, 2011).

More obvious horror novels, such as those by popular writer Stephen King, have built a following for the genre. King is perhaps the most widely known and prolific horror writer in American history. His stories, many of which have been made into feature films, tell of scary nightmares, like creepy clowns, but also of more everyday violence, like child abuse, sexual assault, and bullying. Although he had faced numerous lawsuits accusing his work of inspiring real-life violence, law in the United States has generally protected novelists from blame in cases of murder or suicide. Even more so, books like *American Psycho* (1987) have been said to glorify violent, abusive behavior, in particular against women.

Literature not only allows readers to escape their lives for a short time, but it also has great power to shed light on injustices, to offer creative solutions to social issues, and to help readers envision a better world. At the same time, literature can reinforce stereotypes, glorify violence, and immerse readers in violent, negative spaces. Rather than bans or censorship of controversial text, most scholars favor media literacy, or the development of skills in how to interpret various texts, in order for literature to be used in its most positive way.

Laura L. Finley

Further Reading

Adin, Mariah. 2014. *The Brooklyn Thrill-Kill Gang and the Great Comic Book Scare of the 1950s.* Santa Barbara, CA: Praeger.

"Banned Books that Shaped America." n.d. *Banned Books Week.* http://www.bannedbooksweek.org/censorship/bannedbooksthatshapedamerica

Bates, S. 2011. "'Catch-22' Author Joseph Heller: "How Did I Feel about the War? I Enjoyed It?" *The Guardian*, October 24. https://www.theguardian.comty an/books/2011/oct/25/catch-22-author-enjoyed-war

Butler, R. J. 1986. "The Function of Violence in Richard Wright's Native Son." *Black American Literature Forum 20*(1/2), 9–25.

Goodfriend, W. 2011. "Relationship Violence in 'Twilight.'" *Psychology Today*, November 9. https://www.psychologytoday.com/blog/psychologist-the-movies/201111/relationship-violence-in-twilight

Greene, A. 2014. "Stephen King: The Rolling Stone Interview." *Rolling Stone*, October 31. http://www.rollingstone.com/culture/features/stephen-king-the-rolling-stone-interview-20141031

"History of Comics Censorship, Part 1." n.d. *Comic Book Legal Defense Fund.* http://cbldf.org/resources/history-of-comics-censorship/history-of-comics-censorship-part-1/

"History of Comics Censorship, Part 6." n.d. *Comic Book Legal Defense Fund.* http://cbldf.org/resources/history-of-comics-censorship/history-of-comics-censorship-part-6/

Morais, B. 2011. "The Never-Ending Campaign to Ban 'Slaughterhouse Five.'" *The Atlantic*, August 12. https://www.theatlantic.com/entertainment/archive/2011/08/the-neverending-campaign-to-ban-slaughterhouse-five/243525/

Telegraph Reporters. 2016. "Edgar Allan Poe: The Master of Horror Writing." *The Telegraph*, April 20. www.telegraph.co.uk/books/authors/edgar-allan-poe-the-master-of-horror-writing/

Ancient Greek Literature and Culture

Although much attention has been paid to violence in modern literature, ancient Greek poetry is replete with violence. References to violence were many, although live performances operated on an informal code that prohibited the depiction of an actual death or the inflicting of blows on another person. There's even a Greek god of death, Thanatos, and a god of the Underworld, Hades.

Greek tragedies often focused on war, as did Euripides's *Trojan Women* and Sophocles's *Electra.* Characters are not only engaged in war but also in avenging those who were lost in war, as is Electra, who lost her father, Agamemnon, and her mother, Clytemnestra. The classic tale of Oedipus also offers insights into violence, as readers are asked to ponder whether he was destined to kill his father and marry his mother. The Battle of the Titans, called the Titanomachy, was a war between the Titans and the Olympic gods, led by Zeus. Gaea, wife of Titan leader Uranus, seeks revenge after her husband incarcerated two of her children. She tells them to castrate their father and overthrow him, which her son Cronus does. Cronus took over the throne from his father, but constantly feared that he would be overthrown as well, so became a brutal tyrant just as Uranus had been. His wife, Rhea, hides their child, Zeus, in a cave so that he is not tormented by his father. Zeus grows up and leads the rebellion against his father.

Likewise, the story of Odysseus features violence, albeit justified by his capture by the Cyclops. Like many Greek tales, not only is violence used by the antagonists but also by the protagonists as a way to escape or for revenge. Yet religious doctrine prohibited extensive coverage of violence, and, as mentioned, convention held that live audiences should not see any person inflicting a blow.

The star of Greek mythology, Zeus, is, as some have proclaimed, a serial rapist. Medusa, a notoriously evil character, likely became that way after enduring a violent sexual assault. Stories tell of the attempted rape of the warrior-goddess Athena. Additionally, Persephone's husband kidnapped and raped her. However, these instances were often referred to with benign verbs, like "seduced."

The original Olympic Games in Greece, now celebrated for inspiring global unity, were full of drama and violence. David Clay Large, an Olympic historian, has said, "The world of the ancient Olympics was so embroiled in constant fighting back and forth between rival city-states that every time the Olympics took place there was fear of some kind of attack, some kind of disruption." While there was a pact to stop fighting during the games, it was often violated, like when in "364 BC when soldiers from the city of Elis actually invaded the Olympics grounds in order to retrieve protection rights over the games, that had been taken away from them in the years before. So there was a bloody battle going on right during the wrestling competition." Allegations of black magic were also common (Woolf, 2016).

Lysistrata is a Greek comedy by Aristophanes. It tells the story of creative action by women trying to stop the fighting during the Peloponnesian War. Tired of their men battling all the time, the women essentially go on a sex strike, denying any sexual activity with the men until they stop fighting. It has been referenced in many forms of popular culture and inspired actual Lysistratic actions, a tool for nonviolent social change.

Laura L. Finley

See also: Game of Thrones; Lee, Spike; Shakespeare, William

Further Reading

Haynes, N. 2014. "Violence, Destiny and Revenge: Why Ancient Greeks Still Rule the Stage." *The Guardian*, May 4. https://www.theguardian.com/commentisfree/2014/may/04/violence-revenge-ancient-greeks-rule-stage

Katz, E. 2017. *Enraged: Why Violent Times Need Ancient Greek Myths.* New Haven, CT: Yale University Press.

Pierce, K., & Deacy, S. 2002. *Rape in Antiquity: Sexual Violence in the Greek and Roman Worlds.* New York: Bloomsbury Academic.

Schecter, V. 2012. "The Darker Side of Greek Myths." *Huffington Post*, May 29. https://www.huffingtonpost.com/vicky-alvear-shecter/the-darker-side-of-greek-_b_1389773.html

Sommerstein, A. 2004. "Violence in Greek Drama." *Ordia Prima, 3*, 41–56.

Woolf, C. 2016. "The Ancient Olympics Were Dirty, Violent, Corrupt Affairs. There Was Even Regular 'Doping.'" *PRI*, August 5. https://www.pri.org/stories/2016-08-05 /ancient-olympics-were-dirty-violent-corrupt-affairs-there-was-even-regular -doping

Brave New World

Brave New World is a dystopian novel by English author Aldous Huxley. Published in 1932 and set in London, it focuses on the dangers of a society in which people are psychologically manipulated and where babies are created through artificial wombs in "hatcheries." Procreation is outlawed, but indiscriminate sex is normal. There are predetermined classes, and the totalitarian government keeps citizens docile through the near-constant consumption of a drug called Soma. One of the main characters, Bernard Marx, a psychologist, is a vocal critic of Soma. He, with Lenina Crowne, a worker at a hatchery, take a visit to a reservation in New Mexico, where they meet "natural born" people and see the remnants of what is a clear reference to life as it was in the 1930s. They are very interested in the role of disease and the natural aging process, which is foreign to them, but two people they encounter there, Linda and John, are desperate to see their brave new world. When they get to London, John, who is considered a "savage," becomes a celebrity, as does Bernard for keeping him. Eventually, Bernard, his friend Helmholtz, and John all must face the "Resident World Controller for Western Europe," Mustapha Mond, who says that Bernard and Helmholtz are to be exiled. John moves himself to near exile and attempts to purify with self-flagellation. Lenina, to whom he is both attracted and hates, comes to see his bizarre behavior, and he beats her with a whip, encouraged by a frenzied crowd. The next morning, disturbed by what he has done, John hangs himself.

Many have compared *Brave New World* to George Orwell's dystopian novel, *1984.* Yet while Orwell criticized a world in which the government controlled everything, Huxley's novel is more concerned with people having so much information they don't know what to do with it. Instead of using pain to control, as in *1984*, Brave New World features pleasure, in the form of Soma, as a tool of control. *Brave New World* made *The Guardian*'s list of top 10 most banned books in 2010. It was banned almost immediately after publication by Ireland and Australia and in many U.S. public schools. The ban in Ireland was focused on the sexual content, but in the United States, some of the concern was about derogatory language, stereotypes, and misinformation about Native Americans.

Huxley wrote a sequel, *Brave New World Revisited*, in 1958. In it, he concluded that the world was becoming more like that depicted in his novel than he even anticipated, citing overpopulation and the frequent use of prescription drugs. In his third and last novel, *Island* (1962), he explores some of the same issues as the previous two but offers alternatives. Rather than drugs for exploitation and manipulation, *Island* shows them being used for enlightenment. As opposed to mandatory reproductive control, *Island* features readily available contraception. As such, it is considered a utopian novel, not a dystopian one.

Huxley is also known for his 1954 essay "The Doors of Perception," which chronicled his own experiment with the psychedelic plant extract mescaline (Schaub, 2017).

Media critic and philosopher Neil Postman wrote about the comparisons between *1984* and *Brave New World* in his 1985 book *Amusing Ourselves to Death: Public Discourse in the Age of Show Business*. In commenting about the book 75 years after publication, author Margaret Atwood noted, "*Brave New World* is either a perfect-world utopia or its nasty opposite, a dystopia, depending on your point of view: its inhabitants are beautiful, secure and free from diseases and worries, though in a way we like to think we would find unacceptable." After World War II, Huxley criticized himself for having offered only two options—the savagery of the reservation or the brave, new but controlled world. This likely influenced the direction he took in the other two novels (Atwood, 2007).

Laura L. Finley

See also: Dystopian Young Adult Literature and Film; *Fahrenheit 451*; *Mad Max* Films; *1984*; Vonnegut, Kurt

Further Reading

Atwood, M. 2007. "Everybody Is Happy Now." *The Guardian,* November 17. https://www .theguardian.com/books/2007/nov/17/classics.margaretatwood

Flood, A. 2011. "Brave New World among Top Ten Books Americans Most Want Banned." *The Guardian,* April 12. https://www.theguardian.com/books/2011/apr/12/brave -new-world-challenged-books

Petri, A. 2011. "For 'Banned Books Week,' Two Reasons to Ban Brave New World." *The Washington Post,* September 28. https://www.washingtonpost.com/blogs/compost /post/for-banned-books-week-two-reasons-to-ban-brave-new-world/2011/09/28 /gIQAViSe5K_blog.html?utm_term=.d3884e0fb315

Postman, N. 1985. *Amusing Ourselves to Death: Public Discourse in the Age of Show Business.* New York: Penguin.

Schaub, M. 2017. "Happy Brave New Birthday, Aldous Huxley!" *LA Times,* July 26. http:// beta.latimes.com/books/jacketcopy/la-et-jc-aldous-huxley-20170726-story.html

Call of the Wild, The

The Call of the Wild is a novel by Jack London (1876–1916), published in 1903. It is set during the 1890s Klondike Gold Rush in the Yukon, Canada, and follows the protagonist, Buck, a dog. Buck has been stolen from his home in California and sold to be a sled dog in Alaska. He fights to survive not just the elements but the other dogs and abusive people throughout the story, which is based loosely on the year London spent in the Yukon. It was first serialized in the *Saturday Evening Post* then published as a book one month later. It has been adapted to cinema numerous times since 1923.

Buck has been well taken care of by his family, the Millers, until he is sold by the gardener's assistant, Manuel, who does so to satisfy his gambling addiction. He is first put in a crate and starved as he is shipped to Seattle, and upon release attacks the overseer, a "man in a red sweater, who responds by beating him badly so as to teach Buck to respect the 'law of the club.'" He is then sold to two Canadians, Francois and Perrault, who take him to Canada and train him as a sled dog. Many of the other sled dogs help Buck, but a bitter rivalry erupts between him and Spitz, who Buck eventually beats in a fight. The pack responds by killing Spitz and making Buck the leader of the team. The Canadians get new orders and sell the team to another man, who works them hard on long, tiresome journeys with heavy loads. After that, Buck is sold to a trio of stampeders who are clueless about surviving the wild, making life again hard for him and the team. They meet John Thornton, an experienced outdoorsman, who tells the trio not to cross the river. Buck senses danger, and he is exhausted and starving, so he refuses to move. One of the trio, Hal, beats him, but Thornton intervenes and takes Buck. Although Buck survives, the trio and the other dogs all fall into the river and drown. Thornton nurses Buck back to health, and Buck responds by being loyal, even saving Thornton when he falls into a river. As Thornton takes Buck with him on trips to pan for gold, people offer him money to race, which he wins, and even for purchase, but Thornton will not give Buck up. While Buck is out exploring one night he finds that a group of Natives, the Yeehat, have killed Thornton and others at their camp. Buck avenges the loss, killing the Natives, and then he is attacked by a pack of wolves. Buck wins that fight as well, then follows a timber wolf and his pack into the wild, returning each year as the Ghost Dog of the Northland Legend, mourning at the site where Thornton was killed.

The Guardian named *Call of the Wild* number 35 on its list of 100 best books. It is challenged for its dark tone and the bloody violence that Buck is involved in throughout the book. Also, it is often challenged as to its age-appropriateness, as a book about a man and a dog may seem fitting for young audiences but the dark themes are not. It was banned in Italy and Yugoslavia and burned in bonfires in Nazi Germany in the late 1920s and early 1930s because it was considered "too radical" ("Banned Books that Shaped America," n.d.).

London died at the young age of 40, having written 50 books in 20 years but living dangerously, with frequent drinking and drugs. *The People of the Abyss* (1903), *White Fang* (1906), and *The Road* (1907) were among London's other most popular stories.

Laura L. Finley

See also: Crucible, The; Poe, Edgar Allan; Steinbeck, John

Further Reading

"Banned Books that Shaped America." (n.d.). *Banned Books Week.* http://www.banned booksweek.org/censorship/bannedbooksthatshapedamerica

McCrum, R. 2014. "The 100 Best Novels: No. 35—The Call of the Wild by Jack London (1903)." *The Guardian,* May 19. https://www.theguardian.com/books/2014/may/19 /100-best-novels-call-of-the-wild-jack-london

Yang, H. 2015. "Psychoanalysis of Jack London's The Call of the Wild and White Fang." *English Language Teaching, 8*(11), 42–46. https://files.eric.ed.gov/fulltext/EJ1080 306.pdf

Catch-22

Catch-22 is a novel published in 1961 by American author Joseph Heller (1923–1999). It is a satire set during World War II that describes events from different points of view and out of sequence. The novel is more than 500 pages long and features more than 50 characters. The primary character is Captain John Yossarian, who is a bombardier for the United States in the fictional 256th squadron. Heller himself was a bombardier, so the book was inspired by his experience. It showcases the challenges Yossarian and the other men face in trying to stay sane and survive to return home. Over time, Yossarian fears his commanding officers more than the Germans he is fighting, mostly because as he flies more and more missions, his colonel, Cathcart, keeps upping the number of required missions before a soldier can leave the war. Yossarian believes he will never reach that number, which will continue to be raised. The Catch-22 is a clause which states that pilots don't have to fly if they are certified as insane, but that fear is rational so being driven crazy by it is not grounds for insanity. "The result, put simply, is that no one can get off the ride."

The book has been criticized for being overly positive in its depiction of the Germans, but Heller has said that any antiwar sentiment was directed at the Cold War and the Korean War, not World War II. Others have said that more than a criticism of war, the book is a disavowing of God. Others see it as more critical of excessive bureaucracy. The book ends with Yossarian remembering a bombing raid that resulted in a young enlisted man bleeding to death. Critic Chris Cox wrote, "But it's only near the end, when Yossarian finally gives in and reflects fully on the episode—its gruesome details and savage lack of meaning—that the novel is transposed into a tragic key. Sure, it's been funny. But all along the comedy has been an expression of horror; it springs from outraged, stupefied humanity. There seems to be something up for grabs in *Catch-22*'s circular logic—where madness begets laughter, and laughter begets madness—that makes me immediately go back and read it again; which is an impulse I think Heller, Yossarian, and the rest of the gang would understand" (Cox, 2011). Readers have applauded the book's style for matching the lunacy that is war.

Heller was asked how he felt about the war when he was in it, and he responded, "Much differently than Yossarian felt and much differently than I felt when I wrote the novel. . . . In truth I enjoyed it and so did just about everyone else I served with, in training and even in combat. I was young, it was adventurous, there was much hoopla and glamour; in addition, and this too is hard to get across to college students today, for me and for most others, going into the army resulted immediately in a vast improvement in my standard of living." He made more money in the military than in his job as a filing clerk and enjoyed the prospect of travel. He enlisted at age 19 and flew on the Italian front, like his character Yossarian, flying some 60 combat missions. It took Heller most of the 1950s to write the book after being contracted by Simon & Schuster when they approved of a sample chapter (Bates, 2011). The Ohio town of Strongsville banned the book in 1972, citing indecent language. The ban was removed in 1976.

Catch-22 was made into a feature film in 1970, starring Alan Arkin as Yossarian.

Laura L. Finley

See also: Fahrenheit 451; Vonnegut, Kurt; War Films

Further Reading

Bates, S. 2011. "'Catch-22' Author Joseph Heller: "How Did I Feel about the War? I Enjoyed It?" *The Guardian,* October 25. https://www.theguardian.com/books/2011/oct/25/catch-22-author-enjoyed-war

Cox, C. 2011. "Catch-22: 50 Years Later." *The Guardian,* October 10. https://www.theguardian.com/books/2011/oct/10/catch-22-50-years-joseph-heller

Driscoll, M., & O'Carroll, E. 2012. "30 Banned Books that May Surprise You." *Christian Science Monitor*, October 3. https://www.csmonitor.com/Books/2012/1003/30-banned-books-that-may-surprise-you/Catch-22-by-Joseph-Heller

Jordison, S. 2016. "Catch-22's Crazy Style Reflects the Madness of War." *The Guardian*, August 16. https://www.theguardian.com/books/booksblog/2016/aug/16/catch-22s-crazy-style-reflects-the-madness-of-war

Rosenbaum, R. 2008. "Seeing Catch-22 Twice." *Slate,* August 2. http://www.slate.com/articles/life/the_spectator/2011/08/seeing_catch22_twice.html

Crucible, The

The Crucible is a play by American playwright Arthur Miller (1915–2005), first performed on Broadway in 1953, for which it won a Tony Award for Best Play. It is loosely based on the Salem witch trials of 1692–1693, and is also an allegory to the era of McCarthyism in the time period in which Miller wrote. Led by Joseph McCarthy, the U.S. government, and in particular, the House of Representatives' Committee on Un-American Activities, investigated many artists, including Miller, for being sympathetic to communism during the Cold War. McCarthy was convicted of contempt of court for refusing to identify others as potential communist sympathizers.

The Crucible is focused on a group of women and girls who are engaged in non-traditional behavior, like dancing in the forest, and are discovered by the local preacher, Reverend Samuel Parris. Parris's 10-year-old daughter Betty becomes motionless, seemingly catatonic, and rumors quickly circulate that the women, led by an enslaved woman from Barbados, Tituba, are involved in witchcraft. Parris and others believe that, besides Tituba, the ringleader is his niece, Abigail Williams, whom Parris has adopted. Wealthy residents of the town, Thomas and Ann Putnam, insist that it is witchcraft and not just dancing, as Abigail claims, and they coerce Parris to bring in Reverend John Hale, a demonology and witchcraft expert. Meanwhile, Betty briefly rouses but is so distraught she attempts to jump out the window. Abigail threatens the girls, asking them to stick to the story that it was only dancing, even though in reality, the meeting in the woods was intended to conjure a spell against Elizabeth Proctor, the wife of the man Abigail has been having an affair with, which resulted in her firing as a servant to that home. Abigail believes that John still has feelings for her, as she does for him, but once she confronts him, it is clear that he does not.

Things escalate, as Mrs. Putnam, who has lost many babies, continues to blame witchcraft for these losses. In a classic case of groupthink, the other citizens line up to accuse not just the girls, but also a farmer, Giles Corey, who has been fighting with the Putnams over property, and Rebecca Nurse, a woman too outspoken for her time, of being involved in witchcraft. Amidst it all Reverend Hale arrives and begins investigating. Under pressure, Abigail says that Tituba forced her to drink blood. As an enslaved woman with little power, no one believes Tituba, and she breaks down, claiming the devil has bewitched the town. Tituba accuses Sarah Good and Sarah Osborne of witchcraft, and Mrs. Putnam agrees, citing Osborne as her former midwife. Abigail then names Bridget Bishop, who accuses George Jacobs. This concludes the first act of the play.

Act Two begins with narration comparing Puritan fundamentalism to the Cold War McCarthyism. It then opens to the Proctors' home, where John and Elizabeth are distraught that almost 40 people have been arrested for witchcraft based on Abigail's and the other women's accusations. Abigail told him the allegations were not true, but John does not know how to disclose that fact, given that they were never to see one another again alone. Elizabeth is disturbed because she believes John still harbors feelings for Abigail, and he can, in her eyes, not redeem himself if he does. Meanwhile, Elizabeth has been accused. Reverend Hale interviews them all. Abigail has claimed that Elizabeth stabbed her with a needle while engaged in witchcraft. This angers John, who finally realizes that the truth must come out no matter the consequence.

Act Three opens 37 days later, during the trial of Martha Corey for witchcraft. John and others announce that the girls are lying. Reverend Hale is even disturbed, wondering why the accused are not allowed to defend themselves. John admits to the affair, asserting it is the primary motivation for Abigail's lies, and Hale agrees, but the town officials refuse to change their focus. The girls go crazy in the courtroom, and a deeply upset John is arrested.

Act Four shows the town jail three months later. Many of the villagers have been charged with witchcraft. Some have confessed, seeing no alternative, and have been given lengthy prison terms and forced to relinquish their property to the government. Twelve have already been hanged. John Proctor and six others are set to be hung the following morning because they refused to confess. The play ends with John and others being hung.

There are varying theories to explain the Salem witch trials. Some argue it was about property disputes, whereas others assert that it was about isolationism, as the community was deeply fearful of their Native neighbors. Still others say it was a debate between those who wanted a more progressive society and those who preferred something similar to the religious fundamentalism of Britain.

In reality, 18 individuals were executed and some 150 accused during the Salem witch trials. In 1711, the Massachusetts Colony passed legislation restoring the names of those accused and providing restitution to their heirs (Salem Witch Trials, n.d.). A 2002 revival of *The Crucible* starred Liam Neeson and Laura Linney. There was a 1957 film adaptation, and Miller himself directed a 1996 version starring Daniel Day-Lewis, Paul Scofield, and Winona Ryder. It received an Academy Award nomination for Best Screenplay.

When he wrote *The Crucible*, several of Miller's plays were already being boycotted and banned. In 1949, Miller won the Pulitzer Prize and many other awards for *Death of a Salesman*. Other Hollywood and Broadway stars were also targeted by the McCarthy purges, including Edward G. Robinson, Paul Robeson, Lillian Hellman, Charlie Chaplin, Aaron Copland, Dashiell Hammett, John Garfield, Ruth Gordon, and Edward Dmytryk.

Miller remained a controversial figure, turning down a 1965 invitation to witness President Lyndon B. Johnson signing the Arts and Humanities Act as a protest against the president's escalation of the Vietnam War. In a telegram to Johnson, he said, "The signing of the Arts and Humanities bill surely begins [a] new and fruitful relationship between American artists and their government. But the occasion is so darkened by the Viet Nam tragedy that I could not join it with clear conscience. When the guns boom, the arts die" (Dreler, 2016).

Laura L. Finley

See also: *Buffy the Vampire Slayer*; *Call of the Wild, The*; *Harry Potter* Books and Film Series; *Lord of the Flies*; Morrison, Toni; Poe, Edgar Allan; Steinbeck, John; *Things Fall Apart*; Walker, Alice

Further Reading

Adams, R. 2012. "The Crucible: Arthur Miller's Classic Still Scalds." *World Socialist Web Site,* June 29. https://www.wsws.org/en/articles/2012/06/cruc-j29.html

Dreler, A. 2016. "Playwright Arthur Miller, Dead for a Decade, Is Still Stirring Controversy." *Huffington Post,* October 19. https://www.huffingtonpost.com/peter-dreier/playwright-arthur-miller-is-still-stirring-controversy_b_8331464.html

Miller, A. 1996. "Why I Wrote 'The Crucible.'" *The New Yorker,* October 21. https://www.newyorker.com/magazine/1996/10/21/why-i-wrote-the-crucible

"Salem Witch Trials." n.d. *History.com.* http://www.history.com/topics/salem-witch-trials

Fahrenheit 451

Fahrenheit 451, published in 1953, is a dystopian novel written by American author Ray Bradbury. It describes a society in the future in which books are prohibited, and firemen burn any they find. The title comes from the fact that paper catches fire and burns at 451 degrees Fahrenheit. The main character is a fireman named Montag, who tires of his work and becomes disillusioned with the destruction of not just books but knowledge. Montag also grows upset at the high-speed, low-intellect life that is now common. Throughout the book, Montag learns that books were gradually phased out—first dumbed down to accommodate the shortened attention span generated by the growth of mass media, and then eventually prohibited completely. He quits and joins a resistance group that is attempting to memorize and share the world's great literary, historical, and cultural works.

Montag first begins to question his work after meeting a new, teenage neighbor, Clarisse McClellan, who is a free-thinker and independent spirit. The two become friends, and Montag grows to look forward to their conversations, where Clarisse reveals that she is made fun of for her interests and forced to go to therapy because she is different. Then Clarisse goes missing.

Another pivotal event is when Montag and the firemen respond to a book-filled home and the old woman who lives there refuses to surrender her books. Instead, she sets herself on fire. Montag is moved by her commitment and takes a book from the scene. At the same time, he is questioning his marriage, as his wife, Mildred, is addicted to sleeping pills and the hedonistic lifestyle. It turns out Mildred knows what happened to Clarisse: her family moved away after Clarisse was hit by a speeding car and killed.

A distraught Montag is visited by his boss, Captain Beatty, who comes to suspect he has a book. Beatty threatens Montag that if a fireman has a book he will be asked to burn it within 24 hours or else his peers will burn his house down. Beatty leaves, and Montag tells Mildred he has a stash of books hidden in their air-conditioning duct. She panics and tries to destroy them, but he says they should both read the books to see if they have value before destroying them. As they read, Montag wonders whether the books might contain important messages that can save society from what he sees as its inevitable destruction. Mildred is not interested, instead setting up time with friends to watch mass media.

Montag decides to seek help, and remembering an old English professor he met once named Faber, goes to find him. Returning home, he finds Mildred and her friends watching the "parlor walls," which are gigantic televisions. They are unable to engage in meaningful conversation, which solidifies to Montag that they are ignorant and callous, even about an upcoming war that should make them worried and upset. Montag hides his books, then returns to the firehouse, where he hands Beatty a book he thinks will cover for the one he believes Beatty knows he stole. This does not work, however, as Beatty sends a fire truck to Montag's house and commands him to destroy it, saying that his wife and friends reported his ownership of books. Rather than be upset for her husband, Mildred is only concerned about the destruction of her parlor wall. Beatty also discovers that Montag has been communicating with Faber through an earpiece and threatens to hunt him down. Montag ends up burning his boss, knocking out his coworkers, and escaping the scene.

Faber encourages Montag to flee to the countryside, where other exiled book lovers live. There he meets a group of drifters, led by a man named Granger. They have memorized books so that they can share the information with others to create a better society. They watch as the city burns, hopeful that their efforts will help.

Fahrenheit 451 has won many awards, including the 1954 American Academy of Arts and Letters Award in Literature. It has been adapted into a spoken word performance, for which Bradbury won a Grammy nomination in 1976. It has also been adapted for film, radio, stage play, and even a computer game. In 2007, Bradbury received a special Pulitzer Prize for his "distinguished, prolific and deeply influential career as an unmatched author of science fiction and fantasy." Bradbury did not attend, as he was upset that he was not allowed to give a speech (Ray Bradbury, 2018).

Written during the era of McCarthyism, most believe that Bradbury was concerned about the threat of book burning in the United States. Further, Bradbury was horrified by the Nazi book burnings before and during World War II, although the author says it was not this that was the impetus for the book. Instead, Bradbury has said that he was most worried about the increasing role of mass media in the United States and its destruction of people's interest in reading. He criticized mass media for teaching "factoids" (Ray Bradbury, 2018). "They stuff you with so much useless information, you feel full," said Bradbury (Flock, 2011). *Fahrenheit 451* is often taught in junior high and high schools. In an ironic twist, the novel was published with several words changed and 75 modified passages. Only this version was available between 1973 and 1979. An angered Bradbury insisted that the original version be published, which has been available in print since (Ray Bradbury, 2018).

Laura L. Finley

See also: Brave New World; Dystopian Young Adult Literature and Film; *Mad Max* Films; *1984*; Vonnegut, Kurt

Further Reading

Flock, E. 2011. "'Fahrenheit 451,' 50 Years Later, Still Sharply Divides Readers over Ray Bradbury." *The Washington Post,* August 26. https://www.washingtonpost.com /blogs/blogpost/post/fahrenheit-451-50-years-later-still-sharply-divides-readers -over-ray-bradbury/2011/08/26/gIQAn596fJ_blog.html?utm_term=.2759d6e005b9

Johnston, A. 2007. "Ray Bradbury: Fahrenheit 451 Misinterpreted." *LA Weekly,* May 30. http://www.laweekly.com/news/instead-of-being-put-down-these-feral-cats-are -being-put-to-work-8963106

"Ray Bradbury." 2018. *Pulitzer.* http://www.pulitzer.org/winners/ray-bradbury

Faulkner, William

William Cuthbert Faulkner (1897–1962) is an American author known for his novels and short stories that were set largely in the South. Faulkner wrote for decades and received numerous awards, including a Nobel Prize in Literature in 1949. He donated part of his winnings to establish the PEN/Faulkner Award for Fiction. His first published story, "A Rose for Emily," is one of the most famous. Faulkner is best known for his novels *The Sound and the Fury* (1929), *As I Lay Dying* (1930), *Light in August* (1932), and *Absalom, Absalom!* (1936). He also wrote two collections of short stories and poetry, and collaborated on several screenplays, including *Mildred Pierce* (1945), *To Have and Have Not* (1944), and *The Big Sleep* (1946). Faulkner is known for using stream of consciousness in his writing, and in addition to the Nobel Prize, he won two Pulitzers.

Although he wrote for some time prior, it wasn't until the publication of his novel *Sanctuary* in 1931 that Faulkner gained a real reputation. *Sanctuary* describes the rape of a young woman with a corncob, which oddly turns her into a prostitute.

The Sound and the Fury is unique in that it follows four characters through the same experience, showcasing each person's perspective. It is notoriously difficult to read, starting with the character Benjy, a 33-year-old who was described as "severely retarded." Because Benjy doesn't fully understand the world around him, the reader must piece together what is happening from various clues that jump around over 30 years of Benjy's life. In sum, the novel tells the story of the decline of a family, the Compsons, who retain obsolete attitudes about race, class, and sex well past the end of the Civil War in the 1860s. One of the perspectives in the book is that of Dilsey, the Black servant who works for the Compsons. It was named the sixth-greatest English-language book by the Modern Library in 1998 (Churchwell, 2012).

Some of Faulkner's other stories took on racial violence. *Dry September* is about a lynching in which a Black man had been accused of raping a White woman. Published in 1931, it allows readers to see what was typically the case: no rape happened, but White women who engaged in promiscuous sex or were adulterers often claimed to have been raped by Black men to draw attention away from their behavior. White men, quick to defend the alleged "honor" of the women, responded by attacking and lynching the accused. At the time newspapers often featured gruesome photos of lynchings, but Faulkner's story does not depict the moment of the lynching or the dead body.

Faulkner's 1930 novel *As I Lay Dying* has faced bans due to "God's name being used in vain," abortion, profanity, promoting secular humanism, and obscenity. One Kentucky school banned the book even though the school board members admitted they had not read it (Spillman, 2012).

One poll of writers and critics named Faulkner's *Absalom, Absalom!* the "greatest Southern novel ever written." Set in 1909, it tells the story of a Southern boy, Quentin, who moves north to study at Harvard. He has a Canadian roommate, Shreve, to whom he relays tales told to him about slavery, violence, and interracial marriage. Like other Faulkner works, it used racial slurs multiple times. Some have said the novel is "the most serious attempt by any white writer to confront the problem of race in America" (Sullivan, 2012).

Laura L. Finley

See also: Lord of the Flies; Steinbeck, John; *To Kill a Mockingbird*

Further Reading

Chavers, L. 2013. "Violent Disruptions: Richard Wright and William Falkner's Racial Imaginations." (PhD dissertation). Boston, MA: Harvard University. https://dash .harvard.edu/bitstream/handle/1/11169797/chavers_gsas.harvard_00841_11139 .pdf?sequence=1

Churchwell, S. 2012. "Sarah Churchwell: Rereading "The Sound and the Fury" by William Faulkner." *The Guardian*, July 20. https://www.theguardian.com/books/2012 /jul/20/sound-fury-william-faulkner-rereading

Milica, I. 2012. "Racial Violence in William Faulkner's *Dry September* and Harper Lee's *To Kill a Mockingbird*." *Lingua Culture*, 1, 103 20.

Spillman, R. 2012. "On William Faulkner's *As I Lay Dying*." *PEN*, October 15. https://pen .org/on-william-faulkners-as-i-lay-dying/

Sullivan, J. 2012. "How William Faulkner Tackled Race—And Freed the South from Itself." *The New York Times*, June 28. http://www.nytimes.com/2012/07/01/magazine/how -william-faulkner-tackled-race-and-freed-the-south-from-itself.html

West, B. 2013. *Crowd Violence in American Modernist Fiction: Lynchings, Riots, and the Individual Under Assault*. Jefferson, NC: McFarland.

King, Stephen

Stephen King is perhaps the most widely known writer of horror novels in the United States. Born in 1947, King has published more than 50 novels which feature a wide array of violence, perpetrated by a host of realistic and less-realistic characters. Many have been adapted into feature films as well. King has sold at least 350 million books, although early in his career he faced tremendous criticism from reviewers who did not see horror as a legitimate genre.

King's first novel, *Rage*, was authored when he was still a high school student in 1965, although it wasn't published for more than a decade. *Rage* tells the story of a troubled high school student who seeks revenge on those who tormented him. He brings a gun to school, holds his algebra class hostage, and kills several faculty members. *Rage* has been linked to four school shootings:

- An April 1988 incident in which a California high school student held his humanities class hostage. He told police he got the idea from *Rage*.

- In September 1989, a Kentucky high school student held his classmates hostage for nine hours, also apparently trying to reenact the novel.

- In February 1996, 14-year-old Barry Loukaitis, inspired by *Rage*, shot and killed his algebra teacher and two classmates in Moses Lake, Washington.

- In December 1997, 14-year-old Michael Carneal fired on a prayer group at his school in Paducah, Kentucky, killing three. He had a copy of *Rage* in his locker.

Although King has stated that he does not believe the story was a catalyst for these incidents, he pulled it from a 1985 collection of four stories in which it had been included out of concern that it was "an accelerant" (Adwar, 2014).

Aside from *Rage*, which he published under the pseudonym Richard Bachman, King's oldest novel is *Carrie*, the story of a high school misfit, Carrie White, who seeks revenge on her tormenting peers during the high school prom, where she uses the telekinetic powers she discovers she has. It was made into a film in 1976, with Sissie Spacek starring as Carrie. In 1975, King published *Salem's Lot*, which depicts a man returning to his home town only to find it overrun by vampires. *The Shining*, published in 1977, told the story of a family that moves into a hotel because the father has taken the position of caretaker. They find out the hotel is full of evil forces that seek to claim the protagonist's son, Danny. In 1980, the novel was adapted into a film, directed and produced by Stanley Kubrick, and featuring Jack Nicholson and Shelley Duvall as the caretaker, Jack Torrance, and his wife, Wendy. Director Martin Scorsese has ranked it as one of the 11 scariest films of all time, although King was not happy with the adaptation.

In 1978, King wrote *The Stand*, an apocalyptic novel about a strain of influenza created to instigate a biological war that kills more than half the population. One year later, King published *The Dead Zone*, about a man who emerges from a coma clairvoyant and with precognition abilities. Christopher Walken and Martin Sheen starred in the 1983 film adaptation. King published *The Long Walk* in 1979 under the pseudonym Richard Bachman. Similar to *Lord of the Flies* and later, *The Hunger Games* trilogy, it is a dystopian novel featuring a grueling contest involving 100 teenage boys. It is a physical and psychological trial, and many die on the walk.

In 1983, King published *Pet Sematary*, which was nominated in 1984 for a World Fantasy Award for Best Novel. It was adapted into a film in 1989. It is the creepy tale of dying pets and humans at an American Indian burial ground. King published *It* in 1986, which tells the tale of seven children who are tormented by various scary characters. "It" most frequently appears as a scary clown to entice vulnerable children, and the novel and later television series (1990) starring Tim Curry as Pennywise the Clown are considered among King's scariest works. The novel won numerous awards, including the British Fantasy Award in 1987. *Publishers Weekly* listed *It* as the best-selling book in the United States in 1986.

King published *Misery* in 1987, which was made into a feature film in 1990 starring Kathy Bates and James Caan. Bates won the Best Actor Oscar for her performance as Annie, a deranged woman who takes in author Sheldon after a winter car accident. Annie becomes increasingly obsessed with keeping Sheldon with her, and she inflicts various forms of violence on him in the process.

King is also the author of more than 200 short stories, most of which have been published in collections. His son, Joe Hill, is also a horror writer. In a 2014 interview, King claims that his worst books are *Tommyknockers* and *Dreamcatcher*, both of which he wrote when he was grappling with drug addiction (to cocaine and oxycontin, respectively) (Greene, 2014). Many are unaware that King authored *Rita Hayworth and the Shawshank Redemption,* which was the basis for the 1994 film *The Shawshank Redemption* that has been rated among the best of all time.

In 2014, King published *Mr. Mercedes*, less a horror book and more a detective novel. It won the 2015 Edgar Award for Best Novel from the Mystery Writers of America and was selected for a Goodreads Choice Award in 2014 in the "Mystery and Thriller" category. It was the first in a trilogy about a retired policeman who is taunted by a murderer. It was followed by *Finders Keepers* (2015) and *End of Watch* (2016).

In 2015, King was awarded a National Medal of Arts from the United States National Endowment for the Arts. He is a big fan of the band the Ramones and has referenced them multiple times in his novels. He also loves AC/DC and other heavy metal bands.

Although he has expressed concern about the influence of his work on teen readers and viewers, in April 2008 King spoke out against Massachusetts HB 1423, a bill that would have restricted or banned the sale of violent video games to anyone under the age of 18. King stated that he had no personal interest in video games particularly; however, he criticized the proposed law, which he sees as an attempt by politicians to scapegoat pop culture. He has also voiced opposition to the Tea Party, promoted more gun controls, and supported wealthy individuals being taxed at higher rates.

Laura L. Finley

See also: Murder, She Wrote; Poe, Edgar Allan; Scandinavian Crime Novels

Further Reading

Adwar, Corey. 2014. "This Stephen King Novel Will Never Be Printed Again after It Was Tied to School Shootings." *Business Insider,* April 1. http://www.businessinsider.com/school-shootings-drove-stephen-king-to-take-rage-off-shelves-2014-3

Greene, A. 2014. "Stephen King: The Rolling Stone Interview." *Rolling Stone*, October 31. http://www.rollingstone.com/culture/features/stephen-king-the-rolling-stone -interview-20141031

King, S. 2014. "Stephen King: Tax Me for F@%&'s Sake!" *The Daily Beast*, April 30. http:// www.thedailybeast.com/articles/2012/04/30/stephen-king-tax-me-for-f-s-sake .html

Lord of the Flies

Lord of the Flies is a 1954 novel by British author William Golding (1911–1993), who won a Nobel Prize in Literature in 1983 for his novels. *Lord of the Flies* was initially met with little interest from many publishing companies, nor was it an immediate success. Upon its release in September 1954, *Lord of the Flies* sold only 4,662 copies. The novel eventually sold 65,000 copies by 1962. Yet today, the novel has sold millions of copies worldwide and has been translated into all the major languages, as well as many minority languages. The novel has been critically well received. It was named in the Modern Library 100 Best Novels, reaching number 41 on the editor's list, and 25 on the reader's list. It was also listed at number 70 on the BBC'*s* The Big Read poll in 2003, and *Time* magazine named it one of the 100 best English-language novels from 1923 to 2005. *Lord of the Flies* has also been cited as number eight on the American Library Association's list of banned and challenged classics. William Golding's book has been challenged and successfully banned on a host of grounds, ranging from profanity to excessive violence. There have been three film adaptations based on the book and a fourth adaptation, to feature an all-female cast, was announced in August 2017 by Warner Bros.

The book takes place during an unspecified nuclear war. It portrays group-think and a descent into barbarism. A group of English boys are stranded on a deserted island far from modern civilization and are struggling to develop their own society. Eventually the children fall back into a primitive state. Ralph is the protagonist of the book, and Jack is the antagonist. Ralph represented order and a positive leadership. He wanted to act peacefully and valued the good of the group. On the other hand, Jack wanted control and power over everyone and everything on the island, representing savagery.

Parents, school administrators, and others have criticized the language and violence in the novel. The major theme of the book is that humans are innately evil. Also, bullying is rampant throughout the book. Golding implies that people are naturally prone to being savage and cruel and that there is no hope of redemption for humankind. The kids, who have to hunt for food, enjoy the brutal hunt and slaughter of a pig; this makes them want to go hunting every day. Their rational motive to acquire meat to eat is overtaken by an irrational drive to kill solely for the sake of it.

In the novel, there are two murders. The first is the murder of Simon, a shy and sensitive boy, the only innately good character in the book. They kill him while brutally chanting "Kill the beast! Cut his throat! Spill his blood! Do him in!" ignoring his crying (Golding, 1954, p. 118). The beast represents their savagery. Simon was the only one who realized the beast was the evil within each of them, and Ralph was the only one who felt remorse for what the other children did to Simon. Simon's death was an accident, but Piggy's was not.

Many of the characters are bullied throughout the book, especially Piggy. He is immediately set apart from everyone else in the novel because of his appearance. Piggy was known as the "fat boy," and the verbal abuse quickly changed to physical, with his glasses being stolen and broken. In his murder scene, Piggy asks, "Which is better to have rules and agree, or to hunt and kill?" (Golding, 1954, p. 141). Then, Jack lets Roger drop a boulder on Piggy, killing him.

In addition to the violence, many people think that the book promotes a pro-slavery ideology, and they point this out as the wrong messages to teach children. For example, at the end of the book when the boys are being rescued, the naval officer who spoke to the boys said, "I should have thought that a pack of British boys—you're all British, aren't you?—would have been able to put up a better show than that" (Golding, 1954, p. 157). In other words, he wouldn't expect the kind of behavior the kids displayed because they are British. Also, the children apply face paint, and in an early edition of the novel, Piggy uses a racial slur referring to their appearance. The line was changed, however, to "a pack of painted Indians" (Golding 1954, p. 141), which is not much better. Additionally, as the children sharpen their spears and make face paint, they ask if they should have drums as well; they are copying what they have learned about "savages" from the people and media around them.

Dr. Stephanie van Goozen, a professor of developmental psychology at Cardiff University who has conducted extensive research into aggression in children, stated that *Lord of the Flies* could only have been written about boys. She said, "[F]rom the age of two or three, girls start to control themselves and regulate their emotions a bit more. Boys, on the other hand, have violent responses much higher up in their repertoire of behavior," and it arises more easily in stressful situations (Simons, 2014). Thus it is less likely that a group of girls would partake in the activities that the boys did in the novel. But this does not mean that girls are more enlightened than boys, according to van Goozen. She claims that "it is not socially acceptable for girls to bite and fight when they are growing up, so they find more complex ways of expressing indirect aggression" (Simons, 2014). She believes that if *Lord of the Flies* focused on a group of girls, there would have been more gossiping and social exclusion.

Golding gave three reasons as to why he wrote the book with all boys, some of them quite misogynistic. The first is that he had the experience of being a little boy, a brother, a father, and a grandfather, not a girl, sister, mother, etc. His second reason is that he felt that a group of boys parallels society more closely than a group of girls. He believes that "women are foolish to pretend they are equal to men, they are far superior and always have been. But one thing you can't do with them is take a bunch of them and boil them down, so to speak, into a set of little girls who would then become a kind of image of civilization, of society" (Golding, n.d.). Lastly, he said, "[I]f they'd been little boys and little girls, we being who we are, sex would have raised its lovely head," and he didn't want the book to be about sex (Golding, n.d.).

Many parents, school administrators, and other critics do not think that *Lord of the Flies* is an appropriate novel for their children to read. They think that the violence in the book is too gruesome and graphic, and that readers will become negatively influenced by the book. However, the book is still widely read in high school by many students, helping them to understand the problem of evil and how people live together in society.

Laura L. Finley

See also: Crucible, The; Dystopian Young Adult Literature and Film; Faulkner, William; Steinbeck, John

Further Reading

Golding, W. n.d. "Introduction to the Lord of the Flies." *YouTube*. https://www.youtube.com /watch?v=vYnfSV27vLY&feature=youtu.be Video.

Golding, W. 1954. *Lord of the Flies*. London: Faber and Faber.

Lombardi, E. 2018." Why Does Lord of the Flies Continue to Get Banned in Schools?" *ThoughtCo*, February 19. https://www.thoughtco.com/lord-of-the-flies-banned -challenged-740596

Macek III, J. 2015. "'Lord of the Flies' Is an Inferior Take on William Golding's Classic Novel." *Pop Matters*, April 28. http://www.popmatters.com/review/192544-lord-of -the-flies/

Simons, J. W. 2014. "Why Lord of the Flies Speaks Volumes about Boys." *Telegraph*, September 17. http://www.telegraph.co.uk/men/thinking-man/11101515/Why-Lord-of -the-Flies-speaks-volumes-about-boys.html

Smith, S. E. 2016. "Challenged Book: Lord of the Flies." *Meloukhia*, March 25. http:// meloukhia.net/2011/05/challenged_book_lord_of_the_flies/

Mexican Crime Novels

Crime novels in Mexico often express frustration at the lack of justice and the corruption of police. A genre of crime novel has been called narcoliterature, which focused on the realities of drug culture and tells fictional but realist stories. Narcoliterature novels are among the top-selling books in Mexico and to the U.S. Spanish-speaking market. Authors maintain that such novels help readers understand what is going on, as they read much like investigative reports. The genre is influenced by *corridos*, or colorful ballads, about Mexico that often also focused on the drug trade and, in many cases, glamorized the cartels. It is also influenced by journalistic efforts, in particular by the late Jesus Blancornelas, who founded the magazine *Zeta* in Tijuana in 1980. It was known for its coverage of the political corruption that gave rise to and allowed the cartels to prosper. Mexican author Yuri Herrera has said, "It's important to talk about these difficult topics whether we like it or not. In that sense this literature can help create citizens who reflect on our problems and hopefully come up with solutions" (Orozco, 2014). Fans and critics sometimes praise narcoliterature for its brutal depictions and for showing the "grey zone" where organized crime and the state are both perpetrators.

Yet narcoliterature has not always been met with applause. Blancornelas received many death threats and survived an attempted assassination. Since 2010, at least 30 journalists and media personnel have been murdered in Mexico, in particular in the violent area of Sinaloa (Orozco, 2014). Critics also contend that these books glorify the drug life and depict authorities as the enemy. Further, they argue that narcoliterature often oversimplifies complex issues.

Recommended narcoliterature includes *Los Senores del Narco* (in English, *Narcoland: The Mexican Drug Lords and Their Godfathers*) by Anabel Hernandez; *La Reina del Pacific* (*The Queen of the Pacific*), by Julio Scherer Garcia; *El Cartel de Sinaloa* (*The Sinaloa Cartel*) by Diego Enrique Osorno; *El Narco En Mexico* (*The Narco in Mexico*) by Ricardo Ravela; *El Jefe de Jefes* (*The Boss of Bosses*) by Jose Manuel Valenzuela; *Historia del Narcotrafico en Mexico* (*History of the Narcotrafico in Mexico*) by Guillermo Valdes Castellanos; and *El Ultimo Narco* (*The Last Narco: Inside the Hunt for El Chapo, the World's Most Wanted Drug Lord*) by Malcolm Beith (Orozco, 2014).

Author Juan Pablo Villalobos has argued that the name narcoliterature should not be used, as it has negative connotations and results in good books being dismissed as merely one more "drug book" (Villalobos, 2012).

Laura L. Finley

See also: Breaking Bad; Latin American MCs; *Miami Vice*; Narcocorridos; Scandinavian Crime Novels; Spanish-Language Television

Further Reading

Esch, S. 2014. "In the Crossfire: Rascon Bando's Contraband and the 'Narcoliterature' Debate in Mexico." *Latin America Perspectives,41*(2), 161–76.

Miranda, C. 2014. "Days of the Dead: Time to Say 'Enough' to the Days of Extreme Narco-Culture." *LA Times,* November 12. http://www.latimes.com/entertainment/arts /miranda/la-et-cam-days-of-the-dead-the-future-of-narco-culture-20141110 -column.html

Orozco, G. 2014. "Narcoliterature Explores Realities of Mexico's Drug Culture." *Chicago Tribune,* May 20. http://www.chicagotribune.com/lifestyles/books/chi-narcolitera tura-20140530-story.html

"Tragic Realism: The Rise of Mexican Narcoliterature." *The Conversation.* https:// theconversation.com/tragic-realism-the-rise-of-mexican-narcoliterature-16375

Villalobos, J. 2012. "Against Narcoliterature." *The PEN*, April 19. https://www.englishpen .org/pen-atlas/against-narcoliterature/

Wilson, L. 2017. "The Best Recent Crime Novels—Review Roundup." *The Guardian,* March 31. https://www.theguardian.com/books/2017/mar/31/the-best-recent-crime -novels-review-roundup

Morrison, Toni

American novelist Toni Morrison (1931–), born Chloe Ardelia Wofford, is the multiaward-winning author of several books. Her earliest book, *The Bluest Eye*, published in 1970, was adopted by the City University of New York's Black Studies Department along with other college programs. Morrison's next book, *Sula* (1975), earned her a nomination for the National Book Award, and she earned critical acclaim for her third book, *Song of Solomon* (1977). It was chosen for the Book of the Month Club, an accolade not given to a Black writer since Richard Wright's *Native Son* (1940). Morrison also received a National Book Critics Circle Award for *Son of Solomon*. *Tar Baby* (1981), Morrison's fourth book, was also well received. During the 1980s, Morrison taught English at several college campuses and wrote her first play, *Dreaming Emmett*, about the murder of Black teenager Emmett Till in 1955 by a group of White men. It was first performed at the State University of New York in Albany, where Morrison was teaching at the time. In 1987 Morrison published *Beloved*, which earned her the Pulitzer Prize and the American Book Award in 1988. In 1993, Morrison received the Nobel Prize for Literature, the first Black woman to win that prize, and in 1996 she was selected to give the Jefferson Lecture by the National Endowment for the Humanities, its highest honor. President Barack Obama presented Morrison with the Presidential Medal of Freedom in 2012, and in 2016, she received the PEN/Saul Bellow Award for Achievement in Fiction.

The Bluest Eye is the story of Pecola Breedlove, a Black girl living in small-town Ohio in 1941 who feels she is ugly due to the color of her skin so she prays for blue eyes. It was banned from many schools and libraries because it describes her parents constantly fighting, then Pecola's father, an abusive alcoholic, Cholly, rapes her, leaving her pregnant.

Beloved is the first in what is often considered a trilogy. It is based on the true story of a slave, Margaret Garner, who had escaped and was being pursued by slave hunters. Rather than have her two-year-old daughter raised in slavery, the woman kills her, but is captured before she can commit suicide. *Beloved* tells the story through the eyes of the dead baby, who has come back to haunt the woman and her family. When Morrison failed to win the National Book Award or the National Book Critics Circle Award, 48 Black critics and authors, including poet Maya Angelou, wrote a letter of protest in *The New York Times*. Morrison says that the three books should be read together, not because they follow the same characters but for their themes (Putnam, 2011).

Jazz, the second novel in the trilogy, was published in 1992. It is about a love triangle in New York City during the Harlem Renaissance. *Paradise*, the third novel, was released in 1997. It focuses on the citizens of an all-Black town. Although the trilogy has been popular since each of the books was released, a 1998 film adaptation of *Beloved* starring Oprah Winfrey and Danny Glover gained it even more attention, even though the film was a box office flop.

It was some years after *Paradise* that Morrison published *A Mercy* (2008), about conflicts in the Virginia colonies in 1682. In 2012 she published *Home*, which she dedicated to her son, Slade, who had died during the writing of it. It is set after the Korean War and focuses on a Black veteran who tries to save his sister from undergoing medical experiments by a White doctor. Morrison's 11th novel, *God Help the Child*, was published in 2015. It is about a woman in the fashion industry who has long been tormented by her mother for her skin being too dark.

Violence is a significant factor in the lives of the people Morrison writes about, and many use it as a form of resistance to abuse they have endured. This is especially true when they encounter threats to their children. Sexual abuse of children is a common theme in Morrison's novels, yet the characters are strong and resilient in the face of deep trauma. Morrison said about *The Bluest Eye*: "Little black girls were never taken seriously in books, they were always jokes," Morrison noted.

"But I wanted to read a book where they were taken seriously, so I had to write it" (Collette, 2013).

Morrison, who has never disavowed the label "Black" author, still actively speaks out about racial oppression. In a 2015 interview, she reflected, "You understand, don't you [. . .] that this is not new—it's in the press. Which is good but it's always been that way. I have sons. They have to say 'Sir' if a police officer stops them. You know . . . strategies for getting around" (Hoby, 2015). She expressed concern about the end of President Obama's term and issued her hope that Hillary Clinton would win the 2016 election.

Laura L. Finley

See also: Crucible, The; Native American Literature; *Native Son*; *Their Eyes Were Watching God*; *Things Fall Apart*; *To Kill a Mockingbird*; *Uncle Tom's Cabin*; Walker, Alice

Further Reading

"Banned: The Bluest Eye." 2017. *PBS.* http://www.pbs.org/wgbh/americanexperience /features/banned-bluest-eye/

Collette, M. 2013. "Toni Morrison: 'Goodness' More Powerful than Violence, Hate." *Northeastern University News*, January 22. https://news.northeastern.edu/2013/01/toni -morrison/

Hoby, H. 2015. "Toni Morrison . . . 'I'm Writing for Black People, I Don't Have to Apologise.'" *The Guardian*, April 25. https://www.theguardian.com/books/2015/apr/25 /toni-morrison-books-interview-god-help-the-child

Nurse, D. 2015. "Book Review: Toni Morrison's Violent New Novel." *MacLeans*, April 26. http://www.macleans.ca/culture/books/book-review-toni-morrisons-violent-new -novel/

Putnam, A. 2011. "Mothering Violence: Ferocious Female Resistance in Toni Morrison's The Bluest Eye, Sula, Beloved, and A Mercy." *Black Women, Gender & Families,* 5(2): 25–43.

Native American Literature

Historically, literature about Native Americans tended to rely heavily on stereotypes. Three common stereotypes, which were also used in film, television, and other forms of popular culture, are the bloodthirsty savage, the noble savage, and the half-breed. Popular authors, especially writers of Western novels, used these because they reflected how many thought about Native Americans. The fiction of James Fennimore Cooper, Zane Grey, Charles Brockden Brown, and Owen Wister are all replete with such stereotypes, which served to desensitize readers to the plight of Native Americans in the United States. Literature by Native Americans helps correct some of the misconceptions and includes some highly acclaimed novels. Many of the most famous Native American authors weave their rich culture into their books and shed light on the many forms of violence common on reservations as well as the cultural violence perpetrated by the U.S. government.

Louise Erdrich is a renowned Native American author. Her novel, *The Round House*, tells the story of a Native American teenager whose mother is raped. In trying to figure out who perpetrated the assault on his mother and why, the boy learns a lot about how sexual assault is treated in general and on reservations. Given that Native women are overrepresented as victims of sexual assault, books such as this can shed important light on the topic.

Perhaps the most well-known Native American author is Sherman Alexie. His novel *The Absolutely True Diary of a Part-Time Indian* (2007) tells the story of Junior, a poor 14-year-old living on Spokane Indian Reservation but who attends an all-White school off-reservation. It is partly autobiographical and chronicles Junior's experience as the only non-White kid in the school. He is bullied, gets into a fight with his best friend on the reservation, and develops a crush on a popular girl. He also details the death of family members due to alcoholism, a common problem on reservation land. It is often taught in middle and high schools but has been criticized, challenged, and even banned in some schools due to "excerpts on masturbation" and "vulgarity, racism, and anti-Christian content." Others have claimed that the book is "encouraging pornography" ("Banned . . . ," n.d.). It was banned in most U.S. libraries in 2014, despite winning the National Book Award in 2007. Alexie has responded to the bans, saying that "book banners want to control debate and limit the imagination. I encourage debate and celebrate imagination" (Flood, 2015).

Another Alexie book, *Flight,* is more humorous. It tells the story of a boy who calls himself Zits. He is half Native American and lives in a foster home. The story is centered on violence, however, as Zits develops the power to read people's minds during violent encounters after he opens fire in a bank lobby. He also wrote the screenplay for the film *Smoke Signals* (1998). Alexie has recently faced controversy, as several women have accused him of sexual misconduct (Neary, 2018).

Another renowned Native American writer and poet is Leanne Simpson, author of *Islands of Decolonial Love* (2013). It is a collection of short stories and poetry that addresses the oppression of Native peoples and environmental injustices in the United States and Canada. Simpson is also an activist who has been involved in the indigenous rights group Idle No More.

Indigenous Hawaiian Haunani Kay-Trask is the author of several nonfiction books and poetry collections that address discrimination against and oppression of Native Hawaiians. She also writes about activism against U.S. imperialism.

Sarah Deer is a lawyer, professor, author, and advocate. Her book, *The Beginning and End of Rape: Confronting Sexual Violence in Native America* (2015), is a collection of essays about the high rates of rape, domestic violence, and sexual trafficking of indigenous people and the destruction of Native justice systems. Deer was a leading voice in the 2013 reauthorization of the Violence Against Women Act, which extended protections to Native American victims of domestic violence.

Brenda Child's work focused on the boarding schools as well as Ojibwe activism. Her book *Boarding School Seasons: American Indian Families, 1900 to 1940* (1998) compiled letters between parents and children to document the trauma experienced by these families and the abuse children endured at the boarding schools.

Leslie Marmon Silko is a novelist, essayist ,and poet. She writes about the Laguna Pueblo and their struggles.

Laura L. Finley

See also: Morrison, Toni; *Native Son*; *Their Eyes Were Watching God*; *Things Fall Apart*; *To Kill a Mockingbird*; *Uncle Tom's Cabin*; Walker, Alice

Further Reading

Beck, A. 2017. "15 Indigenous Feminists to Know, Read, and Listen To." Bitch, September 18. https://www.bitchmedia.org/article/15-indigenous-feminists-know-read-and-listen

"Banned: The Absolute True Story of a Part-Time Indian." n.d. *PBS*. http://www.pbs.org/wgbh/americanexperience/features/banned-absolutely-true-diary-part-time-indian/

Coloumbe, J. 2014. "'The Efficacy of Humor in Sherman Alexie's 'Flight': Violence, Vulnerability and the Post-9/11 World." *Melus, 39*(1): 130–48.

Cotton, L. n.d. "American Indian Stereotypes in Early Western Literature and the Lasting Influence on American Culture." (MA thesis). Waco, TX: Baylor University. https://baylor-ir.tdl.org/baylor-ir/bitstream/handle/2104/5247/Lacy_Cotton_masters.pdf?sequence=1

Flood, A. 2015. "Sherman Alexie Novel Tops List of Books Americans Most Want Censored." *The Guardian*, April 13. https://www.theguardian.com/books/2015/apr/13/sherman-alexie-novel-tops-list-of-books-americans-want-censored-2014

Neary, L. 2018. "'It Just Felt Very Wrong': Sherman Alexie's Accusers Go on the Record." *NPR,* March 5. https://www.npr.org/2018/03/05/589909379/it-just-felt-very-wrong-sherman-alexies-accusers-go-on-the-record

Whitehouse, P. C. 2016. "Violence and Frontier in Twentieth Century Native American Literature." (PhD dissertation). Warwick, UK: University of Warwick.

Native Son

Native Son (1940) is a novel written by the Black American author Richard Wright. It is set in the south side of Chicago in the 1930s and follows the protagonist, 20-year-old Bigger Thomas. It has been both applauded and criticized for its depiction of crime and criminal justice, or injustice, for Black men. Although it was written decades ago, those themes still resonate today.

Bigger Thomas lives in a run-down apartment with his brother, sister, and mother. The book opens with a violent chase after a rat in the home. Later that day, Bigger sees Mr. Dalton for a new job that he needs to support his family. Before the interview he tells his friend Gus in the poolroom that he feels whites will do something terrible to him. They and two other friends, G. H. and Jack, plot how to rob a White man, and even though they are all scared none admit it to each other. Bigger and Gus go to a movie, then Gus attacks Bigger and they fight, so the planned robbery is off.

Bigger gets the job with Mr. Dalton but is unsure how to behave in front of the wealthy White man and his blind wife, even though they try to be kind to him. He is intimidated by their daughter, Mary, who is a communist and belongs to a union. That night, Bigger drives Mary to meet her communist boyfriend, Jan. They invite him to join them and are nice, but he feels uncomfortable, as he knows he is simply supposed to be their chauffer. Jan and Mary get drunk and make out in the back seat, and Bigger has to carry Mary to her bedroom when they get home. He can't resist the temptation and kisses her just as Mrs. Dalton enters. He is scared she will know what he is doing, despite being blind, so he covers Mary's face with a pillow, accidentally suffocating her. He decides to tell everyone that Jan took her into the house that night, then determines he should hide the body so he decapitates it and tries to put it in the house's furnace.

Bigger goes back to work but is acting oddly, and his girlfriend, Bessie, suspects he was involved with Mary's disappearance. Meanwhile, Mr. Dalton has hired a private detective, Mr. Britten, who interrogates Bigger and pits him and Jan against each other. Bigger becomes increasingly upset when he learns that Mr. Dalton owns the rat-infested apartment where his family lives. He writes a fake kidnapping note and slips it under the Dalton's door. They call the police, who come to the house with journalists. Bigger is then ordered to take the ashes from the furnace and make a new fire. Terrified that they will know Mary's body is in there, he pokes around, leaving the room full of smoke. An upset journalist grabs the shovel, pushes Biggers aside, and finds Mary's bones and earring in the furnace. Bigger flees, running to Bessie to confess. She says she's sure the White people will think he raped Mary before killing her. They run together, and while they are in an abandoned building Bigger rapes Bessie then decides to kill her. He runs through the city, alone and with no money. He sees newspapers covering the crime and knows that whites hate him for it; Blacks do as well, as he has shamed his race.

Bigger is finally caught and sent to prison. Jan visits him and offers him an attorney, Max Through these conversations, Bigger starts to reexamine his views of White people. Bigger is found guilty and sentenced to death, although he has come to terms with his fate by the end of the book.

While the novel features violence perpetrated largely by the Black character, Bigger, it also emphasizes that structural violence in the form of racism creates a system whereby whites objectify Blacks. *Native Son* has been applauded as a tool for not only understanding Black violence but also the violence of the law (Tuitt, 2000). Further, *Native Son* introduced much of mainstream America to the ghetto conditions in which many Blacks lived. It was well received, selling 215,000 copies in its first three weeks after publication. At least eight different states have seen bans on the book due to its "violent and sexually graphic" content ("Banned Books that Shaped America," n.d.).

Author James Baldwin criticized *Native Son* as a "[p]amphlet in literary disguise" and argued that the depiction of Bigger Thomas did nothing to transcend stereotypes of Black men. W.E.B. Du Bois criticized Wright for penning such a provocative commentary on race. Wright purposely used exaggerated characters to shock White America, the intended audience, into racial awareness (Matthis & Mishra, 2015).

Laura L. Finley

See also: Morrison, Toni; Native American Literature; *Their Eyes Were Watching God*; *Things Fall Apart*; *To Kill a Mockingbird*; *Uncle Tom's Cabin*; Walker, Alice

Further Reading

"Banned Books that Shaped America." n.d. *Banned Books Week.* http://www.bannedbooks week.org/censorship/bannedbooksthatshapedamerica

Butler, R. 1986. "The Function of Violence in Richard Wright's Native Son." *Black American Literature Forum, 20*(1/2): 9–25.

Matthews, K. 2014. "Black Boy No More? Violence and the Flight from Blackness in Richard Wright's Native Son." *Modern Fiction Studies, 60*(2): 276–95.

Matthis, A., & Mishra, P. 2015. "James Baldwin Denounced Richard Wright's 'Native Son' as a 'Protest Novel.' Was He Right?" *The New York Times*, February 24. https://www.nytimes.com/2015/03/01/books/review/james-baldwin-denounced-richard-wrights-native-son-as-a-protest-novel-was-he-right.html

Nnaemeka, O. 1992. "Richard Wright: Climate of Fear and Violence." *The Western Journal of Black Studies, 16*(1): 14–20.

Tuitt, P. 2000. "Law and Violence in Richard Wright's Native Son." *Law & Critique, 11*(2): 201–17.

"Violence and Identity in Richard Wright's Native Son." n.d. *Bowling Green University Archives.* https://scholarsarchive.byu.edu/cgi/viewcontent.cgi?article=1060&context=english_symposium

1984

In 1949, George Orwell (1903–1950) published *1984*—a novel depicting a fictional dystopian society in Airstrip One, a province of Oceania. The setting of the text was in London, the chief city of Airstrip One, which was subjected to a ruthless, totalitarian government. Orwell was inspired to write *1984* following the dictatorships of Joseph Stalin in the U.S.S.R. and Adolf Hitler in Germany during World War II. In the novel, Orwell aimed to warn the Western world of the dangers of living under the rule of a totalitarian government, something he experienced firsthand. According to the Mid-Continent Public Library, *1984* ranks as high as the fifth most challenged novel of all time. The novel has been banned in several countries since its publication due to its strong sexual content, controversial politics, and vivid depictions of violent themes, including war, rape, and torture.

The novel begins by introducing the protagonist Winston Smith. Winston is employed by the Ministry of Truth and is responsible for revising and distorting historical documents in favor of Big Brother and the Inner Party to manipulate the general public. In this way, anything stated by the Inner Party is irrefutable. The citizens of Oceania, predominately those who work for the government, are closely monitored by telescreens, hidden microphones, and the Thought Police; any subtle form of contempt of the government leads to severe punishment or death. As a form of secret rebellion, Winston acquires a diary and documents his frustrations of working under an oppressive regime. Winston knows that those engaged in counterrevolutionary activities, or *thoughtcrime,* are condemned to death or mysteriously disappear, or *vaporize*, so any nervous expression or tic was a punishable offense. There was no escape from Big Brother.

Later, Winston inconspicuously receives a note from Julia, Winston's love interest, professing her love for him. Love and sexual feelings were ordered to be repressed in this society, thus Winston hallucinated of "smashing a pickax right in the middle of it [Julia's face]" (Orwell, 1950, p. 112). Although forbidden, Winston and Julia planned to meet for several affairs in the country to avoid detection by hidden microphones and telescreens. During one such meeting, Winston expresses to Julia his desire to rape and murder her and "smash her head with a cobblestone" (Orwell, 1950, p. 121). Julia reveals to Winston that she does voluntary work a few evenings a week for the Junior Anti-Sex League despite her lack of belief and frequent sexual encounters with Party members. She also shares with Winston a piece of chocolate that she acquired from the "black market" (Orwell, 1950, p. 121). Ultimately, Winston confides in Julia the same antigovernment sentiment that she has. "I hate purity, I hate goodness. I don't want any virtue to exist anywhere. I want everyone to be corrupt to the bones" (Orwell, 1950, p. 125).

Julia and Winston meet with O'Brien, a member of the Inner Party, and share with him their distaste for the government and their plans to overthrow it. In a book by the founder of the Inner Party, Winston learns about how the Big Brother regime brainwashes the "proles" by engaging in a continuous and fictional war. This continuous warfare, with poverty and mass casualties, prevents the masses from becoming educated and promotes their reliance on the powerful elite. Moreover, the text explains how technology is created to manipulate public opinion and enforce complete loyalty to the State. Shortly afterward, Winston and Julia are arrested by the Thought Police and are both taken to the ironically named Ministry of Love to be tortured into confession.

While incarcerated, Winston and other inmates are subjected to extreme physical and psychological violence and starvation. Winston also learns that O'Brien had betrayed him. Winston confesses to a variety of crimes against the government, including things he didn't do, in order to avoid further torment. When summoned to the infamous Room 101, Winston is brutally tortured by O'Brien. "You have been kicked and flogged and insulted, you have screamed with pain, you have rolled on the floor in your own blood and vomit. You have whimpered for mercy, you have betrayed everybody and everything. Can you think of a single degradation that has not happened to you?" (Orwell, 1950, p. 273). Winston is then strapped to a chair to face his worst fear: rats that were to attack his face. "They will leap onto your face and bore straight into it. Sometimes they attack the eyes first. Sometimes they burrow through the cheeks and devour the tongue" (Orwell, 1950, p. 285). Finally, Winston submits to O'Brien and the Inner Party and denounces his love for Julia. He is then let free. The novel ends with the description of how Winston finally understands the smile on Big Brother's face and that he now loves Big Brother. Winston is no longer a threat to the totalitarian regime; he now believed that two plus two equaled five.

The violent themes depicted in the text were the subject of widespread criticism. In 1950, the novel was banned and burned in the U.S.S.R. for political reasons, but was reintroduced in 1990 after revisions. During the Cold War, the United States underwent a period of challenging and banning the novel, which resulted in a Minnesota teacher being fired for not removing the novel from his reading list. In 1981, the novel was challenged in Jackson County, Florida, for being "pro-communist" and containing "sexually explicit content." In 2017, a Jefferson County,

Idaho parent challenged the novel citing "violent, sexually charged language." As of September 26, 2017, the administration determined that the novel did support the content standards for the government course ("Officials: No, the Book '1984' . . . ," 2017). Presently, *1984* is ranked number nine on the American Library Association's Banned and/or Challenged Books list.

In June 2017, a theatrical version of *1984* debuted on Broadway. Olivia Wilde, Tom Sturring, and Reed Birney starred as Julia, Winston, and O'Brien, respectively. Olivia Wilde reportedly suffered a dislocated rib and broken tailbone and Tom Sturring suffered from a broken nose during the earlier runs of the show. Moreover, several audience members have fainted and vomited during the graphic torture scene of Winston in Room 101, and others have been left terrified. Security guards patrolled the theater to manage the audiences' reactions and to prevent fights.

Despite the controversy, *1984* has played a prominent role in American popular culture. The novel has inspired music, television shows, movies, books, and art. Artists such as Marilyn Manson, David Bowie, Coldplay, and Rage Against the Machine have depicted elements of the novel in their music such as Big Brother, the Thought Police, Julia, and two plus two equals five. *Big Brother*, a U.S. television series, was also inspired by *1984.* The show involves contestants who are frequently under surveillance and have no connection to the "outside world" who complete tasks for their chance to win a grand prize. Moreover, *N1984ineteen Eighty-Four* has also inspired a variety of texts to include Anthony Burgess's *1985* and Graham Gardner's *Inventing Elliot*.

In early 2017, *1984* was sold out on Amazon following the inauguration of President Donald Trump. President Trump's counselor, Kellyanne Conway, stated that Sean Spicer used "alternative facts," a reference to a technique that the government in the book used to control the truth, when he made statements regarding the audience at President Trump's swearing-in ceremony. This event has catalyzed a wave of nervous readers during a time when fake news and media reports have infiltrated American society much like Orwell predicted in 1949.

In summary, despite the violent themes depicted in *1984,* including physical torture, psychological manipulation, rape, and explicit sexual content, the novel still remains a significant contribution to the American public school system and society overall.

Natalie Sosa-Ortiz

See also: Brave New World; Dystopian Young Adult Literature and Film; *Fahrenheit 451*; *Mad Max* Films; Vonnegut, Kurt

Further Reading

American Library Association. n.d. "Banned and/or Challenged Books from the Radcliffe Publishing Course." http://www.ala.org/Template.cfm?ContentID=136590&Section =bbwlinks&Template=%2FContentManagement%2FContentDisplay.cfm

Banned Library. 2017. "Banned 79—Nineteen Eighty-Four (1984) by George Orwell." http://www.bannedlibrary.com/podcast/2016/12/28/nineteen-eighty-four-1984-by -george-orwell

Larkin. A. 2017. "Stage Version of '1984' Makes Audiences Faint, Vomit, Scream." *CNN*, June 26. http://www.cnn.com/2017/06/26/us/1984-broadway-opening-trnd/index .html

"Officials: No, the Book '1984' Has Not Been Banned at East Idaho High School." 2017. *Idaho State Journal*, September 26. https://idahostatejournal.com/news/local /officials-no-the-book-has-not-been-banned-at-east/article_ed0afc07-8450-5103 -bb34-1ae168101722.html

Orwell, G. 1950. *Nineteen Eighty-Four.* New York: Signet Classics.

Poe, Edgar Allan

American poet, writer, editor, and literary critic Edgar Allan Poe (1809–1849) is best known for the macabre. He is considered the first horror writer, although his work included science fiction and detective fiction elements as well. He is also considered the first American to try to make a living as an author, which did not go particularly well during his lifetime. Part of the problem was that copyright law was weak, so publishers often produced unauthorized copies of his work for which he made no money.

A significant influence in Poe's life was in 1935, when he married his 13-year-old cousin, Virginia Clemm, when he was 26. Throughout his life he struggled with alcoholism and depression, and he was especially distraught when Virginia died of consumption, today called tuberculosis, in 1947. Poe was found delirious in the streets of Baltimore two years later and was taken to the hospital, where he died. His death remains a mystery.

Poe's "The Murders in the Rue Morgue" is considered to be the first modern detective story. It was published on April 20, 1841. It features a giant ape with horrifying teeth, a killer of women. Feminists have critiqued his work as misogynistic, although surely it was a reflection of the time. Some even blamed Poe for inspiring Jack the Ripper or of being a killer himself. Poe's narrators are always men, most of whom are damaged or traumatized. His "Tell-Tale Heart," considered a classic today, was rejected by the *Boston Miscellany* before *The Pioneer* paid $10 for it. It is a brutal tale of a man's eye that is so hideous that it drives the narrator to murder.

His first horror story, "Berenice" (1835), is about a man who is obsessed with his late-wife's teeth so he digs them up from her grave. Yet, sadly, she was not actually dead but instead had been buried alive. Poe was likely influenced by a story about grave diggers who were caught stealing the dentures of corpses in 1833. In "The Fall of the House of Usher" (1839), Poe tells the story of a man who disposes of the body of his twin sister in their ancestral home, another nod to real-life incidents. "The Pit and the Pendulum" (1842) is about torture during the Spanish Inquisition, where those accused of heresy would be tortured until they confessed. "The Masque of the Red Death," released the same year, is about a plague that is killing peasants in gruesome fashion. It was likely influenced by Poe's survival of the cholera epidemic of 1832. A popular topic for Poe was being buried alive, one he visited at least five times, including in his 1844 story "The Premature Burial." Poe was a master of odd deaths, like the narrator's wife in "The Black Cat" (1843), whose head is split open by an axe and the body enclosed in the wall of a cellar. The old man in "Imp of the Perverse" (1845) dies from inhaling fumes in an unventilated room. In "Hop-Frog" (1849), the King, dressed in an ape costume, is winched and burned alive.

Poe's work has influenced other major artists, including the Sherlock Holmes stories and director Alfred Hitchcock. There are also Poe societies and museums around the world. There are more than 170 film and television adaptations of Poe's works (Edgar Allan Poe, 2008). Poe is also referenced in other popular culture, including the movies *The Crow, The Lost Boys, Last of the Mohicans, Nightmare Before Christmas,* and more. A 2012 movie called *The Raven* featured John Cusack as Poe. It is a fictional plot but one that plays on Poe's love of the macabre as well as his romanticism.

Laura L. Finley

See also: Call of the Wild, The; *Crucible, The*; Hitchcock Alfred; King, Stephen; *Murder, She Wrote*

Further Reading

"Edgar Allan Poe." 2008. *The Guardian,* July 22. https://www.theguardian.com/books/2008/jun/12/edgarallanpoe

Kennedy, J. 2001. *Historical Guide to Edgar Allan Poe.* New York: Oxford University Press.

Lenman, J., Frost, A., & Kynvin, J. 2012. "Edgar Allan Poe Death Scenes—Graphic." *The Guardian,* August 7. https://www.theguardian.com/books/graphic/2012/aug/07/edgar-allan-poe-death-graphicSemtner, C. 2014. "13 Haunting Facts about Edgar Allan Poe's Death." *Biography.com*, October 6. https://www.biography.com/news/edgar-allan-poe-death-facts

Telegraph Reporters. 2016. "Edgar Allan Poe: The Master of Horror Writing." *The Telegraph,* April 20. www.telegraph.co.uk/books/authors/edgar-allan-poe-the-master-of-horror-writing/

Scandinavian Crime Novels

Some of the most popular crime fiction novels in the 2000s have been written by Scandinavian novelists. These authors tell interesting and sordid tales that are internationally popular, but that critics say overestimate the amount of violent crime in Scandinavian countries. Scandinavian countries are known for their low rates of violent crime, and Sweden, Denmark, and Norway routinely rate among the most peaceful countries on the planet.

One of the most famous authors of recent times is the late Stieg Larsson, author of *The Girl with the Dragon Tattoo* series featuring protagonist Lisbeth Salander. This series was tremendously popular due to the complex and interesting storylines. Salander is a powerhouse in that she is terrifically smart yet socially awkward, due to the abuse she witnessed and experienced as a child and as a teen. She teams with reporter Mikael Blomqvist to help solve a mysterious death in the first book, *The Girl with the Dragon Tattoo* (2005), and in subsequent books more is revealed about how she came to be so intense and damaged and why she is so eager to seek revenge on the many men in her life who have hurt her. Although the series sheds light on why Salander is the way she is, it makes clear that as a protagonist, she is not hesitant to use violence. She breaks into the home of the man who is responsible for her becoming a ward of the state, and since he assaulted her, she violently assaults him and carves into his body disturbing comments as a means of retribution. Other books in the series include *The Girl Who Played with Fire* (2006) and *The Girl Who Kicked the Hornet's Nest* (2007). Larsson died of a heart attack in 2004, just before the first book was published in Sweden. Found notes for other books were then released as *The Girl in the Spider's Web* (2015) and *The Girl Who Takes an Eye for an Eye* (2017) by David Lagercrantz. The series raises attention to issues of domestic violence, sexual trafficking, and police and institutional corruption. Before authoring the series, Larsson was a journalist specializing in right-wing extremism and neo-Nazism, which definitely influenced the series. Throughout the books Larsson integrates statistics about domestic violence and sexual assault in Scandinavia. The first book was adapted for film in 2011, with Rooney Mara starring as Lisbeth Salander.

Jo Nesbø is another best-selling Scandinavian author. His novels, which are centered on rogue police officer Harry Hole, feature complex plots, brutal murders, and police corruption. Hole is a complicated character, as he suffers from drug and alcohol addiction and gets into trouble frequently, but his rogue actions are often effective when more traditional efforts are not. Hole is not afraid to use violence, although it is always presented as justified in order to apprehend a violent criminal. There are 11 books in the Harry Hole series. Nesbø has also written other crime thrillers. In 2017, a film adaption of Nesbø's book *The Snowman* was released, starring Michael Fassbender as Harry Hole. *The Guardian* film critic Peter Bradshaw called it "a serviceable, watchable thriller, with very gruesome images, coagulating around psychopathologies of father obsession and son obsession" (Bradshaw, 2017).

Karin Fossum, first a poet, is the author of a successful series of novels based on a police inspector, Konrad Sejer. There are 13 books in the series, which focus on various violent crimes in Norway. Fossum has been called "the queen of crime" in that country, and her main character, Sejer, is different from many crime novel protagonists in that he is a mild-mannered widower who is unfailingly polite and appreciates order. Like other Scandinavian crime novels, Fossum's series calls attention to social issues like class inequality, immigration, and sexism.

Other popular Scandinavian authors include Henning Mankell, Arnaldur Indridason, Hakan Nesser, and Sjowall and Wahloo, a husband and wife team.

Laura L. Finley

See also: King, Stephen; Mexican Crime Novels; *Murder, She Wrote*; Rape Films; *Serial*

Further Reading

Bradshaw, P. 2017. "Fassbender Plays It Cool in Watchable Jo Nesbø Thriller." *The Guardian*, October 12. https://www.theguardian.com/film/2017/oct/12/the-snowman-review-michael-fassbender-tomas-alfredson-jo-nesbo

Crace, J. 2009. "Move Over, Ian Rankin." *The Guardian*, January 22. https://www.theguardian.com/books/2009/jan/23/scandinavian-crime-fiction

The Economist Staff. 2010. "Inspector Norse." *The Economist*, May 11. http://www.economist.com/node/15660846

Guttridge, P. 2008. "Let's Play Corpse and Robbers." *The Guardian*, January 6. https://www.theguardian.com/books/2008/jan/06/fiction.features

Rich, N. 2009. "Scandinavian Crime Wave." *Slate*. http://www.slate.com/articles/arts/culturebox/2009/07/scandinavian_crime_wave.html

Shakespeare, William

William Shakespeare is arguably the world's most famous English writer. Shakespeare was born on April 23, 1564, in Stratford-upon-Avon, England. He began his successful career by 1585. His early writings consisted of mainly comedies and histories. He then converted into writing the darker style of tragedies. In regard to literature, a tragedy is a "branch of drama that treats in a serious and dignified style the sorrowful or terrible events encountered or caused by a heroic individual" (Conversi & Sewall, 2017). Some of Shakespeare's most famous tragedies are *Romeo and Juliet* and *Othello.*

While Shakespeare's works are undoubtedly some of the best works in literature of all time, they tend to have an underlying theme of violence. His tragedies showed acts of violence on many levels, including warfare, rape, murder, suicide, and mutilation. This use of violence operates on multiple levels, including intrapersonal, interpersonal, institutional, and societal.

Shakespeare's tragedies are commonly taught to students of all ages throughout the world. But there is a huge issue concerning whether students should be taught literature with such content. Whereas some scholars have attacked the use of violence in Shakespeare's work, some have defended it as a representation of the historical period. He was simply informed by his life experiences in the 16th century. Some scholars argue it is a learning and deterring mechanism, stating that "his heroes make free choice and [are] free to turn back, but they move toward their doom relentlessly" (Conversi & Sewall, 2017).

Shakespeare lived during and is often associated with the Elizabethan era, between 1558 and 1603, while Queen Elizabeth I reigned. Queen Elizabeth took the throne following the culmination of the English Reformation, which was a religious and political movement in which the Church of England wanted to break away from the authority of the Roman Catholic Church. During this time, many violent outbreaks occurred. People were persecuted over their religious and political affiliations.

The Elizabethan era is also referred to as the "Golden Age" or English Renaissance due to a rebirth of culture, literature, and the arts. The article, "Women, Violence, and English Renaissance Literature," "maintains that the Renaissance shift from violence and militarism to verbal artistry precipitates male frustrations that vented themselves into violence against women that was both literary and real" (Ahern, 2003, p. 722). These tragedies just "legitimize violence and negatively stereotype women" (Deats, 1991, p. 79).

Shakespeare brought to light the issues of domestic violence during the era in his writing of *Othello.* Othello is married to Desdemona. Roderigo, who is a suitor of Desdemona's, becomes very angry and jealous over the marriage and seeks revenge. He goes out on a mission to convince Othello that Desdemona has been unfaithful to him. Although untrue, Othello becomes fully convinced of her infidelity after Roderigo's extreme scheme. They even go as far as to deem Desdemona as a "whore." Othello feels so betrayed that one night he stands over his wife who was lying in bed and smothers her to death. Shortly after, Othello learns that her infidelity was false, and he cries in despair and stabs himself out of guilt and sorrow.

Although written hundreds of years ago, the accounts in this story are not unlike the domestic violence epidemic that society is facing today. According to The National Coalition Against Domestic Violence, 72 percent of all murder-suicides involve an intimate partner. Out of these victims, 94 percent are female (NCADV, n.d.). Domestic violence and abuse go far beyond homicide, including the violent acts of rape; assault; stalking; and financial, verbal, and psychological abuse. The issue is so large because "domestic violence is prevalent in every community, and affects all people regardless of age, socioeconomic status, sexual orientation, race, religion or nationality" (NCADV, n.d.). One in three women and one in four men have been physically abused by an intimate partner, and these statistics shall not be desensitized.

Another famous tragedy by Shakespeare is *Romeo and Juliet,* a story about two star-crossed lovers living in the northern Italian city of Verona. Although it is one of the most famous and well-known love stories, *Romeo and Juliet* includes a great deal of violence. To begin, Verona itself has a history of violence due to territorial and power struggles. The Romans, Etruscans, Gauls, Carthaginians, and many others had fought many battles and wars over this.

In Verona live the Montague and the Capulet families. Romeo is a Montague, and Juliet is a Capulet. These two families have had a deep hatred and have feuded for centuries. The hatred is so deep that members of each household are ready to kill at any moment. The story begins with a brawl between the family's servants, which sets the tone for the relationship. Initially, Romeo was in love with another woman named Rosaline. He finds out that she was going to be at a party and decides he must go see her. The party is at the Capulets' home, so Romeo must attend disguised in full costume. When he gets to the party, he sees Juliet and they immediately fall in love.

Due to this feud, Romeo and Juliet's love is absolutely forbidden. The two lovers decide they cannot live without each other and devise a plan to run away from Verona together. Juliet, with the help of the Friar, drinks a potion that will cause her to appear dead, but she will actually wake up within two days. At that point Romeo is supposed to meet her in the vault, and they will run away together. Unfortunately, Romeo did not receive the letter that contained full disclosure of the plan. When he arrives at the vault, he assumes Juliet is truly dead. Romeo decides there is no way he can live without Juliet and drinks poison so he will die and they will be together forever. After he dies, Juliet wakes up. When she sees Romeo's dead body lying there, she stabs herself and takes her own life.

In a sense, the story of *Romeo and Juliet* has romanticized and dramatized the use of violence. There is something enticing about a forbidden relationship and two individuals going against their family's wishes, all in the name of love. At the end of the story, the Montagues and Capulets decide they will end the feud, yet it has taken the death of their two children to do so. *Romeo and Juliet* has captured the attention of so many that is has been replicated and reenacted several times.

Other violent Shakespeare plays include *Titus Andronicus, Macbeth, King Lear*, and *Julius Caesar*.

Although Shakespeare's portrayal of violence can be attributed to a number of different historical factors, it still causes controversy today. After five centuries, much of the violence featured in Shakespeare's literature is similar to the issues our society has today.

Laura L. Finley

See also: Ancient Greek Literature and Culture; *Game of Thrones*

Further Reading

Ahern, S. 2005. "Women, Violence, and English Renaissance Literature: Essays Honoring Paul Jorgensen." *Renaissance Quarterly, 58*(2), 722.

Barish, J. 1991. "Shakespearean Violence: A Preliminary Survey." In *Themes in Drama: Violence in Drama,* 101–121.

Branam, H. 2016. *William Shakespeare.* Salem, MA: Salem Press Biographical Encyclopedia.

Conversi, L. W., & Sewall, R. B. 2017. "Marlowe and the First Christian Tragedy." *Britannica,* April 21. https://www.britannica.com/art/tragedy-literature/Marlowe-and-the-first-Christian-tragedy

Jennifer, F. 2013. "'O Blood, Blood, Blood': Violence and Identity in Shakespeare's 'Othello.'" *Medieval & Renaissance Drama in England,* 240.

Munson Deats, S., & Tallent Lenker, L. 1991. "From Pedestal to Ditch: Violence against Women in Shakespeare's Othello." *The Aching Hearth: Family Violence in Life and Literature,* 79–93.

National Coalition Against Domestic Violence (NCADV). n.d. https://ncadv.org/statistic

Shaw, R. L. 2004. "Making Sense of Violence: A Study of Narrative Meaning." *Qualitative Research in Psychology, 1*(2), 131–51. doi:10.1191/1478088704qp009oa

Steinbeck, John

John Ernst Steinbeck, Jr. (1902–1968) was an American author who wrote 27 books. This includes 16 novels, 6 nonfiction books, and 2 short story collections. His most widely known books are *Tortilla Flats* (1935), *Of Mice and Men* (1937), *Cannery Row* (1945), *East of Eden* (1952), and *The Grapes of Wrath* (1939), for which he won a Pulitzer Prize. Steinbeck also won the 1962 Nobel Prize in Literature.

Most of Steinbeck's books are set in central California and feature working-class protagonists who struggle with various injustices. He has been applauded for his efforts to draw attention to the marginalized and dispossessed, generating empathy for not just people but also for the environment.

Of Mice and Men is one of Steinbeck's most popular books and is based on his own experience as a migrant worker. It tells the story of George Milton and Lennie Small, migrant workers during the Great Depression. George is small and intelligent and he takes care of Lennie, who is a giant of a man with a mild mental disability. Lennie worships George. Lennie loves small animals but often does not realize his own strength so accidentally kills them, which frustrates George. The two are hired by a ranch, with George initially saying that they were cousins. Over time, he reveals to another worker, Slim, that they are not actually cousins and that they have had to leave other positions because Lennie got them in trouble. They were fired from their last job because Lennie touched a woman's dress and was accused of rape. The two dream of having some land of their own, but circumstances always work against them. On the ranch is Curley, their boss's aggressive son, and his wife, to whom Lennie is attracted. At one point Curley attacks Lennie, who crushes his fist, but otherwise George is starting to trust him more and begins leaving him alone while he goes into town with the other ranch hands. Curley's wife continues to flirt with the men and especially Lennie, then threatens to have him lynched. The next day, Lennie accidentally kills his new puppy while stroking it. Then, the wife comes in and lets Lennie stroke her hair, but gets upset and, again not realizing what he is doing, Lennie breaks her neck then runs away.

George rushes to find Lennie, knowing that they'd both be in trouble if the other ranch hands got to him. Knowing they will never realize their dreams, George kills Lennie moments before Slim and the others reach them.

Of Mice and Men was well received and was adapted to film in 1939 and 1992. The 1992 film starred Gary Sinise as George and John Malkovich as Lennie. Yet it has been challenged many times, with critics complaining about "profanity," "morbid and depressing themes," and the author's alleged "anti-business attitude." Others have called it "derogatory towards African Americans, women, and the developmentally disabled" (Scales, 2017).

The Grapes of Wrath (1939) is also set in the Great Depression. It focuses on the Joads, a poor family of tenant workers who are forced from their Oklahoma home due to economic woes. They hit the road to California with other "Okies" and a preacher named Casy, in search of work and a better life. The grandma and grandpa both die along the treacherous road west. When the Joads get there they find California awash with workers in need of jobs and they are treated very poorly. Conditions in the migrant camps are horrific. Casy becomes a labor organizer and tries to start a union and is brutally beaten during a strike. Tom Joad, who had only recently been released from prison for homicide, kills Casy's attacker then flees.

The Grapes of Wrath was also well received, earning Steinbeck a Pulitzer Prize and a National Book Award. It also helped bring the La Follette committee to California to investigate migrant housing conditions. It has sold more than 14 million copies. It was not entirely applauded, however, as the Associated Farmers of California called it a "pack of lies" and "communist propaganda" (Chilton, 2015). It was banned for a short time by Joseph Stalin in the Soviet Union, because the ruling Communist Party "was troubled by the thought that it showed that even the most destitute Americans could afford a car" (Chilton, 2015). Steinbeck was put under FBI surveillance and received death threats. Many libraries banned the book, and some towns even hosted book burnings. Darryl Zanuck purchased the film rights for *The Grapes of Wrath* for $75,000 but decided to hold the premiere in New York instead of California out of safety concerns. The film, directed by John Ford, received glowing reviews. Steinbeck applauded Henry Fonda's performance as Tom Joad, and Steinbeck and Fonda remained friends until Steinbeck died in 1968.

Bruce Springsteen wrote a song in 1995 called "The Ghost of Tom Joad," which was later recorded by Rage Against the Machine. Other Steinbeck books take on striking workers (*In Dubious Battle*, 1936), the environment (*Sea of Cortez*, 1941), and the Cold War (*A Russian Journal*, 1948).

Laura L. Finley

See also: Call of the Wild, The; *Crucible, The*; Faulkner, William; *Lord of the Flies*; Vonnegut, Kurt

Further Reading

Chilton, M. 2015. "The Grapes of Wrath: 10 Surprising Facts about John Steinbeck's Novel." *The Telegraph*, September 16. http://www.telegraph.co.uk/books/authors/john -steinbeck-grapes-of-wrath-what-you-should-know/

Scales, J. 2017. "Banned: Of Mice and Men." *PBS*, September. http://www.pbs.org/wgbh /americanexperience/features/banned-of-mice-and-men/

Shillinglaw, S. 2014. "The 13 Best John Steinbeck Books." *Publisher's Weekly,* April 14. https://www.publishersweekly.com/pw/by-topic/industry-news/tip-sheet/article /61688-the-13-best-john-steinbeck-books.html

Their Eyes Were Watching God

Black novelist and writer Zora Neale Hurston (1891–1960) wrote the novel *Their Eyes Were Watching God* in 1937. It was written during the Harlem Renaissance era, which was a time of social and cultural explosion for Black Americans. The novel gradually became popular in Black American literary history. It was inspired by Hurston's personal life experiences of love, finding her identity, and overall emotional distress. In 2005, the novel inspired the film with the same title starring the award-winning actress, Halle Berry. It has been praised as a feminist novel because of how the main character (Janie Crawford), a beautiful young Black woman, goes through many trials and tribulations in her life to finally gain her confidence and find her voice in the end.

Throughout the novel, *Their Eyes Were Watching God* covers various themes that tie into violence. Domestic violence, sexism, coercion, anger, and verbal and physical abuse are some of the themes found in the book. Janie Crawford's story begins to unfold at the age of 16, when her grandmother forces her to marry an older man, a farmer named Logan Killicks. Her grandmother wanted her to have the life and opportunities that she never had and was confident that Mr. Killicks would be able to provide stability and security for Janie. Despite Janie's reluctance, she gave in to her grandmother's request and married the farmer. She was miserable and completely unhappy due to Logan verbally abusing her by calling her spoiled, ugly, and useless day after day. He then treats her like a mule anytime that she complains and refuses to help him work on his farm. While Janie experienced painful physical abuse, the novel clearly shows how domestic violence occurs in different ways. Janie was mistreated both verbally and physically, which affected her self-esteem and her overall mental health.

Janie meets another man named Joe Starks, and they run off to get married and move to Eatonville, Florida. Just when Janie thought that she was escaping from trouble and suffering, it became even worse for her. Joe became well known in the community very quickly and was elected mayor. His position of power and respect in the community had a negative impact on his marriage with Janie. He publicly humiliates her by controlling what she says and does. He forces her to cover her hair and serve him as if she was a slave.

Throughout Janie's marriages she plays the role of a submissive and compliant wife. She continues to endure emotional, physical, and psychological effects in her relationships. Janie's third marriage, to "Tea Cake," seemed like it was going to be the love affair that she always wanted, but this, too, was another traumatizing event for Janie. She runs off with him, and they relocate to the Everglades. Tea Cake becomes jealous and beats her. Janie stays in the relationship because of the love that she has for Tea Cake and even realizes that she, too, became jealous when another woman took interest in Tea Cake. Janie ends up killing him in an act of self-defense because he tried shooting her first. "In Janie Mae Crawford, Hurston rejects 19th- and early 20th-century stereotypes for women and creates a protagonist who though silenced for most of her life ultimately finds her own voice" ("National Empowerment for the Arts Big Read," n.d.).

From the beginning of the book, Janie flashes back and shares her story of these marriages with a friend named Phoeby back home in Eatonville. Her motive to share these relationships was to express how relationships can go through obstacles. There are still opinions about what the title of the novel means, but the main concept seems to be that Black Americans (including Janie) during this time were in darkness because of the maltreatment that they encountered, but their eyes were still watching God.

Hurston wrote this novel in Haiti while studying an African religious practice, writing it over just seven weeks. Zora Neale Hurston's relationship with one man in particular was her inspiration for the story. Hurston did not originally receive positive reviews, but the novel was "rediscovered" in the 1970s. Many Black authors during the Harlem Renaissance felt that Hurston oversimplified the Black characters in this novel. Despite Hurston's struggle to get her novel published, she received positive feedback for the style of writing and dialect and won a Guggenheim Fellowship.

The book sold fewer than 5,000 copies before its rediscovery. Nonetheless, today, it is recognized as Zora Neale Hurston's most influential and powerful piece of literature and often listed as reading for high school students.

Francesca Gerard

See also: Morrison, Toni; Native American Literature; *Native Son*; *Things Fall Apart*; *To Kill a Mockingbird*; *Uncle Tom's Cabin*; Walker, Alice

Further Reading

Department of Justice. 2006. "Women of Color Network Facts & Stats: Domestic Violence in Communities of Color." June. http://www.doj.state.or.us/wp-content/uploads/2017/08/women_of_color_network_facts_domestic_violence_2006.pdf

Kamara, A. 2017. "Their Eyes Are Watching God: Critical Reception." *Emory Scholar Blog*, February 21. https://scholarblogs.emory.edu/eng210zoranealehurston/2017/02/21/their-eyes-are-watching-god-critical-reception/

"National Empowerment for the Arts Big Read." n.d. https://www.arts.gov/partnerships/nea-big-read/their-eyes-were-watching-god

Tasharofi, P. 2014. "Domestic Violence in Zora Neale Hurston's Their Eyes Were Watching God: A Feminist Reading." *International Journal of Applied Linguistics and English Literature*, 3(4), 120–27.

Things Fall Apart

Writer Chinua Achebe (1930–2013) published *Things Fall Apart* in 1958 to depict both the pre- and post-colonial life of the Igbo society in Umuofia—a fictional village in Nigeria—during the late 19th century. Achebe was inspired to contest the Western (predominately British) perception of Africa as a "primitive" and "barbaric" society "without culture or history" as it was depicted in Joseph Conrad's *Heart of Darkness* (1899). *Things Fall Apart* is considered to be an archetypal African novel despite its original publication in the English language, and has been the subject of criticism due to its depictions of colonialism and violence.

Achebe first depicted what the Igbo society was like prior to the arrival of the British. The novel begins with an elaborate description of Okonkwo, who is a notorious wrestler among the nine villages; Okonkwo's hypermasculine identity is fueled by a fear of being anything like his father, Unoka—a man perceived as "weak" and "feminine" due to his many unresolved debts. Okonkwo was devoid of emotion unless it was anger and was depicted throughout the text as a volatile, fearless character. He expected strict subservience from his three wives and masculinity and strength from his sons—especially Nwoye, Okonkwo's oldest son. Throughout the text, Nwoye is repeatedly physically threatened for exhibiting signs of "weakness" or "femininity." "'Do you think you are cutting up yams for cooking?' he asked Nwoye. 'If you split another yam of this size, I shall break your jaw. You think you are still a child. I began to own a farm at your age'" (Achebe, 1994, p. 32). A later scene depicts Okonkwo and his sons sitting with him in his *obi* telling them "masculine stories of violence and bloodshed" (Achebe, 1994, p. 53). Shortly after that, Nwoye heard that Ikemefuna was to be taken home the following day, and Nwoye "burst into tears, whereupon his father beat him heavily" (Achebe, 1994, p. 57). Ikemfuna is a 15-year-old from a neighboring clan who is to be given up for sacrifice.

Moreover, Okonkwo is reprimanded by the village priest for beating his wife, Ojiugo, during the Week of Peace—a great offense to the gods and ancestors of the Igbo society. Also, to atone for the death of a Umuofian man's wife, Okonkwo intimidates a neighboring village into providing Umuofia with a virgin female and a young lad, Ikemefuna, who would be raised by Okonkwo and later sacrificed. The village elder, Ezeudu, warns Okonkwo to not play any role in the killing of Ikemefuna; however, Okonkwo, out of fear of appearing weak, kills him with a machete despite Okonkwo's fondness for Ikemefuna. Okonkwo and his family are exiled from Umuofia following Okonkwo's accidental shooting of a 16-year-old boy while Okonkwo mourns the loss of his father, Ezeudu, at his funeral. Consequently, Okonkwo's compound, animals, and barn are all demolished in a fire for offending the village's great goddess. In summary, Achebe sought to depict a precolonial society that was civilized where violence and "savagery" are behaviors that are not condoned.

During Okonkwo's exile, British colonialists introduce Christianity into Umuofia. The Christians don't condone the killing of twins (as the Umuofians did due to their cultural beliefs) and were able to acquire many converts—especially women. To Okonkwo's dismay, his oldest son, Nwoye, is among the converts. Okonkwo feels helpless about his inability to preserve his culture during his time in exile. However, upon his return to Umuofia, Okonkwo takes note of how the new religion, government, and trading stores have made Umuofia almost unrecognizable to him. During the annual worship of the earth goddess, Enoch creates a conflict between the clan and the church when he tears off an *egwuwu*'s mask that results in the killing of an ancestral spirit. In retaliation, Enoch's compound is burned down, and the band of *egwuwus* burn down the Christian church (without the intention of harming the Christians). The district commissioner then has the leaders, including Okonkwo, imprisoned, where they are starved, taunted, and shaved as punishment. They can only be released if the village paid a fine of 250 bags of cowries, or else they will be hanged in public. The village pays the White men, and the Umuofian leaders are released from imprisonment.

In a final attempt to preserve their culture, many Umuofians convene in the marketplace the following day to "root out the evil" that has penetrated their land. Suddenly, a White messenger arrives and orders the meeting to cease. In a fury, Okonkwo draws his machete and decapitates the messenger, stares at the dead man, and walks away. The district commissioner then arrives at Okonkwo's compound with soldiers and court messengers, but he finds a small crowd of men instead. After demanding Okonkwo, the district commissioner is led to a tree where Okonkwo has hanged himself. Ironically, the men ask the district commissioner to get Okonkwo down and bury him according to their custom; it is an abomination against the Earth to bury a man who has committed suicide in the Umuofian village. The novel ends with the district commissioner making note of his experiences in Africa and his plans to write a book titled *The Pacification of the Primitive Tribes of the Lower Niger*.

The violent themes portrayed in *Things Fall Apart*, including domestic violence, war, and suicide, have been the subject of literary criticism across the globe. For example, during the 2011–2012 school year, Centennial High School in Burleson, Texas, sought to ban *Things Fall Apart*. The following reasons were cited: violence or horror; politically, racially, or socially offensive; and offensive to religious sensitivities. However, despite the action made against the novel, it is still read in high schools across the United States without restriction.

Things Fall Apart also received criticism for its "marginalization of women." In the novel, Okonkwo is depicted as pressing a gun against his wife's head and pulling the trigger (although he purposefully missed) to intimidate his wife. Moreover, Uzowulu was repeatedly beaten during her pregnancy, which resulted in a miscarriage. Achebe also included descriptions of Nneka, who repeatedly gave birth to twins; because twins are condemned in Igbo society, the newborn twins were left abandoned to die in the Evil Forest. Despite these violent depictions of female subservience, critics applauded the text for its contextual accuracy. Dr. Grace Igbokwe indicated that these portrayals of violence are very much a reality in African culture—especially when a younger woman is wed to an older man. Igbokwe praised *Things Fall Apart* for its detailed representation of everyday life and indicated that this truth is "what literature is all about" (Igbokwe, 2013).

Students in universities across the United States have demanded what are referred to as "trigger warnings" on class content. Trigger warnings refer to disclaimers alerting an audience of potential traumatic subject matter. Oberlin College recently published an official document advising its faculty members to be mindful of potential triggers to students and to "be aware of racism, classism, sexism, heterosexism, ableism, etc." and to remove material that may trigger students if it does not directly correspond with learning objectives. *Things Fall Apart* was indicated as a text that may trigger students who have been subjected to "racism, colonialism, religious persecution, violence, suicide, and more" (Jarvie, 2014). However, critics have argued that the growing use of trigger warnings has created a university climate of hypersensitivity and paranoia that prevents students from openly discussing conflicting values (Lukianoff & Haidt, 2015). Ultimately, schools have retained *Things Fall Apart,* despite its violent themes, because of its academic value: it "exposes students to a unique point of view and foreign cultural experience and serves to expand their [students'] base of world literature" (National Endowment for the Humanities, 2013).

Finally, many critics have commented on the significance of Okonkwo's suicide. Did this event truly make the Igbo society fall apart? Many Nigerians were offended by Achebe's controversial depiction of an Igbo leader, Okonkwo, ending his life as a metaphor of the decimation of the Igbo culture. Achebe's illustration of things "falling apart" following Okonkwo's suicide was adamantly opposed by many Nigerians who felt that Nigerian students should instead be taught the importance of "holding the center together." *Things Fall Apart* was ultimately banned in Malaysia and Nigeria because of Achebe's depiction of colonialism and its consequences.

In summation, despite the criticism that *Things Fall Apart* received for its portrayal of communal, domestic, and political violence, this novel received worldwide acclaim. Originally published in English, the novel has been translated into more than 50 languages and has sold more than 10 million copies. Although Achebe's work is based on a fictional village in Nigeria, critics appreciate Achebe's authentic narrative about Nigerian life and his attempt to shatter European stereotypes and misperceptions about Africa.

Natalie Sosa-Ortiz

See also: Crucible, The; Morrison, Toni; Native American Literature; *Native Son*; *Their Eyes Were Watching God*; *To Kill a Mockingbird*; *Uncle Tom's Cabin*; Walker, Alice

Further Reading

Achebe, C. 1994. *Things Fall Apart.* New York: First Anchor Books.

ACLU. 2012. "Free People Read Freely: 16th Annual Report in Celebration of National Banned Books Week." *ACLU*, January 10. https://www.aclutx.org/sites/default/files/field_documents/20120110bannedbooksfinal.pdf

Igbokwe, G. 2013. "Chinua Achebe's 'Things Fall Apart': A Timeless Piece." *Sahara Reporters*, April 23. http://saharareporters.com/2013/04/23/chinua-achebe%E2%80%99s-%E2%80%9Cthings-fall-apart%E2%80%9D-timeless-piece

Jarvie, J. 2014. "Trigger Happy." *New Republic*, March 3. https://newrepublic.com/article/116842/trigger-warnings-have-spread-blogs-college-classes-thats-bad

Jefferess, D. 2001. "Violence, Culture, and Politics." *Peace Review, 13*(2), 195–200.

Lukianoff, G., & Haidt. J. 2015. "The Coddling of the American Mind." *The Atlantic*, September. https://www.theatlantic.com/magazine/archive/2015/09/the-coddling-of-the-american-mind/399356/

National Endowment for the Humanities. 2013. "A 'New English' in Chinua Achebe's 'Things Fall Apart.'" *National Endowment for the Humanities*, October 29. https://edsitement.neh.gov/lesson-plan/new-english-chinua-achebes-things-fall-apart

To Kill a Mockingbird

To Kill a Mockingbird is a novel by Harper Lee (1926–2016), published in 1960, the height of the civil rights movement. It is set in Maycomb, Alabama, during the Great Depression. The story is told through the eyes of a six-year-old little girl, Scout. She lives with her brother, Jem, and their father, Atticus Finch, who is a prominent lawyer in town. In the house on the corner there lived a man, Boo Radley, who everyone in the town claimed to be violent and dangerous. Neither Scout, Jem, nor their friend, Dill, who lived across the street, had ever seen this man, but they believed the scary stories about him. People said that Boo ate animals and probably would kill anyone who came close to him. One night as Scout and Jem walked to a school dance, a man attacked them. In the midst of the scuffle another man came to the rescue and saved their lives. Scout had fallen down during the fight but as she got up she saw a man carrying her brother home; she ran back home to find her brother lying in the bed. Her dad, Atticus, asked her who brought Jem home and at first she was confused but then she saw a shadow behind the door. She quickly turned and pointed and said "Hey, Boo." Scout and her father quickly realized that Boo was quiet and concerned, not scary. Boo was mistreated as a child, and his father kept him locked up in the basement. Anytime the kids would sneak over to their lawn, Boo's father would come out with a gun and would occasionally shoot it.

Another part of the plot focuses on a criminal trial. Atticus was a defense attorney in their town and he was asked to take on a case about a rape victim. The rape victim was a White girl, and the man accused of the act was a Black man. Atticus knew it would be hard to win the case but he was willing to try. Throughout the trial, Atticus spent nights in front of the jail reading over the case and also watching over Tom, the defendant, to keep him safe from a lynch mob. The truth was that the victim's father saw her kiss Tom and didn't like it so he was trying to punish her; however, he said the complete opposite during the trial, and both his story and his daughter's kept changing throughout the trial. Atticus proved that the person who assaulted her was left-handed and that Tom couldn't even use his left hand because of an injury several years prior. Despite all the evidence, the jury still found Tom guilty. Tom was killed trying to escape.

Although *To Kill a Mockingbird* is considered a classic, it has long been controversial. It has faced numerous challenges and book bans due to the rape and the language used in it. The American Library Association named it the 21st most banned book of the 2000s (Mosbergen, 2017). It was adapted into a film in 1962 with Gregory Peck starring as Atticus.

The novel was praised for offering a different look at the South. "Her novel gives us a particular point of view of an independent southern woman's voice and we don't have anything quite like that from other southern women writers," said Julia Eichelberger, Professor of Southern Literature at College of Charleston. Former president Barack Obama and his wife, Michelle, commented, "Through the uncorrupted eyes of a child, she showed us the beautiful complexity of our common humanity, and the importance of striving for justice in our own lives, our communities, and our country" (Shapiro, 2016). Yet it is not universally applauded. Novelist Toni Morrison has critiqued *Mockingbird* as yet again emphasizing a "white savior." Colin Dayan of *Al Jazeera* wrote, "The popularity and heart-warming poignancy of *To Kill a Mockingbird* buries the very real activism and resistance of Black citizens in Alabama and throughout the South right at the time that Lee wrote her story" (Spaeth, 2015).

Lee's next book, *Go Set a Watchman*, was written prior to *Mockingbird* but was not published until 2015. Whereas *Mockingbird* shows Atticus Finch as a symbol of courage, morality, and racial equality, *Watchman* depicts Finch, some 20 years later, as a racist who has attended some meetings of the Ku Klux Klan. The book was an instant hit, but many disliked this more complex look at the heroic Finch.

Shanquia Hilson

See also: Falkner, William; Morrison, Toni; Native American Literature; *Native Son*; *Their Eyes Were Watching God*; *Things Fall Apart*; *Uncle Tom's Cabin*; Walker, Alice

Further Reading

Mosbergen, D. 2017. "School District Scrubs 'To Kill a Mockingbird' Because It Makes People Feel 'Uncomfortable.'" *Huffington Post,* October 16. https://www.huffing tonpost.com/entry/biloxi-to-kill-a-mockingbird_us_59e4974ce4b03a7be581e2a8

Shapiro, E. 2016. "Harper Lee: The Impact of 'To Kill a Mockingbird.'" *ABC News*, February 19. http://abcnews.go.com/US/harper-lee-impact-kill-mockingbird/story?id =37055512

Spaeth, R. 2015. "Is To Kill a Mockingbird Racist?" *The Week,* July 17. http://theweek.com /articles/566893/kill-mockingbird-racist

Uncle Tom's Cabin

Uncle Tom's Cabin; or, Life Among the Lowly is a novel by American author Harriet Beecher Stowe. Published in 1852, historians claim that its antislavery message helped prompt the Civil War. Stowe was a teacher at the Hartford Female Seminary and was actively involved with abolitionist efforts. Some 300,000 copies were sold in the United States and 1 million in Great Britain in the first year after publication. *Uncle Tom's Cabin* was the best-selling novel, and the second-best-selling book overall, of the 19th century, following only the Bible. It inspired plays of the same name and was translated into every major language.

Before publication as a book, *Uncle Tom's Cabin* appeared as a serial for 40 weeks in *The National Era,* an abolitionist periodical. Stowe expanded the story for the book. The novel tells the story of Uncle Tom, a Black slave, and through him and other slaves depicts the vileness that is slavery and the ability of humans to overcome. Stowe was inspired by real accounts of the slave experience, including the story of Josiah Henson, a slave who escaped from a Maryland plantation and fled to what is today Ontario, Canada. There he helped other fugitive slaves.

In the novel, Kentucky farmer Arthur Shelby is struggling so he decides they need to sell two slaves: Uncle Tom, who has a wife and children, and Harry, the son of his wife's slave, Eliza. Eliza overhears the plans to sell her son and leaves with him. Tom is sold on a riverboat headed down the Mississippi. On the boat he befriends a White girl, Eva; her father, Mr. St. Clare, buys Tom and moves him with the family to New Orleans. Meanwhile, Eliza meets up with her husband, George Harris, who had previously run away, and they attempt to flee to Canada. They are caught by slave hunter Tom Loker, who George shoots. Eliza insists that they get him medical attention at a nearby Quaker settlement. This kind treatment leads Loker to change his beliefs about slavery.

In New Orleans, after Mr. St. Clare dies, Tom is sold to Simon Legree, a vicious plantation owner. Legree takes Tom and another slave he bought at the auction, Emmeline, to rural Louisiana. Legree orders Tom to whip his other slaves, and Tom refuses, which results in a brutal beating. Legree vows to crush Tom's faith in God, but Tom won't waver. He encourages Cassy, another slave, and Emmeline to leave. When they escape, Legree orders his overseer to kill Tom. As he is dying, Tom professes that he forgives his killers, which humbles them and turns them to Christianity. Too late, George Shelby, the son of Arthur, arrives to buy Tom's freedom. In the end, Cassy and Emmeline meet George Harris's sister, and Cassy discovers that Eliza is her long-lost daughter who had been sold as a child. They all travel to France and then to Liberia, a nation created by former slaves, while George Shelby frees all of his slaves.

Critics point out that *Uncle Tom's Cabin* popularized stereotypes that live on today, including the dark-skinned "mammy," the "pickaninny" children, and especially the "Uncle Tom," or the dutiful servant to a White master. That term has taken on a particularly negative connotation and is used today to refer to Black men who have "sold out," or who act "too White." This notion of Uncle Tom, dramatically different from the portrayal in the book, came into use in the early 1900s (Stuteville, 2005).

Yet Stowe's book is credited with turning the North toward abolition and paving the way for an antislavery president in Abraham Lincoln. *Uncle Tom's Cabin* showcased the love of Black families at a time when they were often portrayed as sex-crazed and violent. Not surprisingly, the book was unpopular in the South, with many authors, politicians, and others issuing responses about the alleged "good" of slavery. And while it galvanized the North, defensiveness may also have rallied the South to secede (Reynolds, 2011). It was a capital offense to own a copy in Kansas. After the Civil War, the book became less popular, until it was reprinted in 1948. It was not very popular during the civil rights era, and fewer history instructors used the text, with some taking issue with the frequent use of racial slurs. The 1970s saw a resurgence, led largely by feminist academics. In addition to showcasing the violence of slavery, reports showed that performances of *Uncle Tom's Cabin* were often met with violence (Frick, 2010).

Some have expressed concern that *Uncle Tom's Cabin* has waned in popularity. In 2004, only 18,000 copies were sold, about half of what were sold in 2001.

Yet Walter B. Hill, Jr., a senior archivist at the U.S. National Archives and Records Administration who specializes in Black history, says, "It is not in any danger of passing out of the American memory. You cannot teach the history of slavery without a reference to *Uncle Tom's Cabin*. It belongs in any discussion on the civil rights movement, which came about in rejection of laws that discriminated against people of color. Those laws were connected to slavery" (Stuteville, 2005).

Laura L. Finley

See also: Morrison, Toni; Native American Literature; *Native Son*; *Their Eyes Were Watching God*; *Things Fall Apart*; *To Kill a Mockingbird*; Walker, Alice

Further Reading

Frick, J. 2010. "The Representation of Violence and the Violence of Representation: *Uncle Tom's Cabin* on the American Antebellum Stage." *New England Theater Journal*, 21–40. http://utc.iath.virginia.edu/interpret/exhibits/frick/frick.html

Reynolds, D. 2011. "Did a Book Start the Civil War? 'Uncle Tom's Cabin' Is a Testament to the Power of Culture." *New York Daily News*, April 11. www.nydailynews.com/opinion/book-start-civil-war-uncle-tom-cabin-testament-power-culture-article-1.112605

Stuteville, G. 2005. "'Uncle Tom' Today: From Slavery to Obscurity." *National Geographic News*, February 17. https://news.nationalgeographic.com/news/2005/02/0217_050218_ngm_uncletom.html

Vonnegut, Kurt

Kurt Vonnegut Jr. (1922–2007) was an American author who published 14 novels, five plays, three short story collections, and five nonfiction books in his 50 years writing. His most famous work is *Slaughterhouse-Five* (1969), an antiwar novel. Like several other novelists who wrote antiwar books, Vonnegut spent some time at war. Rather than wait to be drafted, he joined the Army in March 1943 and was trained to fire howitzers. He was then sent as an intelligence scout with the 106th Infantry Division to the war in Europe and fought in the December 1944 Battle of the Bulge. More than 500 members of the division were killed and some 6,000 were captured by the Germans, including Vonnegut and about 50 other American soldiers. He was sent to a prison camp in Saxony, France, then to Dresden, where he lived in a slaughterhouse and worked in a factory while the city was constantly bombed by Allied forces. Nearly 90 percent of the city's center was destroyed. Vonnegut only survived one fierce attack by hiding in a meat locker three stories underground. After the attack he and others were sent to clean up the bodies in the streets, then were evacuated to Le Havre, France. Vonnegut returned to the United States and was awarded a Purple Heart before being discharged.

The protagonist of *Slaughterhouse-Five* is Billy Pilgrim, who, like Vonnegut, survived the attack on Dresden. The shock of his experience makes Billy "unstuck in time," so he must relive the same experiences day after day. Julia Whitehead, the executive director of the Kurt Vonnegut Memorial Library, says the book is intended to "impress upon readers that we keep making the same mistake and it doesn't have to be that way" (Morais, 2011).

Slaughterhouse-Five was widely read by peace activists during the Vietnam War. In a 1987 interview, Vonnegut said he was determined to write about war without romanticizing it, using humor instead. He criticized war propaganda and romantic depictions of the glory of war. In a 1991 interview, shortly after the Gulf War, Vonnegut said he was saddened by what he saw in America. "We have become such a pitiless people," Vonnegut lamented. "And I think it's TV that's done it to us. When I went to war in World War II, we had two fears. One was we would be killed. The other was that we might have to kill somebody. And now killing is Whoopee. It does not seem much anymore. To my generation, it still seemed like an extraordinary thing to do, to kill" (Vitale, 2011).

It is meant as a critique of war, but ironically, the repeated calls to censor or ban the book strike a chord as well. *Slaughterhouse-Five* has been banned or challenged at least 18 times. A circuit judge in Oakland County, Michigan, called it "depraved, immoral, psychotic, vulgar, and anti-Christian" when it was banned in the Oakland public schools in 1972. The Drake Public School Board in North Dakota burned 32 copies in 1973. The Island Trees school district of Levittown, New York, removed *Slaughterhouse-Five* and eight other books from its high school and junior high libraries, calling it "anti-American, anti-Christian, anti-Semitic, and just plain filthy." This resulted in the *Board of Education v. Pico* case in 1982, in which the U.S. Supreme court ruled 5–4 that the board's restrictions violated the First Amendment (Morais, 2011).

Wesley Scroggins, an associate professor at Missouri State University who home-schools his own children, referred to *Slaughterhouse-Five* as "a book that contains so much profane language, it would make a sailor blush with shame. The 'f word' is plastered on almost every other page. The content ranges from naked men and women in cages together so that others can watch them having sex to God telling people that they better not mess with his loser, bum of a son, named Jesus Christ" (Morais, 2011).

A biography about Vonnegut written by Charles Shields called *And So It Goes* paints a less kind picture of the author. Vonnegut is depicted as cruel to his wives, distant from his children, and angry and depressed. Shields also claims that for all of Vonnegut's comments against war, he had no problem investing in companies that made napalm. Some suggest he was bitter out of survivors' guilt.

Laura L. Finley

See also: Catch-22; Fahrenheit 451; Mad Max Films; 1984; Steinbeck, John; War Films

Further Reading

Chilton, M. 2014. "Banned Books Week Celebrates Kurt Vonnegut." *The Telegraph,* September 23. http://www.telegraph.co.uk/culture/books/booknews/11115041/Banned-Books-week-celebrates-Kurt-Vonnegut.html

Harris, P. 2011. "Kurt Vonnegut's Dark, Sad, Cruel Side Is Laid Bare." *The Guardian,* December 3. https://www.theguardian.com/books/2011/dec/03/kurt-vonnegut-biography

Morais, B. 2011. "The Never-Ending Campaign to Ban 'Slaughterhouse Five.'" *The Atlantic,* August 12. https://www.theatlantic.com/entertainment/archive/2011/08/the -neverending-campaign-to-ban-slaughterhouse-five/243525/

Vitale, T. 2011. "Kurt Vonnegut: Still Speaking to the War Weary." *NPR,* May 31. https:// www.npr.org/2011/05/31/136823289/kurt-vonnegut-still-speaking-to-the-war -weary

Walker, Alice

Alice Malsenior Walker (1944–) is an American novelist, poet, and short story writer best known for *The Color Purple* (1982), for which she won a Pulitzer Prize for Fiction and the National Book Award. Walker also wrote 13 other novels, nine poetry collections, and 12 nonfiction books. She is also an activist who has long spoken out about racial and gender inequality.

Walker's parents insisted that their daughter receive an education despite living as sharecroppers who worked the fields in the Jim Crow era. The family also had a long tradition of storytelling, which influenced Walker to begin writing when she was eight. The Walkers struggled, and in 1952, Alice was accidentally wounded in her right eye by a BB gun fired by one of her brothers. Because the family had no car, it was a week before a doctor could see her, and by that time Alice was permanently blind in that eye. She was stared at and bullied by kids after a layer of scar tissue formed over the eye, making her self-conscious. Walker turned to poetry and writing for solace. She attended Spelman College, a historically Black school in Atlanta, on a full scholarship but then transferred to Sarah Lawrence College in New York, from which she graduated in 1966. Again, Walker faced adversity, having an abortion the summer before her senior year that left her severely depressed. Out of it came her first book of poetry, *Once*, which was published in 1968.

Walker had become interested in the civil rights movement while at Spelman and was particularly inspired by one of her professors, the renowned Howard Zinn, and by meeting Dr. Martin Luther King, Jr. After college she returned to the South and helped with welfare rights campaigns, children's programs, and voter registration drives in Mississippi. She married, had children, and worked as a writer-in-residence at two colleges as well as a consultant on Black history to the Friends of the Children of Mississippi Head Start program. She resumed writing for publication as an editor at *Ms.* magazine. In 1970, Walker published her first novel, *The Third Life of Grange Copeland*, an abusive sharecropper. Her second novel, *Meridian*, published in 1976, is based on Walker's experience in the civil rights movement and focuses on activists in the South.

It was *The Color Purple* in 1982 that really ignited Walker's career. Set in the 1930s and 1940s, it tells the story of Celie, a Black woman who is abused by her father (she later learns he is not her biological father), who twice impregnates her. He takes the kids from her and then marries her off to Albert, who she calls "Mister," who continues to abuse her. Celie is not attractive and is constantly told that, so she lacks confidence. The book is somewhat graphic in its depiction of what can only be called sexual assault, as she by no means enjoys the sexual encounters with her husband. He also routinely beats her and even instructs his children that the best way to get women to behave is to beat them. The only joy in her life is her sister Nettie, but when Celie is concerned that Mister will take advantage of Nettie, she sends her off and Nettie ends up in Africa. Throughout the novel Celie writes letters to Nettie, describing how she is raising Mister's kids, but never receives a response. She learns toward the end that Nettie did write back but that Mister kept the letters from her. As times goes by, the novel introduces two strong Black women, Sofia, who marries Mister's son, Harpo, and Shug Avery, a beautiful singer who is occasionally Mister's mistress and who takes a liking to Celie. Yet even as strong as Sofia is, she, too, is the recipient of violence. When she stands up to the mayor's White wife, she is beaten brutally.

Walker was the first Black woman to win the Pulitzer Prize for Fiction. In 1985, *The Color Purple* was adapted into a film directed by Steven Spielberg, starring Whoopi Goldberg, Danny Glover, and Oprah Winfrey. It was also made into a Broadway musical. Walker explained where the title came from in an interview for National Public Radio:

> Because when I was writing the novel, I lived way in the country in Boonville, California, and I went walking through the redwoods and swimming in the river and noticed that in nature purple is everywhere. And it's interesting because we tend to think that in nature you would see more red, yellow, white, you know, all of those colors. But actually, purple is right there. And in that sense, it's like the people in the novel. You think that they are unusual, that what's happening to them is unusual, but actually it's happening somewhere on your block almost every minute. All the trouble, all of the trials and tribulations of Celie are happening to people all over the planet right now. (Goodman, 2012)

Walker continues to engage in activism and to be an outspoken critique of racism and sexism. On March 8, 2003, which was International Women's Day and the evening before the U.S. invasion of Iraq, Walker was arrested along with 26 others at a protest outside of the White House. In 2009 she traveled to Gaza with the antiwar group Code Pink, where they delivered aid and tried to persuade Israel and Egypt to relinquish their hold on Gaza. She supports the Boycott, Divestment and Sanctions (BDS) campaign against Israel that is designed to pressure the country to afford greater rights to Palestinians.

Laura L. Finley

See also: Crucible, The; Morrison, Toni; Native American Literature; *Native Son*; *Their Eyes Were Watching God*; *Things Fall Apart*; *To Kill a Mockingbird*; *Uncle Tom's Cabin*

Further Reading

Goodman, A. 2012. "Alice Walker on 20th Anniversary of 'The Color Purple': Racism, Violence against Women Are Global Issues." *Democracy Now!,* September 28. https://www.democracynow.org/2012/9/28/alice_walker_on_30th_anniv_of

Priya, K. 2014. "Violence in Alice Walker's *The Color Purple*." *IOSR Journal of Humanities and Social Science, 19*(7), 51–54.

Watkins, M. 1982. "Some Letters Went to God." *The New York Times,* July 25. http://www.nytimes.com/books/98/10/04/specials/walker-color.html

6

Violence in Video Games

Introduction

Scholars, parents, and activists have all expressed concern about both the short- and long-term effects of playing video games, which are widely popular with children and youth, especially boys. An estimated 90 percent of children play video games, and in the age group of 12 to 17, some 97 percent do. It is clear that these games have grown increasingly violent, with studies showing that approximately 85 percent of video games feature violent content (Grossman & DeGaetano, 2014). An exploration of just the titles of the games indicates violent content, as popular games include *Manhunt, Thrill Kill*, and *Mortal Kombat*. First-person-shooter games are among the most popular, bringing in an estimated $5 billion annually (Keim, 2013). Many also feature sexual content, and an estimated one-third of all video games include sexual violence. Research clearly shows a link between playing violent video games and aggression, decreased empathy, moral engagement, and reduced prosocial behavior, but is not entirely clear whether it actually increases violent behavior.

According to Colonel David Grossman, video games were created by the U.S. military in order to improve the "kill ratio" during violent conflicts. After World Wars I and II, the military analyzed how many soldiers fired their weapons and how frequently they did so compared to how many enemy soldiers were killed. They found a significant discrepancy and concluded that soldiers, even those facing an armed enemy, find it difficult to shoot to kill. As such, they would often shoot to wound or even fire warning shots. Over time, the military tried different tactics to increase the kill ratio, and ultimately concluded that the more lifelike the training simulations, the better at killing soldiers became.

With the advent of new technology, video games became more violent and realistic in the 1990s. *Doom,* released in 1992, allowed players to kill simulated people rather than just monsters and demons. The *Duke Nukem* series permitted the shooter, "Duke," to walk through pornography shops and to use posters of scantily clad women as target practice. Advanced players can earn Duke "bonus points" for killing naked prostitutes. *Redneck Rampage* allows users to perpetrate massacres against farmers and farm animals. *Manhunt 2* includes a basement sex club where characters, typically sexy women, are tortured. *Grand Theft Auto* allows players to have sex with prostitutes, then beat them up and run over them with cars. *Call of Duty*, a military-based first-person-shooter game that features scantily clad women, is played almost exclusively by males (80 percent), and 21 percent of that population is ages 10 to 14 (Stanton, 2016).

Many studies have been conducted to test whether playing violent video games or viewing violent movies decreased empathy, as measured by participants' willingness to help others. In one study, participants played either a violent or nonviolent video game and then overheard a staged fight that resulted in (fake) injury. The difference between those who played the violent game and those who played the nonviolent game was not statistically significant, but the violent game players who did agree to help took longer to do so and rated the potential for injury as less serious. In an analysis of 33 studies that involved 3,033 participants, researchers found a statistically significant relationship between video game violence and violent behavior for males, females, children, and adults alike. They also found a temporary decrease in prosocial behavior among those who played violent video games. A 2010 study by researchers with the National Institute of Neurological Disorders found that regular use of violent video games makes youth less sensitive to violence, more accepting of violence, and more likely to commit aggressive acts. A study of sixth- through eighth-grade boys who played *Mortal Kombat* exhibited increased aggressive behavior. Another study in 2004 found that eighth- and ninth-grade boys who played violent video games were more hostile and more prone to get into fights. A 2013 report by the American Psychological Association (APA) found a link between playing violent video games and aggression, but no clear evidence that it leads to actual violent behavior. It reviewed 150 studies and found a general decrease in empathy and prosocial behavior as well. Both the APA and the American Academy of Pediatrics advise parents against allowing youth to play violent video games.

Many of the worst school shooters were avid players of violent video games. For example, Eric Harris and Dylan Klebold, the Columbine killers, as well as Adam Lanza, the man responsible for the Sandy Hook Elementary massacre, were all avid players of violent video games. Harris and Klebold even wrote some code for the game *Doom*. A decade prior, Evan Ramsey, who killed a student and his principal and wounded two others at his Alaska high school, told interviewers that playing *Doom* made it hard for him to see the reality of gun violence, because in the game when you shoot a character he keeps getting back up. Norwegian mass murderer Anders Breivik also played violent video games. He even referred to the game *Call of Duty* as a training simulation. Virginia Tech shooter Seung-Hui Cho was a fan of the violent game *Counterstrike*. Copies of the violent game *Manhunt* were pulled from store shelves after parents blamed it for their son's death in July 2004. It turns out, however, that the copy of the game that was found in a bedroom actually belonged to the victim, Stefan Pakeerah, and not the shooter.

While there are parental advisories on games, many ignore them. Europe has a stricter advisory system. Advocates have been pushing Congress to enact further restrictions. The Entertainment Software Association opposes additional restrictions, calling the data about violence unclear. In 1997, parents of the victims killed by school shooter Michael Corneal filed a lawsuit against several manufacturers of video games. The suit was dismissed in 2001.

In 2011, the Supreme Court considered the constitutionality of California's ban on the sale of specific violent video games to children without parental consent in *Brown v. Entertainment*. The Court ruled 7–2 that the ban violated the First Amendment. In 2005, California had created an act that placed a ban on the distribution of video games to minors due to sexual and violent content. It authorized a $1,000 fine for all retailers found in violation. Before it could be implemented, however, it was contested by people who felt it was unnecessary censorship and too vague.

The case began when California Deputy Attorney General Zackery P. Morazzini appealed a court decision to block the act. He referred to this as a First Amendment issue, arguing that video game content was closely related to obscenity. Further, he noted that a developing brain did not have the capacity to understand that the game was not reality. The court ruled against Morazzini and the state.

In 2007, Arnold Schwarzenegger, governor of California at the time, appealed the 2005 ruling, which became known as the Ninth Circuit Appeal, in the court case *Video Software Dealers Association v. Schwarzenegger*. That court ruled that the law was unconstitutional, noting that the state had no evidence proving that psychological harm or brain damage had occurred in the minors who played violent video games. Schwarzenegger once again appealed the decision in 2009, and was joined by 11 other states interested in enacting similar laws.

Much of the debate before the court centered on comparing video games to movies and books to determine if they deserved the same protections. Currently, there are restrictions on movies and radio, but not on books. Counsel representing the video game industry asserted that video games were similar to graphic and disturbing fantasy books and thereby should not be censored.

Critics contend that many youth and even adults who are avid players of violent video games do not act out violently. They assert that it is other factors such as mental illness and bullying that are the primary cause of an offender's violent behavior. Further, they argue that pointing to violent media absolves offenders from taking responsibility for their own behaviors and is a form of censorship. Some consider the outcry against violent video games to be another moral panic, just like earlier ones about comic books and the role-play game *Dungeons & Dragons*. Additionally, critics contend that youth who choose to play violent video games may have a predisposition toward aggression. Some even argue that playing video games can reduce violence, as it keeps these kids busy. Cunningham, Englestatter, and Ward (2016) looked at crime rates in the weeks following the release of a new violent video game and found that there was no evidence of an increase and perhaps even a slight decrease. Others simply contend that more research is needed in this area.

Further Reading

Anderson, C., & Bushman, B. 2001. "Effects of Violent Video Games on Aggressive Behavior, Aggressive Cognition, Aggressive Affect, Physiological Arousal, and Prosocial Behavior: A Meta-Analytic Review of the Scientific Literature." *Psychological Science, 12*(5), 353–59.

Casey, M. 2015. "Do Violent Video Games Lead to Criminal Behavior?" *CBS News*, August 17. http://www.cbsnews.com/news/do-violent-video-games-lead-to-criminal-behavior/

Cunningham, S., Englestatter, B., & Ward, M. 2016. "Violent Video Games and Violent Crime." *Southern Economic Journal, 82*(4), 1247–65.

Durham, M. 2008. *The Lolita Effect.* Woodstock, NY: Overlook Press.

Grossman, D., & DeGaetano, G. 2014. *Stop Teaching Our Kids to Kill: A Call to Action against TV, Movie, & Video Game Violence.* New York: Harmony.

Jaccarino, M. 2013. "'Training Simulation': Mass Shooters Often Share Obsession with Violent Video Games." *Fox News*, September 12. http://www.foxnews.com/tech/2013/09/12/training-simulation-mass-killers-often-share-obsession-with-violent-video-games.html

Keim, B. 2013. "What Science Knows about Video Games and Violence." *PBS Nova*, February 28. http://www.pbs.org/wgbh/nova/next/body/what-science-knows-about-video-games-and-violence/

Scutti, S. 2016. "Do Video Games Lead to Violence?" *CNN*, July 26. http://www.cnn.com/2016/07/25/health/video-games-and-violence/

Singular, S., & Singular, J. 2015. *The Spiral Notebook: The Aurora Theater Shooter and the Epidemic of Mass Violence Committed by American Youth.* Berkeley, CA: Counterpoint.

Stanton, R. 2016. "Do Video Games Make Children Violent? Nobody Knows—And This Is Why." *The Guardian*, March 9. https://www.theguardian.com/technology/2016/mar/09/do-video-games-make-children-violent-nobody-knows-and-this-is-why

Strenziok, M., Krueger, F., Deshpande, G., Lenroot, R., van der Meer, E., & Grafman, J. 2010. "Front-Parietal Regulation of Media Violence Exposure in Adolescence: A Multi-Method Study." *Social, Cognitive and Affective Neuroscience* (online version). http://scan.oxfordjournals.org/content/early/2010/10/18/scan.nsq079.full

Call of Duty

The *Call of Duty* video game franchise is the most popular war/shooter game in history. This franchise has been making war-based video games since 2003, and as of 2016, had sold over 250 million copies and made over $15 billion. Millions of people have spent billions of dollars in order to get their violent fantasies fulfilled (Crecente, 2014). The *Call of Duty* franchise has been called the most realistic first-person-shooter game in history; a new video game is released every year.

Most *Call of Duty* games have story modes based on events throughout U.S. history. For example, *Call of Duty 4: Modern Warfare* takes place in the Middle East, with U.S. soldiers fighting the Taliban and other terrorist forces. *Call of Duty: Black Ops* is set during the Cold War and includes CIA operations to gain intelligence on enemies.

Many critics of violent video games, and especially of the *Call of Duty* franchise, have stated that this type of violent media has produced disastrous results. One of the most disturbing cases was that of Anders Breivik, who killed 77 people in Norway. He claimed that he trained for the event by playing *Call of Duty* 16 hours a day for 16 months, perfecting his marksmanship and getting comfortable with the idea of killing large numbers of people (Pidd, 2012). The U.S. military has also been known to use this video game to train soldiers for combat.

Another example of how the game is said to promote real-life violence is when Mohamed Merah, a French gunman, killed three soldiers and four civilians.

According to the gunman's wife, he compulsively played *Call of Duty* before going on his killing spree. In the United States, Adam Lanza, who killed 20 children and six adults at Sandy Hook Elementary School in a Newtown, Connecticut elementary school, was obsessed with the *Call of Duty* franchise and the weapons that he could use while playing it. According to several witnesses, the shooter would spend hours locked in the family basement playing *Call of Duty* (Zakarin, 2012).

Another concern is that playing video games like *Call of Duty* has a negative effect on the brain. Researchers at the University of Montreal found that, in their sample of 51 men and 46 women who played *Call of Duty* and other action games for a combined total of 90 hours, the grey matter in the hippocampus area of the brain atrophied, which may be linked to schizophrenia, depression, and Alzheimer's (Roe, 2017).

On the other hand, there are those who claim that this video game and others in general actually help people. Some studies show that *Call of Duty* can help with cognitive simulation, especially if used in moderation, because the games are goal based and therefore they continuously motivate people to stay active and focused. Players also feel good about themselves because they are rewarded for accomplishing goals, improving their problem solving (Walters, 2015).

Laura L. Finley

See also: Doom; Fallout; Half-Life; Portal; Quake

Further Reading

Crecente, B. 2014. "Call of Duty Franchise Tops $10 Billion, Advanced Warfare Sales Not Released." *Polygon*, November 20. https://www.polygon.com/2014/11/20/7253589/call-of-duty-franchise-tops-10-billion-advanced-warfare-sales-not

Pidd, H. 2012. "Anders Breivik 'Trained' for Shooting Attacks by Playing Call of Duty." *The Guardian*, April 19. https://www.theguardian.com/world/2012/apr/19/anders-breivik-call-of-duty

Roe, D. 2017. "Violent, Aggressive Video Games Like 'Call of Duty' May Be Damaging Your Brain." *Men's Health*, August 9. https://www.menshealth.com/health/violent-video-games-damage-brain-call-of-duty

Underwood, K. 2012. "Call of Duty WWII: Using History to Sell Violence." *The Trumpet*, May 28. https://www.thetrumpet.com/15859-call-of-duty-wwii-using-history-to-sell-violence

Walters, N. 2015. "Playing These 6 Video Games Could Help Improve Your Problem-Solving Skills." *Business Insider*, November 18. http://www.businessinsider.com/video-games-that-help-improve-problem-solving-skills-2015-10

Zakarin, J. 2012. "Sandy Hook Shooter Linked to Violent 'Call of Duty' Games, Sparking Debate." *Hollywood Reporter*, December 18. http://www.hollywoodreporter.com/news/sandy-hook-shooter-linked-violent-404576

Diablo

Diablo is an action video game known for its violence. It was first released by Blizzard Entertainment in 1996. The game is set in a fictional kingdom called

Khanduras, and the player journeys through 16 levels in order to get to hell and face off against the Lord of Terror, Diablo. *Diablo II* was released in 2000, and *Diablo III* in 2012. It can be played solo or by up to four players. The *Diablo* series has sold more than 18.5 million copies worldwide (John, 2009).

The game features three classes of characters, the warrior, the rogue, and the sorcerer, each with unique skills. Warriors specialize in hand-to-hand or close-quarters fighting and are known for their strength. Rogues are weapons masters who are also able to disarm traps. Sorcerers are best at spells. Players can choose from a variety of weapons, including bows, swords, maces and clubs, shields, and more. *Diablo III* added a new class, monks, who specialize in martial arts, as well as new enemies, including the Fallen Lunatic, a demon who stabs itself in the chest then explodes, damaging the player. In addition to the actual violence of the game, critics have noted the violent art that is featured on the box, which shows "a glowing, snarling red devil with ram's horns on his head and tiny yellow eyes" (Kent, 1997).

Despite being notorious for bloody violence, the game's director, Jay Wilson, says he would allow his nine-year-old daughter to play it. He applauds the game for its design and argues that it does not prompt users to engage in actual violence (John, 2009).

New research suggests that it may not be playing violent games but rather the frustration felt by those who don't play well or don't understand how to win a game that results in aggression. Oxford researchers found that being bad at a nonviolent version of a game induced more rage than did playing a violent one that included adequate instructions. Users have applauded the *Diablo* series for its careful instruction and ease of play.

Laura L. Finley

See also: Final Fantasy; Legend of Zelda, The; World of Warcraft

Further Reading

John, T. 2009. "Why Designer of Gory Diablo III Lets His Daughter Play." *Wired*, August 24. https://www.wired.com/2009/08/diablo-iii/

Kent, S. 1997. "Cyberplay: Why Do So Many Games Have Devil Imagery?" CNN Interactive, May 30. http://edition.cnn.com/SHOWBIZ/9705/29/cyber.lat/

Tassi, P. 2014. "At Long Last, Video Game Aggression Linked to Losing, Not Violence." *Forbes*, April 8. from https://www.forbes.com/sites/insertcoin/2014/04/08/at-long-last-video-game-aggression-linked-to-losing-not-violence/

Doom

Doom is a first-person-shooter game first released in 1993. It was one of the first of its kind, and is known for its science fiction/horror theme. Several notorious shooters have been linked to the game, but proponents maintain it is simply fast-paced, action-packed fun. *Doom II: Hell on Earth* was released in 1994, and several expansion packs have been released since. *Doom III* was released in 2004.

Players are space marines who fight invading demons from hell. Marines have a variety of weapons they can use, including their fists, pistols, chainsaws, a shotgun, a rocket launcher, a plasma rifle, and various types of armor. One description of the most recent version of *Doom* reads: "'Brutal' is probably even an understatement.

This is a game where you crush the skull of a demon in the first three seconds of waking up when the game starts. You get a shotgun a minute later and then you're blowing apart demons left and right, then chainsawing them in half, and doing horrific executions where you rip off their arms and beat them to death with them, or just punch their heads clean off when all else fails" (Tassi, 2016).

Negative attention was focused on *Doom* in 1999, after Eric Harris and Dylan Klebold killed 12 classmates and a teacher before shooting themselves at Columbine High School in Littleton, Colorado. They were avid players of the game, which the U.S. military uses to train soldiers. Harris and Klebold had even dressed in trench coats and made a videotape of themselves simulating *Doom*. Harris allegedly created a game level based on the floor plan of Columbine High School, and investigators found several homemade versions of the game on Harris's website. Harris also created a level that outlined his own neighborhood and located the home of his classmate, Brooks Brown, as the primary target that was to be destroyed, Brown's parents alleged in a complaint they filed with the sheriff's department against Harris in early 1998. Further, Harris listed "professional doom and doom2 creator" as his hobbies on his America Online account profile (Simpson & Blevins, 1999).

It was not the first time school shooting had been linked to violent video games. A lawsuit in Kentucky against 25 video game companies alleged that the shooter, Michael Carneal, who was 14, killed three students at Heath High School in 1997 because he was influenced by playing violent video games. The lawsuit was dismissed. A group of people filed a similar lawsuit on behalf of Dave Sanders, the teacher killed at Columbine, and other victims, seeking $5 billion in damages from 25 companies. It was also dismissed (Ward, 2001).

Studies after Columbine have shown mixed results. Some research has found that players of violent games do engage in more violent behavior. Yet others assert that aggressive young men gravitate to these games but that the games are not to blame for their behavior (Radford, 2000).

Laura L. Finley

See also: Call of Duty; Fallout; Half-Life; Quake; World of Warcraft

Further Reading

Radford, T. 2000. "Computer Games Linked to Violence." *The Guardian*, April 24. https://www.theguardian.com/uk/2000/apr/24/timradford

Simpson, K., & Blevins, J. 1999. "Did Harris Preview Massacre on 'Doom?'" *Denver Post*, December 4. http://extras.denverpost.com/news/shot0504f.htm

Tassi, P. 2016. "Doom's Uncomplicated Violence Stands Out in Today's Gaming Landscape." *Forbes*, May 14. https://www.forbes.com/sites/insertcoin/2016/05/14/dooms-uncomplicated-violence-stands-out-in-todays-gaming-landscape/

Ward, M. 2001. "Columbine Families Sue Computer Game Makers." *BBC*, May 1. http://news.bbc.co.uk/2/hi/science/nature/1295920.stm

Fallout

Fallout is a video game series created by Interplay Entertainment. A postapocalyptic South California serves as the setting for users to role-play as they navigate various challenges while avoiding the ever-lurking threat of nuclear annihilation. *Fallout* was released in 1997, and then was followed a year later by *Fallout 2*. *Fallout 3* and *4* were introduced in June and November 2015. There is also a massive multiplayer online role-playing game (MMORPG) version and several spinoff versions.

The protagonist of *Fallout* is the Vault Dweller, whose task is to recover a water chip in Wasteland that is needed to replace one in their underground shelter. In seeking the chip, he fights off mutants who are controlled by a monster called Master. *Fallout 2* features a descendant of the Vault Dweller, the Chosen One, who must save their village from drought and famine and then from the Enclave, a power-obsessed group of remnants from the U.S. government before the apocalypse. It includes several enhanced game-playing features, including random popular-culture jokes. *Fallout 3* picks up 30 years after *Fallout 2*. This time the protagonist is the Lone Wanderer who searches for his father. This game includes 3D graphics that allow players to engage in real combat.

Fallout 3 was praised for the freedom it allows players in choosing their action. Reporter Klaus Kneale put it this way:

> There is nothing so sacred in Fallout 3 that you can't steal, kill, destroy, or break into it. Previous sandbox games would make certain characters impervious to death, so the storyline could progress through their actions, or would make certain areas inaccessible until you reached the proper point in the plot to enter them. But Fallout 3 does away (almost completely) with this notion. Important characters can be killed, stealth rules are liberal enough that you can steal anything (at the loss of a little karma), and when a shady man in the corner of a bar suggests you nuke the city you're in, you not only can do it, but if you do, you'll be treated to the best in-game explosion ever. (Ewalt, 2008)

Fallout 4 is set in the year 2287 and follows the Sole Survivor. It features not only a depressing post-apocalyptic setting but also grim humor and strange creatures that are quite different from previous versions. Users have an estimated 30 square miles to explore and can hear about 110,000 lines of spoken dialogue. One description of playing *Fallout 4* reads: "A flash, so bright you see the bones of your hand, and a violent, invisible force that throws you to the ground. Darkness. A terrible heat follows. A hatch opens beside you. You fall in. You smell smoke and singed hair. Blind and burning, your last thoughts are of your wife: Did she hold our baby tight? Blackout" (Mozuch, 2015). Some have referred to it as a work of art, due to its striking visuals.

Despite the obvious violence in these games, industry officials and players defend them, arguing that they allow individuals to grapple with ethical and moral reasoning, addressing such questions as "Do colonies of irradiated lepers deserve to live in isolation or does the threat of a pandemic justify genocide?" (Mozuch, 2015).

Laura L. Finley

See also: Call of Duty; Doom; Half-Life; Portal; Quake; Tomb Raider

Further Reading

Ewalt, D. 2008. "Review: Fallout 3." *Forbes*, October 28. https://www.forbes.com/sites/digitaldownload/2008/10/28/review-fallout-3

Mozuch, M. 2015. "'Fallout 4' Is the Most Complex Entertainment of Our Day, But Does that Make It Art?" *Newsweek*, November 2. http://www.newsweek.com/2015/11/13/fallout-4-todd-howard-389473.html

Thier, D. 2015. "'Fallout 4': What Makes This Series So Special." *Forbes*, June 10. https://www.forbes.com/sites/davidthier/2015/06/10/fallout-4-what-makes-this-series-so-special/

Final Fantasy

Final Fantasy is a video game series that premiered in Japan in 1987 and includes 15 games as well as several sequels, prequels, and spinoffs. Each game is set in a different fictional universe. All are role-playing games, with some more tactical, others shooter games, and still others massive multiplayer online games. It is among the most popular video game series, as well as the most violent, as tested by researchers (Haninger, Ryan, & Thompson, 2004).

At least one actual shooting has been linked to playing *Final Fantasy.* Sixteen-year-old Spanish teenager José Rabadán Pardo murdered his father, his mother, and his sister on April 1, 2000, when he was allegedly on an "avenging mission" given to him by the main character. *Final Fantasy VII* was blamed for the murder of a married couple and the kidnapping of a 15-year-old girl by two German teenagers who called themselves Sephiroth and Reno after the game. Investigators found a copy of it in the house of one of the perpetrators, prompting calls to ban the game.

The game features random "battle screens" in which player characters fight enemies until one side is defeated, with the body count tallied on-screen. Its plot centers on a corrupt company that is draining the planet's resources and conducting dangerous and violent experiments on people. A mercenary named Cloud is the protagonist of the game. Sephiroth is an artificially created warrior that must be defeated by Cloud.

After a school massacre in Parkland, Florida, on February 14, 2018, pundits and policy makers renewed their attention to the role of violent video games. President Donald Trump has said he believes they are a factor, and members of the video game industry scheduled meetings with him in March 2018. Players and industry officials argue that this attention to video games is inappropriate and shifts the focus from gun control or mental health issues. In fact, some have warned for decades, since video games were brought up as a reason for some of the school shootings in the mid-to-late 1990s, that there was essentially a culture war against video games. Further, defenders maintain that since all the foes in the *Final Fantasy* games are not real, it is different from games featuring violence against real-looking characters. Because the games are marketed heavily in Japan, where the first *Final Fantasy* was released, critics also note that rates of teen violence in Japan are quite low, suggesting there's no real connection.

Laura L. Finley

See also: Legend of Zelda, The; *Minecraft*; *Portal*; *Super Mario Bros.*; *Tomb Raider*; *World of Warcraft*

Further Reading

Crecente, B. 2018. "Video Games Remain an Easy Out for Politicians, But Change Will Come with Time." *Rolling Stone*, March 6. https://www.rollingstone.com/glixel /features/guns-violence-and-video-games-change-will-come-with-time-w517512

Fisher, M. 2012. "Ten-Country Comparison Suggests There's Little to No Link between Video Games and Gun Murders." *The Washington Post*, December 17. https://www .washingtonpost.com/news/worldviews/wp/2012/12/17/ten-country-comparison -suggests-theres-little-or-no-link-between-video-games-and-gun-murders

Haninger, K., Ryan, M., & Thompson, K. 2004. "Violence in Teen-Rated Video Games." *Medscape General Medicine*, 6(1), e28. https://www.medscape.com/viewarticle /468087

Macias, A. 2017. "Final Fantasy VII Blamed for Double Homicide in Germany." *Wired*, January 17. https://www.wired.com/2007/01/final-fantasy-v/

Global Video Games

Around the world, concerns that playing violent video games can stimulate aggressive behavior have been levied, often as a result of an act of violence such as a mass shooting. Although some research does suggest an increase in aggression and a decrease in empathy among heavy players, other research indicates that playing games that are frustrating, rather than violent, specifically, is more likely the cause of aggressive behavior. Or it may be that kids who are predisposed to violent behavior are drawn to playing such games. Given that very high percentages of young men, and many young women as well, play violent video games, the relationship between playing and violent behavior is clearly somewhat complex. Although debate continues about the effect of playing these games, some countries have moved to censor or even ban them (Scutti, 2016).

In the United States, a host of mass shooters have been linked to violent video games. In 2016 in Munich, Germany, 16-year-old David Sonboly shot and killed nine people. He was an avid player of a first-person-shooter game, *Counter Strike: Force*. Sonboly said he was inspired by Anders Breivik, who said he "trained" by playing the video game *Call of Duty: Modern Warfare* before he shot and killed 77 people at a youth camp on the island of Utøya, Norway, on July 22, 2012. Breivik says he used a "holographic aiming device" while playing the war game, which helped to develop his "target acquisition." Breivik also admitted to taking a year off in 2006 and 2007 to essentially play another war game, *World of Warcraft*, full time. Incarcerated for a 21-year sentence, Breivik threatened in 2014 to go on a hunger strike if prison officials did not grant him access to better video games.

Countries vary as to how they regulate video games. In China, video games are wildly popular, as it has the world's largest market for games and some of the largest video game companies. A country known for media censorship, there are also regulations that apply to video games. Any type of media that violates the basic principles of the constitution, disturbs the social order, or infringes on the rights of others is subject to censorship. Beginning in 2000, China banned video game consoles, but that ban was lifted in 2015. It had been in place because lawmakers believe that the 3D worlds produced in such games were bad for the mental and physical development of children. China also screens the content of games and requires the removal of imagery deemed to be offensive. For instance, parts of *World of Warcraft* were removed in China.

Australia bans the sale of video games that promote illegal activity, and the law allows for the banning of games for sexual or violent content. Brazil, along with many other countries, has banned *Grand Theft Auto*. In Germany, games that use symbols of unconstitutional organizations, such as Nazi imagery, are prohibited, and many popular games featuring Nazi hunters have had to be altered to comply with the law. In Venezuela, all violent video games are banned, and importing, producing, or selling them can result in a prison sentence of up to five years.

In Cuba, another country known for media censorship, video games may also be subject to bans or restrictions, in particular if they portray the government in a negative fashion. The government was concerned about *Call of Duty: Black Ops* when it was released in 2009, as the first-person-shooter game is set in the Cold War and the mission for players is to assassinate former Cuban leader Fidel Castro. Cuba's state-run media accused the United States of using the game for continued propaganda against Castro. Similarly, the Mexican state of Chihuahua banned the game *Tom Clancy's Ghost Recon Advanced Warfighter 2* in 2007 because it negatively depicted the region, featuring a kidnapping by Latin American gangs.

Laura L. Finley

See also: Call of Duty; Grand Theft Auto; World of Warcraft

Further Reading
AFP. 2014. "Anders Behring Breivik Threatens Hunger Strike to Get Better Video Games." *The Telegraph*, February 15. https://www.telegraph.co.uk/news/worldnews/europe/norway/10640466/Anders-Behring-Breivik-threatens-hunger-strike-to-get-better-video-games.html

News Desk. 2010. "Blacklisted: The World's Banned Video Games." *PRI*, December 29. https://www.pri.org/stories/2010-12-29/blacklisted-worlds-banned-video-games

Pidd. H. 2012. "Anders Breivik 'Trained' for Shootings by Playing Call of Duty." *The Guardian*, April 19. https://www.theguardian.com/world/2012/apr/19/anders-breivik-call-of-duty

Reuters. 2016. "Munich Gunman, a Fan of Violent Video Games, Rampage Killers, Had Planned Attack for a Year." *CNBC*, July 25. https://www.cnbc.com/2016/07/24/munich-gunman-a-fan-of-violent-video-games-rampage-killers-had-planned-attack-for-a-year.html

Risen, T. 2015. "Game On: China Lifts Console Ban, But Not Censorship." *U.S. News & World Report*, July 27. https://www.usnews.com/news/articles/2015/07/27/china-lifts-video-game-console-ban-but-not-censorship

Scutti, S. 2016. "Do Video Games Lead to Violence?" *CNN*, July 26. http://edition.cnn.com/2016/07/25/health/video-games-and-violence/index.html

Ziv, S. 2017. "Nazi-Killing Video Game 'Wolfenstein II' Censored in Germany." *Newsweek*, November 2. http://www.newsweek.com/nazi-killing-video-game-wolfenstein-ii-censored-germany-70052

Grand Theft Auto

The *Grand Theft Auto* video game series began in 1997. Since its inception, each game within the series has had improved graphics, but the amount of violence has also increased. The main character(s) in each game must go through a number of usually violent missions in order to win. Although the storyline varies with each game, the underlying plot is still the same: crime must be committed in order to get attention, in order to gain respect and power, and in order to succeed or win. *Grand Theft Auto II* was released in 1999, *III* in 2001, *IV* in 2008, *V* in 2013, and *VI* in 2014. Additional versions have been made for PlayStation and other software packages. The games are widely popular, with *Grand Theft Auto V* grossing $1 billion in its first three days on the market (Saar, 2014).

The majority of the games in the series begin with the storyline of a poor male character, usually white (although more recent versions of *Grand Theft Auto* feature a few main characters that are Black). They are typically portrayed as an outcast to their friends, family, and society at large, much like the demographics of perpetrators in real life. During game play, the character(s) find a way to make money in order to buy property, usually through completing missions in which they have to assassinate someone, or by beating up random characters while walking down the street. The game allows players the freedom to roam around the city in between missions, which often means they are going around town causing terror or killing innocent civilians. Throughout the duration of the game the character is able to earn his respect back from his family, friends, and even the other characters in his neighborhood by acquiring wealth or power. In each level of the game the characters complete different missions in order to claim dominance, power, and success. After completing certain missions, the former antagonists are then viewed as protagonists or heroes.

The police in the *Grand Theft Auto* games respond to all of the terror that is being caused to the city, but once a player is arrested or killed by the police, the game restarts. This may give the illusion that if you get caught by the police or get killed in real life, you'll either be reborn or will be let go. The scenarios and graphics, and thus the violence, are life-like.

Critics maintain that the *Grand Theft Auto* series glorifies violence against women. *Grand Theft Auto V* allows a gamer to purchase a woman to perform various sex acts; the character is incentivized to kill her afterward to get his money back. One *Huffington Post* commentator wrote, "*GTA V*'s new standard for ramped-up, graphic violence against women comfortably exists in our rape culture, and reifies the distinct ways in which women and girls are propertied, humiliated, and abused" (Saar, 2014). Target and Walmart in Australia pulled the game from shelves after several sexual assault survivors started a petition on change.org calling for its removal.

A study published in 2016 assigned 154 male and female high schoolers to play one of three types of games: video games that contained both violence and sexism (two *Grand Theft Auto* games), games with violence but not sexism (*Half Life 1* or *Half Life 2*), and games without violence or sexism (*Dream Pinball 3D* or *Q.U.B.E. 2*). After they played, the researchers asked each of the players to say how much they identified with the character they were controlling and showed them a photo of a girl who they said had been beaten up by a boy, asking the players to rate how empathetic they felt toward her. The boys who played the violent and sexist games were more likely to report identifying with the character and less likely to report empathy for the girl in the photo. The girl players did not show the same results (Sifferlin, 2016).

Rather than copycat the violence or desensitizing players, some maintain that playing games like *Grand Theft Auto* allows people to take out their pent-up frustrations on the characters in the game, because in real life you're unable to restart all over again. The game allows players to release their frustrations toward the world onto a more "controlled" setting.

Laura L. Finley

See also: Call of Duty; Global Video Games; *Half-Life*; *Quake*

Further Reading

Saar, M. 2014. "Grand Theft Auto V and the Culture of Violence against Women." *Huffington Post*, December 9. https://www.huffingtonpost.com/malika-saada-saar/grand -theft-auto-v-and-the-culture-of-violence-against-women_b_6288528.html

Sifferlin, A. 2016. "Here's What Sexist Video Games Do to Boys' Brains. *Time*, April 13. http://time.com/4290455/heres-what-sexist-video-games-do-to-boys-brains/

Tassi, P. 2014. "GTA V and the Ethics of Mass Murder." *Forbes*, December 11. https://www .forbes.com/sites/insertcoin/2014/12/11/gta-5-and-the-ethics-of-mass-murder/

Half-Life

Half-Life is a series of first-person-shooter games. It was released in 1998, and was followed by a sequel, *Half-Life 2*, in 2004. The first game is set in a fictional research facility in New Mexico, where Gordon Freeman is a theoretical physicist involved in experiments that allow extraterrestrial visitors to attack the facility, killing most people there. Freeman and a few survivors try to flee, but the military is brought in to keep them there, even killing those who try to escape. Freeman ultimately does get out and finds his way to the other planet, Xen, where he tries to eliminate the leader, Nihilanth. *Half-Life 2* is set 20 years later, when more aliens have invaded and conquered Earth, subjugating the humans to live in internment camps. Freeman again battles to destroy the aliens.

One study that included *Half-Life 2* found that games that include more frustration, such as poor directions or counterintuitive moves, resulted in players having more aggressive reactions. The aggression was worst for those who played more than three hours each day, resulting in them having little real-life interactions. The researchers even created a nonviolent version of *Half-Life 2*, where instead of shooting or blowing up enemies, they would be tagged and then would simply evaporate. This made no difference in the aggression; rather, it was those who were not given a tutorial beforehand so that they were familiar with the controls and game mechanics who felt less competent and more aggressive. "If developers can design more effective game-play processes then it could be possible to minimise a player's feelings of exasperation and irritation—admittedly something good developers will want to achieve in any case," said Richard Wilson, chief executive at Tiga, a British video game trade body (Lee, 2014).

Unlike many other violent video games, *Half-Life* has not been accused of being sexist.

Laura L. Finley

See also: Call of Duty; Doom; Fallout; Grand Theft Auto; Portal; Quake

Further Reading

Lee, D. 2014. "Aggression from Video Games "Linked to Incompetence." *BBC*, April 7. http://www.bbc.com/news/technology-26921743

Place, N. 2016. "Study: Video Games Are Making You Sexist." *Daily Beast*, April 14. https://www.thedailybeast.com/study-video-games-are-making-you-sexist

Legend of Zelda, The

The Legend of Zelda, often referred to as "Zelda," is a series of action-adventure video games published by Nintendo. It is a fantasy in which the protagonist, Link, seeks to rescue Princess Zelda from the evil Ganon. Along the way he collects clues, solves mysteries, and defeats enemies. Originally released in Japan in 1984, it was released in the United States in 1986. Available on various formats, it is a bestseller for Nintendo. The series now includes 19 games and a number of spinoffs.

While many have praised it as one of the best games ever, some have criticized the games for being classist, sexist, and racist. It is critiqued for promoting women as "damsels in distress" who must be saved by males. The abduction of Zelda is indeed a violent act, and Link must shoot dragons and ghosts as he enacts his rescue plan. Critics believe that since Nintendo is supposedly a family-friendly company, such depictions and acts of aggression are inappropriate. In contrast, some players believe the game contains too little violence and blood, even for a game rated "E" for everyone.

The most recent game in the series, *Legend of Zelda: Breath of the Wild,* has been applauded for its beauty and sophistication, yet also critiqued for being too violent for the age groups to which it is marketed. Players constantly switch weapons (stick, club, sword, bow, etc.) depending the environment and which foe they are fighting. The Computer Entertainment Ratings Organization (CERO), Japan's ratings board, noted the game's sexual content, crime, and violence.

Zelda has been linked to at least one incident of real-life violence. In 2014, a man named Eugene Thompson was arguing with his girlfriend. She called her estranged husband over, and Thompson ended up chasing the man with a replica of Link's sword from *Zelda*. Thompson stabbed him in the chest and in the leg as the two scuffled, leaving him in serious condition.

Laura L. Finley

See also: Final Fantasy; Minecraft; Portal; Super Mario Bros.; Tomb Raider

Further Reading

Gibson, E. 2017. "Children and Video Games: A Parent's Guide." *The Guardian*, May 11. https://www.theguardian.com/technology/2017/may/11/children-video-games -parents-guide-screentime-violence

Hochschartner, J. 2013. "'The Legend of Zelda" Is Classist, Sexist and Racist." *Salon*, October 5. https://www.salon.com/2013/10/05/the_legend_of_zelda_is_classist_sexist _and_racist/

Hoggins, T. 2017. "The Legend of Zelda: Breath of the Wild Review: 'One of the Finest Video Games Ever Made.'" *The Telegraph*, March 3. http://www.telegraph.co.uk /gaming/reviews/legend-zelda-breath-wild-review-one-finest-video-games-ever/

Kain, E. 2014. "Man Stabbed with Replica Zelda Master Sword in Serious Condition." *Forbes*, March 4. https://www.forbes.com/sites/erikkain/2014/03/04/man-stabbed -with-legend-of-zelda-master-sword-in-critical-condition/#104fa1887716

Minecraft

Minecraft, created by Swedish game designer Markus "Notch" Persson, is a video game that was first released in 2009. Players build a world with different cubes and occasionally engage in combat with various creatures. Players can select between survival mode (where they have to build and maintain their world), creative mode (where they have unlimited resources to build the world and can even fly), adventure mode (which includes playing custom maps created by other players), and spectator mode (where they move around without fear of collisions or gravity). The game is popular with elementary school and middle school students, and has even been used in schools and other educational settings. There are more than 100 million users worldwide.

Proponents maintain that, like Lego blocks, *Minecraft* helps stimulate creativity. It may also teach real-life skills of strategy and resource management, allowing players to engage in cost-benefit analyses. Players must also be patient and must persevere. Although many play it solo, with online options it can be played with others, hence developing teamwork skills. Because it runs on computers, smartphones, and tablets in addition to other gaming systems, it can be played anywhere. And although there are monsters, they are cartoon-like; the game even features a "peaceful" mode that allows one to turn off all the enemies. No blood or gore is involved. *Mother Jones* magazine considers *Minecraft* largely nonviolent. "Slash your way through zombies and other creepy creatures if you so choose, but violence is mostly avoidable. In Minecraft, you create the world you want to live in" (Raja, Caldwell, & Connolly, 2013).

Not all people believe that *Minecraft* is so innocent, however. In March 2015, the Family and Social Policies Ministry of Turkey recommended banning the game because there was concerns that kids might replicate the violence they use against the creatures who attempt to destroy their creations. "Although the game can be seen as encouraging creativity in children by letting them build houses, farmlands and bridges, mobs [hostile creatures] must be killed in order to protect these structures. In short, the game is based on violence," the ministry's report said (Linshi, 2015).

Laura L. Finley

See also: Final Fantasy; Legend of Zelda, The; Portal; Super Mario Bros.

Further Reading

Komando, K. 2015. "5 Things Minecraft Teaches Kids (Plus One Bad Thing, Too)." *Fox News*, January 10. http://www.foxnews.com/tech/2015/01/10/5-things-minecraft -teaches-kids-plus-one-bad-thing-too.html

Linshi, J. 2015. "Why This Country Might Ban Minecraft." *Time*, March 11. http://time .com/3740378/turkey-minecraft/

Raja, T., Caldwell, M., & Connolly, M. 2013. "10 Nonviolent Video Games that Kick (Metaphorical) Butt." *Mother Jones*, September 21. http://www.motherjones.com/media /2013/09/12-totally-kick-ass-violence-free-video-games/

Portal

Portal is a video game system developed by Valve Corporation and released in 2007. It involves a series of puzzles that the protagonist, Chell, must solve. She is being held in a lab and is subject to various experiments. Chell is taunted by an artificial intelligence called Genetic Lifeform and Disk Operating System, or GLaDOS. The game has been praised for its originality and for featuring a female protagonist. *Portal 2* was released in 2011.

Unlike most video games, Chell is not hypersexualized or a victim. She wears normal clothes, unlike most female characters in video games, who are typically scantily clad. Commentator Joe McNeilly (2007) noted, "In the rare event that a female character is playable, she serves as an object of male fantasy." Although it is a shooter game, Chell's primary weapon is a portal gun, which opens doorways instead of shooting bullets. No armies of bad guys are in pursuit. McNeilly notes that this is a dramatic difference from other first-person-shooter games. "The Portal Gun creates connections rather than destroying life. It is through innovative placement of these connections, or portals, that goals are achieved or enemies overcome" (McNeilly, 2007). Additionally, although GLaDOS manipulates Chell, the experiments are more emotionally dangerous than physically violent. The game does feature physical violence in the form of security turrets that are located throughout the facility that open fire whenever they see Chell. Critics and players alike have praised *Portal* for being more like a puzzle or escape room experience than a traditional shooter game, with many saying that playing the game makes them feel smart.

In *Portal 2*, there are new items at the research facility that Chell must combat. GLaDOS issues scornful remarks as players navigate the new challenges. Reviewer Nick Cowen (2011) wrote, "Valve has created a masterpiece in *Portal 2*. The depth of content, the mind-bending mechanics and fantastic experience are almost certain to satisfy ardent fans of the first game; and to all newcomers to the series, it's as simple as this: prepare to have your mind blown. Over and over again."

See also: Call of Duty; Doom; Fallout; Half-Life; Legend of Zelda, The; Minecraft; Quake; Super Mario Bros.; Tomb Raider

Laura L. Finley

Further Reading

Cowen, N. 2011. "Portal 2-Review." *The Guardian*, April 19. https://www.theguardian.com /technology/gamesblog/2011/apr/19/portal-2-game-review

Huntemann, N., & Payne, N. 2010. *Joystick Soldiers: The Politics of Play in Military Video Games*. New York: Routledge.

Larchuk, T. 2011. "Portal 2: A Student Video Game All Grown Up." *NPR*, April 1. https:// www.npr.org/2011/04/19/135511250/portal-2-a-student-video-game-project-all -grown-up

McNeilly, J. 2007. "Portal Is the Most Subversive Game Ever." *GamesRadar*, December 7. https://www.gamesradar.com/portal-is-the-most-subversive-game-ever/4/#article -body

Stanton, R. 2016. "Do Video Games Make Children Violent? Nobody Knows—And This Is Why." *The Guardian*, March 9. https://www.theguardian.com/technology/2016 /mar/09/do-video-games-make-children-violent-nobody-knows-and-this-is-why

Quake

Quake is a first-person-shooter game first released in 1996. It can be a single-player or multiplayer game. Trent Reznor, a musician with the band Nine Inch Nails and a music producer, voices the protagonist, Ranger, who must stop an enemy called "Quake," who sends death squads to kill humans. Ranger must fight as he collects four magic runes to stop the invasion of Earth. The realms that players enter include caves, dungeons, and various other gothic-looking contraptions. *Quake II* was released in 1997, *Quake III* in 2000, and *Quake IV* in 2005. There are other spinoff versions as well.

Quake was modeled from 3D, a first in action video games, allowing for a 360-degree view. That technology is said to have paved the way for other first-person-shooter games like *Call of Duty*. It was also one of the first to host competitive gaming events and was a catalyst for the development of multiplayer action. Players often organized teams, or clans. *Quake* also allows "camping," or hiding in a trafficked spot on a multiplayer map in order to ambush enemy players.

Quake has been described as one of the most graphically violent games. "Extra 'packs' for the game can be downloaded from the Internet should you wish to add more blood, more gore and bigger and better weapons. You can scan in a face of your pal and put it on the person you're shooting in the game. Some people have put in the face of their teacher from class photos," explains 14-year-old Michael, a player. He went on, "Then you can cut off their heads and kick them around or use them as head grenades to explode another person." *Quake* has also been accused of promoting sexism. "Disturbingly like pornography, they [women] are either helpless victims or scantily clad sex objects" (McVeigh, 2000).

One study in which researchers had participants play *Quake II* and took measures of their anger before, during, and after play found that playing did increase feelings of anger in some but not in others, and the majority of participants saw no change. Researchers found that the effects were mediated by how the player was feeling before playing as well as his or her temperament (Unsworth, Devilly, & Ward, 2007).

Some gamers who are religious have expressed concern about playing games with such violence and depictions of devils. As a result, some have attempted to create their own games. The Columbine school shooters, Eric Harris and Dylan Klebold, were said to have been avid players of *Quake*.

Laura L. Finley

See also: Call of Duty; *Doom*; *Fallout*; *Grand Theft Auto*; Goth and Industrial Music; *Half-Life*; *Portal*

Further Reading

Davis, M. 2005. "Christians Purge Video Game Demons." *BBC*, May 24. http://news.bbc .co.uk/2/hi/americas/4534835.stm

Davison, J. 2016. "How 'Quake' Changed Video Games Forever." *Rolling Stone*, June 22. https://www.rollingstone.com/culture/news/how-quake-changed-video-games -forever-20160622

McVeigh, T. 2000. "Games Do Make Kids Aggressive." *The Guardian*, April 23. https:// www.theguardian.com/uk/2000/apr/23/tracymcveigh.theobserver

Unsworth, G., Devilly, G., & Ward, W. 2007. "The Effect of Playing Violent Video Games on Adolescents: Should Parents Be Quaking in Their Boots?" *Psychology, Crime & Law, 13*(4): 383–94.

Super Mario Bros.

The goal of the games in the *Super Mario Bros.* series is to save the Princess Peach while defeating evil-looking monsters. Although the characters in the games are cartoon-like and cute, players manipulate them through a series of violent acts as they try to score points, move on to the next level, and win the game.

Video game violence is "the new kid on the block" when it comes to the media violence literature, having only emerged in the late 1980s and early 1990s. Research shows that over 90 percent of America's adolescents own a video game system and over 60 percent play video games for at least 30 minutes a day. Boys play video games far more often than do girls; they play for about an hour a day, while girls play for under 15 minutes a day (Fraser, Padilla-Walker, Coyne, Nelson, & Stockdale, 2012). Following a crash in the video game industry in 1983, the Nintendo Entertainment System was then released in 1985 and met widespread success. *Super Mario Bros.* is the primary trademark of Nintendo.

In the original game, the main character, Mario, faces obstacles that prevent him from getting to the princess. He has monsters to jump on, and he has to defeat his nemesis, Bowser, in different levels to advance. Then Mario has to defeat Bowser again in the final round in order to save the princess.

Since the success of the original *Super Mario Bros.* game, several successors have been released, with each new Nintendo platform receiving at least one version of the game. The violence in the game series dramatically escalated in the early 2000s, as new tools and techniques were developed for users playing Mario and for Bowser.

In the early 1990s, Nintendo introduced *Mario Kart*, a game in which various Mario characters compete in car races, collecting items to help themselves or hurt their competitors. Like *Super Mario Bros.*, Nintendo has continued to release updated versions of *Mario Kart*. Some argue that *Mario Kart* is teaching children that reckless driving is cool. The latest version, *Mario Kart 8 Deluxe*, includes a battle mode and allows a choice of drivers such as Baby Mario, Baby Luigi, and Baby Peach, younger versions of standard *Super Mario Bros.* characters.

The games in the *Super Mario Bros.* series also involve using items as boosters to aid players in becoming faster, more dangerous, or invincible. For example, mushrooms are used to make Mario (or other characters) bigger and harder to kill; flowers can make Mario shoot fire, and stars make Mario invincible. Critics contend that, through these games, Nintendo deceives and deludes our youth that drugs will put their lives on the fast track. The *Mario Kart* games also use weapons such as banana peels, grenades, and bombs to prevent other drivers from catching up to them.

Still other critics contend that these games normalize violence against animals. The animal rights activist organization People for the Ethical Treatment of Animals (PETA) urged people to boycott *Super Mario Bros. 3D Land* because of its Tanooki suit, which it argues glorifies abuse of tanukis, which are real-life raccoon dogs that are often beaten and skinned alive for their fur (Kain, 2012).

On the other hand, there are some benefits to playing games like *Super Mario Bros.* and *Mario Kart*. *Mario Kart* might aid in real-life driving skills. According to Laura Aratani, a *Huffington Post* commentator, action-based video games force the gamer to respond to visual cues. In one experiment, subjects were asked to play a *Super Mario Bros.* game like *Mario Kart* for hours to see if there was any change of behavior. The results showed that some action-based games can improve precision and response amplitude of visuomotor control (Aratani, 2016).

Laura L. Finley

See also: Legend of Zelda, The; *Minecraft*; *Portal*

Further Reading

Aratani, L. 2016. "Study Confirms 'Mario Kart' Really Does Make You a Better Driver." *Huffington Post*, July 18. https://www.huffingtonpost.com/entry/video-games-better-driver-study_us_5789766fe4b03fc3ee5105fc

Fraser, A. M., Padilla-Walker, L. M., Coyne, S. M., Nelson, L. J., & Stockdale, L. A. 2012. "Associations between Violent Video Gaming, Empathic Concern, and Prosocial Behavior toward Strangers, Friends, and Family Members." *Proquest, 41*(5), 636–49.

Kain, E. 2012. "PETA Pokémon Protest Isn't a First—5 Other Silly Anti-Video Game Protests from the Animal Rights Group." *Forbes*, October 10. https://www.forbes.com/sites/erikkain/2012/10/10/peta-pokemon-protest-isnt-a-first-4-other-silly-anti-video-game-protests-from-the-animal-rights-group/

Tomb Raider

Tomb Raider is an action-adventure video game series first released in 1996. The protagonist is Lara Croft, an archaeologist who searches for ancient treasures. An updated remake was issued in 2007, and a film version of the story, starring Angelina Jolie as Lara Croft, was released in 2001. Another version is scheduled for release in 2018, with Alicia Vikander as Lara Croft. A *Tomb Raider* Barbie doll was even introduced in February 2018, in advance of the reboot.

Players of the video game control Croft as she searches for artifacts across the world. Along the way she must solve puzzles and fight dangerous animals and creatures. Croft is highly skilled and can not only operate deadly weapons but also engage in martial arts and other evasive techniques. She often faces burning, drowning, electrocution, impaling, and other horrors. While the original game included violence, the makers of an updated version in 2013 were allegedly under pressure to include more violence. They deny that there was any such pressure (Press Association, 2013).

Aside from the violence, one of the biggest criticisms of *Tomb Raider* is the sexualization of the characters. In the video game and the film, Lara Croft fights through a variety of challenges, all while wearing skimpy clothes or bathing suits. Such depictions are typical of the male-dominated gaming industry. One study of 571 female video game characters from 1989 to 2014 found that 1995 was the peak of hypersexualization, and that female characters were often nude, had overenlarged breasts and hips, and had unrealistically narrow waists. This is perhaps due to the fact that only 30 percent of the gaming industry involved women, largely in low-ranking positions, and the vast majority of players are male (Strum, 2016). Critics contend that although she is positioned as an empowered woman, Lara Croft has always been there for men's enjoyment. Some have argued that Lara Croft is a feminist, as her clothing has become less sparse over time, and her character was likely influenced by the Swedish singer Neneh Cherry and the comic book character Tank Girl. Studies have repeatedly shown that video games reinforce sexist attitudes.

Laura L. Finley

See also: *Fallout*; *Final Fantasy*; *Legend of Zelda, The*; *Minecraft*; *Portal*

Further Reading

Huntemann, N. 2000. *Game Over: Gender, Race and Violence in Video Games*. Documentary film. Media Education Foundation.

Press Association. 2013. "Tomb Raider Firm Denies Pressure to Include More Violence." *The Guardian*, March 3. https://www.theguardian.com/technology/2013/mar/03/tomb-raider-violence

Schmidt, G. 2016. "Girl Power? For Lara Croft, It's a Complicated Legacy." *The New York Times*, November 25. https://www.nytimes.com/2016/11/25/arts/girl-power-for-lara-croft-its-a-complicated-legacy.html

Strum, L. 2016. "Study Tracks 31-Year History of Female Sexualization in Video Games." *PBS*, July 8. https://www.pbs.org/newshour/science/study-tracks-31-year-history-of-female-sexualization-in-video-games

World of Warcraft

World of Warcraft (*WoW*) is a 3D massively multiplayer online role-playing game (MMORPG), first released in 2004. It is among the most popular video games around the world, featuring elements of fantasy, science fiction, steampunk, and more. Players control a character avatar who fights monsters, zombies, aliens, werewolves, and other players and characters to complete quests. It is known for being challenging to gamers as well as for its violence. The game has some 12 million users worldwide (Martinez, 2010).

Critics assert that the realism of the game can influence real-life violence. In 2011, Anders Behring Breivik, a right-wing extremist, killed 77 people when he went on a shooting sprees in Norway. Breivik was allegedly obsessed with the game, which he was said to do "full-time," some seven hours per day. In a manifesto, Breivik expressed concern about the influence of Islam on Western Europe and argued that people should play the game to prepare for an alleged upcoming "invasion" of Muslims. Other incidents have drawn a link between the game and real-life violence. In 2010, two Canadian teens allegedly raped and murdered an 18-year-old, Kimberly Proctor, and were influenced by the game. They also bragged about it on *WoW* forums.

Studies have shown that violent video games may increase aggression, but exactly how they are linked remains unclear. The game has also been linked to other sordid behavior. In 2010, Houston mom Laurie Alexander was accused of using *WoW* to solicit sex from an underage boy. The game has also been used, or versions revised, for military training.

Yet critics contend that the game, played by such a wide audience, cannot possibly be the impetus for violence, given that most players do not act out after playing. In fact, given its global nature, some assert that *World of Warcraft* does more good than harm, helping players to communicate in different languages and to get along with people from all backgrounds.

Laura L. Finley

See also: Diablo; *Doom*; *Final Fantasy*; Global Video Games; *Quake*

Further Reading

Almendrala, A. 2017. "It's Not the Video Games that Are Making You Angry, You're Just Bad at Them." *Huffington Post*, December 6. https://www.huffingtonpost.com/2014/04/08/violent-video-games_n_5112981.html

Jaslow, R. 2013. "Violent Video Games and Mass Violence: A Complex Link." *CBS News*, February 18. https://www.cbsnews.com/news/violent-video-games-and-mass-violence-a-complex-link/

Martinez, E. 2010. "'World of Warcraft' Played Role in Teens' Rape, Murder of Canadian Girl Kimberly Proctor, Experts Say." *CBS News*, October 29. https://www.cbsnews.com/news/world-of-warcraft-played-role-in-teens-rape-murder-of-canadian-girl-kimberly-proctor-experts-say/

Peckham, M. 2012. "Norway Killer Played World of Warcraft, Which Probably Means Nothing at All." *Time*, April 17. http://techland.time.com/2012/04/17/norway-killer-played-world-of-warcraft-which-probably-means-nothing-at-all/

Recommended Resources

BOOKS

Badley, L. 1995. *Film, Horror, and the Body Fantastic*. Westport, CT: Greenwood.

Barker, M., & Petley, J (Eds.). 1997. *Ill Effects: The Media/Violence Debate*. New York: Routledge.

Benedict, H. 1992. *Virgin or Vamp: How the Press Covers Sex Crimes*. Oxford, UK: Oxford University Press.

Boyle, K. 2005. *Media Violence: Gendering the Debates*. London: Sage Publications.

Carter, C. 2003. *Violence and the Media*. Philadelphia: Open University Press.

Clover, C. 1992. *Men, Women and Chainsaws: Gender in the Modern Horror Film*. Princeton, NJ: Princeton University Press.

Dines, G. 2010. *Pornland: How Porn Has Hijacked Our Sexuality*. Boston: Beacon Press.

Durham, M. 2008. *The Lolita Effect*. Woodstock, NY: Overlook Press.

Ehrlich, S. 2003. *Representing Rape: Language and Sexual Consent*. Oxford: Routledge.

Fowles, J. 1999. *The Case for Television Violence*. Thousand Oaks, CA: Sage.

Freedman, J. 2002. *Media Violence and Its Effect on Aggression: Assessing the Scientific Evidence*. Toronto, ON: University of Toronto Press.

Gay, R. 2014. *Bad Feminist: Essays*. New York: Harper Perennial.

Goldstein, J. (Ed.). *Why We Watch: The Attraction of Violent Entertainment*. New York: Oxford University Press.

Grossman, D., & DeGaetano, G. 2014. *Stop Teaching Our Kids to Kill: A Call to Action against TV, Movie, & Video Game Violence*. New York: Harmony.

Groves, B. 2002. *Children Who See Too Much: Lessons from the Child Witness to Violence Project*. Boston: Beacon.

Haaken, J. 2010. *What Does Storytelling Tell Us about Domestic Violence? Hard Knocks: Domestic Violence and the Psychology of Storytelling*. London: Routledge.

Haskell, M. 1987. *From Reverence to Rape: The Treatment of Women in the Movies*. Chicago: The University of Chicago Press.

Horeck, T. 2004. *Public Rape: Representing Violation in Fiction and Film*. London: Routledge.

Jones, G. 2002. *Killing Monsters: Why Children Need Fantasy, Super Heroes and Make-Believe Violence.* New York: Basic.

Kellner, D. 1995. *Media Culture: Cultural Studies, Identity and Politics between the Modern and the Postmodern.* New York: Routledge.

Kimmel, M. 2008. *Guyland: The Perilous World Where Boys Become Men.* New York: Harper.

Kirsch, S. 2006. *Children, Adolescents, and Media Violence: A Critical Look at the Research.* Thousand Oaks, CA: Sage.

Magestro, M. 2015. *Assault on the Small Screen: Representations of Sexual Violence on Primetime Television Dramas.* London: Rowman & Littlefield.

Moorti, S. 2002. *Color of Rape: Gender and Race in Television's Public Spheres.* Albany: State University of New York Press.

Potter, J. 2002. *The 11 Myths of Media Violence.* Thousand Oaks, CA: Sage.

Quart, A. 2004. *Branded: The Buying and Selling of Teenagers.* New York: Basic Books.

Raphael, J. 2013. *Rape Is Rape: How Denial, Distortion, and Victim Blaming Are Fueling a Hidden Acquaintance Rape Crisis.* Chicago: Lawrence Hill Books.

Robson, P., & Silbey, J. (Eds.). 2012. *Law and Justice on the Small Screen.* West Sussex, UK: Hart Publishing.

Sanday, P. 2011. *A Woman Scorned: Acquaintance Rape on Trial.* New York: Anchor.

Sielke, S. 2002. *Reading Rape: The Rhetoric of Sexual Violence in American Literature and Culture, 1790–1990.* Princeton, NJ: Princeton University Press.

Singular, S., & Singular, J. 2015. *The Spiral Notebook: The Aurora Theater Shooter and the Epidemic of Mass Violence Committed by American Youth.* Berkeley, CA: Counterpoint.

Sternheimer, K. 2003. *It's Not the Media: The Truth about Pop Culture's Influence on Children.* Boulder, CO: Westview.

Steyer, J. 2002. *The Other Parent: The Inside Story of the Media's Effect on Our Children.* New York: Atria.

VIDEO AND FILM RESOURCES

Beyond Good and Evil: Children, Media, and Violence Times
> Available from Media Education Foundation, focuses on how good and evil are depicted in news and entertainment media.

California Newsreel: www.newsreel.org
> Seller of documentary videos on an array of topics.

Dreamworlds 3
> Documentary from Media Education Foundation addressing sexism, racism, and violence in music videos.

The Empathy Gap: Masculinity and the Courage to Change
> A follow-up to Media Education Foundation's *Generation M*, this documentary examines how misogynistic messages in popular culture reduce men's ability to empathize with women.

Films for the Humanities and Sciences: www.films.com
> Seller of videos generated by independent producers on various topics in the humanities and sciences.

Game Over: Gender, Race and Violence in Video Games
> Focuses on the depiction of race, gender and violence in popular video games. Available from Media Education Foundation.

Generation M
> Looks at misogyny and sexism in American media. Documentary available from Media Education Foundation.

Hip Hop: Beyond Beats and Rhymes
> Shows how hip-hop and the culture surrounding it promotes destructive gender stereotypes. Also highlights hip-hop artists who have and are challenging this culture of exploitation.

Joystick Warriors
> Media Education Foundation documentary addressing the link between militarism, war, violence, and video games.

Killing Us Softly 4
> Documentary from Media Education Foundation focusing on sexism and misogyny in advertisements.

The Mean World Syndrome
> Focuses on how repeated exposure to violent news and entertainment media increases fear. Available from Media Education Foundation.

Media Education Foundation: www.mediaed.org)
> Provides educational documentaries available for purchase by schools, universities, and libraries on social issues.

Militainment, Inc.
> Documentary focuses on how media promotes militarism. Available from Media Education Foundation.

Pornland: How the Porn Industry Has Hijacked Our Sexuality
> Documentary from Media Education Foundation addressing the unrealistic depictions in pornography and the impact on viewers.

Rape Myths on Trial
> Focuses on how rape myths that are disseminated in media and popular culture affect rape trials.

What Next? Violence in the Media (http://www.pbs.org/video/2320526646/)
> PBS *Frontline* episode focusing on what research says about the effect of violent media.

Wrestling with Manhood
> Shows how World Wrestling Entertainment uses sexist and homophobic narratives that promote bullying and violence.

TED TALKS

Ashley Judd: How Online Abuse of Women Has Spiraled Out of Control: https://www.ted.com/search?q=media+violence
> Shares personal stories and statistics related to revenge pornography.

Ione Wells: How We Talk about Sexual Assault Online: https://www.ted.com/search
?q=media+violence
Shows how social media can help survivors heal and change rape culture.

Jean Kilbourne: The Dangerous Ways Ads See Women: https://tedxinnovations.ted
.com/2015/05/27/spotlight-tedx-talk-the-dangerous-ways-ads-see-women/
Showcases Kilbourne's work on misogyny, sexism, and violence in
advertisements.

ORGANIZATIONS

American Booksellers Foundation for Freedom of Expression: www.abffe.org
Promotes free speech, press, and expression and provides resources to
resist censorship.

American Civil Liberties Union (ACLU): www.aclu.org
Promotes civil rights as laid out in the U.S. Constitution and opposes censorship of speech, press, and expression.

American Psychological Association (APA): www.apa.org
Society of psychologists that advances the field and promotes human
welfare.

Cato Institute: www.cato.org
Libertarian organization that opposes government regulation of media.

Center for Media and Public Affairs: www.cmpa.com
Educational and research organization that studies media and public policy, in particular entertainment media and the news.

Center for Media Literacy: www.medialit.org
Nonprofit organization that provides educational materials to promote critical analysis of media.

Center for Media Studies: www.mediastudies.rutgers.edu
Focuses on how media affects contemporary society, emphasizing how
media can best serve the public interest.

Center for the Digital Future: www.digitalcenter.org
Devoted to providing data-based recommendations for sound communications policies.

Entertainment Software Ratings Board (ESRB): www.esrb.org
Self-regulating body for the entertainment software industry involved with
rating video and computer games based on age-appropriateness and content.

Federal Communications Commission (FCC): www.fcc.gov
Independent governmental agency responsible for regulating telecommunications, including radio, television, wire, satellite, and cable.

Film Advisory Board: www.filmadvisoryboard.org
Promotes family-oriented film, video, books, and other media.

The Free Expression Policy Project (FEPP): www.fepproject.org
Part of the Democracy Project at the Brennan Center for Justice at NYU
School of Law, FEPP offers education and resources related to free speech,
copyright, and censorship issues.
Conducts research on free speech, censorship, and copyright issues.

Lion and Lamb Project: www.lionlamb.org
>Works to reduce the marketing of violent media and games to children.

Media Coalition: www.mediacoalition.org
>Defender of the First Amendment, including access to violent and sexual content.

Mediawatch: www.mediawatch.com
>Devoted to decreasing racism, sexism, and violence in media.

Motion Picture Association of America (MPAA): www.mpaa.org
>Responsible for movie ratings in the United States.

National Cable and Telecommunications Association (NCTA): www.ncta.com
>Major trade association for the cable industry, works to resist restrictions on cable content.

National Center for Children Exposed to Violence (NCCEV): www.nccev.org
>Provides training and awareness around violence in life and in media.

National Coalition Against Censorship: www.ncac.org
>Alliance of nonprofit organizations that promotes free thought, speech, press, and expression.

National Institute on Media and the Family: www.mediafamily.org
>Provides data and resources related to children and the media.

Parents Television Council (PTC): www.ParentsTV.org
>Promotes monitoring and regulations of television supported by many parents.

TV-Turnoff Network: www.tvfa.org
>Nonprofit organization encouraging Americans to reduce their time spent watching TV and supports engaging in outdoor or other family-centered activities.

About the Editor and Contributors

THE EDITOR

LAURA L. FINLEY is Associate Professor of Sociology & Criminology at Barry University in Miami, Florida. She is the author, co-author, or editor of 20 books, numerous book chapters, and journal articles, and is a syndicated columnist with *PeaceVoice*. In addition, Dr. Finley is involved with a number of organizations devoted to peace, justice, human rights, and gender equality.

THE CONTRIBUTORS

KESHA BASSUE is studying criminology at Barry University.

RICHARD CIBRAN earned a bachelor's degree in sociology from Barry University and is pursuing graduate work.

JHALAND FRANCOIS earned a bachelor's degree in criminology from Barry University.

FRANCESCA GERARD is a social worker earning a master's degree at Barry University.

SHANQUIA HILSON is studying criminology at Barry University.

JAZMIN MEDINA-MORALES is studying criminology at Barry University.

NAREN NAVARRO is studying sociology at Barry University.

BRENDAN NEWMAN is a student at Miami University in Ohio and an intern with the Peace and Justice Studies Association.

DINA ODEH is studying criminology at Barry University.

MEGAN-MARIE PENNANT is studying criminology at Barry University.

ISABEL RAPISARDO-CALVO, a native of Spain, is studying criminology at Barry University.

KATELYN SCHEIVE is a student at Miami University in Ohio.

NATALIE SOSA-ORTIZ is pursuing a master's degree in criminal justice from Florida International University and is an adjunct professor there.

GINA THOMPSON is earning a master's degree in liberal studies at Barry University.

CHELSEA WAGNER is studying criminology at Barry University.

Index